Elizabeth M. Moys

Moys Classification and Thesaurus for Legal Materials

Elizabeth M. Moys

Moys Classification and Thesaurus for Legal Materials

Fifth edition

Revised and expanded by
Diana Morris
Helen Garner
Sarah Wheeler

DE GRUYTER
SAUR

ISBN 978-3-11-025453-2
e-ISBN 978-3-11-025137-1

Library of Congress Cataloging-in-Publication Data
A CIP catalog record for this book has been applied for at the Library of Congress.

Bibliographic information published by the Deutsche Nationalbibliothek
The Deutsche Nationalbibliothek lists this publication in the Deutsche Nationalbibliografie; detailed bibliographic data are available in the Internet at http://dnb.dnb.de.

Typesetting: Dr. Rainer Ostermann, München
Printing: Hubert & Co. GmbH & Co. KG, Göttingen
♾ Printed on acid free paper
Printed in Germany

MIX
Papier aus verantwortungsvollen Quellen
FSC® C016439

www.degruyter.com

Dedicated to the memory of Elizabeth M. Moys – a hard act to follow

Contents

Editorial Board — 1

Introduction — 3

Introduction to the First Edition — 5

How to use the Schedules — 25

Synopsis — 35

Schedules

K	Journals and Reference Books — **43**
KA	Jurisprudence — **47**
KB	General and Comparative Law — **49**
KC	International Law — **52**
KD	Religious Systems — **74**
KE	Ancient and Medieval Law — **80**
KF	Common Law – Primary Materials – British Isles — **85**
KG	Common Law – Primary Materials – America — **90**
KH	Common Law – Primary Materials – Australasia — **96**
KL	Common Law – Treatises – General — **97**
KM	Common Law – Treatises – Public Law — **106**
KN	Common Law – Treatises – Private Law — **134**
KP	Preferred Jurisdiction — **184**
KR	Africa — **185**
KS	Latin America — **189**
KT	Asia and Pacific — **191**
KV	Europe — **196**
KW	European Union Law — **200**
KZ	Non-Legal Subjects — **211**
Appendix	Criminology — **212**

Tables

Table I – Primary Materials — **219**
Table II – Secondary Materials — **221**
Table III – Dates — **225**
Table IV – Common Law Jurisdictions — **226**

Indexes

Editorial Board

Diana Morris, BA(Hons), MCLIP: was Librarian and then Research Services Manager at Slaughter and May (solicitors in the City of London) from 1985 to 2007, having previously worked on contract in Zimbabwe for two years and held posts in public and commercial libraries in London. Since then she has worked freelance abstracting journal articles for a legal database. Publications include a research index for the Prime Minister's Scientific Liaison Office in Harare, co-ordination of the Zimbabwean contributions to *Periodicals in Southern African Libraries*, and more recently a part chapter on cataloguing and classification in the *BIALL Handbook of Legal Information Management*. She was a member of the Editorial Board for the 3rd edition of *Moys Classification and Thesaurus for Legal Materials*, published in 1992.

Helen Garner, BA(Hons), PGDip: has been the Information Resources Librarian at the Bodleian Law Library since August 2004, having previously worked for over ten years at Freshfields Bruckhaus Deringer in London. She started her professional career as a cataloguer at the Foreign and Commonwealth Office before moving to the Royal Institution of Chartered Surveyors. Helen is a member of the BIALL Publications Committee.

Sarah Wheeler, MA: has been Assistant Librarian at the Supreme Court of the United Kingdom since it opened in 2009, with responsibility for cataloguing. Previously she worked at the Ministry of Justice Library before gaining an MA in Library and Information studies from University College London in 2009.

Additional corresponding members:

Jacqueline Elliott, BA, Dip. Ed(Tas), LLB(Hons) (Adel), ALAA: was Court Librarian at the High Court of Australia from 1985 to 2005. Previously she worked as Law Librarian at the University of Papua New Guinea (UNPG) 1982–85; was Deputy Law Librarian, University of Adelaide, 1974–82; and Assistant Law Librarian, University of the West Indies (Cave Hill Campus, Barbados), 1970–73 (where she initiated the use of Moys). During her years at UPNG she made two collecting trips to the Pacific Islands to gather material to start up the Pacific Law Collection in the Law Library at UPNG, Port Moresby. She maintained her contacts with the Pacific jurisdictions until her retirement in 2005 and for many years was Coordinator of the Pacific Twinning Project of the Australian Law Librarians' Group (now ALLA). Ms Elliott edited *Australian Law Librarian* 1993–95 and published

Pacific Law Bibliography (2nd edn., Hobart: Pacific Law Press) in 1992 and *Papua New Guinea Statutes in Force as at 31 December 1991* (UPNG Library) in the same year. She also wrote several articles on Pacific legal bibliography and was a member of the Board of the International Association of Law Libraries for five years. During her time at the High Court of Australia she conducted a number of Moys seminars in all states of Australia and after her retirement continued to do so until 2010. She was also a corresponding member of the Editorial Board for both the 3rd and 4th editions of *Moys Classification and Thesaurus for Legal Materials.*

Gail Griffin, NZLA Cert.: has been a cataloguer at Russell McVeagh (private law firm in Auckland, New Zealand) since 1991. Previously she was a cataloguer at the Secondary Teachers' College Library, University of Auckland Library, Business Archives, and an independent contractor for mainly small specialist government and private collections. Publications include indexes for New Zealand photographic journals. She has run seminars/workshops for new Moys users, including *Moys Classification – An Introduction*, and *Moys Classification – How You Can Use It*, which included a practical classification component.

Introduction

This is the first edition to be prepared under the auspices of BIALL after the sad passing of Betty Moys in 2002. I was an Editorial Board member for the 3rd edition published in 1992, but apart from the continuing help from Jacqueline Elliott (formerly of the Australian High Court Library) as a corresponding member, a new Board was assembled for this edition.

I have retained much of Betty's introduction from the previous edition, including the first two sections of the Introduction to the first edition, reprinted on request from librarians in Australia and New Zealand, with a few minor changes. Naturally, some of what was said there is now out of date, as are some of the bibliographical references.

I have also left unchanged Betty's explanation of the scheme's facet structure, reproduced below.

Facet structure

The secondary materials for each modern system are divided first into public and private law, a distinction which is almost universally known. Broadly, private law is concerned with the relations between persons, natural or corporate, while public law concerns relationships between the individual and the state.

Public law falls conventionally into three main groups: constitutional, administrative and criminal law. Each of these is divided by its own criteria of the rights, duties, topics and procedures which are involved. Criminal procedure is a sub-class of Criminal law and procedure.

Private law is arranged into groups of topics, following conventions which are fairly generally accepted by common lawyers, and not usually too different from the conventional classification of Civil lawyers. Thus, contract and tort (or obligations in the Civil law) and property are almost universal areas of legal activity. The growing body of law dealing with broadly social matters, such as health, education, labour law and social welfare have been placed alongside certain other matters affecting the legal position of the individual under the class heading Persons and Social Laws. One group of topics where there may be less agreement between lawyers in the United Kingdom and the United States is that of commercial law. In this scheme, topics are grouped by subject area, rather than by the sources of the legal rules governing them, so the topics of commercial law, such as company law, monopolies, sale of goods, insurance, banking, investment, transport and communications (now including computer law in general) are all in the main

class Commercial law. Civil and general procedure form another class, at the end of the Private Law group of classes.

Common tables have been provided for use at any required point. Those for Courts (Table V) and Persons (Table VII) should *not* be used where the court or the type of person is the main topic of the book, but rather where the court or person is one part only of a complex subject. Further explanation of the use of the tables can be found below.

Criminology, being strictly a sociological rather than legal study, is assigned to the Appendix. The schedule there can be used on its own, if required, or used at the end of one of the main classes, as instructed in the Appendix and in the relevant places in the schedules.

Index-Thesaurus

The Index-Thesaurus is presented in a format similar to that of the previous edition, expanded to include more references.

Updating

Many readers will already be aware of the email list *lis-moys-users*, which has been in operation for several years. The list provides a forum for anyone interested to make suggestions for amendment and improvement of the scheme, as well as being a general discussion forum. Its current address for sending messages is: lis-moys-users@jiscmail.ac.uk

Diana Morris
June 2012

Postscript

The preparation of this edition was eased immeasurably by the help, support and encouragement of Sarah Spells, Chair of the BIALL Publications Committee, who died suddenly after a short illness in September 2012. She will be greatly missed by all who knew her.

Introduction to the First Edition

Part 1: Principles of Library Classification for Law Books

In compiling a library classification for any special subject, whether it be law, engineering or literature, the general rules of classification, such as the exclusiveness of categories and the comprehensiveness of the sum total of categories, must be observed. The nature of the particular literature and the way it is used in libraries assume great importance, and must be thoroughly studied before any attempt is made to establish the basic outline of a classification scheme. The way specialists in the subject classify it themselves must also be studied, although a classification scheme for books will not necessarily be identical as other factors, such as form of publication, must be taken into account.

The classification of law itself has long been a subject of controversy. It is virtually impossible to divide the subjects of law into neat watertight compartments, as there is inevitably a great deal of overlapping of different aspects of subjects. For example, the law of insurance can be treated as a subject in its own right, or it can be regarded as an aspect of contract law, commercial law, tort, maritime law, the law of inland or air transport or criminal law. It is partly for this reason that legal practitioners, both in England and America, have tended to resist the introduction of subject classification in their libraries. As recently as 1955, an American survey showed that at least 39 per cent of law school libraries in the United States used no subject classification [Jennett, C. Subject classification in law libraries – a survey – 1955. 49 *Law Lib. J.* 17–20].

The advantages of subject classification for law libraries are similar to those for general libraries, namely that it improves the usefulness of the books to the reader by enabling him to find information on a particular topic, even if the specific volumes he asks for are not available, and that the strength and weaknesses of a library's bookstock are immediately apparent, so that a well rounded collection can more easily be developed. Lawyers frequently know the author of the books they want, or think they want, but if the books are arranged alphabetically by author, readers are likely to miss other, possibly more recent, books on the subject which might be helpful to them. Alphabetical order is, in any case, less simple than is usually supposed. For example, Clarke, Hall and Morrison's *Law relating to children and young persons* could be shelved at Clarke or Hall or, according to the present editor, at Morrison. A subject number, such as 347.42 or KN176, is safer, and more meaningful.

There are, of course, limitations to the advantages to be gained by classifying law books, most of which are inherent in all library classification. One of the most obvious is that no shelf arrangement can fully bring out all aspects of all the

books. However good the classification scheme used, the individual book can be put in only one place on the shelves. It will be alongside books which are similar in some respects and widely separated from others which are similar in different respects. A good subject catalogue is essential to bring out all useful aspects of a book's contents. Once it is agreed that a collection of law books should be classified, the principles underlying the arrangement to be adopted should be examined. There are two main types of library classification scheme: the traditional, enumerative kind exemplified by the Dewey Decimal Classification and the Library of Congress Classification, and the more modern faceted kind, such as the Colon Classification of S.R. Ranganathan. Whether a law library classification scheme is to be enumerative or faceted, it should follow certain general principles, which are discussed below.

The legal system

Library users almost invariably approach the study of a subject of law in the context of the law of a particular jurisdiction, and only very rarely from the point of view of comparative law. Therefore, the classification approach usually adopted for many other main subjects, namely giving primacy to various subjects and sub-arranging them either by traditional sub-division methods or by facet analysis, is inappropriate for law. This principle is reinforced by the fact that, apart from some very general books and philosophical and comparative works, law books are concerned with particular individual systems of law, such as English law, French law, Brazilian law, Indonesian law, Egyptian law, Roman law or Hindu law. There are two chief types of legal system: national systems and non-national systems.

The term "national system: is not strictly correct here, but is used throughout to mean the system of law applicable to a particular modern jurisdiction. A jurisdiction frequently coincides with a nation state, but does not necessarily do so. For example, the United Kingdom, although not a federal state, contains three separate jurisdictions: England and Wales, Scotland and Northern Ireland. The United States, as at present constituted, contains 51 jurisdictions – the federal nation state and the fifty constituent States. A wider jurisdiction can also exist when there is no sovereign federal government, as in East Africa, where the East African Common Services Organisation has jurisdiction in certain matters without sovereignty.

By "modern" jurisdiction is meant one that has existed since about 1800 AD, although it is not necessarily still extant, or may have been divided or merged into other jurisdictions. For example, legislation was passed over a period of many years applicable to Afrique Occidentale Française and, although this jurisdiction

no longer exists, a place must be available for these volumes in a classification scheme. On the other hand, it seems logical that books on the law of Serbia or Montenegro before 1919 should be treated as belonging to the history of modern Yugoslav law.

The second category, non-national legal systems, consists of subjects such as international law, Hindu law, Islamic law and other systems which do not coincide with modern national boundaries, such as classical Roman law, medieval Germanic law, and the special Dutch developments of Roman law in the seventeenth and eighteenth centuries.

The usual classification practice is to place general subjects before specialised subjects, and general books before specialised books. Therefore, very general works, books on legal philosophy, comparative works and books on non-national legal systems should be placed at the beginning of any classified arrangement, followed by the books on national legal systems, arranged by system. In other words, the first characteristic of division is the legal system. A regional arrangement of national systems is clearly preferable to alphabetical arrangement, as it can allow for future federations, amalgamations of states or other political developments.

Naturally, the legal systems of countries which share historical links tend to have common features. Many systems of law, from all parts of the world, belong to one or other of two main families: the civil law systems derived from the law of the late Roman empire, and the common law systems derived from the common law of England. [The term "common law" is used here to mean the whole system of law including statutes and equity, developed in England. In the schedules and elsewhere in the introduction, the term usually means the whole family of systems based on the English common law. In the United States, the term "Anglo-American law" is frequently used.] In addition to systems which are firmly based on one of these European systems, many others in Asia and Africa have been influenced, in varying degrees, by European law. In fact, according to Professor Lawson, "it is only in a few isolated territories, such as Saudi Arabia and Afghanistan, that nonwestern law remains pure" [Lawson, F.H. *A common lawyer looks at the civil law*. Ann Arbor, University of Michigan Press, 1955].

The civil law systems can be divided into two main groups: those influenced by the French *Code Napoléon* and those influenced by the German *Bürgeliches Gesetzbuch*. The French group includes the Belgian, Italian, Spanish, most Latin American systems and the Egyptian civil law. The German group includes the Austrian, Swiss, many East European systems and Japanese and Turkish civil law. A number of legal systems, which were originally civil law systems, have been subject to outside influences, notably Scots law, Roman law in South Africa, Sri Lanka and Guyana and the laws of Quebec and Louisiana, Puerto Rico, the

Panama Canal Zone and the Philippines. All these have been geographically or politically connected with common law countries and their legal systems have been partially hybridized [Lawson, op. cit.].

It is, no doubt, because "there are considerable differences in the substantive laws of the two main representatives of the civil law world" [Ryan, K.W. *An introduction to the civil law.* Brisbane, Law Book Company of Australasia, 1962] that no known Anglo-American or European classification scheme treats all civil law systems together. There seems no reason why this should be done, although a place must be provided for books on civil law systems as a whole. Nevertheless, a scheme published in South Africa in 1966 provides, in addition to the classes for South African law, two separate foreign law classes, one for common law and one for civil law [Dannenbring, R. *The classification of law books in the University of South Africa library.* Pretoria, University of South Africa, 1965].

Common law systems

The common law was taken by English settlers or administrators to every continent, and in many places it took root and flourished, not only in countries settled originally by people from Britain, but also in more alien surroundings. The famous Indian Penal Code is a good example, and was subsequently adopted by nine other jurisdictions. Lawyers still feel to a remarkable extent that they serve a common system, whether they are in Accra, Bombay, Idaho, Manchester or Sydney. The legal systems derived from the English common law are therefore generally felt to be more homogeneous than the civil law systems, but because of the large number and variety of systems which have been influenced by the common law, the arrangement of books on the law of the countries concerned presents some considerable problems.

One of the basic features of the common law is that judges determine what the law actually is as well as applying it to particular cases. That "there is, indeed, a sort of general common law" applicable in many countries, is proved by the fact that judges in one country can and frequently do consult decisions from other countries in the system to determine the law applicable to cases before them [Elias, T.O. *British colonial law: a comparative study of the interaction between English and local laws in British dependencies.* London, Stevens, 1962]. In most countries, this is a matter of custom, but the practice is sometimes given statutory force, for example in the Ghana Interpretation Act [Interpretation Act, 1960 (C.A.4) section 17(4)]. Such reference is by no means confined to the use of English cases by overseas courts; it may equally involve reference to an Indian case in deciding a case from New Zealand, [Vajesingji v. Secretary of State for

India (1924) L.R. 51 Ind. App, 357 at 360 applied in Hoani etc. v. Acten District Maori Land Board [1941] A.C. 308 at 324] the application of a Canadian case to a New Zealand case, [Clelland v. Clelland [1944] 4 D.L.R. 703 applied in Joe v. Young [1964] N.Z.L.R. 34], reference to an Australian case by a Canadian court, [Re Farmers' Settlers' Co-operative Soc. Ltd., City Bank of Sydney v. Barden (1908) 9 S.R. (N.S.W.) 41 distinguished in Thoresen v. Capital Credit Corporation Ltd. (1964) 43 D.L.R. (2d) 97], or the citation of a Gold Coast case in an English case [Kwaku Mensah v. R. [1946] A.C. 83 cited in R. v. Porritt [1961] 1 W.L.R. 1372]. This process was greatly assisted in the Commonwealth by the work of the Judicial Committee of the Privy Council.

Not all the countries concerned have adopted the common law wholesale. Generally speaking, this happened only in those countries whose population consisted at the relevant time of British settlers. In African and Asian countries, the parts of the common law system relating to economic activity and the criminal law have usually been adopted, while the local customary law of landed property and family law has often been retained. In some countries the legal mixture contains elements of still further systems. For example, the civil law of Sri Lanka is based on Roman-Dutch law, considerably influenced by English law, together with some elements from Islamic, Hindu and Sinhalese law, while the criminal law is fundamentally English; the law of Uganda is a mixture of local legislation, various African tribal laws, common law as applicable in England in 1902, and certain British and Indian legislation specifically adopted in Uganda.

To complicate the problem, the quirks of history have left some pockets of non-common law jurisdiction in the midst of some of the basically common law countries, notably Quebec and Louisiana with their French-based systems in Canada and the United States, and Scotland, the Isle of Man and the Channel Islands, which are more or less within the area of the United Kingdom.

The areas in which the common law is to be found can, therefore, be divided into three main categories:

1. those whose legal systems are entirely, or almost entirely based on the common law, i.e. England, Ireland, Canada, the United States, most of the West Indies, Australia and New Zealand;
2. those whose legal systems consist of a mixture, in various proportions, of the common law and other systems e.g. India, Cyprus, Guyana, Nigeria;
3. those areas within a basically common law jurisdiction which have retained their own non-common law systems, albeit influenced to some extent by the common law, e.g. Scotland, Quebec, Louisiana.

For the reasons outlined earlier, several English and American classification schemes group common law jurisdictions together in some way, separately from

the rest of the world. While the grouping together of common law books can be very useful to readers, especially in any of the countries in the common law sphere of influence, the differences between the three categories of jurisdiction described above present a serious problem: which of these jurisdictions should be included in the common law section of the classification and which, if any, should be excluded? If all three types of jurisdiction are included, any large or medium-sized library will find a considerable number of books which do not deal with common law being placed alongside the common law books. This is undesirable, as it partly defeats the purpose of keeping common law books together, and is likely to be confusing, or even dangerous, for laymen and students starting their studies.

On the other hand, if a strict differentiation is made between books dealing with common law and books dealing with other systems, regardless of geography, the books on the law of countries with mixed systems, notably India and the African states, will be shelved in two or more separate places. This may not be a special disadvantage in other countries, but is hardly likely to be acceptable in the countries concerned. As the present tendency in these countries is for the law to be revised and developed along national lines, it seems probable that their legal systems will gradually diverge further and further from the common law system. Therefore, it seems best to treat the mixed systems as if they were separate national systems, rather than grouping them with the basic common law countries.

There is no ideal solution to the problem. It is understood that the Library of Congress proposes to adopt the simplest solution, disregarding the common features of the system and arranging books strictly by jurisdiction. Any library which prefers to keep common law books together must accept some sort of compromise. The arrangement suggested as avoiding the least desirable results of the two extreme solutions discussed above, while keeping together most of the books which are likely to be used in conjunction by lawyers and research workers, is to define the common law section of the classification as the countries belonging to the first category listed above, leaving books from jurisdictions in the second category to be classified separately by national system.

The two main objections to this proposal are that some important common law books, such as those on Indian criminal law and company law will be excluded, and that some non-common law books, such as those from Quebec, will be included. The first seems to be the lesser objection, as the number of volumes concerned would, in most libraries be small, and their connection with common law could be brought out in the subject catalogue. The other objection, concerning the category three jurisdictions, is more intractable. If, for example, Scots law books were placed in a separate Scottish section, this would not contain the whole law of Scotland, because laws of the United Kingdom as a whole, such as

electoral legislation, apply to Scotland. But Scots law books should not be placed alongside their English or Australian counterparts with no distinction. A possible solution might be to allow books from the category three jurisdictions to remain in the common law section, denoted by special symbols, such as S for Scotland or Q for Quebec, after the standard class mark.

Sub-division of the legal system

It has been established by reference to both the nature and use of legal literature that the first characteristic of division is the legal system. Within each legal system, the next question is the extent to which division should be, in traditional terminology, by subject, form, geographical area or date or, in the facet formula, how facets such as personality, energy, space and time are to be applied. Again, it is necessary to study the form and use of law books. It is clear that chronology is normally significant only for historical books and for the detailed shelf arrangement of publications such as successive editions of revised statutes, conference proceedings etc. Something like geographical treatment has, by means of defining national legal systems, already been used and although provision will still be needed for local sub-division within the area of a jurisdiction, this is of relatively minor importance.

An examination of the contents of law books leads to an analogy with literature. In one sense, the terms "literature" and "law" refer to abstractions, but in another sense it is true to say that a volume of Shakespeare's plays or Milton's poems is itself literature, and similarly that a volume of statutes is itself law. On the other hand, Dover Wilson's *What happens in Hamlet* is a book about literature and *Chitty on contracts* is a book about law. For convenience, these two basic types of law books are referred to throughout as primary materials and secondary materials respectively. This is not a distinction based strictly on form or on subject, but rather on the special nature of the contents of law books and their use. A simple definition of primary and secondary materials is that the former contain the law itself, are books *of* law and can be quoted in court, and that secondary materials are books *about* law and cannot normally be quoted in court. This is, of course, an over-generalisation and cannot be strictly applied to every volume usually included in either group, but it serves to highlight the basic differences.

At this point, the analogy with literature must be abandoned. Whereas there are few practical difficulties in classifying together both the volumes of Shakespeare's works and the biographies and critical monographs about his work, the same does not apply to legal literature. In all countries, but especially in common law jurisdictions, primary legal materials are very frequently published in

serial form, whereas most secondary materials are in the form of monographs or multi-volume sets of limited dimensions. The idea of trying to place monographs alongside the annual volumes of statutes which contain the legislation referred to is so ludicrous that it is quite obvious that the two kinds of books cannot be mixed. Therefore, primary and secondary materials must be treated separately in any classification scheme.

Primary materials

Primary materials should be arranged by the form of their contents. They contain two main kinds of texts: legislative texts, whether these are codes, statutes or subsidiary rules and regulations; and reported decisions of courts of law or administrative tribunals. Both types of publication require very full indexing services of various kinds, such as indexes, digests and citators. It is essential for law library readers that these service volumes should always be placed beside the true primary materials to which they relate, and they are therefore included here in the term "primary materials". What exactly constitutes primary materials varies from one jurisdiction to another. It is a special feature of the common law system that much of the law is to be found in the reported decisions of the judges in cases before the courts. On the other hand, in many civil law jurisdictions the law is embodied in detailed codes, which are theoretically intended to provide a certain answer for every eventuality. In these countries, judicial decisions usually have less force than in common law countries. It is interesting to note, however, that in some European countries the position has already changed considerably: "French law has become almost as much a system of judge-made law as English law . . . German judges can be just as daring" [Lawson, op. cit.].

In many common law jurisdictions a consolidation of the statute law is compiled and published at intervals of about ten years or more. The form and arrangement of these compilations, or revised editions of statues vary, but the object is always to provide in a convenient form the total valid legislation of the jurisdiction, i.e. all statutes which are in force, omitting all clauses or complete acts which have been repealed, and incorporating changes made by amending legislation. Arrangement is sometimes chronological, as in the British *Statutes Revised*, but is more usually by subjects alphabetically. If several revised editions are held, they should be arranged in chronological order.

In addition to legislation, both main and subsidiary, a law library is almost certain to contain volumes of parliamentary debates, government gazettes etc., which are necessary for the full understanding and interpretation of legislation. In an independent law library, this material should be placed close to the legisla-

tive texts, but in a general library it is more likely to be shelved in the political science section.

In arranging reported decisions, it is necessary to distinguish between decisions of the courts of law and those of administrative bodies, which usually have less authority and are frequently subject to review by the courts. Law reports must also be distinguished from casebooks, which are usually single volumes containing a selection of cases illustrating a particular subject, and designed to be used by students in conjunction with subject monographs. Casebooks are not intended for official use; they are textbooks, and should be classified with other secondary materials, by subject.

Digests are a specialised form of legal publication, mostly produced in common law jurisdictions (but are also published in some European countries, notably France and Italy), which are extremely valuable to all law library readers. In form, they are somewhat like encyclopaedias, being arranged alphabetically by subject. However, instead of articles, a digest consists of a series of brief statements of what the law is thought by the editor to be, with copious references to the law reports, and sometimes statutes, on which these assertions are based. Their function is normally to act as subject indexes to a wide range of law reports, although a few digests are confined to a single series of law reports, e.g. *Digest of the United States Supreme Court Reports*. Digests of the latter kind should be placed next to the reports they index, while more general digests should follow the body of reports for the jurisdiction.

Secondary materials

All other law books are secondary materials, including dictionaries, directories, histories, bibliographies, commentaries, monographs, casebooks and journals. With the exception of journals, which will be discussed below, most secondary materials should be arranged by subject, proceeding from the general to the special. Therefore, general works on the legal system and administration of justice, together with books on legal history and the legal profession are best placed before the books on specific legal topics.

Most legal systems recognise certain major fields of law, such as constitutional law, criminal law, property law and commercial law, but delimitation and nomenclature vary enormously. When the more detailed sub-division of legal topics is considered, the variations in concepts, classification of topics and nomenclature become increasingly prolific. The production of a library classification taking full account of all these differences, with the schedule for each legal system individually tailored, would be an immense task for a team of specialists.

Fortunately, it is unnecessary to seek such a perfectionist conclusion, as the theoretical objections to adopting a common pattern of arrangement for the books on various national systems of law seem to be losing strength.

The present tendency is towards emphasising the features shared by legal systems, rather than their disparities. As one of the chief American law classification workers has observed, "modern developments tend to wipe out many of [the] incompatibilities between legal systems of heterogeneous origins. Effective administration and effective use of a global collection of legal literature require that the arrangement of subject matter under various jurisdictions follow the same principles, and be as reciprocal as circumstances will permit, even at the risk of minor theoretical flaws" [Ellinger, W.B. Some observations on classification theory in the development of Class K. 57 *Law Lib. J.* 360 and 364]. In other words, the use of standard methods for the subject arrangement of books from various jurisdictions is acceptable, either using traditional tables of the type found in other classes of the Library of Congress scheme or by employing the techniques of facet analysis. In either case, the resultant scheme should if possible agree with the consensus of the specialists in the field. This consensus is sometimes difficult to discover, and the compiler of a classification scheme may sometimes be forced to take decisions himself about the most convenient placing of disputable subjects, using his knowledge of the literature and its use.

In dealing with the arrangement of specific legal topics, the concept of public law and private law may be found useful. This distinction, which is much clearer in the civil law than in the common law, is between the public law regulating the relations of the citizen and the state, and the private law regulating relations between the individual members of society, singly or in groups. Public law is usually taken as consisting of constitutional law and administrative law with, sometimes, the addition of criminal law. The term is used in the fuller sense here throughout. Private law consists of property law, obligations (contract and tort), personal and family law and commercial and civil procedure law. The distinction between public and private law can be useful to the classifier, if only by providing convenient names for groups of sub-classes, although it has little practical value for the lawyer, and developments in the last 50 years or so have blurred it very considerably.

Governments now regulate many private activities, which used to be the sole province of private law. In the United States, in particular, government regulations of this type have been regarded as public law, and several American law classification schemes place them under public law. This has the unfortunate result that the "public" and "private" aspects of the law of a particular subject, such as the relations between landlord and tenant, or between employers and workers, are widely separated. The phenomenon of massive government regulation of many activities of the private citizen has obviously come to stay, and the

treatment of this type of law as public law is no longer useful, at least as far as common law jurisdictions are concerned, "where [public and private law] penetrate each other everywhere" [Lawson, op. cit.]. It is greatly preferable to treat the substance of administrative regulations together with the specific topics concerned, leaving only the constitutional, organisational and procedural aspects under the heading "administrative law and procedure".

With this proviso, the terms public law and private law can be useful in determining the order of subjects, so that an orderly progression is made either from constitutional and administrative law to criminal law and the various branches of private law, or vice versa.

Legal journals

The contents and subject coverage of legal journals varies widely. In content they are clearly secondary materials, but in form they are nearer to primary materials, and there is a good case, on the grounds of convenience to both readers and library staff, for shelving journals next to primary materials. Most legal journals, except those specialising in subjects such as jurisprudence or comparative or Roman law, are concerned mainly with the law of the country of publication. If these journals are to be classified, the most suitable place for them is between primary materials and treatises within each legal system.

However, the question arises as to the extent to which journals should be classified at all. Opinion seems to be divided on the value of classifying legal journals by country, even to the extent suggested in the previous paragraph. A reader looking for a journal usually has a reference to a specific article. He wants to locate a particular volume quickly, preferably without having to look up a call number. The titles of many journals give no indication of the country of origin, e.g. *Criminal Law Review, Journal of Public Law, Law and Contemporary Problems, New Law Journal*, and therefore classification by jurisdiction can be a positive hindrance. General browsing through periodicals, except the current issues, is comparatively rare, even in an academic library, and ease of finding is more important to most readers than subject classification.

A survey conducted in Ghana in 1960 among both practising and academic lawyers produced a two-thirds majority in favour of arranging all journals in one alphabetical title sequence. While this is by no means conclusive, there do seem to be good arguments for treating journals in a different way from all other law books, and placing them all together, unclassified. Each library should choose whichever arrangement, either by legal system or unclassified, seems best suited to its own circumstances.

Non-national legal systems

Special schedules are needed for the classes allocated to general works and non-national legal systems, but some of the principles and procedures mentioned above can be applied. For example, the literature of international law includes its own primary materials, with treaties taking the place of legislation. While specially constructed schedules are necessary for the equivalent of legislative texts in systems such as Islamic law or Roman law, the standard tables compiled for the arrangement of the subjects of national legal systems can be used for many non-national systems, including the conflict of laws, and also for comparative law.

One subject which requires special mention is the conflict of laws, sometimes known as private international law. As its name implies, this is generally an international subject, but is also sometimes regarded as a part of national law, especially in federal states. This applies particularly to the rules regulating the conflicts between the laws of the various states in the United States. It is quite acceptable to place most conflict books with the national system, if so desired, keeping only those of wider application in an international class. It is equally possible to place all conflict books in a non-national class and sub-divide, where appropriate, by jurisdiction. There are several reasonable places for conflict of laws and no absolute best.

Part 2: Principal Features of the New Scheme

This classification scheme is an attempt to put the principles discussed above into practice. While the scheme has a clear bias towards the common law system, especially as developed in Britain and the British-settled Commonwealth countries, such as Canada and Australia, it has been provided with various features, described below, designed to make it more widely acceptable. It is not intended for any particular type of library, either for students, academic lawyers or practising lawyers. It is designed however, to be suitable either for a specialist law library or for the law section of a general library which is using either the Library of Congress Classification or the Dewey Decimal Classification for the rest of its books.

In the English-speaking world outside the United States there are relatively few fully organised law libraries which are outside academic institutions. There are, it is true, other great libraries, notably those of the Inns of Court in London, but even in England they are clearly outnumbered by the libraries of the university law faculties. In the newer overseas Commonwealth countries, court and bar libraries are usually small, and the degree of organisation varies widely. Fine

practitioners' libraries, of the type operated by some large American law firms, are virtually non-existent outside North America. The new classification scheme was originally compiled for use in a university library, with other academic libraries in mind, but suitability for practitioners' libraries was also considered.

In the Commonwealth as a whole, probably more academic libraries use the Library of Congress classification scheme for their general collections than any other single general scheme. This is particularly true of the newer universities, both in Britain and overseas countries, many of which are establishing law faculties. In addition, some of the older universities are reclassifying their stock by the Library of Congress scheme. It is well known that, although a great deal of work has been done on it, the law class of the Library of Congress classification has not yet been published, and therefore the libraries mentioned above are without an established scheme for classifying their law collections.

For these reasons, the new scheme was deliberately designed to fit into a general library classified by the Library of Congress scheme. The basic method of the scheme follows the enumerative pattern of the Library of Congress, and the notation for Class K is constructed on the principles used in its other classes. Thus, within each lettered class, the numbers run serially, although a few decimal sub-divisions of them are used. In certain sections, notably the classes for non-common law legal systems, blocks of numbers are indicated in the schedules, and sub-division is by means of tables printed at the end of the schedules. Numbers in Tables I and II are used serially, in the same way as in the schedules.

In any classification scheme, the process of division must proceed in an orderly fashion, using the various characteristics of division one at a time. Even with a basically enumerative classification, it can be said that "the total subclasses resulting from the application of a single characteristic [may be] called a facet" [Mills, J. *Modern outline of library classification*. London, Chapman and Hall, 1960]. This fact tends to be hidden in a scheme such as that of the Library of Congress in a welter of repeated detail. For example, specific numbers are provided in a great many places throughout the schedules to represent the application to particular subjects of facets such as place or time. Because of the practical requirement of fitting into libraries using the Library of Congress scheme for other subjects, the same kind of repetition occurs in the new scheme, particularly for the facet of legal form, containing such foci as casebooks or forms and precedents. Specific numbers have been allocated to these foci in the traditional manner, at the most appropriate places throughout classes KB to KN. However, as a move towards the construction of a faceted law classification, tables for two special facets, courts and legal form, have been added. The use of these tables is explained below.

Basic structure of the scheme

The list of classes shows how closely the structure of the scheme adheres to the principles set out in the first part of the introduction. The classes are arranged in three main groups. Books of a general nature come first, followed by books concerned with legal systems which do not belong to individual modern nation states, even approximately. The classes in this first group are:

K	Journals and reference books
KA	Jurisprudence
KB	General and comparative law
KC	International law
KD	Religious legal systems
KE	Ancient and medieval law

The second group which, in most libraries, would contain the bulk of the books, consists of all modern national legal systems, divided into two systems, the common law and all the rest. The common law section is defined as consisting of the countries with "pure" common law systems. As the scheme was intended for use in countries whose legal systems showed at least considerable influence of the common law, six classes were allocated to the common law section. One class was allocated to each of the remaining four continents, and another was set aside for the law of any particular country, usually the home country, which seemed to require special treatment. The classes in the second group are:

KF–KN	Common Law
KP	Own country (optional alternative)
KR	Africa
KS	Latin America
KT	Asia and Pacific
KV	Europe

The remaining group consists of a single class, KZ, to provide for non-legal books which may be possessed by specialist law libraries. General libraries should not use class KZ.

Within each national legal system, the separate treatment of primary and secondary materials has been carefully maintained. For practical convenience, the alternative place for journals is at the end of the primary materials section, although it is fully realised that this is terminologically incorrect. The common law is treated as a whole, and can be used to illustrate the method of subdivision of secondary materials. However, it was felt necessary to depart from strict application of the basic principles when arranging the primary materials from

common law jurisdictions. Many more readers want to find both the statute and case law of one jurisdiction together rather than statutes from many jurisdictions. Therefore common law primary materials are divided by jurisdiction before form. Three classes are allocated to common law primary materials: KF for the British Isles, KG for North America and the West Indies and KH for Australasia.

The remaining three classes are used for the secondary materials of common law arranged by subject. Class KL is for general surveys and a number of general subjects, such as administration of justice and legal history, while classes KM and KN are devoted to public and private law respectively. As explained above, these terms have no particular significance, but are used as convenient labels for groups of legal topics.

The common law classes are:

Primary materials

KF	British Isles
KG	Canada, U.S.A., West Indies
KH	Australia, New Zealand

Treatises, etc.

KL	General and legal history
KM	Constitutional, administrative and criminal law
KN	Private law

The method of arrangement for each of the other modern systems of law is similar to that for the common law, but fewer numbers are used. Each jurisdiction has been allocated a block of either 150, 80, 50 or 20 numbers, the size of the block being based on an estimate of the amount of literature that might be held in a British library which was interested in the country concerned. Thus, more numbers are given to countries such as France, India and South Africa than to Chile or Mongolia. Very small countries, whose output of legal literature is not large, and sub-divisions of countries are given smaller blocks of numbers. Tables I and II are used in combination for the detailed arrangement of books within each country. Table I deals with primary materials by form, and Table II is for the subject arrangement of secondary materials. The arrangement of forms and subjects respectively in the tables follows closely that in KF to KN, described above, except that no provision for jurisdictional division is needed. The use of the tables is described in detail below.

Adaptability

Certain special features have been built into the scheme to make it adaptable for use in different kinds of libraries, such as independent libraries of courts, legal societies and law schools as well as the legal sections of general public or academic libraries. These features include the provision of optional numbers for non-legal subjects, an optional class for the law of a preferred country, a method of simplification to help smaller libraries, and certain numbers throughout the scheme being left blank to allow for possible future developments. The scheme attempts to provide places for all books that may be found in an independent law library. As well as law books, such libraries usually have collections of books on related subjects, including sociology, politics and history, and some have substantial collections of literature, philosophy and other subjects. Class KZ has been set aside for this type of material, but it is recommended that if the non-legal collection is substantial, it should be classified by one of the published general classification schemes (simplified as may seem necessary), rather than using class KZ. General libraries should not use class KZ.

Books on a number of subjects very closely connected with law, such as legal bibliography, law libraries, forensic medicine and criminology are likely to be held by any library, general or special, which has a collection of law books. In general classification schemes, some or all of these subjects are placed in non-legal classes, such as bibliography, librarianship, medicine and sociology. General libraries using this scheme should decide whether placing these books in the law class or the other classes will be more convenient for their readers. The numbers provided for these subjects in class K may, therefore, be regarded as optional by general libraries.

The scheme has an obvious English-speaking common law bias, and is more likely to interest libraries in Commonwealth countries than elsewhere. However, in case any library might consider using the scheme, if it were not for the fact that the provision in the schedules for its own jurisdiction was inadequate or unsuitable, a whole class, KP, has been set aside as an optional alternative. This class, which comes between the sections for the common law and the rest of the world, is available so that any library which requires special treatment for the books of its own jurisdiction may achieve this, while using the printed schedules for the remainder of its books. It is therefore possible to withdraw all the volumes for, say, Scotland, Nigeria, New South Wales, Malaya or France from the main schedules and devise a special schedule for them in KP.

Experience shows that a librarian classifying books in a field with which he is relatively unfamiliar usually finds a detailed classification scheme easier to apply than a broad one. Although many legal treatises deal with large branches of

law such as contracts, criminal law or company law, a number of monographs are published every year on relatively detailed topics, such as future interests, charter parties, the continental shelf or Magna Carta. Theses, pamphlets and articles are frequently devoted to similar, or even smaller, segments of law. Therefore the scheme has been worked out in considerable detail. While it is true that monographs are never likely to be published on many of the minor topics listed, no one can tell when an offprint, inaugural lecture or dissertation on any of them may be published. In the notation for these details, decimal numbers have been used on a larger scale than is normal in the Library of Congress scheme. This provides an easy method for small libraries to simplify the scheme. It is suggested that, while large libraries should use the full numbers given, small libraries should ignore most of the decimal numbers, using only the full numbers of which they form the sub-divisions. Further simplification can be achieved by ignoring larger sub-division of subjects, as seems suitable, and placing books under the more general numbers. For example, the schedule for contracts in class KN, omitting the decimal sub-divisions, is:

KN	10	Contract – General
	11	Casebooks
		Special aspects
	13	Formation
	14	Parties
	15	Enforceable and unenforceable contracts
	16	Discharge of contracts
	17	Remedies
	18	Special kinds of contracts

Any library not wishing to use the full schedule could use KN13 to cover all subjects contained in KN13 to KN18, thus retaining only three numbers, KN10, KN11 and KN13 for contracts. A very small library might decide to put all books on contracts in KN10. This method of simplification can be used very easily at any place in any class. Apart from the omission of decimals, it is not recommended that any of the numbers in the schedules should be abbreviated. As they are in numerical sequence in each class, shortening numbers, unless done with the utmost care, could lead to great confusion. The best procedure is the deletion of blocks of numbers preferring to use the general number which covers the whole section. Addictions and changes to the schedules will obviously be needed from time to time, because no classification scheme can provide for all likely future developments in either the subject or its literature. In an effort to make the scheme hospitable to at least some future developments, numbers have been left free throughout the scheme. Where blank numbers are not available, it will be possible to

extend the use of decimal or alphabetical sub-division to provide for some further additions. It is hoped that arrangements can be made for the publication of occasional supplements.

The decimal version

A number of university libraries which use the Dewey Decimal Classification finds the law class unsatisfactory, and it was suggested that a parallel version of the new scheme using decimal notation should be prepared. This required the telescoping of the seventeen legal classes (by definition the non-legal class was not needed) into ten decimal classes. This was simply achieved by putting together in one general class the subjects contained in the first three fairly general classes of the class K scheme, by using a single class instead of three, for common law primary materials, and by combining the four classes allocated to continents into another single class. The result is very different from the Dewey Decimal scheme, whose law class is:

340	General and comparative law
341	International law
342	Constitutional law
343	Criminal law subjects sub-arranged by country
344	Martial law
345	U.S. primary materials
346	U.K. and Commonwealth primary materials
347	Private law subjects, sub-arranged by country
348	Religious law
349	Rest of world – primary materials, by country, sub-arranged by form

Although a few minor changes had to be made to the schedules to fit them into the different pattern of the Decimal Classification, the basic shapes of the two versions of the new scheme are very similar:

	K version	Decimal version
General and non-national systems		
Journals and reference books	K)	
Jurisprudence	KA)	340
General and comparative law	KB)	
International law	KC	341
Religious legal systems	KD	342
Ancient and medieval law	KE	343

Modern national legal systems		
Common law		
Primary materials	KF–KH	344
Treatises, etc.		
General	KL	345
Public law	KM	346
Private law	KN	347
Own country	KP	348
Other countries	KR–KV	349

In this way, the basic arrangement by legal system has been maintained in the decimal framework, in contrast to the Dewey subject-oriented arrangement. The Dewey scheme's tables of standard divisions for countries are used in classes 344, for common law jurisdictions, and 349 for the rest of the world. For further sub-division of these classes, two tables, similar to Tables I and II in the K version, are provided. Table E gives nine numbers for arranging common law primary materials, and Table F distributes the nine numbers, with some decimal sub-divisions, over the whole field of primary and secondary materials. The resulting numbers are not unduly long, compared with those in some other classes of the Dewey scheme, or with parallel numbers in the K version, e.g.

	K version	**Decimal version**
English sessional statutes	KF 22	344.42022
US federal administrative decisions	KG 376	344.7308
Victorian state digests	KH 159	344.94509
Egyptian criminal law	KR 533	349.6205
Nigerian property law	KR 1442	349.66907
Indian constitutional law	KT 1577	349.5404
German civil code	KV 1625	349.430141
Soviet labour law	KV 3624	349.47077

The schedules for the remaining classes have been given in outline only, to avoid unnecessary repetition. Any library requiring more detail can subdivide any number decimally, using the K schedules for the subject as a guide. An example is given above, where the number obtained from Table F for German codes is 349.43014, and an extra "1" has been added to indicate civil codes. Similarly, the number for maritime law (common law) is 347.82. Should it be desired to sub-divide this, a schedule such as the following could be produced very quickly:

347.82 Maritime law
.821 Casebooks
.822 Shipping, seamen, etc.
.823 Collisions at sea
.824 Salvage
.825 Marine insurance
.826 Ports and harbours
.827 Carriage of goods by sea
.828 Fisheries

How to Use the Schedules

The layout of the schedules and the two notations should be self-evident, with the K notation to the left and the 340 notation to the right of the page. Some words are printed in italics, not to give them special emphasis but to indicate that they are necessary parts of the classification, such as facet indicators, which are not to be used as terms in the index-thesaurus. Most of the remaining terms in the schedules may also be used for alphabetical cataloguing or indexing.

Experienced librarians should encounter no special difficulties in finding their way round the scheme. It is, however, advisable that they should have ready access to a good legal dictionary and should have looked at least one of the introductions to the nature of legal literature which are available to first year law students.

The first step in building up a class number is to determine which legal system is dealt with by the book or document. The nature of the book as either a primary or secondary source is usually obvious. Generally, if it is not one of the types of publications listed in Table I, it can be assumed to be secondary in nature. Primary materials are sub-arranged by legal form: legislation, law reports, etc. Secondary materials are arranged by subject.

It is worth pointing out that books should *never* be classified by reference to the title alone. In the first place, the title frequently gives no indication of the legal system covered. Secondly, as can be seen from a scrutiny of the index-thesaurus, legal terminology includes a considerable number of homographs, such as: charges, defence, discovery, interests, maintenance and security. It is therefore essential to examine the context in which the words of the title operate.

Form or subject

A substantial proportion of modern legal primary sources are published in serial form: current legislation, law reports and the indexes, citators and digests to go with them. As these serial collections cover wide subject areas within their jurisdictions (even such subject-oriented series as *Road Traffic Reports*) they should always be placed in the appropriate form division of the primary sources section for the jurisdiction.

Most individual statutes and regulations are also published separately as individual pamphlets. Any library may obtain copies of all or some of these pamphlets in order to place them on the subject shelves. In this case, they can be easily distinguished from other pamphlet material by using the Table VI,

e.g.
Subject of document Water Act, 1989 (text)

Water	KN90	347.333
Statute (Table VI)	.Z14	.Z14
Full number	KN90.Z14	347.333.Z14

General or specific number

Unless the library has taken a policy decision to use a broad classification (see page 21) books should be classified as specifically as possible. In the schedules, following normal practice, the general precedes the specific. Therefore, numbers following the number which at first sight appears to be correct should always be inspected in case one of them provides a more specific place which fits the book better.

On the other hand, if the book covers several aspects of a subject or several related subjects, it should be placed in the most specific number which encompasses the subjects covered by the book. For example, a book on tax havens should be placed at KM336.75, but if it also dealt at some length with offshore funds and dividend-stripping, it should be placed in the more general number KM336.7.

For a book which deals with the law of two or more jurisdictions, see the notes at the beginning of Comparative Law, KB100/340.5.

Alphabetical sub-division

At some numbers, where logical sub-division has reached its practical limit, the schedules specify alphabetical arrangement, e.g. “By topic, A–Z”, “By city, etc., A–Z”. Usually one or two examples are given, when topic division is specified, leaving the classifier to devise his or her own Cutter numbers, as needed. The examples provided are not intended to be prescriptive.

The cutter numbers are constructed as follows:

after the initial letter S							
for the second letter	a	ch	e	hi	mop	t	u
use number	2	3	4	5	6	7–8	9

after other initial consonants							
for the second letter	a	e	hil	o	rs	u	wy
use number	3	4	5	6	7	8	9

after initial vowels

for the second letter	abc	dfg	ilm	n	p	r	stu	y
use number	2	3	4	5	6	7	8	9

For example:

Subject of document The coffee trade

Foreign trade	KN253	*or*	347.61
Commodities	KN253.8, A–Z		347.616, A–Z
Coffee	.C6		.C6
Full number	KN253.8.C6		347.616.C6

Subject of document International terrorism

International crimes	KC215–8	*or*	341.36
Others, A–Z	KC218		341.369
Terrorism	.T4		.T4
Full number	KC218.T4		341.369.T4

Where alphabetical arrangement of countries or other jurisdictions is specified, reference should be made to the Cutter numbers provided in the Index of Jurisdictions for the K notation or to the Dewey Decimal Classification geographic table for the 340 version. For example:

Subject of document Australian national legal bibliography

National legal bibliography	K61–76	*or*	340.04
Australasia, A–Z	K75		
Australia	.A82		(DDC) .94
Full number	K75.A82		340.0494

Subject of document Lives of English judges

Biography	KB10–15	*or*	340.31–3
Collections, by country	KB11		340.32
England	.E65		(DDC) .42
Full number	KB11.E65		340.3242

Where arrangement by cities or towns is required, Cutter numbers should be supplied by the classifier, for both types of notation. For example:

Subject of document Local government of Vancouver

Local government	KM361–91	*or*	346.6
Particular cities	KM391		346.69
Vancouver	.V27		.V27
Full number	KM391.V27		346.69.V27

Use of the Tables

Tables I and II

Each non-common law jurisdiction is listed in classes KR to KV, with a block of numbers and a letter against its name in the schedules, e.g. Kenya KR3101–50 (C), Malaysia KT3201–80 (B), France KV1101–1250 (A). A block of numbers has been allocated to each country and the letter indicates which section of Tables I and II is to be used for arranging the material for that country, state, province etc. For class 349 in the decimal version, Table I and II, section F must be used for each jurisdiction.

In applying the Tables, it will be seen that the numbers in Tables I and II follow on from each other, with Table I for primary sources and Table II for the secondary sources of the same jurisdiction. The number found in the Tables is NOT added to the first number in the block, but is SUBSTITUTED into the given block of numbers, as shown by the following examples:

Subject of document Land tenure in Kenya

Kenya	KR3101–50 (C)	*or*	349.6762
Land tenure (Table IIC)	29.2		(IIF) 0711
Full number	KR3129.2		349.67620711

Subject of document Malaysian tax law

Malaysia	KT3201–80 (B)	*or*	349.595
Taxation (Tale IIB)	32.5		(IIF) 0472
Full number	KT3232.5		349.5950472

Subject of document French civil code

France	KV1101–1250 (A)	*or*	349.44
Civil code (Table IA)	25		(IF) 0141
Full number	KV1125		349.440141

Subject of document Spanish fisheries law

Spain	KV821–900 (B)	*or*	349.46
Fisheries (Table IIB)	73		(IIF) 0884
Full number	KV893		349.460884

England and Wales and the United States (federal only) have been provided with full schedules for primary sources at KF1–99 and KG301–99 respectively. For the other common law jurisdictions, as defined on page 8, blocks of numbers are provided for primary materials *only* in classes KF to KH or in class 344. These are subarranged by Table I in exactly the same way as is described above, except that for the decimal notation Table IE is used. For example:

Subject of document Constitution of Canada (official text)

Canada (primary materials)	KG1–60(A)	*or*	344.71
Constitution (text)(IA)	14		(IE) 012
Full number	KG14		344.71012

Subject of document Digest of Victorian law

Victoria (primary materials)	KH141–60(B)	*or*	344.945
Digests (IB)	19		(IE) 095
Full number	KH159		344.945095

Table III – Dates

This Table for dates may be used at any number where it is desired.

Table IV – Common law jurisdictions

This Table may be used at any relevant number, if required, but there are many places in the schedules where its use is suggested (i.e. *By jurisdiction* [Table IV]).

In each case the range of numbers given for the decimal notation refers to the Dewey Decimal Classification Classification geographic table. For example:

Subject of document The New Zealand legal profession

Common law – general	KL	*or*	345
Legal profession			
by jurisdiction	KL51–70		170094–9
New Zealand (Table IV)	18		(DDC) 93
Full number	KL68		345.1700993

Table V – Courts

This Table may be used at any number, if required. For example:

Subject of document Procedure in youth courts

Procedure, by court	KN361–9	*or*	347.921–9
Youth courts (Table V)	7.1		7.1 (10 numbers)
Full number	KN367.1		347.927.1

Subject of document Social security offences in the magistrates' courts

Crimes	KM540–565	*or*	346.85–88
Offences against public finance	KM564		346.886
Social security offences	KM564.5		346.8865
Magistrates courts (Table V)			
1 number	.X53		.X53
Full number	KM564.5.X53		346.8865.X53

Tables VI, VII and VIII

These can be used at any number, if required. For example:

Subject of document Libel actions

Libel	KN38.21	*or*	347.2481
Actions (Table VI)	.Z7		.Z7
Full number	KN38.21.Z7		347.2481.Z7

Subject of document Women in trade unions

Trade unions	KN195	*or*	347.48
Women (Table VII)	.Q22		.Q22
Full number	KN195.Q22		347.48.Q22

Subject of document Conference on New Zealand constitutional law

Constitutional law, by jurisdiction	KM61–79	*or*	346.14–9
New Zealand (Table IV)	18		(DDC) .93
Conference (Table VIII)	.004		.004
Full number	KM78.004		346.193.004

Methods of linking subjects

Complex subjects which cannot be dealt with by using the Tables can be classified by linking the class numbers for their constituent elements, employing the symbols : and + in the same way as in the Universal Decimal Classification. For example a book on sexual discrimination in relation to schools could be KN184.2 : KM208.2, or possibly KM208.2 : KN184.2, whichever arrangement seems to fit the particular book best. In a classified catalogue, both class marks should appear.

A book covering subjects from two different sections of the schedules, and not suitable to be classed under comparative law, could be dealt with by using + to join the two class numbers. For example, a book on the law of scientific research and patents could be either KN184.7 + KN114.1 or KN114.1 + KN184.7.

Terms in the thesaurus can be linked in the same ways (see page 251).

Extending the Tables

It is not possible to reproduce the schedules in any detail in the Tables. Libraries which need more detail are recommended to devise their own extensions to the sections they need. Supposing the library of an organisation specialising in energy resources wishes to classify books on the laws of the OPEC states in the Persian Gulf, such as Kuwait. Class KT gives Kuwait only twenty numbers, KT1101– 2000, to be divided by Table ID and IID, which assigns 16.33 to "Natural resources, energy", making the number for the subject KT1196.33. This is not likely to be suf-

ficient for the specialist library, so the main schedules should be examined and an extended schedule for Table IID number 16.33 devised, such as:

16.33	Natural resources, energy
16.331	Energy policy
16.332	Coal
16.333	Oil and gas
16.334	Concessions
16.335	Exploration, oil rigs
16.336	Refineries
16.337	Distribution, pipelines, oil tankers
16.338	Alternative energy sources
16.339	Others, A–Z

Thus, oil refineries in Kuwait would be KT1196.336.

Similarly, a library needing more detail for the classification of tax law in South Africa might devise an extended schedule, such as:

South Africa	KR4201–4350
Tax law (Table IIA)	84.5
Normal number	KR4284.5
Extended schedule:	
84.5	Tax law
84.51	Liability to tax
84.52	Types of income
84.53	Types of person (Table VII)
84.54	Assessment, collection, avoidance
84.545	Allowances
84.55	Personal taxes
84.551	Income tax
84.552	Inheritance taxes
84.56	Company taxes
84.57	Capital taxes
84.575	Property taxes, stamp duties
84.58	Indirect taxes
84.585	Sales taxes
84.59	Customs and excise

Thus, income tax in South Africa would be KR4284.551.

We do ask libraries which devise special schedules of this type to post the details on *lis-moys-users*, so that all users will know what is happening. The information would also be invaluable when the next edition is being compiled.

Changed Numbers

The scheme is generally hospitable to new subjects, with the result that relatively few numbers need to be changed from one edition to another. However, for the 5th edition the decision was taken to update the structure of the scheme from KN84/347.326 to KN98.99/347.3599 to allow for the addition of a construction law section and the potential expansion of environmental law and natural resources, which are now adjacent to each other. Inevitably this will be unpopular with some users who may not have the resources to undertake a reclassification project. Anyone in this position is of course at liberty not to implement the changes at this time and to continue as they are, using whatever local adaptation they have adopted to classify materials in this area. Alternatively they could opt to use some of the new numbers (e.g. those for climate change) while leaving the overall arrangement unchanged.

Below is a summary of the basic structure of this part of the scheme, with the new numbers on the left and original numbers on the right, in italics. Classifiers are referred to the Index-Thesaurus and the schedules themselves for more detail.

KN84	Construction law	*KN84–88*	*Natural resources and energy*
KN85–88	Landlord and tenant		
KN89–92	Natural resources and energy	*KN89*	*Estate management*
KN93	[left unused for future expansion]	*KN90–93*	*Landlord and tenant*
KN94	Environmental law		*[same]*
KN95	Environmental protection		*[same]*
KN96	Planning		*[same]*
KN97	Environmental health		*[same]*
KN98	Agricultural law		*[same]*
KN99	Agricultural produce		*[not used before]*

Other changed numbers

4th edition		5th edition
K79	Bibliographical research	K32
KN83.8	Building and civil engineering contracts	KN84.4
KN267.3	Third parties (partnerships)	KN267.6
KN308.3	Regulatory bodies	KN309.1
KN308.5	Compliance	KN309

Dewey notation

During the preparation of this edition it was found that the Dewey notation had become muddled in places, leading to duplication of numbers, sequences out of place, and some incorrect Index entries. These have now been corrected and more guidance given where Dewey numbers need to be constructed. One area of the schedules particularly affected is that from Legal dictionaries (currently 340.03) to Legal research, Law reform (currently 340.0894–9) where the sequence has been completely renumbered. Classifiers are referred to the schedules for more detail.

Synopsis

Schedules

K	**Journals and Reference Books**	**340**	
1–28	Journals		.01
29–79	Bibliography		.02–04
80–90	Library and information science		.05
100–107	Legal writing, publishing		.06
110–114	Abbreviations, etc		.07
120–126	Dictionaries, etc		.08
140	Encyclopedias (general)		.089
150–180	Directories		.09
200	Maps, etc.		.099

KA	**Jurisprudence**	**340**	**.1**

KB	**General and Comparative Law**	**340**	
10–22	Biography, memoirs etc		.31–35
30–35	Legal miscellany		.37
40–66	Popular accounts		.4
100–250	Comparative law		.5–6

KC	**International Law**	**341**	
10–65	Primary materials		.11–16
71–76	Reference materials		.17
80–86	General works		.19
	Public international law		
100–136	General, history, theory etc		.2–23
140–199	The State		.24–31
200–209	Human rights		.33
210–219	International criminal law		.35–39
220–239	International economic law		.4–43
240–242	Social laws		.44–442
243	Environmental law		.444–4444

245	Nuclear energy		.448
250–255	Transport		.45
256–259	Communications		.46
260–277	International maritime law		.47–48
280–284	Outer space		.49
300–317	International relations		.5–53
320–329	Diplomacy		.54–5
330–339	Treaties		.56–9
340–1199	International organisations		.6
1200–1319	International disputes, courts etc		.7
1350–1425	War		.8
2000–2150	Conflict of laws		.9

KD	**Religious Legal Systems**	**342**	
10–39	General		.1
60–890	Jewish law		.2
100–590	Christian churches		.3–6
600–680	Islamic law		.7
700–780	Hindu law		.8
800–980	Others		.9

KE	**Ancient and Medieval Law**	**343**	
5–20	General		.1
21–29	Ancient Near East		.2
30–95	Hellenistic law		.3
100–250	Roman law		.1
251–300	Byzantine law		.5
310–340	Other ancient European systems		.6
350–380	Medieval and Pre-Napoleonic European law		.7
400–480	Roman–Dutch law		.8
500–540	Others		.9

KF–KN	**Common Law**	**344–347**	
KF	Primary materials	344	
KG	British Isles		
KH	Canada, US, West Indies		

	Treatises		
KL	General	345	
1–44	Legal system		.1
50–119	Legal profession		.17
130–149	Legal education		.178
155–179	Legal research, law reform		.19
200–319	Administration of justice		.2–7
400–480	Legal history		.8–9
KM	Public Law	346	
1–29	General		.01
	Constitutional and administrative law		
31–141	General		.1–2
171–207	Citizens		.3–35
208–229	Civil and human rights		.36
231–259	Government		.37–8
300–307	Administrative law		.4
331–359	Public finance, taxation		.5
361–391	Local government		.6
400–416	Military law		.7
	Criminal law and procedure		
500–565	General, crimes		.8
570–690	Criminal procedure, law enforcement		.9
KN	Private Law	347	
(1)–(4)	Conflict of laws (alternative)		(.1–4)
10–25	Contract, agency		.1
30–39	Tort		.2
	Property		
50–58	General		.3–3057
60–98	Real property		.31–35
100–118	Personal property		.36–37
120–143	Inheritance and succession		.38–39
	Persons and social laws		
150–169	Persons		.4
170–176	Family law		.42
180–182	Social services, education		.43–.445
185	Public health, medical law		.446–9

186	Controls in the public interest	.45
190–198	Industrial law and relations	.46
200–235	Equity	.5
	Commercial law	
250–256	General, trade, etc	.6–619
260–279	Business associations, industries	.62–64
280–287	Sale of goods	.65–67
290–295	Insurance	.68–69
300–315	Finance, investment	.7
320–329	Transport (non-maritime)	.81–82
330–338	Maritime law	.86
340–349	Communications law, computer law	.84–89
350–399	Procedure (general and civil)	.9

KP–KW	**Other Modern Legal Systems**		
KP	Preferred Jurisdiction	348	
KR	Africa	349	.6
KS	Latin America		.8
KT	Asia And Pacific		.5
KV	Europe		.4
KW	European Union Law (Alternative)		

KZ	**Non-Legal Subjects**

Appendix

Criminology

Tables

Index of Jurisdictions

Index-Thesaurus

Schedules

K Journals and Reference Books 340

Note:
Some general libraries may prefer to place in another part of the library some of the material here, such as Library and Information Science K80–99/340.05 or Dictionaries, K120–6/340.08.

Journals

1 *By title*, A–Z .01

Notes:
1. As an alternative to placing all journals, regardless of legal topic, country of origin, etc., together in K1, numbers are provided in other classes, e.g. KA1, KF99 and in the Tables.
2. Numbers K2–27/340.02–8 are free for the arrangement of journals by language, or other criterion, if desired.
3. Indexes to an individual journal should be placed with the journal.
4. Some journals include law reports. If the reports predominate, treat as law reports, otherwise as journals.

28 Indexes, abstracts (*to two or more titles*) .019

Bibliography

Notes:
1. Include here library catalogues, union lists, etc.
2. As an alternative to placing subject bibliographies here, numbers are provided in other classes, e.g. KA5, KC71 and in the Tables.

29 *General and non-legal* .02
30 Legal bibliography .021
31 Journals .022
32 Bibliographical research .023
(For legal research *use* KL155/345.08)
40 *Non-national legal systems, etc.* .025
Divide by the main classification, classes KA–KE/340–343, thus:
Bibliography of jurisprudence:
K40:KA or 340.025:340.1
Bibliography of space law:

K	Journals and Reference Books	340
40	*Non-national legal systems, etc*	0.25
	K40:KC280 or 340.025:341.49	
49–60	*Subjects of public and private law*	.033-9
	Divide by Table IID, e.g.	(Table IIF)
	K49.4 Legal profession	.0331
	K52.2 Taxation	.03472
	K57.6 Industrial law	.0378
	National legal bibliography	.044-9
61	Commonwealth	(DDC
62	England and Wales (*and UK as a whole*)	Table 2)
63	Scotland	
64	Ireland	
71	United States	
72	Rest of America, by country, A–Z	
73	Africa, by country, A–Z	
74	Asia and Pacific, by country, A–Z	
75	Australasia, by country, A–Z	
76	Europe, by country, A–Z	

Library and Information Science

80	*General works*	.05
81	Associations	.051
.9	*by name*, A–Z, e.g.	.0519
	.B5 BIALL	
82	Directories of libraries and librarians by country, A–Z	.052
84	Library administration	.054
.1	Government	.0541
.2	Finance	.0542
.4	Staff	.0544
.5	Buildings, accommodation	.0545
.6	Furniture, equipment	.0546
85	*Special types of library operations*	.055
	by operation, A–Z, e.g.	
	.C3 Cataloguing	
	.I5 Information work	
86	Use of computers and technology	.056
.2	Systems management	.0562

K	Journals and Reference Books	340
86	Use of computers and technology	.056
.4	Online services	.0564
.6	Library networks	.0566
90	*By country*, A–Z	.059
	Legal Writing, Legal Publishing	
	(*see also* Law of publishing KN345/347.88)	
100	Legal language, plain language	.06
.5	Semiotics, law and linguistics	.0605
	(If preferred, *use* KA70.L5/340.16.L5)	
101	Legal composition, legal opinion writing	.061
102	Palaeography, manuscripts	.062
103	Artificial intelligence	.063
104	Translation	.064
105	Publishing, bookselling	.065
.1	Electronic publishing, desktop publishing	.0651
.2	Authorship, punctuation guides, etc.	.0652
.3	Copy editing	.0653
.5	Proof-reading	.0655
.7	Tabling	.0657
.8	Indexing	.0658
.9	Bookselling	.0659
106	*Individual firms*, A–Z	.066
107	Directories	.067
	Abbreviations	
110	General lists	.07
112	Legal abbreviations	.072
114	Citation manuals	.074
	(i.e. how to construct or construe citations. Citators should be placed with the appropriate law reports, etc.)	
	Dictionaries	
	(*see also* Legal dictionaries under jurisdictions)	
120	English, Legal	.08

K Journals and Reference Books 340

Dictionaries

121 Polyglot .081

122 *Other languages*, A–Z, e.g. .082

.L3 Latin

123 Synonyms, antonyms, thesauri .083

124 Proverbs, legal maxims, phrases .084

125 Quotations .085

126 *Others*, A–Z, e.g. .086

.C5 Chemistry

.E2 Economics

140 **Encyclopedias: General** .089

Directories

(including Who's Whos, Law Lists, etc)

Lawyers

150 *Multinational* .09

151 *By jurisdiction*, A–Z .091

Legal associations

160 *General* .092

161 *Multinational* .093

162 *By jurisdiction*, A–Z .094

165 Higher education, law schools .095

166 *By jurisdiction*, A–Z .096

168 Legal services .097

180 *Non-legal directories, by subject*, A–Z .098

200 **Maps, Atlases, Plans** .099

KA Jurisprudence 340

KA		340
(1)	*Journals* (alternative to K1/340.01)	(.101)
(5)	*Bibliography* (alternative to K40/340.025)	(.102)
10	*General works*	.1
	(It is recommended that all general works, regardless of the school of legal theory to which the author subscribes, should be placed here. KA40–49/340.14 should be reserved for critical and historical works about jurists, rather than for their own writings)	
	Special subjects	
19	Historical jurisprudence	.12007
21	Legal concepts	.121
22	Content of law	.122
23	Sources of law	.123
24	Legal personality	.124
25	Legal rights and obligations, liability as a concept	.125
26	Causation	.126
27	Law: The state	.127
28	Judicial process	.128
29	Law: Force	.129
30	*Others*, A–Z, e.g.	.1295
	.E6 Equality before the law	
34	Rule of law	.1298
35	Justice, natural justice	.13
37	Law: Justice	.132
38	Morality: Justice	.134
40	*Schools of legal theory*	.14
41	Natural law, social contract	.141
42	Command: law	.142
43	Idealism	.143
44	Positivism	.144
	Political theories of law	
47	Fascist jurisprudence	.145
48	Communist jurisprudence, socialist jurisprudence	.146
49	*Others*, A–Z, e.g.	.147
	.F4 Feminist	
	.P6 Post modernism	
50	*National schools of legal theory by country*, A–Z	.1479
55	Legal logic, legal reasoning	.148

KA Jurisprudence 340

KA		DDC
59	Critical legal studies	.149
60	Sociology of law	.15
61	Public opinion : Law	.151
62	Public policy : Law	.152
63	Social psychology	.153
64	Civil rights	.154
65	Civil disobedience, opposition to immoral laws	.155
66	Animal rights	.156
67	Multiculturalism	.157
70	*Law in relation to other subjects, by subject*, A–Z, e.g.	.16
	.A7 Arts, literature, music	
	.D4 Development	
	.E2 Economics	
	.E3 Education	
	.E8 Ethics	
	.G4 Geography	
	.H5 History	
	.L5 Linguistics, semiotics	
	.P5 Philosophy	
	.P6 Politics	
	.P7 Psychology	
	.S3 Science	
	.S4 Sexuality	
	.S6 Sociology	
90	Law as a profession (Place here philosophical works only. For the legal profession in a particular jurisdiction *use* KL/345 or Table II)	.19
100–199	Criminology (Optional alternative. The same one hundred numbers, with the "hundred" figure suitably adjusted, can be used at *either* KB300–399, *or* KM700–799.)	

The schedule is printed as the Appendix.

KB General and Comparative Law 340

(1)	*Journals* (alternative to K1)	(.301)
(5)	*Bibliographies* (alternative to K40/340.025)	(.302)

Biography, Memoirs etc.

(As an alternative, biographies reflecting on a particular subject may be placed with the subject, using Table VIII)

	Collections	
10	*General*	.31
11	*By country*, A–Z	.32
15	*Individuals*, A–Z	.33
	under each:	
	.A1 Autobiography, memoirs	
	.A11 Diaries	
	.A12 Letters	
	.A13 Conversations	
	.A14 Speeches	
	.A2–Z Biographies, by author or editor	
21	Genealogy	.34
22	Heraldry	.35

30	**Legal Miscellany, Essays etc.**	**.37**
31	Oratory	.371
32	Poetry, drama	.372
33	Fiction	.373
34	Humorous writings	.374
35	Pictures, sketches, cartoons, photographs	.375

Popular Accounts

Note:
This section is optional, likely to be used by libraries which prefer to keep books intended for laypersons separate from those for professional readers.

40	*General*	.4
45	*By jurisdiction*, A–Z	.41

KB General and Comparative Law 340

Popular Accounts

	Trials	
60	*Collections*	.42
61	*By jurisdiction*, A–Z	.43
	Individual	
65	Criminal, *by defendant*, A–Z	.45
66	Civil, *by best known name*, A–Z	.46

Comparative Law

Notes:

1. Place here books which treat in a comparative manner the law of two or more legal systems from different regions (non-common law).
2. For common law jurisdictions, use KL for general works and KM-KN for individual subjects.
3. The distinction between common law and non- common law may be ignored if it seems preferable to keep all such books together.
4. Books which deal with the law on specific subjects in different jurisdictions without comparing them may be treated the same way as comparative works if desired.

100	*General works*	.5
105	Conferences, by date (Table III)	.51
	(Place here multinational conferences which are not confined to any particular topic or system of law)	
110	Associations	.52
111	*Bar associations*	.521
112	*Others*, A–Z	.522
115	Unification of private law	.53
	(General works only; subjects should be placed in KB161–250/340.6)	
120	Civil law : Common law	.54
121	Civil law systems	.55
	(As a whole and compared with each other. For individual systems *use* KR–KV/349)	

KB General and Comparative Law 340

122	Eastern law : Western law	.56
125	Ancient law : modern law	.57
130	Customary law (General works only. For the customary law of an individual area, tribe etc. *use* KL8 or the appropriate jurisdiction)	.58
140	Legal pluralism	.59
141	Colonial laws (General works only. Place the law of a particular colony in the appropriate jurisdiction)	.591
161–250	*Special subjects* (Use Table IIA, numbers 61 to 150, adding 100 to each, e.g. KB164 Legal professions compared KB177 Political systems, democracy fascism, socialism, communism, etc. KB184 Comparative tax law KB222 Comparative education law (Note: as an alternative, for a library holding only a small quantity of foreign material, the subject numbers for the library's home jurisdiction may be used with .009 from Table VIII)	.6 (Table IIF)

300–399 Criminology

(Optional alternative. The same one hundred numbers, with the "hundred" figure suitably adjusted, can be used at *either* KA100–199, *or* KM700–799.)

The schedule is printed as the Appendix.

KC International Law 341

	Primary Materials	.1
(1)	Journals (alternative to K1)	(.11)
	Treaties	
	(Texts of treaties, conventions and other international agreements. For works about treaties *use* KC330–339/341.56–9)	
	Collections	.12
10	General and multilateral, by first word of best known form of citation, A–Z, e.g.	.121
	.H4 Hertslet's Commercial Treaties	
	.U5 United Nations Treaty Series	
12	*By jurisdiction*, A–Z	.122
	Single treaties	
	Multilateral	
14	Peace treaties, by date (Table III) then by name e.g. .F19.V4 Versailles Treaty 1919	.124
16	*Others*, by date (Table III)	.126
18	*Bilateral*, by date (Table III) then by first named party, A–Z	.128
19	*Indexes*	.129
	Law reports	
20	*General collections* (i.e. cases from several courts) by best known citations, A–Z, e.g.	.13
	.I5 International Law Reports	
	International courts	
	(Reports and related official documents only. For works about the courts *use* KC1210–1249/341.71–4)	
	Permanent Court of International Justice	
21	*Official series* A–Z, by letter and number	.131.A1–6
22	*Unofficial series, collections* etc.	.131.A7–Z
	e.g. .H8 Hudson's World Court Reports	
	International Court of Justice	
23	*Official series* A–Z, by letter and number or date	.132.A1–4
24	*Unofficial series, collections, etc.*	.132.A7–Z

KC	International Law	341
27	Inter-American Court of Justice	.133
28	European Court of Justice	.134
	(May alternatively be placed in KV or KW)	
29	European Court of Human Rights	.135
30	European Commission of Human Rights	.1355
35	*War crimes courts*, A–Z, e.g.	.136
	.N8 Nuremberg International Military Tribunal	
37	*Other international courts*, A–Z	.137
38	*Individual cases*, by date (Table III) then by name, e.g.	.138
	.F27.L6 'Lotus' case, 1927	
39	Cases on international law decided by national courts, by jurisdiction, A–Z	
	Arbitration cases etc.	
	(Reports and official documents only. For works about international arbitration *use* KC1250–79/341.73–4)	
40	*General collections*	.14
	Permanent Court of Arbitration	.141
41	*Official series*	.141.A1–A4
42	*Non-official collections*, e.g.	.141.A7–Z
	.S3 Scott's Hague Court Reports	
47	*Other "permanent" arbitral bodies,* A–Z	.142
48	Claims commissions, mixed arbitral tribunals, *ad hoc* bodies, A–Z	.143
49	*Individual cases*, by date (Table III) e.g.	.148
	.E93 Behring Sea fisheries, 1893	
	Digests, indexes	
50	*Serially published*, by title, A–Z	.15
55	*Others*, by editor or compiler, A–Z	.155
	International conferences	
60	*Collections*	.161
65	*Individual conferences*, by date (Table III) e.g.	.165
	.F44 Dumbarton Oaks Conference, 1944	
	under each:	
	.A1–5 Official reports, proceedings etc.	
	.A6–Z Non-official publications	

KC International Law 341

70	**Reference Materials**	.17
(71)	Bibliographies (alternative to K40)	(.171)
72	Dictionaries	.172
73	Encyclopedias	.173
	Directories	
	(Diplomatic and consular personnel etc.)	
75	*International*	.175
76	*By country*, A–Z	.176
	International Law as a Whole	
	(i.e. both public and private)	
80	*General works*	.19
82	Sources	.192
.1	International custom	.193
86	International law: municipal law	.196
	Public International Law	
100	*General works*	.2
	Legal history	
102	*General works*	.21
	By period, under each classic author, except Grotius:	
	.A1 Collected works	
	.A2 Selections	
	.A3–Z4 Individual works, by title	
	.Z5–Z9 Biography and criticism	
103	*Up to about 1500 AD*	.211
104	*1500 AD to Grotius*	.212
	(e.g. Machiavelli, Vittoria, Belli, Ayala, Suarez, Gentili)	
105	Grotius (1583–1645)	.213
	De Jure Belli ac pacis	
.1	Texts, *by editor*, A–Z	.2131
.2	Commentary and criticism	.2132

KC	International Law	341
105	Grotius (1583–1645)	.213
.3	Other texts, A–Z	.2133
.5	General biography and criticism	.2135
106	*From Grotius to about 1814* (e.g. Zouche, Pufendorf, Bynkershoek, Wolff, Vattel)	.214
	The State	
107	1815–1900	.215
108	1901–1918	.216
109	1919–1945	.217
110	1946–	.218
	Theory and practice of international law by particular groups	
121	Fascists, Nazis etc.	.221
122	Communists, socialists, etc.	.222
123	*By country*, A–Z, e.g. .J17 Japanese practice of international law	.223
124	*Others*, A–Z, e.g. .C3 Catholic; .I8 Islamic	.224
	Special aspects	.23
130	Codification	.231
132	Consent	.232
133	Compliance	.233
135	Individuals (as subjects of international law, *see also* Human rights KC200–8/341.33)	.235
136	Supranationality	.236
140	The State	.24
141	*As a physical entity*	.25
142	National territory	.252
.1	Accretion (e.g. creation of polders)	.2521
.2	Discovery	.2522
.3	Occupation (Civil only; for military occupation *use* KC1400/341.87)	.2523
.4	Settlement	.2524
.5	Colonisation	.2525
.6	Annexation	.2526
.7	Conquest	.2527
143	Frontiers	.253

KC	International Law	341
144	National waters	.254
.1	Territorial sea	.2541
.2	Continental shelf	.2542
.3	Exclusive economic zones	.2543
.5	Drainage basins	.2545
	(For national airspace *use* KC253.3/341.4531)	
145	Islands	.255
.1	Artificial islands	.2551
146	Landlocked states	.256
150	*As a legal entity*	.26
151	Sovereignty	.261
.1	Act of State	.2611
152	Equality	.262
153	*Status of special types or groups of states*	.263
.1	Commonwealth	.2631
.2	Federations	.2632
.3	Papacy	.2633
.4	Micro-states	.2634
154	Dependent states	.264
.1	Colonies	.2641
.2	Protectorates	.2642
.3	Mandates	.2643
.4	Trust territories	.2644
.5	Leased territories	.2645
.6	Condominiums	.2646
.7	International zones	.2647
.8	Associated states	.2648
155	Partition	.265
156	Mergers	.266
160	State succession	.27
161	Transfer of sovereignty	.271
162	Self-determination, referendums	.272
163	New states, division of states	.273
164	Recognition	.274
170	Servitudes	.28
171	Extraterritoriality	.281
172	Concessions	.282
173	Free zones	.283

KC	International Law	341
174	Neutralised zones, demilitarised zones	.284
180	State responsibility	.29
185	Jurisdiction	.291
186	Friendly military personnel	.292
189	*Other aspects*, e.g.	.299
	.G6 Government in exile	
	.H4 Heads of state	
190	Nationality	.31
191	Acquisition, naturalisation	.311
192	Loss, denaturalisation	.312
193	Dual nationality	.313
194	Statelessness	.314
195	Passports, visas	.315
.5	Refugee passports	.3155
196	Diplomatic protection	.316
197	Aliens, deportation	.317
199	Migration, free movement	.319
.5	People smuggling	.3195
200	Human rights (Use Table VII as appropriate)	.33
201	*Special topics*, A–Z e.g. .P7 Privacy	.331
202	Rule of law	.332
203	International protection	.333
204	Discrimination (use Table VII as appropriate)	.334
205	Refugees, displaced persons (*see also* Statelessness KC194/341.314)	.335
206	Asylum; asylum seekers	.336
207	Slavery	.337
208	Human trafficking	.338
209	Prisoners (*see also* Prisoners of war KC1415/341.885)	.339
210	International criminal law	.35
212	Criminal jurisdiction	.352
213	Extraterritorial crime	.353
.2	Crime on the high seas, piracy	.3532
.3	Crime on aircraft, hijacking	.3533
.4	Crime in outer space	.3534
214	Extradition, fugitive offenders, *by country*, A–Z	.354

KC	International Law	341
215	International crimes, crimes against humanity	.36
216	Genocide, ethnic cleansing	.361
217	War crimes (*see also* Geneva Conventions KC1411/341.881)	.362
218	*Others*, A–Z, e.g.	.369
	.D5 Disappearances, kidnapping, secret killing	
	.T4 Terrorism	
	.T6 Torture	
219	International criminal courts (General works. For reports of cases *use* KC20–55/341.13–5)	.39
.1	*Individual courts*, A–Z, e.g.	.391
	.I5 International Criminal Court	
	.R9 International Criminal Tribunal for Rwanda	
	.Y8 International Criminal Tribunal for the former Yugoslavia	
.5	Sentences, e.g. death penalty	.395
220	International economic law	.4
222	Finance, capital movements	.41
223	Debts	.411
.1	Drago doctrine	.4111
.2	War debts	.4112
224	Taxation	.412
.1	Double taxation	.4121
225	Tariffs	.413
.1	Customs unions (Theory only; for particular organisations *see* Index)	.4131
.8	Free trade	.4138
226	Credit, international banks (Theory only; for particular banks *see* Index)	.414
.1	Gold Clause	.4141
.3	Money laundering	.4143
227	Investment	.415
.1	Foreign investment from individual countries, *by country*, A–Z	.4151

KC	International Law	341
227	Investment	.415
.2	Foreign investment to individual countries, *by country*, A–Z	.4152
228	Development law	.4154
230	Trade	.42
231	Commercial agreements	.421
	(Theory only; for texts *use* KC10–18/341.12)	
.1	Reciprocity	.4211
.2	Favoured nation clause	.4212
.9	*Special subjects*, A–Z, e.g. .A7 Art	.4219
232	Raw materials	.422
233	Contracts	.423
.1	Calvo clause	.4231
234	Cartels, multinational companies	.424
235	Dumping	.425
236	Intellectual property, industrial property	.43
	(For World Intellectual Property Organisation *use* KC648/341.6458; for TRIPS *use* KC641–5/341.645)	
.1	Copyright, Berne Convention	.431
.2	Patents	.432
.3	Trade marks	.433
.4	Cultural property	.434
.5	Designs	.435
.9	*Special topics*, A–Z, e.g.	.436
	.G4 Genetically modified organisms	
237	Economic development	.437
238	Expropriation	.438
239	*Other matters*, A–Z, e.g.	.439
	.E8 Espionage, industrial	
240	Social laws	.44
241	Public health	.441
.1	Drugs	.4411
.3	Toxic materials	.4413
242	Industrial law	.442
243	Environmental law	.444
.1	Pollution (generally; for sea pollution *use* KC269/341.474)	.4441

KC	International Law	341
243	Environmental law	.444
.2	Wildlife conservation, biodiversity	.4442
.3	Conservation of sites of historical interest	.4443
.4	Conservation of resources, sustainable development (For resources of the sea and seabed *use* KC276–7/341.48)	.4444
.5	Climate change, global warming	.4445
245	Nuclear energy (peaceful) (For nuclear weapons *use* KC1392/341.862)	.448
250	Transport	.45
.5	Carriage of goods (in general) (For carriage of goods by road *use* KC252.8/341.4528; by air *use* KC253.8/341.4538; by sea *use* KC272.8/341.4758)	.4501
251	Railways	.451
.2	Rail tunnels	.4512
252	Roads, bridges, tunnels	.452
.1	Motor vehicles	.4521
.8	Carriage of goods by road	.4528
253	Air law	.453
.2	Airspace, overflight	.4532
.3	Supersonic flight	.4533
.4	Navigation, flight control	.4534
.5	Aircraft	.4535
.6	Flight crews	.4536
.8	Carriage of goods by air	.4538
254	Flights	.454
.1	Non-scheduled flights	.4541
.3	Charter flights	.4542
.5	Private flights	.4544
255	Scheduled flights	.4545
.1	Routes, cabotage	.4546
.3	Fares	.4547
.4	Aircraft servicing	.4548
.5	Security	.4549

KC	International Law	341
	(For International Air Transport Association *use* KC1193/341.6985)	
256	Communications	.46
.1	Mails	.461
	(For Universal Postal Union *use* KC571–5/341.638)	
257	Telecommunications	.462
	(For International Telecommunications Union *use* KC581–5/341.6385)	
.2	Telephone, telegraph, telex, fax	.4622
.5	Submarine cables	.4625
.6	Electronic data interchange	.4626
.7	Networks, Internet, electronic mail	.4627
.8	Satellites	.4628
258	Media, broadcasting	.464
.5	Radio	.465
259	Television	.466
.1	Cable television	.4661
.2	Satellite television	.4662
260	International maritime law, law of the sea	.47
	(For International Maritime Organisation *use* KC591–5/341.639)	
263	International waters	.471
264	High seas	.4715
265	Straits, bays, (*in general*)	.472
266	*Individual*, A–Z, e.g.	.4725
	.B6 Bosphorus	
	.P4 Persian Gulf	
267	Rivers, canals (*in general*)	.473
	Individuals, A–Z, e.g.	
	.D3 Danube	
	.P3 Panama Canal	
	(For drainage basins *use* KC144.5/341.2545)	
269	Sea pollution	.474
272	Ships	.475
.1	Nationality	.4751
.2	Flags of convenience	.4752
.3	Immunities, government ships	.4753

KC	International Law	341
272	Ships	.475
.4	Searches	.4754
.5	Arrest of ships	.4755
.6	Ship safety	.4756
.8	Carriage of goods by sea, Hamburg Rules, Rotterdam Rules, etc.	.4758
273	Seamen, crews	.476
274	Navigation, rules of the road at sea	.478
.1	Collisions	.4781
.5	Lighthouses, lightships	.4785
275	Wrecks, salvage	.479
276	Natural resources of the sea and seabed	.48
.1	Fisheries	.481
.2	Whaling	.4812
.3	Sealing	.4813
277	Seabed resources	.482
.1	Oil and gas	.4821
.2	Coal	.4822
.3	*Other minerals*, A–Z	.4823
280	Outer space	.49
282	Overflight	.492
284	Satellites, space stations	.494
.1	Space research	.4941
.2	Communications satellites (*see also* KC257.8/341.4628 and KC259.2/341.4662; for spy satellites, *use* KC1355.5/341.825 and KC1306/341.7845)	.4942
	International relations	
300	*General works*, inter-continental relations	.5
.4	Conferences (General works only. *See also* names of particular conferences in the index)	.504
	By region	
302	Africa	.512
.1	North Africa	.5121
.2	East Africa	.5122
.3	West Africa	.5123
.4	Central Africa	.5124

KC	International Law	341
302	Africa	.512
.5	Southern Africa	.5125
303	Asia	.513
.1	East Asia and Pacific	.5131
.2	South-East Asia	.5132
.3	Central (India etc.)	.5133
304	Middle East	.514
305	Europe	.515
.1	Eastern, Balkans	.5151
.2	Central	.5152
.3	Western	.5153
.4	Northern	.5154
306	America	.516
.1	North (e.g. Monroe Doctrine)	.5161
.2	Central, Caribbean	.5162
.3	South and Latin America in general	.5163
.4	South Atlantic (e.g. Falkland Islands)	.5164
307	Australia and New Zealand	.517
308	Polar regions	.518
309	Others	.519
.1	Communist bloc	.5191
.5	Developing countries, Third World	.5195
.7	Buffer states	.5197
310	*By country*, A–Z	.52
312	Peace movements	.53
	(For peace conferences *use* KC60–5/341.16)	
.1	Carnegie Endowment for International Peace	.531
.2	*Others*, A–Z, e.g.	.532
	.C3 Campaign for Nuclear Disarmament	
313	Disarmament	.533
	(For talks and treaties *use* KC336/341.58)	
.5	Arms limitation	.5335
314	World federation	.534
316	Alliances	.536
	(General works only. *See also* names of particular alliances in the index)	
317	Non-alignment, de-alignment	.537
	(*see also* Neutrality KC1360/341.83)	

KC International Law 341

320	Diplomacy	.54
322	Privileges, immunities	.542
.1	Legations (i.e. *buildings*)	.5421
.2	Diplomatic quarters (i.e. *districts*)	.5422
323	Diplomats	.55
	(For privileges and immunities *use* KC322/341.542)	
324	Ambassadors	.551
325	Ministers, Secretaries, attaches, *other staff*	.552
326	Consuls	.553
.1	Consular courts	.5531
327	Agents, special representatives	.554
328	Information services, media, etc.	.555
329	*By country*, A–Z	.557
	Treaties	
	(Theory and history of all kinds of international agreements including talks and negotiations. For texts of treaties and agreements *use* KC10–18/341.12)	
330	*General works*	.56
333	Formation	.561
.1	Parties	.5611
.2	Ratification	.5612
.4	Entry into force	.5614
.5	Amendment	.5615
334	Effect of treaties	.57
.1	Binding nature of treaties on parties/ compliance	.571
.2	Municipal law (i.e. *national law*)	.572
.3	Third parties	.573
.4	Interpretation	.574
336	*By subject matter*	.58
.1	Armaments, disarmament, non-proliferation, arms limitation	.581
.2	Non-aggression	.582
.3	Frontiers	.583
.5	Culture	.585
.6	Environment	.586

KC	International Law			341
336	Treaties *by subject matter*			.58
	(For commerce, navigation, etc. *use* KC231/341.421)			
	(For peace treaties *use* KC1425/341.895)			
.9	*Others*, A-Z			.589
338	*Special aspects*			.59
.1	Reciprocity			.591
.2	Pacta sunt servanda			.592
.3	Termination			.593
.4	Breach of treaty, supervision of treaty			.594
.5	State succession (i.e. *effect of*)			.595
.6	War (i.e. *effect of*)			.596
.7	Jus cogens			.597
339	History, practice, *etc. by country*, A–Z			.599
	International organisations			
340	*General works*			.6
343	Membership			.611
344	Privileges, immunities			.612
345	Regulation of the internal operation of international organisations			.613
346	Officials			.614
349	*By subject*, A–Z, e.g.			.619
	.E2 Economic			
	Individual organisations, under each:-			
		5 Nos.	1 No.	Cutter No.
	Constitution, charter	1	.A1	1
	Debates, proceedings	2	.A2	2
	Annual reports, statistics	3	.A3	3
	Other official documents	4	.A4	4
	Books about the organisation	5	.A5	5
	(Journals should be placed under their subject)			
	Relation to individual countries, *by country*, A–Z			
	World-wide organisations			
351–5	League of Nations			.62
356–60	Assembly			.6211
361	*Committees*, A–Z			.6212
366–70	Council			.6213

KC	International Law	341
371	Permanent Mandates Commission	.6214
376–80	Secretariat	.6215
381	*Other organs*, A–Z	.6219
401–5	United Nations	.622
406–10	General Assembly	.623
411	*Committees*, A–Z	.6239
416–20	Security Council	.624
421	*Committees*, A–Z	.6249
431–5	Economic and Social Council	.625
436	*Commissions*, A–Z	.6259
441–5	Trusteeship Council	.626
446	*Committees*, A–Z	.6269
448	Disarmament Commission	.627
450	International Law Commission	.628
451–5	Secretariat	.629
456	High Commission for Refugees	.6292
458	Relief and Works Agency	.6293
460	Unicef	.6294
465	United Nations Commission on International Trade Law	.6295
501–5	Unesco	.631
511–5	International Labour Organisation/Office	.632
521–5	Food and Agriculture Organisation	.633
531–5	World Health Organisation	.634
536	International Narcotics Control Board	.6345
541–5	World Meteorological Organisation	.635
551–5	International Atomic Energy Agency	.636
561–5	International Civil Aviation Organisation	.637
571–5	Universal Postal Union	.638
581–5	International Telecommunications Union	.6385
586	Intergovernmental Bureau for Informatics	.6386
591–5	International Maritime Organisation (*Previously* Intergovernmental Maritime Consultative Organisation)	.639
596	United Nations Conference on Law of the Sea	.6396
597	International Seabed Authority	.6397
601–5	International Bank for Reconstruction and Development	.64

KC	International Law	341
611–5	International Monetary Fund	.642
621–5	International Finance Corporation	.643
631–5	International Development Association	.644
641–5	GATT, GATS, World Trade Organisation (Place here works about the TRIPS agreement)	.645
646	United Nations Conference on Trade and Development	.6456
647	United Nations Industrial Development Organisation	.6457
648	World Intellectual Property Organisation	.6458
649	*Other UN specialised agencies, related organisations, funds and entities*, A-Z	.64585
650	Organisation of Petroleum Exporting Countries	.6459
	Regional organisations	
705	Africa	.65
711–5	Organisation of African Unity	.651
716	African Commission on Human & Peoples' Rights	.6516
721–5	Organisation Africaine et Malgache de Co-opération Economique	.652
736–40	Southern African Development and Co-operation Conference	.656
750	America	.657
751–5	Organisation of American States	.658
756	Inter-American Conference	.6581
757	*Meeting of Ministers*	.6582
758	*Council*	.6583
759	*Secretariat*	.6584
760	*Specialised organs*, A–Z	.6585
761	North American Free Trade Association	.6586
770	Caribbean Community (CARICOM)	.659
771	Organisation of Eastern Caribbean States	.6591
780	South American organisations, A–Z	.6595
800	Asia (including Middle East)	.66
.5	Arab and Muslim organisations in general	.6605
801–5	Arab League	.661
811–5	Gulf Co-operation Council	.6613

KC	International Law	341
816	*Others*, A–Z	.6616
821–5	Central Treaty Organisation	.662
831–5	Colombo Plan	.663
851–5	South East Asia Treaty Organisation	.664
861–5	Association of South-East Asian Nations	.665
880	Australia and New Zealand	.669
881–5	Anzus Pact	.6691
886	*Other Pacific organisations*, A–Z, e.g.	.6695
	.F6 Forum Fisheries	
	.S6 South Pacific Commission	
900	Europe	.67
901–5	North Atlantic Treaty Organisation (NATO)	.671
911–5	Organisation for Economic Co-operation and Development (OECD)	.672
921–5	Council of Europe	.673
926	*Consultative Assembly*	.6731
927	*Committee of Ministers*	.6732
928	Commission of Human Rights	.6733
	(For case reports *use* KC30/341.1355)	
	(For European Court of Human Rights *use* KC1245/341.725)	
929	*Other organs*, A–Z	.6739
931–5	European Central Inland Transport Organisation	.674
941–5	Nordic Council	.675
951–5	Western European Union	.676
961–5	Benelux	.677
981–5	European Free Trade Association	.678
1001–20	European Union *use* Tables ID and IID	.68
	(As an alternative use nos. 1001–9 only with Table C from KW and inserting a decimal point, e.g. KC1001.4 Official Journal.)	
	(If preferred, *use* KV1–50 or KW)	
1021–5	European Coal and Steel Community	.682
1031–5	European Atomic Energy Community	.683
1101–5	Communist Information Bureau	.689
1111–5	Warsaw Pact	.6891

KC International Law 341

KC		341
1121–5	Council for Mutual Economic Assistance (Comecon)	.6892
1131–5	Danube Commission	.6893
1136–40	Conference on Security and Co-operation in Europe	.6895
1150	*Non-governmental organisations*	.69
1151	Inter-Parliamentary Union	.691
1156	European Movement	.692
1161	World Federation of Trade Unions	.693
1166	International Confederation of Free Trade Unions	.694
1171	World Federation of Labour	.695
1176	European Trade Union Confederation	.696
1181	International Chamber of Commerce	.6965
1191	World Council of Churches	.697
1193	International Air Transport Association	.698
1199	*Others*, A–Z	.699
	International disputes (i.e. peaceful settlement, crisis management)	
1200	*General works*	.7
1202	Crisis management	.702
1205	Dispute resolution, remedies	.705
	International courts (Theory and history only. For reports of cases *use* KC20–39/341.13)	
1210	*General works*	.71
1212	Jurisdiction	.712
1214	Procedure, evidence	.714
1216	Judgments (Theory only, see note above)	.716
1218	Enforcement of judgments	.718
	Individual courts	
1220	Permanent Court of International Justice	.721
1225	International Court of Justice	.722
1230	Inter-American Court of Justice	.723
1235	Caribbean Court of Justice	.7235
1240	European Court of Justice (If preferred, *use* KV or KW)	.724
1245	European Court of Human Rights	.725

KC	International Law	341
	(For European Commission of Human Rights *use* KC928/341.6733)	
1249	*Others*, A–Z	.729
1250	Arbitration	.73
1254	Claims	.734
1255	Procedure	.735
1256	Awards (Theory only; for texts *use* KC40–49/341.14)	.736
1258	Enforcement	.738
1260	Arbitration courts	.74
1261	Permanent Court of Arbitration	.741
1269	*Others*, A–Z	.742
1270	Claims commissions	.743
1271	*Individual*, A–Z	.744
1275	Mixed arbitral tribunals	.745
1276	*Individuals*, A–Z	.746
1279	*Other bodies*	.749
1280	International police and forces, multi-national forces	.75
1281	United Nations Forces	.751
1290	*Other peaceful methods of settlement*	.76
.1	Negotiation	.761
.2	Compromise	.762
.3	Conciliation, mediation	.763
1300	Unfriendly measures (short of war)	.77
1301	*Political measures*	.78
1302	Intervention	.782
1303	Retaliation	.783
1304	Suspension of diplomatic relations	.784
1306	Espionage (peacetime)	.7845
1308	Ultimatums	.785
1309	*Others*	.789
1310	*Economic measures*	.79
1311	Embargoes	.791
1312	Sanctions	.792
1313	Pacific blockade	.793
1319	*Others*	.799

KC	International Law	341
	War, armed conflict	
1350	*General works*	.8
1353	Legality; jus ad bellum	.81
1355	*Special aspects*	.82
.1	Aggression, invasion	.821
.2	Declaration of war	.822
.3	Self-defence	.823
.4	Belligerent rights	.824
.5	Espionage	.825
.6	Child soldiers	.8256
.7	Deserters	.826
.8	Enemy aliens	.8261
1356	Trade	.827
1357	Property	.828
.2	Art works	.8282
1360	Neutrality in war (*see also* non-alignment KC317/341.537)	.83
1361	*By country*, A–Z	.831
1365	Civil war, rebellion	.84
1368	Guerrilla warfare	.845
1370	Land warfare	.85
1375	Aerial warfare	.852
1380	Maritime warfare	.854
1381	Submarine warfare	.8541
1385	Blockade, contraband	.8545
1386	Neutral trade, innocent passage	.8546
1388	Prize	.8548
1390	Weapons	.86
1391	Firearms, explosives	.861
1392	Nuclear weapons	.862
1395	Prohibited weapons	.865
.1	Chemical weapons	.8651
.2	Poison gas	.8652
.5	Bacteriological weapons	.8655
1400	Military occupation	.87
1401	Government	.871
1403	Civilians	.873
1404	Property, damage	.874

KC International Law 341

1410	International humanitarian law	.88
1411	Geneva conventions	.881
1412	Red Cross	.882
1413	Internees	.883
1414	Hostages	.884
1415	Prisoners of war	.885
1416	Hospitals	.886
.5	Hospital ships	.8865
1420	Termination	.89
1421	Surrender	.891
1422	Armistice, truce	.892
1425	Peace treaties (Theory only; for texts *use* KC14/341.124)	.895
1427	Reparation	.897

Conflict of Laws

Note:
Place works on international aspects of the conflict of laws here. Works on national aspects, e.g. conflicts between units of a federal state, may be placed here or, alternatively, in KN1–4/347.01–4 or under country using Table II.

2000	*General works*	.9
	By country	
2011–29	Common law countries (Table IV)	
2030	*Other countries*, A–Z	.91A–Z
2050	Jurisdiction, forum shopping (For foreign sovereigns *use* KC189.H4/341.299.H4; for diplomatic immunity *use* KC322/341.542)	.92
2055	Characterisation	.925
2058	Choice of law	.93
2060	Renvoi	.94
2061	Foreign court theory	.945
2065	Domicile	.95
2066	Origin	.951
2067	Choice	.952
2069	*By persons* (Table VII)	.959

KC International Law 341

2070	Foreign law		.96
2071	Proof of foreign law		.961
2079	*By subject* (Table IIF)		.969
2080	Foreign judgments		.97
2082	Enforcement		.975
2085	Foreign arbitral awards		.98
2086	*International arbitration in private cases*		.985
2095–150	*Subjects of private law* Table IIA nos. 95–150, e.g.		.9906–9 (Table IIF)
	2097–8	Contracts	.99063
	2116–9	Family law	.99076
	2135	Bankruptcy	.990869

KD Religious Systems 342

	General	
(1)	*Journals* (alternative to K1)	(.101)
(5)	*Bibliographies* (alternative to K40)	(.105)
10	*General works*	.1
	(For church and state *use* KM58/346.138 *and* Constitutional law in Table II)	
	(For freedom of religion *use* KM206/346.356 *and* Constitutional law in Table II)	
15	*Sources, collections*	.15
18	*By country*, A–Z	.18
	Special subjects, table for use under particular religious systems:	

10 Nos.	1 No.	
1	.1	Church organisation, church government, sects
2	.2	Clergy, monks, nuns
3	.3	Laymen, converts, missions
4	.4	Church property
5	.5	Doctrine, worship, sacraments
6	.6	Criminal law
7	.7	Private law
.2	.72	Obligations
.4	.74	Property, inheritance
.6	.76	Censorship
8	.8	Family law, personal law
.2	.82	Women
.4	.84	Marriage, divorce
.6	.86	Children
.9	.89	Slavery, servitude
9	.9	Courts, procedure

31–39	*Special subjects* (use table above)	.19
	(Use only for works covering several religions)	

KD	Religious Systems	342
	Jewish Law	
60	*General works*	.2
	Sources, texts	
65	*Collections*	.21
66	Torah	.22
.1	Pentateuch	.221
.2	Prophets	.222
.3	Hagiographa, Midrash, *other very early writings*	.223
68	Talmud	.23
.1	Mishnah	.231
.2	Gemara	.232
.3	Halakha	.233
70	*Codes*	.24
.2	Mishneh Torah (*Maimonides*)	.242
.4	Tur (*Jacob ben Asher*)	.244
.6	Shulhan Aruk (*Josef Karo*)	.246
.9	*Others, by date* (Table III)	.249
	Responsa	
75	*Collections*	.25
76	*Individual books, by date* (Table III)	.26
78	*By country*, A–Z	.28
81–89	*Special subjects* (use table after KD18)	.291–9
	Christian Churches	
100	*General works*	.3
105	*Sources, collections*	.305
108	*By country*, A–Z	.308
109	*Special subjects* (use table after KD18), e.g.	.309
	.1 Ecumenical movement	
	Roman Catholic Church (General and western branch)	
110	*General works*	.31
118	*By country*, A–Z	.32

KD Religious Systems 342

	Sources	
120	*Collections*, by date (Table III)	.33
125	*Pre-Corpus juris canonici texts*, by date of first publication (Table III)	.331
130	Corpus Juris Canonici	.34
140	Later, pre-Codex texts	.35
150	Codex Juris Canonici (Use Table III to arrange versions by date of promulgation)	.36
160	*Other official documents*	.37
161	Acta Apostolicae Sedis	.371
162	Papal bulls	.372
163	Papal constitutions	.373
	Reports of cases	
170	*General collections*	.38
171	Papal courts	.381
172	*Other courts*, by country, A–Z	.382
181–189	*Special subjects* (use table after KD18)	.391–9
	Eastern non-orthodox churches	
200	*General works*	.4
205	*Sources*	.41
208	*By country*, A–Z	.415
209	*Special subjects* (use table after KD18)	.42
210	Uniate churches, A–Z, e.g.	.43
	.M3 Malabar Church	
220	*Other churches*, A–Z, e.g.	.44
	.C6 Coptic Church	
	Orthodox Churches	
300	*General works*	.45
305	*Sources*	.455
308	*By country*, A–Z, e.g.	.458
	.G7 Greek Orthodox Church	
	.R8 Russian Orthodox Church	
	.S6 Spiritualism	
309	*Special subjects* (use table after KD18)	.459
	Protestant churches	
	(Arrange individual churches, except Church of England, by table after KD18)	

KD	Religious Systems	342
400–409	*Collections*	.5
410–419	Lutheran churches	.51
420–429	Calvinist churches	.52
	Church of England	
450	*General works*	.6
	Sources	
460	*Collections*, by date (Table III)	.61
	Legislation of the Church	
461	*Before 1603*, by date (Table III)	.621
462	Canons of 1603	.622
463	Canons of 1640	.623
464	*Later amendments*, by date (Table III)	.624
	General Synod Measures (i.e. Church Assembly Measures to 1971)	
465	*Revised editions*, by date (Table III)	.63
466	*Annual volumes*	.636
467	*Individual measures* (prefer subject)	.637
	Legislation of Parliament specifically affecting the Church	
468	*Collections*, by date (Table III)	.64
469	*Individual acts* (prefer subject)	.645
	Reports of cases	
470	*Series, by date* A–Z	.65
471	*Individual reporters*, A–Z	.651
472	*Individual cases*, (for arrangement see note at KF72)	.652
	Special subjects	
477	Common law : canon law	.67
479	Church of England : Roman Catholic Church	.675
481–489	*Other subjects*, use table after KD18	.68
500	*Other Anglican or Episcopalian Churches, by country*, A–Z	.69
510	Free churches (use table after KD18)	.691
520–529	Methodist Church	.6912
530–539	Congregational Church	.6913

KD	Religious Systems	342
540–549	Baptist Church	.6914
550–559	Presbyterian Church	.6915
560–569	Unitarian Church	.6916
570–579	Society of Friends	.6917
580	*Others*, A–Z	.6918
590	*Other churches and sects*, A–Z, e.g.	.6919
	.B7 Brethren	
	.M6 Mormons	
	Islamic Law	
	(Use for general material only; place modern national versions, e.g. Iran, under jurisdiction in KP–KV)	
600	*General works*	.7
610	*Schools and sects*	.71
611	Sunnite law	.711
616	Shiite law	.716
	Sources	
620	*Collections*	.72
621	Koran	.721
622	Sunna, Hadith	.722
623	Ijma	.723
624	Qiyas	.724
	(See also codes and legislation of modern countries, e.g. Egypt, Pakistan)	
631–680	*Special subjects* (Table IIB, numbers 31–80) e.g.	.729
	643 Real property	(Table IIF)
	643.1 Wakf	
	Hindu Law	
	(Use for general material only; place modern national versions under the country in KR–KT)	
700	*General works*	.8
710	*Schools and sects*	.81
712	Dayabhaga	.812
714	Mitakshara	.814
715	*Others*, A–Z	.815

KD	Religious Systems	342
	Sources	
720	*Collections*	.82
721	Vedas	.821
722	Smriti	.822
726	*Others*, A–Z, e.g.	.8229
	.G4 Gentoo	
728	*Commentaries and digests, by author*, A–Z (See also codes and legislation of modern countries, e.g. India)	.823
731–780	*Special subjects* (Table IIB, numbers 31–80) e.g.	.829
	749 Persons and status	(Table IIF)
	749.5 Caste	

	Other Oriental Systems	**.9**
	(Use table after KD18)	
800–809	Buddhist law	.91
820–829	Jain law	.92
840–849	Sikh law	.93
860–869	Parsi law	.94
900–909	Confucian law	.95
920–929	Tao law	.96
940–949	Lamaism	.97
960–969	Shinto law	.98
980	*Others*, A–Z	.99

KE Ancient and Medieval Law 343

Note:
This class comprises legal systems originating in the ancient or medieval periods and which are not clearly identified with any single modern nation state.

(1)	*Journals* (alternative to K1)	(.11)
(3)	*Bibliographies* (alternative to K40)	(.13)
5	*General works*	.15
	Primitive Law	
8	*General works*	.18
9–20	*Special subjects* (Table IID, numbers 9–20)	.19
	Ancient Near East	
	(Before about 540 BC)	
21	*General works*	.2
22	Cuneiform laws	.22
23	Assyro-Babylonian law	.23
24	Sumerian law	.24
25	Persian law	.25
.2	Medean law	.252
26	Greek law (pre-Hellenistic)	.26
27	Egyptian law (pre-Hellenistic)	.27
29	*Others*, A–Z, e.g.	.29
	.C7 Cretan law	
	.H5 Hittite law	
	(For Jewish law *use* KD60–89/342.2)	
	Hellenistic Law	
	(Law of the eastern Mediterranean area between about 450 BC and about 146 BC)	
30	*General works*	.3
33	Papyrology	.33
	Greek law	
40	General works	.34
45	*Sources*	.35

KE Ancient and Medieval Law 343

47	Trials	.355
51–90	*Special subjects* (Table IIC, numbers 11–50)	.36
94	Spartan law	.38
95	Rhodian law	.39

Roman Law

(Place here general materials and works on the Western Empire from about 753 BC to about 600 AD. For the Eastern Empire *use* Byzantine law, KE251–300/343.5)

100	*General works*	.4
	History	
102	*General works*	.41
103	Individual jurists, A–Z	.411
(105)	*By subject* (prefer KE163–250/343.49)	
	Sources, texts codes	
110	Legislation (theory and forms)	.419
111	Literary aspects	.4191
120	*Collections*	.42
125	Twelve Tables (451–450 BC)	.43
128	Lex Aebutia (c. 125 BC)	.435
130	Gaius (c. 161 AD)	.44
135	Constitutio Antoniniana (212 AD)	.45
140	Codex Theodosianus (438 AD)	.46
145	Justinian (527–65 AD)	.47
150	Corpus Juris Civilis	.471
151	Institutiones	.472
152	Digesta	.473
153	Codex	.474
154	Novellae	.475
160	*Later Western texts, by author*, A–Z	.48
163–250	*Special subjects* (Table IIA, numbers 63–150), e.g.	(Table IIF)
	192 Sanctuary	.49055
	213 Persons, coloni	.490751
	216 Family law, patria potestas	.49076
	220 Slavery	.49077

KE Ancient and Medieval Law 343

	Byzantine Law	
	(Roman law as developed in the Eastern empire from about 600 AD to 1453 AD)	
251	*General works*	.5
	Sources	
255	*Collections*	.51
256	Basilica	.52
257	Hexabiblos	.53
259	*Others*, A–Z	.54
261–300	*Special subjects* (Table IIC, numbers 11–50)	.59 (Table IIF)

	Other Ancient European Systems	
310	*General works*	.6
	Germanic law	
	(Up to the end of the migrations about 600 AD. *See also* the legal history of relevant modern jurisdictions)	
320	*General works*	.62
	(For Anglo-Saxon law *use* KL401.2/345.941)	
.1	Burgundian law	.621
.2	Frankish law	.622
.3	Friesian law	.623
.4	Gothic law	.624
.5	Lombard law	.625
.6	Norman law (*see also* KL401/345.941)	.626
	(For Salic law *use* Frankish law)	
.8	Saxon law	.628
.9	Swabian law	.629
321	Scandinavian law, Viking law	.63
330	Celtic law	.65
340	Slavic law	.68

KE Ancient and Medieval Law 343

Medieval and Pre-Napoleonic European Law

Notes:
1. Period from about 600 AD to1804 AD, but varies according to country.
2. Place here general works only. For national or local treatment use the legal history of appropriate modern jurisdictions, e.g. for British Isles *use* KL400/345.8.

350	*General works*	.7
355	Medieval law (about 600–1499)	.72
356	Feudal law	.74
357	Medieval Roman law	.75
359	Reception of Roman law	.76
360	Sixteenth century	.77
370	Seventeenth century	.78
380	Eighteenth century	.79

Roman–Dutch Law

Notes:
1. Special adaptation of Roman law in the Netherlands, originating about 1473 and lasting, in its pure form, until about 1809.
2. For modern national systems based on Roman–Dutch law *see* Guyana, South Africa, Sri Lanka, Surinam.

400	*General works*	.8
	Sources	
410	*Collections*	.82
412	Grotius	.83
415	Voet	.84
420	Bijnkershoek	.85
421	*Others*, A–Z	.86
423–480	*Special subjects* (Table IIB, numbers 23–80)	.89 (Table IIF)

KE	Ancient and Medieval Law	343
	Oriental Laws	
	(*See also* under jurisdiction in KT)	
500	*General works*	.91
509–520	*Special subjects* (Table IID, numbers 9–20)	.92 (Table IIF)
	Other Ancient Systems	
	American aboriginals	
530	*General works*	.94
531	*By tribe*, A–Z	.95
	(For African laws *see* KR)	
540	*Others*, A–Z, e.g.	.99
	.A8 Australian aboriginals	

KF Common Law 344
Primary Materials – British Isles

Notes:
1. If using KF, arrange material for England and Wales by the schedule below and arrange materials for the other jurisdictions by Table I, sub-section A, B, C or D as indicated.
2. If using 344, employ country numbers from the geographic table in the Dewey Decimal Classification and arrange material for each jurisdiction by Table IE.

England and Wales

(including the United Kingdom as a whole)

1 *Official gazettes*

Parliamentary Publications

2 *General*

House of Lords

3 *General, H.L. papers*

4 *Journal*

5 Hansard

6 *Bills*

7 *Committees*, A–Z

House of Commons

9 *General, H.C. papers*

10 *Journals*

11 Hansard

12 *Bills*

13 *Committees*, A–Z

17 Command papers (by command number)

(If preferred, arrange by subject)

Legislation

Statutes

(Note: If held as a series, arrange as below. If preferred, individual Acts, orders etc. may be classified by subject, as should any collection limited to a particular subject)

KF **Common Law** **344**
Primary Materials – British Isles

Revised or collected editions
20 *Modern* (i.e. about 1870 onwards), by date of revision (Table III)
21 *Earlier editions*, by editor, A–Z (if no editor, by title)
22 *Sessional volumes* (official editions)
23 *Non-official editions*, by editor or title, A–Z, e.g.
.H3 Halsbury's Statutes
24 *Private, local and personal acts*
25 *War and emergency legislation*
26 *Indexes, tables*
Subordinate legislation
(See note under Statutes, above)
30 *Revised or collected editions, by date* (Table III)
31 *Sessional or annual volumes* (Official editions)
32 *Non-official editions, by editor or title*, A–Z
33 *Tables of S.I. effects, etc.*
34 *Indexes, other tables*
37 Prerogative instruments
.1 *Royal proclamations and instructions*
.2 *Orders-in-Council*
.3 *Letters patent*
.4 *Others*
40 *Codes* (prefer arrangement by subject)
Local legislation
41 *Counties*, A–Z
42 *Cities, boroughs, districts*, etc. A–Z
Administrative and executive publications
(Place here general publications only; prefer subject arrangement)
45 Legal Officers (opinions etc.)
46 *Other government departments*, A–Z
47 Royal Commissions, *other ad hoc bodies*, A–Z
Law reports
Reports of cases before about 1865
50 Yearbooks, by editor or series, A–Z, e.g.
.M3 Maynard edition

KF Common Law Primary Materials – British Isles 344

51 Court rolls, e.g.
- .C8 Curia Regis rolls
- .P5 Pipe rolls

53 *Collected reports*, by title, A–Z, e.g.
- .E5 English Reports
- .R4 Revised Reports

54 *Individual reporters*, A–Z, e.g.
- .C6 Coke's reports (Q.B. 1572–1616)

Reports of cases from 1865 onwards

55 The Law Reports

(The correct order of shelving the various sets of this series can be found in several legal reference books. The Cutter numbers below are designed to assist with placing the four main sets in the correct order)
- .A6 Appellate
- .C5 Chancery and Equity
- .C6 Common Law (several series 1865–90)
- .P7 Probate etc.
- .W4 Weekly Law Reports
- .Z1 *Indexes*
- .Z5 *Digests*

60 *Other modern general series by title*, A–Z, e.g.
- .A4 All England Law Reports Reprint (1843–1935)
- .A5 All England Law Reports (1936–)
- .L3 Law Times Reports
- .W4 Weekly Notes

65 Modern specialised series, by title, A–Z, e.g.
- .A7 Aspinall's Maritime Law Cases
- .C7 Criminal Appeal Reports
- .T3 Tax Cases

70 State trials, by editor, A–Z, e.g.
- .H6 Howell's state trials

72 *Individual cases*, by date, then name under each case:
- .A1 Decision
- .A2 Briefs
- .A3 Pleadings, arguments etc.
- .A4 Other documents

KF Common Law 344
Primary Materials – British Isles

72 *Individual cases*, by date, then name under each case:
.A5 Appeal papers
e.g. Appeal papers in Abbott v. Philbin
[1961] A.C. 352, would be: KF72.F61.A1.A5
Administrative decisions
75 *Collections, by title or editor*, A–Z
76 *Special, by Ministry, Department etc., by keyword*, A–Z,
e.g.
.E3 Education and Science, Department of
Digests, abridgments (etc.,)
80 *Digests of mainly historical interest* (i.e. published before about 1865) by editor, e.g.
.B3 Bacon's Abridgment
85 *Modern digests*, (i.e. about 1865 –)
(Note: a digest to a particular series of law reports should be placed with the reports in KF55–65)
Arrange by title, A–Z, e.g.
.C9 Current Law
.C91 Consolidation
.C92 Yearbook
.C93 Monthly parts
.C94 Citator
(99) Journals (alternative to K1)

Remainder of The British Isles

Note:
Materials concerning devolution should be placed in KM 82–87 (legislatures) or KM111–114 (executives).

101–160 Scotland (A)
e.g.
102 Scottish Parliament publications
136 Scottish Executive publications

KF Common Law Primary Materials – British Isles 344

161–180 Wales (B)
e.g.
162 National Assembly for Wales:
(Cynulliad Cenedlaethol Cymru) publications
173.1 Assembly Cabinet (Cabinet y Cynulliad) publications
201–260 Ireland (as a whole) (A)
301–360 Northern Ireland (A)
401–460 Irish Republic (A)
501–510 Isle of Man (C)
511–520 Channel Islands (as a whole) (C)
521–530 Jersey (C)
531–540 Guernsey (C)
541–550 Alderney (C)
551–560 Sark (C)

KG Common Law 344
Primary Materials – America

Notes:

1. If using KG, arrange material for the United States by the schedule below and arrange material for the other jurisdictions by Table I, subsection A, B, C or D as indicated.
2. If using 344, employ country numbers from the geographic table in the Dewey Decimal Classification and arrange material for each jurisdiction by Table IE.

1–60	**Canada (A)**
	(Note: include here material covering two or more Provinces, e.g. Western Weekly Reports)
61–80	Alberta (B)
81–100	British Columbia (B)
101–120	Manitoba (B)
121–140	New Brunswick (B)
141–160	Newfoundland (B)
161–180	Nova Scotia (B)
181–200	Ontario (B)
201–220	Prince Edward Island (B)
221–240	Quebec (B)
241–260	Saskatchewan (B)
261–270	Yukon (C)
271–280	Northwest Territories (C)

	United States
301	*Early legislative material* (i.e. pre-1776)
	Congressional publications
302	*Collections*
303	*Bills of both Houses*
304	Congressional Record
	Senate
305	*General papers*
306	*Journal*
307	*History of the bills (i.e. index to journal)*
308	*Bills*

KG Common Law Primary Materials – America 344

309 *Committees*, A-Z
310 *Others*
House of Representatives
312 *General papers*
313 *Journal*
314 *Calendars*
315 *Bills*
316 *Committees*, A-Z
317 *Others*
Constitution (including Amendments)
318 *Official editions*, by date (Table III)
319 *Non-official editions*, by editor or title, A-Z
Legislation
Statutes
(Note: individual statutes are normally classified by subject, unless held as a series, in which case use the appropriate number below)
320 *Official compilations, by date* (Table III)
321 *Non-official compilations, by editor or title*, A-Z
322 Statutes at large
323 *Sessional volumes*
326 *Indexes, tables*
327 *Citations, by title or editor*, A-Z
Subordinate legislation
(General collections only. Subject collections should be placed with subject)
330 Federal Register
331 Code of Federal Regulations
332 *Indexes, tables*
Administrative and executive publications
340 *General works*
341 Department of Justice
342 *Other government departments*, A–Z
343 *Ad hoc commissions, committees* etc. (preferably with the subject)

KG Common Law 344
Primary Materials – America

Law reports

Under each series with five numbers:

1 Main series

2 Supplements

3 Citators

4 Digests and indexes

5 Other materials

350 *Early reports* (i.e. pre-1776)

Reports from both Federal courts and State courts

352 National Reporter System

(Note: if the complete series, or nearly complete series is held, all parts should be placed in KG352. If only a few parts are held and there is no intention of obtaining other parts, the alternative numbers may be used)

Individual series, by title, A–Z, e.g.

.A1–5	Atlantic Reporter
.C1–5	California Reporter
.F11–15	Federal Cases (alternative KG373)
.F21–25	Federal Reporter (alternative KG373)
.F31–35	Federal Supplement (alternative KG373)
.F41–45	Federal Rules Decisions (alternative KG373)
.N21–25	New York Supplement
.S81–85	Supreme Court Reporter (alternative KG364)

357 Other general series, A–Z, e.g.

.A1–5	American Law Reports
.L1–5	Law Reports Annotated

359 *Specialised Series*, A–Z

Federal courts

361 Supreme Courts

362 *Official editions*

363 *Non-official editions*, e.g.

.L3 Lawyers' edition

(364) Supreme Court Reporter (alternative KG352)

KG Common Law Primary Materials – America 344

365 *Citations*
366 *Digests, indexes*
367 *Individual cases*
(For arrangement see note at KF72)
370 Circuit Courts, District Courts, A-Z
371 Court of Appeals, Circuit Court of Appeals
372 *Other Federal courts*, A-Z
373 *Non-official series (see note at KG352)*
(.F11–15 Federal Cases)
(.F21–25 Federal Reporter)
(.F31–35 Federal Supplement)
(.F41–45 Federal Rules Decisions)
374 *Citations, indexes etc.*
375 *Individual cases*
(for arrangement see note at KF72)
Administrative decisions
376 *Collections*
377 *By Department, etc.*, A-Z
Digests
(Place here materials covering Federal courts or both Federal and State courts. Place materials covering several States in KG398 and material for a single State under the State in KG401–1420. Place digests to a particular series of reports with the reports)
380 *Early materials of mainly historical interest*
382 *Modern digests*, e.g.
.A1 American Jurisprudence
.A12 American Jurisprudence 2d
391–398 *Collected State materials* (Table ID) e.g.
391 Constitutions
392 Legislation
(399) Journals (alternative to K1)
Individual States etc.
401–420 Alabama (B)
421–440 Alaska (B)
441–460 Arizona (B)
461–480 Arkansas (B)

KG Common Law 344
Primary Materials – America

481–500	California (B)
501–520	Colorado (B)
521–540	Connecticut (B)
541–560	Delaware (B)
561–580	Florida (B)
581–600	Georgia (B)
601–620	Hawaii (B)
621–640	Idaho (B)
641–660	Illinois (B)
661–680	Indiana (B)
681–700	Iowa (B)
701–720	Kansas (B)
721–740	Kentucky (B)
741–760	Louisiana (B)
761–780	Maine (B)
781–800	Maryland (B)
801–820	Massachusetts (B)
821–840	Michigan (B)
841–860	Minnesota (B)
861–880	Mississippi (B)
881–900	Missouri (B)
901–920	Montana (B)
921–940	Nebraska (B)
941–960	Nevada (B)
961–980	New Hampshire (B)
981–1000	New Jersey (B)
1001–1020	New Mexico (B)
1021–1040	New York (state) (B)
1041–1060	North Carolina (B)
1061–1080	North Dakota (B)
1081–1100	Ohio (B)
1101–1120	Oklahoma (B)
1121–1140	Oregon (B)
1141–1160	Pennsylvania (B)
1161–1180	Rhode Island (B)
1181–1200	South Carolina (B)
1201–1220	South Dakota (B)

KG Common Law Primary Materials – America 344

1221–1240 Tennessee (B)
1241–1260 Texas (B)
1261–1280 Utah (B)
1281–1300 Vermont (B)
1301–1320 Virginia (B)
1321–1340 Washington (state) (B)
1341–1360 West Virginia (B)
1361–1380 Wisconsin (B)
1381–1400 Wyoming (B)
1401–1420 District of Columbia (B)
(For other US territories *see* KS and KT)

Caribbean, etc.

1501–1520 West Indies Federation (1958–62); Commonwealth Caribbean (B)
1521–1530 Barbados (C)
1531–1540 Leeward Islands (C)
1541–1550 Antigua and Barbuda (C)
1551–1560 Montserrat (C)
1561–1570 St. Christopher and Nevis, Anguilla (C)
1571–1580 Virgin Islands (British) (C)
1581–1590 Windward Islands (C)
1591–1600 Dominica (C)
1601–1610 Grenada (C)
1611–1620 St. Lucia (C)
1621–1630 St. Vincent (C)
1631–1640 West Indies Associated States (1967 to various dates) (C)
1641–1660 Jamaica (B)
1661–1680 Trinidad and Tobago (B)
1681–1700 Bahamas (B)
1701–1720 Bermuda (B)
1721–1740 Guyana (B)
1741–1760 Belize (B)
1781–1790 Turks and Caicos Islands (C)
1791–1800 Cayman Islands (C)

KH Common Law 344
Primary Materials – Australasia

Notes:

1. If using KH, arrange material for each jurisdiction by Table I, subsection, A, B, C or D as indicated.
2. If using 344, employ country numbers from the geographic table in the Dewey Decimal Classification and arrange material for each jurisdiction by Table IE.

1–60	**Australia (A)**
61–80	New South Wales (B)
81–100	Queensland (B)
101–120	South Australia (B)
121–140	Tasmania (B)
141–160	Victoria (B)
161–180	Western Australia (B)
181–200	Northern Territory (B)
201–220	Australian Capital Territory (B)
	(For Australian dependencies *see* KT5501–80)
301–360	**New Zealand (A)**
	(For New Zealand dependencies *see* KT5581–620)

KL Common Law Treatises – General 345

Legal System

(Including private law as a whole)

Note:
Where instructions are given to use Table IV, the range of numbers given for the decimal notation refers to the Dewey Decimal Classification geographic table (DDC Table 2).

1	*General works, common law as a whole*	.01
5	*Influence of common law on other modern legal systems*, A–Z	.05
8	Customary law (*current use*)	.08
11–29	*Surveys of common law systems by jurisdiction* (Table IV), e.g.	.094–9
	11 English legal system	
	12 Scottish legal system	
	22 United States legal system	
	.A1 Restatement of the law	
	29 Colonial law	.09.A–Z
30	*Legal compendia, handbooks etc. for special occupations, professions*, A–Z, e.g.	.1
	.A7 Law for architects	
	.M6 Law for motorists	
	.S6 Law for social workers	
	(For the legal status etc. of occupations and professions *use* either KN156/347.416 or KN169.8/347.41898)	
	Special subjects	
31	Common law : equity	.11
32	Precedent, judge-made law	.12
.1	Ratio decided	.121
.2	Persuasive authority	.122
.5	Distinguishment	.125
.9	Obiter dicta	.129

KL Common Law 345
Treatises – General

KL		345
33	Law reporting	.13
.1	Transcription methods	.131
.2	Broadcasting, television, sound recordings, video recordings	.132
.3	Photographs, sketches	.133
.4	Newspaper reporting of cases	.134
.5	Internet services	.135
.9	Headnotes	.139
34	Drafting	.14
.1	Legislation	.141
.2	Documents, forms and precedents	.142
	(General principles only; for particular subjects *use* Z3 from Table VI with the subject number)	
.22	Sealing	.1422
35	Interpretation	.15
.1	Interpretation of legislation (use for mischief rule)	.151
.2	Documents	.152
.5	Legal fictions	.155
.8	Legislative definitions	.158
36	Legislation, statute law reform	.16
	(Use for theory only; for texts *use* KF–KH/344)	
.2	Legislative bills (theory)	.162
.4	Retroactive legislation	.164
.6	Ouster clauses	.166
.9	Autonomic legislation	.167
40	Legal dictionaries, legal encyclopedias	.169
	(*see also* dictionaries at K120/240.08)	
41	Judicial definitions	.1691
42	Encyclopedias	.1692
	(General only; place subject encyclopedias with the subject)	
43	Law Latin	.1693
44	Law French	.1694

KL Common Law Treatises – General 345

Legal Profession

50	*General works*	.17
51–70	*By jurisdiction* (Table IV)	.170094–9
	(For law as a profession in a philosophical sense *use* KA90/340.19)	
80	History	.17005
81	Etiquette, costume, conduct	.17011
82	Legal ethics, professional responsibility	.1702
.2	Lawyer–client relationship	.17022
.5	Duty to accept work	.17025
.7	Pro bono work	.17027
.9	Conflict of interest	.17029
83	Licensing of lawyers, practising certificates, admission to the Bar	.1703
84	Structure. Reform of legal profession (e.g. whether the profession is fused or divided)	.1704
85	Lawyers	.171
	(For special categories of persons *use* Table VII)	
86	Barristers, advocates	.1711
.5	Queens' Counsel	.1712
.8	Pupillage	.1713
.9	Barristers' clerks	.17132
87	Solicitors	.17134
.1	Trainee solicitors, articled clerks	.171341
.2	Legal executives, paralegals	.171342
88	Notaries	.171343
89	Remuneration	.1714
.2	Barristers	.17142
.3	Solicitors	.17143
.4	*Other legal persons*, e.g. notaries	.17144
.5	Contingency fees	.17145
90	Techniques	.172
91	Client interviewing	.1721
92	Briefs	.1722
93	Trial tactics, advocacy	.1723

KL	Common Law Treatises – General	345
94	Restrictive practices	.173
	(rights of audience, two-counsel rule, direct access to barristers etc.)	
95	Complaints	.174
.1	Legal Ombudsman	.1741
.5	Negligence, malpractice	.1745
.8	Indemnity insurance	.1748
96	Law offices	.176
.1	Practice management, chambers administration	.1761
.15	Contracting out of office services	.17615
.2	Use of computers and technology	.1762
.3	Knowledge management	.1763
.4	Records management	.1764
.5	Financial management	.1765
.6	Personnel management	.1766
97	Partnerships, business organisation	.1767
	(including multi-disciplinary partnerships and LLPs)	
.1	Practice mergers	.17671
.2	Multinational practices	.17672
.3	Practice break-ups	.17673
.4	Regulation, Solicitors Regulation Authority	.17674
.5	Risk management and compliance	.17675
.6	Practice strategy	.17676
98	Advertising, marketing	.1768
99	Management of clients' affairs, trust accounts	.1769
	e.g. management of clients' money	
100	Associations	.177
101–119	*By jurisdiction* (Table IV) e.g.	.1774–9
101	England and Wales	
.1	Inns of Court	.177421
.2	Gray's Inn	.177422
.3	Inner Temple	.177423
.4	Lincoln's Inn	.177424
.5	Middle Temple	.177425
.6	Inns of Chancery	.177426
.7	Law Society	.177427

KL	Common Law Treatises – General	345
101	England and Wales (Associations)	
.9	*Others*, A–Z	

Legal Education

130	Legal education and training	.178
131–149	*By jurisdiction* (Table IV) under each:	.1794–9
	.A–.Z General works	
	.1 Law schools, A–Z	
	.2 Examinations, coursework	
	.3 Curriculum	
	.35 Skills training, e.g. moots	
	.4 Special aspects	
	.43 Access courses	
	.46 Continuing education	
	.47 Distance learning	
	.5 Exchange programmes	
	.6 Staff	
	.7 Finance, sponsorship, etc.	
	.8 Professional training	
	Individual training bodies, A-Z, e.g.	
	.C3 College of Law (UK)	
	.I5 Inns of Court	
	.9 Post-qualification training	
	.95 Training directors (in law firms)	

Legal Research, Law Reform

155	*General works*	.19
	(For bibliographical research methods *use* K79/340.04)	
156	Jurimetrics	.191
157	Computers	.192
160	Law reform, codification	.197
	(Place here general works only; class works on the reform of particular subjects with the subject)	
161–179	*By jurisdiction* (Table IV)	.1984–9

KL Common Law Treatises – General 345

Administration of Justice

(Class here works on the organisation, powers and jurisdiction of the courts, the judiciary and other officers. For court rules, procedure etc. *use* KN350–400/347.9 for general and civil matters, and KM570–605/346.978 for criminal matters)

200	*General works*	.2
201–219	*By jurisdiction* (Table IV)	.24–9
220	Courts (*in general*)	.3
	(For procedure *use* KN350–400/347.9–347.9991; for criminal procedure *use* KM570–605/346.9–346.97)	
221–9	*Particular courts* (Table V) e.g.	.301–9
	221 Appeal courts	
	227.1 Youth courts	
	(If required, sub-division may be made using the numbers following KL230/345.3 with an intervening zero, e.g. Terms in Crown Courts KL224.2018/345.342018)	
230	Court management and techniques	.3
.1	*Special aspects*	.31
.11	Court governance	.311
.12	Judicial Councils	.312
.14	Financial management, expenditure, accounts	.314
.16	Audits, audit areas	.316
.17	Personnel management, staff, court administrators	.317
.18	Vacations, terms	.318
.2	Reorganisation	.32
.3	Circuits	.33
.32	Districts	.332
.4	Business	.34
.42	Case load, congestion and delays	.342
.421	Disposal rate	.3421
.422	Case management	.3422

KL		345
	Common Law Treatises – General	
.4	Business	.34
.43	Distribution of business	.343
.47	Case listing, Listing Officers	.347
.48	Use of judicial time	.348
.5	Interpreters, translations	.35
.6	Technology	.36
.61	Computers	.361
.63	Teleconferencing	.363
.69	*Others*, A–Z, e.g.	.369
	.E4 Electronic filing systems	
	.F3 Fax	
	.K5 Kiosks	
.7	Accommodation	.37
.72	Court building	.372
.721	*Specific buildings*, A–Z, e.g.	.3721
	.O4 Old Bailey	
	.R6 Royal Courts of Justice	
.73	Standards/design guides	.373
.74	Facilities	.374
.8	*Other aspects*, A–Z, e.g.	.38
	.P8 Supply of publications	
	(For broadcasting, reporting etc. *use* KL33/345.13)	
240	Judiciary	.4
	(Class here all works on the judiciary except those concerning their constitutional status and powers, for which *use* KM141/346.28)	
.1	Appointment, tenure	.41
.12	Diversity	.412
.2	Salaries	.42
.3	Discipline, impeachment, accountability, conduct, ethics, immunity, performance standards	.43
.4	Retirement, pensions, occupational pensions	.44
.5	Education and training	.45
241	Judges	.46
	(This schedule may need adaptation to meet local needs)	

KL Common Law 345
Treatises – General

KL		345
241	Judges	.46
.1	Superior judges	.461
	(Class here for UK: Lord Chief Justice, Justices of the Supreme Court, Master of the Rolls, Lord Justices of Appeal, President of the Family Division)	
.2	High Court judges (puisne judges)	.462
.21	High Court Masters, District Registrars	.4621
.3	Circuit Judges (UK), Federal District Judges (US)	.463
.32	Recorders, Registrars, District Judges (UK)	.4632
242	Commissioners, Masters etc.	.47
243	Magistrates	.48
.11–.15	*Divide as* KL240.1–5/345.41–45	.4811–15
	e.g. Training of Magistrates KL243.15/345.4815	
.2	Magistrates' clerks	.482
.5	Home duties	.485
244	Assessors, *and others*	.49
250	Legal officers	.5
251	Attorney-General, Solicitor-General	.51
252	Sheriffs	.52
	(Class here works on sheriffs as legal officers. For Scottish sheriffs, i.e. judges, *use* KL241/345.46; for sheriffs as police officers, e.g. in the United States *use* KM615/346.985)	
253	Public prosecutors, District Attorneys, procurators-fiscal (Scotland)	.53
254	Coroners	.54
255	Court officials	.55
259	*Others*, A–Z, e.g.	.59
	.03 Official Solicitor	
	Statistics	
	(Class here all general material on judicial statistics and all statistics related to non-criminal matters. For works confined to criminal statistics *use* KM620–39/346.99)	

KL Common Law Treatises – General 345

KL		345
300	*General works, including statistical method*	.7
.5	*Collected statistics of more than one country*	.71
301–319	*By jurisdiction* (Table IV)	.74–9

Legal History

400	*General works, including the expansion of the Common Law in general*	.8
401–419	*By jurisdiction* (Table IV), e.g.	.94–9
401	England and Wales	
	.1 Regnal years	
	.2 Anglo-Saxon law	
	.3 Domesday Book	
	.4 Magna Carta	
	.5 Yearbooks (Use for history only; for texts *use* KF50/344)	
	.6 Medieval law, feudal law	
	.7 Post-feudal law (to arrange works by date *use* Table III)	
421–480	*Special subjects* (Table IIB, nos. 21–80) (If using class KL notation, it is possible, as an alternative, to use the subject numbers in classes KL, KM and KN with .007 from Table VIII. If using 345 notation the alternative method must be used: e.g. KL432 History of administrative law (alternative KM300.007))	

KM Common Law Treatises – Public Law 346

Public Law in General

Note:
Where instructions are given to use Table IV, the range of numbers given for the decimal notation refers to the Dewey Decimal Classification geographic table.

1	*General works*	.01
5	Public law : private law	.02
11–29	*By jurisdiction* (Table IV)	.04–09

Constitutional and Administrative Law

(Place texts of constitutions and amendments thereto in classes KF–KH/344. For works dealing with constitutional law in a substantially wider context than the Common Law jurisdiction *use* KB177/340.604)

Constitutional law

(For constitutional law by jurisdiction, *use* KM61–79/346.14–9 [Table IV])

31	*General works*	.1
32	Constitutions (theory)	.11
33	Constitutional principles	.12
34	Rule of law	.121
35	Separation of powers	.122
36	Judicial review (general and constitutional) (For judicial review of administrative action *use* KM306/346.46)	.123
37	Constitutional reform	.1234
38	Constitutional conventions (habits)	.12345
39	Political systems (class here democracy, fascism, etc.)	.1235
40	*Types of constitutional structure*	.124
41	Monarchy	.125

KM Common Law Treatises – Public Law 346

42	Parliamentary government	.126
.1	Parliamentary sovereignty	.1261
.2	Ministerial responsibility	.1262
43	Republics	.127
44	Federations	.128
45	Interstate relations	.1285
49	*Others*	.129
50	*Special aspects of constitutional law*	.13
51	Unwritten constitutions	.131
52	Congresses	.132
53	Amendment	.133
54	Treaty-making power	.134
.2	Treaties : municipal law	.1342
56	Referendums	.136
57	Imperial law i.e. present status of pre- independence laws. (For British colonial law, *use* KL29/345.09.A–Z)	.137
58	Church and state (For freedom of religion for the individual *use* KM206/346.356)	.138
59	Flag	.139
61–79	*Constitutional law by jurisdiction* (Table IV)	.14–9
81	*Branches of government* (Note: Use Table IV under any number for works on devolved legislatures, executives etc. For works on the principle of devolution and pre-devolution controversies *use* KM366/346.66).	.2
82	Legislatures, legislative power	.21
.1	Unicameral legislatures	.211
.2	Bicameral legislatures	.212
.3	Upper chamber e.g. House of Lords (UK) Senate (USA)	.213
.4	Lower chamber e.g. House of Commons (UK) House of Representatives (USA)	.214

KM Common Law Treatises – Public Law 346

83	Membership, legislators	.22
.1	Disqualification	.221
.2	Constituencies	.222
.3	Suffrage	.223
.4	Elections	.224
.41	Proportional representation	.2241
.45	Voting	.2245
.46	Voter registration	.2246
.49	*Other systems*	.2249
.7	Non-elected members	.227
.8	Parliamentary groups	.228
.9	Salaries, pensions, expenses, allowances	.229
.92	Conflict of interest	.2292
84	Parliamentary procedure	.23
.2	Standing orders	.231
.3	Speakers	.233
.4	Dissolution of Parliament	.234
.7	Discipline of members	.2347
.8	Publishing etc.	.2348
	e.g. Hansard (theory)	
.85	Broadcasting	.23485
85	Parliamentary privileges	.235
.1	Contempt of Parliament	.2351
86	*Special aspects*	.24
.1	Questions	.241
.2	Legislative investigations	.242
.3	Committees	.243
87	*Accommodation, facilities, and services to legislators and their staff*	.248
.1	Accommodation, buildings	.2481
.2	Communications systems, telephones	.2482
.3	Computer applications	.2483

KM	**Common Law Treatises – Public Law**	**346**
87	*Accommodation, facilities, and services to legislators and their staff*	.248
.5	Assistance for disabled members	.2485
	e.g. assistance for the deaf	
.6	Social and welfare services	.2486
	e.g. refreshment facilities	
.9	*Others*, A–Z, e.g.	.2489
	.T7 Transport services	
111	Executive power	.25
	(For devolved executives *see* note at KM81/346.2)	
112	Heads of state, heads of government	.251
.1	Monarchs, royal succession, regency	.252
.2	Presidents	.253
.3	Prime ministers	.254
.4	Governors	.255
.7	Military governors, dictators	.257
.8	Election, appointment	.258
.9	Impeachment, resignation	.259
113	Cabinet, Privy Council	.26
.1	Coalitions	.261
.5	Secretaries of state	.265
.6	Ministers	.266
114	Executive prerogatives	.27
.2	Veto power	.272
.5	Honours	.275
.9	Crown immunity	.279
141	Judicial power	.28
	(Class here works on the constitutional status and powers of the judiciary; for their appointment, legal status etc. *use* KL240–5/345.4. For judicial review as a constitutional principle *use* KM36/346.123)	
.2	Independence of the judiciary	.282
.4	Decision making	.284
171	Citizens	.3

KM Common Law Treatises – Public Law 346

KM		346
172	Nationality	.31
.3	Allegiance	.313
.31	Registration of births, deaths, marriages etc.	.3131
.32	Census	.3132
.4	Birth	.314
.5	Patriality	.315
174	Naturalisation	.32
.5	Denaturalisation	.325
175	Passports	.328
.1	Identity cards	.3281
.4	Visas	.3284
176	Migration	.33
.1	Quotas	.331
.6	Exit permits	.334
177	Aliens	.336
.3	Illegal immigrants	.3365
.35	Detention centres	.33655
.5	Deportation	.337
.7	Asylum seekers, refugees	.3375
178	Dual nationality	.338
181–199	*Nationality by jurisdiction* (Table IV)	.344–9
201	Civil rights, human rights	.35
	(For civil and human rights by jurisdiction, *use* KM211–229/346.3694–9 [Table IV])	
.2	Bill of rights	.3502
.3	Socio-economic rights	.3503
.5	Cultural rights	.3505
203	Habeas corpus	.353
204	Freedom of speech, freedom of expression	.354
205	Freedom of assembly	.355
206	Freedom of religion, freedom of conscience, conscientious objection	.356
	(Class here works about the individual. For relations between church and state *use* KM58/346.138)	
207	Freedom of the press	.357
	(For censorship *use* KN349/347.898)	

KM Common Law Treatises – Public Law 346

KM		346
208	Equal opportunities, discrimination, minorities (Class here works dealing with categories of individuals. For discrimination in particular places, activities, etc. *use* the number for the place, etc., with KM208/346.36, e.g. discrimination in housing KN96.2:KM208/347.342:346.36)	.36
.1–.7	*By classes of persons* (Table VII) e.g. KM208.2 Sex discrimination *with* KM208.43 *extended as follows*:	.361–7
	208.43 Racial discrimination	.3643
	.431 Aboriginals, indigenous peoples	.36431
	.432 Treaty rights	.36432
	.433 Land claims	.36433
	.434 Self government	.36434
	For customary law *use* KL8/345.08	
209	*Others* by keyword A–Z, e.g.	.368
	.A2 Academic freedom	
	.C6 Right to counsel	
	.I5 Freedom of information	
	.P7 Right of privacy, data protection (If preferred, for data protection *use* KN347.9/347.896)	
	.P8 Right to own property	
211–229	*Civil/human rights by jurisdiction* (Table IV)	.3694–9
231	Government	.37
232	Political parties	.372
.5	Funding	.3725
.8	Pressure groups, lobbying etc.	.3728
233	National security	.373
.1	Defence	.3731
.2	Civil defence	.3732
.3	Emergencies (i.e. political emergencies; for natural disasters *use* KN181.6/347.4416)	.3733
.7	Official secrets	.3737
.8	Intelligence services	.3738

KM Common Law Treatises – Public Law 346

234 Emergency services *in general*, rescue services .3739
(Class specific bodies with the subject e.g.
Police KM615/346.985)
235 Government departments .38
divide A–Z *by department*, e.g.
.H6 Home Office
.R4 Revenue and Customs
.W6 Department for Work and Pensions
(If preferred, *use* KM241.A2–Z/346.384–9)
236 Public administration, public policy .381
.3 QUANGOs, non-departmental public bodies .3813
(class here general works only; place
specific bodies with the subject,
e.g. Land Registry KN72.2/347.3216)
.4 Contracting out .3814
(i.e. the private operation of government
services)
.5 Government purchasing .3815
.6 Public appointments .3816
237 Civil service .382
.3 Management .3823
.5 Salaries, pensions .3825
238 Committees, Royal Commissions, .383
Commissions of enquiry
241–259 *Governments by jurisdiction* (Table IV) .384–9
under each:
.A1 General works
.A2–Z Departments, by keyword
(If preferred, *use* KM235/346.38)
300 Administrative law .4
(For administrative law by jurisdiction,
use KM311–329/346.494–9 [Table IV])
(Class here works on general principles only.
For texts of regulations *use* KF–KH/344;
for works about the regulation of particular
activities, use the numbers for those activities,
e.g. quarantine regulations KN185.6/347.4486)

KM Common Law Treatises – Public Law 346

301	Deregulation	.41
302	Delegation of powers, subordinate legislation	.42
.5	Regulatory agencies (class here general works only; place individual agencies with the subject, e.g. Financial Services Authority KN309.1/347.78691)	.425
303	Administrative tribunals (For administrative courts *use* KL222.5/345.325	.43
.5	Public inquiries	.435
304	Administrative procedure, natural justice	.44
305	Remedies	.45
306	Judicial review (For judicial review as a constitutional principle *use* KM36/346.123)	.46
307	Ombudsmen (Class here general works only; place those with responsibilities in specific areas with the subject, e.g. Legal Ombudsman KL95/345.0665)	.47
.2	Local ombudsmen	.472
311-329	*Administrative law by jurisdiction* (Table IV)	.494–9
331	Public finance (class here public expenditure)	.5
.2	Economic policy (class here monetary policy/monetary control)	.502
.22	Expenditure plans (class here Autumn Statements [UK])	.5022
.3	Control of public expenditure	.503
.4	Financial reporting	.504
.5	Supply procedure, estimates	.505
.52	Cash limits/external financing limits	.5052
.7	Appropriation accounts	.507
.8	Planning totals	.508
332	Budget	.51

KM	Common Law Treatises – Public Law	346
333	Public debt, public funds (General works only; for government securities *use* KN304.2/347.732)	.514
.5	Funding of public projects, e.g. Public–Private Partnerships (PPP), Private Finance Initiative (PFI)	.515
334	Development grants	.518
335	Taxation (For tax systems by jurisdiction, *use* KM341–359/346.594–9 [Table IV])	.52
336	*Bases of taxation* *(N.B. tax authorities are listed as government departments at KM235)*	.521
.1	Liability	.5211
.12	Residence, domicile, foreign nationals	.5212
.15	Double taxation	.5215
.16	*Others*	.5216
.19	Direct and indirect taxation	.5219
.3	*Types of income or wealth*	.523
.31	Earnings, bonuses, profit-related pay, benefits in kind, e.g. company cars	.5231
.32	Business income, profits, added value	.5232
.33	Foreign earnings etc.	.5233
.34	Pensions, annuities, superannuation	.5234
.35	Interest, dividends etc.	.5235
.36	Property, rents, sporting rights, mineral rights etc.	.5236
.37	Royalties, patents, copyright etc.	.5237
.38	Wealth (i.e. 'static' accumulations)	.5238
.39	*Others*	.5239
.4	*Types of persons*	.524
.41–.47	Natural persons: (Add numbers from Table VII directly to KM336.4, e.g. Married couples: KM336.432/346.52432. For trusts and settlements *use* KM336.447/346.52447)	.5241–7

KM Common Law Treatises – Public Law 346

KM		346
336	*Bases of taxation*	.521
	Corporate persons (*use* Table VII with the following changes:)	
.48	Official bodies	.5248
.481	International organisations	.52481
.483	Government (*own*), government departments	.52483
.488	Foreign governments	.52488
.489	*Others*	.52489
.49	Non-official bodies, non-government organisations	.5249
.491	Partnerships, small companies, family companies, close companies	.52491
.492	Joint stock and limited companies, corporations	.52492
.4929	*Special types*, A–Z, e.g.	.524929
	.I5 Insurance companies	
	.P8 Public utilities	
	.T7 Trust companies (Canada)	
	.U5 Unit trusts	
.493	Company groups, mergers, demergers, subsidiary companies	.52493
.494	Foreign companies, resident subsidiaries	.52494
.495	Associations, clubs, friendly societies etc.	.52495
.496	Charities, heritage organisations	.52496
.497	Trade unions, trade associations	.52497
.498	Professional associations	.52498
.499	*Others*, e.g. .S8 Sub-contractors	.52499
.6	Allowances, deductions, exemptions, reliefs	.526
.61	Personal, including married persons, children, blind, disabled etc.	.5261
.62	Payments into trusts, settlements, etc.	.5262
.63	Expenses, interest, mortgages	.5263
.64	Charitable giving, acceptance of valuables in lieu of tax	.5264
.65	Savings, investments, e.g. BES, TEC	.5265
.655	Capital allowances (If preferred, *use* KM337.155/346.5355)	.52655
.66	Loss relief, group relief	.5266

KM Common Law Treatises – Public Law 346

KM		346
336	*Bases of taxation*	.521
.67	Special periods, e.g. opening and closing years of business	.5267
.68	Special industries etc. A–Z, e.g.	.5268
	.A3 Agriculture	
	.F5 Films	
	.O5 Oil and gas	
.69	*Others*, A–Z, e.g.	.5269
	.C6 Covenants	
	.E4 Employee share schemes	
	.E5 Enterprise investment scheme	
	.E5 Entrepreneurs' relief	
	.N4 Negative gearing (Australia)	
.7	Tax avoidance, tax planning, tax saving (For tax evasion *use* KM564.2/346.88621)	.527
.71	Income splitting	.5271
.72	Bond washing, dividend-stripping etc.	.5272
.73	Other securities transfers	.5273
.74	Transfers of assets abroad	.5274
.75	Tax havens, tax shelters	.5275
.76	Offshore funds	.5276
.77	Disclosure of tax avoidance schemes	.5277
.79	*Others*	.5279
.8	Assessment, computations, valuation etc.	.528
.81	Information requirements, returns, forms	.5281
.82	Year of assessment, tax years	.5282
.83	Assessment procedures	.5283
.84	Self-assessment, pay and file	.5284
.86	Carry-back, carry-forward, forward averaging	.5286
.87	Appeals	.5287
.89	Rates of tax, allowances etc.	.5289
.9	Payment/collection of tax	.529
.91	Collection of tax, payment of tax	.5291
.912	Date due	.52912
.914	Overdue tax, interest charges, penalties	.52914
.92	Deduction of tax at source	.5292
.93	Pay As You Earn, earnings	.5293

KM	Common Law Treatises – Public Law	346
336	*Bases of taxation*	.521
.94	Interest, dividends etc.	.5294
.95	Tax audits, investigations	.5295
.96	Tax credits	.5296
.98	Refund of overpaid tax	.5298
.99	*Others*	.5299
337	Particular taxes	.53
	(Divide any tax, if required, by the sub-divisions of KM336/346.52, preceded by a zero, e.g. Personal allowances for Income tax KM337.11061/346.5311061)	
.1	Personal taxes	.531
.11	Income taxes	.5311
.14	Poll taxes, flat-rate taxes, e.g. Community charge (UK)	.534
.15	Capital taxes	.535
.151	Capital gains taxes	.5351
.153	Transfers of assets	.5353
.155	Capital allowances	.5355
	(If preferred, *use* KM336.655/346.52655)	
.159	Wealth taxes (i.e. 'static' wealth)	.5359
.2	Company taxes, corporation taxes	.54
	(For capital taxes *use* KM 337.15/346.535)	
.22	Taxes on profits and income generally	.542
.23	Advance corporation tax	.543
.24	Dividends, distributions, imputation (Australia)	.544
.25	Payroll taxes	.545
.28	Particular industries, A–Z, e.g.	.548
	.M5 Mining	
	.O5 Oil and gas	
.3	Transfer taxes	.55
	(For transfer of commercial assets *use* KM 337.153/346.5353)	
.31	Gift taxes	.551
.33	Inheritance taxes, death duties, estate duty	.553
.35	Tax planning	.555

KM Common Law Treatises – Public Law 346

KM		346
337	Particular taxes	.53
.4	Indirect taxes	.56
.41	Sales taxes	.561
.42	Luxury taxes	.562
.44	Service taxes	.564
.45	Value added tax, goods and service tax (Canada)	.565
.46	Insurance premium tax (IPT)	.566
.5	Stamp duties	.569
.51	Stamp duty reserve taxes (SDRT)	.5691
.52	Stamp duty land tax (SDLT)	.5692
.6	Real property taxes	.57
.65	Rating, valuation (including business rating), council tax	.575
.68	Development gains	.578
.7	Customs and excise	.58
.71	Tariffs, customs duties	.581
.72	Anti-dumping duties	.582
.73	Duty-free importation	.583
.74	Export duties	.584
.76	Excise duties	.586
.761	Tobacco	.5861
.762	Alcohol, spirits, beer	.5862
.763	Bond stores	.5863
.764	Oil and gas, including road fuel duty (For taxes on producers rather than consumers, *use* KM337.28.04/346.548.04)	.5864
.765	Air passenger duty (APD)	.5865
.8	Local taxation (General works only. Place material on particular forms of local taxation under the particular tax, e.g. local sales taxes KM 337.41/346.561; council tax [UK] KM337.65/346.575) (For local government finance in general *use* KM361.2/346.612)	.589

KM **Common Law Treatises – Public Law** **346**

337	Particular taxes	.53
.9	*Others*, A–Z, e.g.	.59
	.A3 Aggregates levy	
	.C5 Climate change levy	
	.E5 Environmental tax e.g. carbon tax	
	.F7 Fringe benefits tax (Australia)	
	.G3 Gambling taxes	
	.L3 Landfill tax	
	.M6 Motor vehicles	
	.P7 Provisional tax (Australia)	
	.S6 Social security taxes (For UK national insurance *use* KN 181/347.44)	
	.W5 Withholding tax	
341–359	Tax systems *by jurisdiction* (Table IV)	.594–9
361	Local government (For local government as a planning authority *use* KN96/347.34) (For local government by jurisdiction, *use* KM371–389/361.684–9 [Table IV])	.6
.1	Local services	.611
.15	Contracting out (i.e. the private operation of local government services)	.6115
.2	Finance (For local government taxation *use* KM337.8/346.59 [follow instructions at that classification])	.612
.3	Purchasing	.613
362	Local government : national government	.62
363	Charters	.63
365	*Types of local authorities* (General works only; place works on particular authorities in KM391/346.69)	.65
.1	Counties	.651
.2	Conurbations	.652

KM	Common Law Treatises – Public Law	346
365	*Types of local authorities*	.65
.3	Cities, towns	.653
.5	Districts	.655
365	*Types of local authorities*	.65
.7	Villages, parishes	.657
366	Regional authorities, devolution	.66
	(General and theoretical works, i.e. those outside the normal range above, restricted to regions within a recognised nation. For devolved governments in national areas, e.g. Scotland, *use* KM371–89/346.684–9)	
.2	Provinces, territories, states etc.	.662
.3	Ad hoc regions	.663
	(e.g. river catchment areas, regional planning areas)	
367	Elected representatives, councillors	.667
368	Local executive	.67
.1	Mayors	.671
.5	Lord Lieutenants, Lieutenant Governors	.675
369	Local elections	.679
370	Local civil servants, officers	.68
371–89	*Local government by jurisdiction* (Table IV)	.684–9
391	*Particular cities, counties etc.*, A–Z, e.g.	.69
	.L6 London	
400	Military law	.7
401	Recruitment	.71
402	Conscription	.715
403	Conscientious objection	.72
404	Militia, territorials, National Guard, reserve forces	.73
405	Courts-martial	.74
	(Works about rules, procedure, etc.; for reports of cases *use* KF–KH/344)	
406	Judge–Advocates	.745
409	Military crimes	.749
.9	*Specific crimes*, A–Z, e.g.	
	.M8 Mutiny	.7495

KM Common Law Treatises – Public Law 346

KM	Subject	346
	Particular services	
410	Naval law	.75
411	Army law	.76
412	Air Force law	.77
413	*Other forces*, A–Z, e.g.	.78
	.C6 Coast Guard (US)	
416	Martial law, military government (class here: military intervention in civil affairs)	.79

Criminal Law and Procedure

KM	Subject	346
500	*General works*	.8
502	Criminal law : tort	.81
503	*Classification of crimes*	.815
.1	Indictable offences	.8151
.2	Felonies	.8152
.3	Misdemeanours	.8153
.4	Arrestable offences	.8154
.5	Summary offences	.8155
.6	Regulatory offences	.8156
.8	Decriminalisation	.8158
504	Criminal law : morality	.818
505	Criminal liability	.82
.1	Mens rea, Actus reus	.821
.3	Duress	.823
.4	Intoxication (alcohol, drugs)	.824
.5	Necessity	.825
.6	Ignorance, mistake, criminal negligence (class here: endangering, omissions)	.826
.7	Recklessness	.827
.9	Strict liability	.828
506	Insane persons (For non-criminal aspects *use* KN155.3/347.4153)	.829
.1	M'Naghten Rules	.8291
.2	Forensic psychiatry (For forensic pathology *use* KM608/346.979)	.8292

KM Common Law Treatises – Public Law 346

506	Insane persons	.829
.3	Diminished responsibility	.8293
.4	Automatism	.8294
507	*Other classes of person* (Table VII) e.g.	.83
	.Q13 Age of criminal responsibility	
	.Q97 Trade unions' liability	
508	Accomplices, accessories	.84
.5	Incitement	.841
509	Attempts	.842
511–29	*Surveys, by jurisdiction* (Table IV)	.844–9
540	Crimes	.85
	Special categories	
.1	Violent crimes	.851
.15	Hate crimes, e.g. homophobic, anti-paedophiles	.8515
.2	Armed crimes	.852
	i.e. use of weapons in crime; for weapons offences *use* KM562.2/346.8832	
.3	White-collar crime	.853
.4	Corporate crime	.854
	(If preferred, *use* KN264.8/347.6268)	
.5	Organised crime	.855
.6	Money laundering	.856
.7	Cybercrime	.857
	(If preferred, *use* KM565.C5/346.89.C5)	
.8	Victimless crime	.858
541	Offences against the person	.86
	(For compensation to victims *use* KM594/346.948)	
.4	Offences against the reputation	.861
.5	Criminal libel	.8612
542	Homicide	.862
.1	Murder	.8621
.2	Manslaughter	.8622
.3	Suicide, abetting suicide, suicide pacts	.8623
.4	Infanticide, concealment of birth	.8624
.5	Criminal abortion	.8625

KM Common Law Treatises – Public Law 346

KM		346
542	Homicide	.862
.6	Euthanasia, mercy killing	.8626
	(For medical law aspects *use* KN185.158/347.446158)	
.8	Lynching	.8628
543	Assault	.863
	(For domestic violence *use* KN175/347.42597)	
.1	Wounding, grievous bodily harm	.8631
.2	Common assault, mugging	.8632
.3	Battery	.8633
.4	Kidnapping	.8634
.42	Child abduction	.86342
.5	Hostage-taking	.8635
.6	False imprisonment, wrongful arrest	.8636
.8	Poisoning	.8638
.9	Duelling	.8639
544	Sexual offences	.864
.01	Consent to/capacity for sexual activity	.86401
.1	Prostitution, brothels	.8641
.2	Sodomy	.8642
.3	Bigamy	.8643
.4	Rape, indecent assault	.8644
.5	Exhibitionism	.8645
.6	Incest	.8646
	(For child abuse *use* KN176.41/347.42641)	
.7	Pederasty	.8647
.9	*Others*, A–Z, e.g.	.8649
	.H3 Harassment, sexual harassment	
	.S2 Sadism	
545	Offences against property	.87
546	Theft	.871
.1	Burglary, housebreaking	.8711
.2	Robbery	.8712
.3	Motor vehicles, hijacking	.8713
.4	Mail	.8714
.5	Theft by finding	.8715

KM Common Law Treatises – Public Law 346

KM		346
546	Theft	.871
.6	*Other forms of theft*, A–Z, e.g.	.8716
	.P5 Pickpocketing	
	.P6 Poaching	
	.S5 Shoplifting	
.7	Housebreaking tools	.8717
.9	Stolen goods	.8719
547	Fraud	.872
.1	Embezzlement	.8721
.2	Deception	.8722
.3	False pretences	.8723
.4	False accounting	.8724
.9	*Other forms of fraud*, A-Z	.8729
548	Arson	.873
549	Criminal damage, vandalism	.874
550	Sacrilege	.875
551	Forgery	.876
	(Place here works dealing with private property. For forging currency etc. *use* KM564.1/346.8861)	
552	Extortion, blackmail	.877
559	*Others*, A–Z	.879
561	Offences against the State	.881
.1	Treason, rebellion	.8811
.2	Subversion, propaganda	.8812
	(class here: hate propaganda)	
.3	Official secrets, espionage	.8813
.4	Trading with enemies	.8814
.5	Foreign enlistment	.8815
.9	*Others*, A–Z, e.g.	.882
	.U5 Uniforms offences	
562	Offences against public order	.883
.1	Riots, affray, unlawful assembly	.8831
.12	Hooliganism	.88312
.13	Sports ground offences	.88313
	(include here: throwing missiles on to the pitch; chanting abuse; pitch invasions;	

KM	Common Law Treatises – Public Law	346
.13	Sports ground offences spectator violence; crowd control. For ticket touting (i.e. unauthorised sale of tickets) *use* KM565.T5/346.89.T5)	.88313
.2	Explosives, weapons, firearms	.8832
.22	Terrorism	.88322
.25	Bomb threats, bomb hoaxes	.88325
.3	Breach of the peace	.8833
.4	Drunkenness, intoxication	.8834
.5	Suspicious persons, vagrancy, begging	.8835
.6	Obstruction	.8836
.9	*Others*, A–Z	.884
563	Offences against justice	.885
.1	Perjury	.8851
.2	Perverting the course of justice	.8852
.3	Contempt of court	.8853
.33	Sub judice	.88533
.4	Jurors (i.e. offences committed by or against jurors)	.8854
.5	Conflict of interest	.8855
.6	Bribery and corruption (If preferred, in a corporate context *use* KN264.8/347.6268)	.8856
.7	Intimidation, witnesses (offences committed by or against witnesses)	.8857
564	Offences against public finance	.886
.1	Counterfeiting	.8861
.2	Tax evasion (For tax avoidance, tax planning use KM336.7/346.527)	.8862
.3	Smuggling	.8863
.4	Excise offences	.8864
.5	Social security offences	.8865
565	*Other offences*, A–Z, e.g.	.89
	.A5 Animals (i.e. offences against)	
	.B5 Blasphemy	
	.C6 Computer crime, cybercrime	

KM	Common Law Treatises – Public Law	346
565	*Other offences*, A–Z, e.g.	.89
	.C6 Conspiracy	
	.D5 Disease transmission	
	.D7 Driving offences	
	.D7 Drug offences	
	.E5 Environmental crimes	
	.H6 Holocaust denial	
	.O2 Obscenity	
	.P6 Pornography	
	.T5 Ticket touting, ticket scalping	
	.T6 Tobacco offences	
	.T7 Traffic offences	
	Criminal procedure	
	(For works covering procedure as a whole, both criminal and civil, *use* KN350–99/347.9. For criminal court systems *use* KL224/345.34)	
570	*General works*	.9
	(Class here works on the criminal justice system in general)	
571	Court rules, forms, procedures	.9.Z72
571.1–9	*By court*, etc. (Table V) e.g.	.9001–9
	Crown Courts KM571.42/346.90042	
573	Criminal jurisdiction	.901
574	Magistrates	.902
579	Defendants	.905
.1	Presumption of innocence	.906
.2	Double jeopardy	.907
.3	Non-legal representatives, e.g. friends	.908
580	Preliminary proceedings	.91
.1	Investigation	.911
.12	Interrogation	.9112
	(Class here: tape recording of interrogation)	
.13	Pre-charge detention	.9113
.14	Surveillance	.9114
.15	Entrapment, agents provocateurs	.9115
.17	Inquests	.9117
.2	Searches, seizures	.912

KM	Common Law Treatises – Public Law	346
580	Preliminary proceedings	.91
.3	Arrest, summonses	.913
.35	Police custody	.9135
.4	Charges	.914
.5	Private prosecutions	.915
.6	Bail	.916
.7	Remands	.917
.8	Alternatives to prosecution	.918
.9	Pre-trial reviews	.919
.92	Pre-trial release	.9192
581	Preliminary hearings	.92
.1	Grand jury	.921
.2	Committal	.922
.4	Disclosure	.924
582	Trial practice	.93
.1	Trial within a trial	.9305
.2	Indictments	.931
.3	Pleas, plea bargaining	.9315
.4	Prosecution	.932
.5	Nolle prosequi	.9325
.6	Joinder and severance	.9326
583	Juries	.933
	(i.e. the structure of the jury and the method of reaching verdicts. For grand juries *use* KM581.1/346.921)	
.1	Selection, summoning	.9331
.12	Exemption	.93312
.2	Challenges	.9332
.4	Directions	.9334
.5	Unanimity, majority verdicts	.9335
584	Defences	.934
.1	Self-defence	.9341
.2	Justification	.9342
.3	Alibis	.9343
	(For insanity as a defence *use* KM506/346.829)	
.4	Disclosures in the public interest	.9344

KM Common Law Treatises – Public Law 346

KM		346
584	Defences	.934
.9	*Others*, A–Z, e.g.	.9349
	.C8 Cultural defences	
	.P7 Procedural defences	
585	Summing up, jury instructions, closing speeches	.935
586	Verdicts	.936
	(i.e. categories of verdicts. For the method of reaching verdicts *use* KM583/346.933	
586	Verdicts	.936
.1	Acquittal	.9361
.12	Costs of accused on acquittal	.93612
.2	Not proven	.9362
.3	Conviction	.9363
587	Sentences	.937
	(Place here general works on sentences. For sentences related to particular crimes *use* crimes, KM540–65/346.85–9. Works on the sociology of sentencing should be placed in Criminology)	
.1	*By type of offender* (Table VII)	.9371
.3	Judicial discretion, mitigation, clemency	.9373
588	Summary trial	.94
.1	Automatic penalties	.941
590	*Procedure related to particular types of offenders* (Table VII) e.g. .Q11 Children	.945
593	Victims of crimes	.947
594	Compensation of victims	.948
.5	Reparation by criminals	.9485
.6	Proceeds of crime	.9486
.7	Confiscation	.9487
.8	State compensation	.9488
.9	Restorative justice	.9489
595	Criminal appeals	.95
596	Prerogative of mercy, reprieves, review of convictions	.956

KM Common Law Treatises – Public Law 346

597	Miscarriage of justice	.957
.3	Quashing convictions	.9573
.5	Retrial	.9575
.8	Free pardon	.9578
.9	Compensation	.9579
599	Legal aid	.959
.1	Public defenders, dock briefs	.9591
.2	Duty solicitors scheme	.9592
.4	Costs	.9594
600	Evidence	.96
	(Criminal cases only; for evidence in general, including civil cases *use* KN390–4/347.961–5)	
601	Material facts	.961
.2	Judicial notice	.9612
602	Burden of proof	.962
.1	Corroboration	.9621
.3	Circumstantial evidence	.9623
.4	Relevance	.9624
.5	Credibility	.9625
.6	Direct evidence	.9626
603	Admissibility of evidence	.963
.1	Constitutional protection, Judges' Rules	.9631
.2	Confessions	.9632
.3	Right to silence, self-incrimination	.9633
.4	Illegally obtained evidence	.9634
.5	Previous convictions, criminal records	.9635
	(For criminal records generally *use* KM617/346.986)	
.55	Spent convictions	.96355
.6	Hearsay	.9636
.7	Computer evidence	.9637
.8	Informers	.9638
604	*Types of evidence*	.964
.3	Identification	.9643
.31	Identity parades, photographs	.9644
.32	Fingerprints, footprints	.9645
.33	Pathological samples	.9646

KM Common Law Treatises – Public Law 346

KM		346
604	*Types of evidence*	.964
.333	DNA profiling	.96463
.34	Voice prints	.9647
.4	Documents	.965
.41	Handwriting	.9651
.42	Typewriters	.9652
.43	Electronic communications	.9653
.5	Recordings	.966
.52	Wire-tapping	.9662
.54	Sound recordings	.9664
.55	Films, video recordings	.9665
.9	Expert evidence	.967
.94	*By type of expert*, A–Z, e.g.	.9674
	.A2 Accountants	
	.M4 Medical experts	
.95	Opinions	.9675
.952	Character evidence, disposition	.96752
605	Witnesses	.97
	(Class here competence and compellability)	
.1	Examination	.971
.12	Oaths, affirmations	.9712
.15	Video-links	.9715
.2	Lie detectors	.972
.3	Hostile witnesses	.973
.4	Affidavits, depositions	.974
.7	Dying declarations	.977
	(For intimidation of witnesses *use* KM563.7/346.8857)	
.8	Witness summons	.9778
.9	*By type of person* (Table VII) e.g.	.978
	.Q51 Physically disabled (deaf, blind etc.)	
607	Forensic science	.9788
608	Forensic pathology	.979
	(For forensic psychiatry *use* KM506.2/346.8292)	

KM	Common Law Treatises – Public Law	346
608	Forensic pathology	.979
.3	Forensic specialisms, A-Z, e.g.	.9793
	.D5 Digital forensics	
	.E5 Entomology	
	.O3 Odontology	
	.T6 Toxicology	
.4	Post mortems	.9794
.5	Forensic laboratories, equipment, etc.	.9795
.8	Forensic physicians	.9798
610	Law enforcement	.98
611	Public peace	.981
612	Crime prevention	.982
614	Private security services	.984
.1	Vigilantes	.9841
.2	Private detectives	.9842
.3	Posses	.9843
.4	Private armies	.9844
.5	*Private forces*, A–Z, e.g.	.9845
	.S4 Securicor	
615	Police	.985
.1	National police, local police	.9851
.2	Police powers	.9852
.25	Police ethics	.98525
.3	Armaments	.9853
.4	Police equipment	.9854
.42	Vehicles	.98542
.6	Relations with the public	.9856
.7	Complaints against the police	.9857
.75	Deaths in custody	.98575
.8	Disciplinary proceedings	.9858
.9	Salaries, conditions of service	.9859
617	Criminal records	.986
	(For criminal records as evidence *use* KM603.5/346.9635)	
620	Criminal statistics	.9865
621–639	*By jurisdiction* (Table IV)	.98694–9

KM Common Law 346
Treatises – Public Law

650	Prison law	.987
	(If preferred, classify using Criminology Appendix)	
651–9	By type of prison (as in Criminology, 80–89) e.g.	.9871
	Open prisons KM653.2/346.987132	
	Prison architecture KM659/346.98719	
660	Prisoners (arrange by Table VII)	.98715
661	Security regulations	.9872
	Divide as in Criminology 92.2 missing out the .2, e.g. Rules KM661.2/346.98722	
662	Disciplinary regulations	.9873
670	Disciplinary proceedings	.9874
	Divide as in Criminology 92.4 missing out the .4, e.g. Fines KM670.2/346.98742	
671	Offences in prison	.987499
	Divide as in Criminology 92.5 missing out the .5, e.g. Riots KM671.3/346.9874993	
680	Prisoners' rights and privileges	.9875
.2	Complaints, requests	.98752
681	Welfare, conditions	.9876
	Divide as in Criminology 93.3–93.9, e.g. Drug abuse KM681.33/346.987633; visits KM681.5/346.98765	
683	Prison life	.987695
	Divide as in Criminology 94 e.g. Prison relationships KM683.3/346.9876953	
684	Prison work	.987697
	Divide as in Criminology 92.7 missing out the .7, e.g. Workshops KM684.2/346.9876972	
685	Release, discharge from prison	.988
686	Reductions for good behaviour	.9881
.5	Remission	.98815
687	Parole	.9882
690	Aftercare, rehabilitation of offenders, treatment of discharged prisoners, offender management	.9885

KM Common Law Treatises – Public Law 346

700-799 Criminology

(Optional alternative. The same one hundred numbers, with the "hundred" figure suitably adjusted, can be used at *either* KA100-199, *or* KB300-399)

The schedule is printed as the Appendix.

KN Common Law Treatises – Private Law 347

Note: for general works on the common law *use* KL/345

	Conflict of Laws	
	(Alternative to KC2000–2150/341.9)	
(1)	*General works*	(.01)
(2)	Choice of law	(.02)
(3)	Domicile	(.03)
(4)	Foreign law, foreign judgments	(.04)
	Contract and Tort	
5	*General works*	.08
	(i.e. covering both contract and tort, sometimes known as 'obligations')	
	Contract	
10	*General works*	.1
13	Formation of contracts	.11
.1	Agreement, promise, intention	.111
.2	Offer, acceptance	.112
.3	Consideration	.113
.4	Terms, covenants, exclusion clauses, releases	.114
.5	Written contracts, oral contracts	.115
.9	Authentication, sealing of contracts	.119
14	Parties, capacity (Table VII), privity of contract	.12
.2	Novation, assignment	.122
.3	Third parties	.123
15	*Enforceability of contracts*	.13
.1	Public policy, illegal contracts	.131
.2	Void contracts	.132
.3	Material facts	.133
.4	Fraud, mistake, non-disclosure, misrepresentation	.134
.5	War: contracts	.135
.6	Duress, undue influence	.136
.7	Disclosure	.137

KN	Common Law Treatises – Private Law	347
15	*Enforceability of contracts*	.13
.8	Unfair, unconscionable contracts	.138
16	Discharge of contracts	.14
.1	Performance	.141
.2	Cancellation, renunciation	.142
.4	Impossibility of performance, frustration	.144
.5	Operation of law (e.g. bankruptcy)	.145
17	Breach of contract, remedies (Table VI)	.148
18	*Special forms of contracts*	.15
.3	Joint contracts	.153
.4	Public contracts	.154
.5	War contracts	.155
.6	Leasing	.156
.7	Suretyship	.157
	(For foreign contracts *use* KC2097–8/341.9906)	
	(Place subject contracts with the subject, e.g. KN84.4/347.3264 for construction contracts)	
20	Quasi-contract	.16
.1	Implied contracts, quantum meruit	.161
.2	Restitution, unjust enrichment	.162
25	Agency	.18
.1	Agents	.181
.2	Power of attorney, enduring power of attorney	.182
.3	Factoring	.183
30	Tort	.2
33	Liability	.21
.1	Fault, accident, proximate cause	.211
.2	Mistake, malice	.212
.3	Negligence, latent damage	.213
.31	Duty of care, breach of duty	.2131
.32	Contributory negligence	.2132
.33	Professional negligence, by profession	.2133
	A–Z, e.g. .M4 Medical negligence	.2135
.4	No fault liability	.214
.5	Public liability	.215
.6	Vicarious liability	.216
34	Parties, capacity (Table VII)	.22

KN Common Law Treatises – Private Law 347

37	Remedies	.23
.1	Damages, compensation, solatium (Scotland)	.231
.15	Actuarial tables	.2315
.2	Replevin	.232
38	*Particular torts*	
.1	Personal injuries	.24
.11	Fatal injuries	.241
.12	Assault, fright	.242
.13	Enticement	.243
.14	Malpractice	.244
.15	Psychiatric injury, post-traumatic stress	.245
.2	Defamation	.248
.21	Libel	.2481
.22	Slander	.2482
.26	Innocent dissemination	.2486
.27	Fair comment	.2487
.28	Apology	.2488
.3	Abuse of legal procedure	.25
.31	Maintenance, champerty	.251
.32	Malicious prosecution	.252
.33	False imprisonment	.253
.4	Deception	.26
.5	Conspiracy (For criminal conspiracy *use* KM565.C6/346.89 C6)	.265
.6	Trespass to land	.27
.7	Trespass to goods	.275
.71	Conversion	.276
.72	Detinue	.277
.73	Trover	.278
.8	Nuisance	.28
.81	Noise, vibration, sonic booms	.281
.9	Privacy infringements, breach of confidence	.289
39	*Others*, A–Z, e.g.	.29
	.A3 Accidental damage	
	.A5 Animals	
	.D3 Dangerous things	

KN	Common Law Treatises – Private Law	347
39	*Others*, A–Z, e.g.	.29
	.E3 Economic torts	
	.O3 Occupier's liability	
	.P7 Product liability	
	.S4 Service defects	
	Property	
50	*General works*	.3
	(i.e. rules applicable to property in general, rather than to real property or personal property specifically)	
52	Classification	.301
	(i.e. into real and personal property)	
54	Ownership, possession	.302
.1	Title (i.e. as a concept)	.3021
.2	Interests, fragmentation of ownership	.3022
.3	Occupation	.3023
.4	Enjoyment	.3024
.5	Co-ownership	.3025
.55	Timesharing	.30255
.6	Powers, management	.3026
56	*Special aspects of property*	.303
.1	Limitations	.3031
.2	Transfer inter vivos	.3032
.3	Gifts, endowment	.3033
.5	Mortgage, charges	.3035
.6	Expropriation, nationalisation	.3036
	(For transfer on death *use* KN120–43/347.38–9)	
.7	Privatisation	.3037
.8	Public policy	.304
58	*Special kinds of property*	.305
.1	Family settlements	.3051
.2	Matrimonial property, dowry	.3052
.3	Commercial property	.3053
.4	Public property	.3054

KN Common Law 347
Treatises – Private Law

58	*Special kinds of property*	.305
.6	Alien property	.3056
.7	Enemy property	.3057
	(For church property *use* KD34/342.194)	
	Real property	
60	*General works*	.31
62	Land tenure	.311
	(For feudal forms of tenure *use* KL/345)	
63	Estates	.312
.1	Freehold	.313
.11	Fee simple	.3131
.12	Fee tail	.3132
.13	Life interest	.3133
.2	Leasehold	.314
	(For landlord and tenant *use* KN85–8/347.327-9)	
.3	Commonhold	.3143
.9	*Others*, A–Z, e.g.	.3149
	.C6 Condominiums	
	.R4 Retirement villages	
64	*Other interests in land*	.315
.1	Equitable interests	.3151
.11	Uses	.3153
.12	Escheat	.3154
.13	Trusts for sale	.3155
.14	Settled land	.3156
.2	Future interests	.316
.21	Reversions	.3161
.22	Remainders	.3162
.23	Executory interests	.3163
.24	Remoteness	.3164
.241	Perpetuities	.31641
.242	Accumulations	.31642
.3	Determinable interests	.3166
.4	Interests upon condition	.3167
.5	Concurrent interests	.3168

KN	Common Law Treatises – Private Law	347
	(For co-ownership *use* KN54.5/347.3025)	
	(For joint tenancies *use* KN87.2/347.3292)	
65	Incorporeal hereditaments, servitudes (i.e. present interests enforceable against the land of another)	.317
.1	Easements	.3171
.11	Light and air	.3172
.12	Rights of way	.3173
	(For access to the countryside in general *use* KN95.13/347.34213)	
.125	Right of access to neighbouring land	.31735
.13	Party walls	.3174
.2	Rent charges	.3182
.3	Profits à prendre	.3183
.4	Pipes, sewers, cables	.3184
.5	Commons, village greens	.3185
.6	Restrictive covenants	.3186
.7	Positive covenants	.3187
.9	*Others*, A–Z, e.g.	.3189
	.S6 Sporting rights	
66	Mortgages	.319
	(For building societies *use* KN305.7/347.767)	
67	Equity release, reverse mortgages	.3191
70	Transfer inter vivos	.32
.7	Vendor and purchaser	.3207
71	Right to alienate	.321
.2	Restraints on alienation	.3212
72	Land titles	.3214
.1	Deeds, abstract of title, investigations, surveying, boundaries, valuation	.3215
.13	Boundaries, hedges, fences etc.	.32153
.15	Neighbours' rights, disputes etc.	.32155
.2	Land registration	.3216
.3	Torrens system	.3217
.4	Native title, aboriginal reserves etc.	.32175
.5	Better title	.3218
.6	Strata titles	.32185

KN	Common Law Treatises – Private Law	347
73	Contract for the sale of land	.322
74	Conveyancing	.3223
.1	Gazumping, gazundering	.32231
.2	Enquiries, searches	.32232
.3	Costs, deposits	.32233
.4	Completion	.32234
.5	Escrows	.3225
.6	Chains	.3226
.7	Standard conditions of sale of land, e.g. Vacant possession	.3227
.8	Estate agents	.32275
.9	Licensed conveyancers, conveyancing agents	.3228
75	*Others*, A–Z, e.g.	.3229
	.E3 Ecclesiastical conveyancing	
	.E4 Electronic conveyancing	
	.M3 Matrimonial conveyancing	
76	*Other methods of transfer*, A–Z, e.g.	.323
	.A2 Accretion	
	.A3 Adverse possession	
	.B3 Bankruptcy	
	.D4 Debts	
	.P7 Prescription	
	(For transfer on death *use* KN120–43/347.38–9)	
79	Extinction of estates and interests	.3231
.1	Bona vacantia, abandonment	.32311
.2	Limitations	.32312
80	Land resources and usage	.324
81	Property development and investment	.3241
82	Public land, land grants, homesteads	.3242
83	Buildings	.325
.1	Houses, flats	.3251
.17	Gardens	.32517
.2	Shops, offices	.3252
.3	Factories, warehouses	.3253
.7	*Others*, A–Z, e.g.	.3257
	.C6 Cold stores	

KN Common Law Treatises – Private Law 347

KN		347
83	Buildings	.325
.9	*Other aspects*, A–Z, e.g.	.3259
	.V4 Ventilation	
84	Construction law	.326
.1	Building control, regulations	.3261
	(If preferred, class under environmental health at KN97.1/347.3451)	
.15	Fire regulations	.32615
	(If preferred, class under environmental health at KN97.11/347.3452)	
.2	Construction industry	.3262
.3	Construction projects	.3263
.4	Construction contracts	.3264
.45	JCT Standard Forms of Building Contract	.32645
85	Landlord and tenant	.327
86	Types of landlord	.328
.1	Private landlords	.3281
.3	Housing associations	.3283
.5	Local authorities	.3285
87	Leases	.329
.1	Creation of leases	.3291
.2	Joint tenancy	.3292
.3	Sub-letting	.3293
.4	Covenants	.3294
.5	Multiple occupation	.3295
.6	Business tenancies	.3296
.7	Private sector tenancies	.3297
.71	Assured tenancies	.32971
.72	Shorthold tenancies	.32972
.73	Regulated tenancies	.32973
	(For agricultural tenancies *use* KN98.1/347.351)	
.8	Termination	.3298
.9	Enfranchisement	.32989
88	*Rights and duties of landlord and tenants*	.3299
.1	Rent	.32991
.11	Ground rent, service charges	.329911
.12	Rent control	.329912

KN Common Law 347
Treatises – Private Law

88	*Rights and duties of landlord and tenants*	.3299
.13	Distress, bailiffs	.329913
.14	Eviction	.329914
.16	Rent review	.329916
.2	Security of tenure	.32992
.25	Tied accommodation	.329925
.3	Fixtures	.32993
.4	Repairs, dilapidations	.32994
.5	Improvements, decorations, home improvements	.32995
89	Natural resources and energy	.33
.1	Energy policy	.331
.3	Energy conservation, renewable energy	.3313
.4	Conventional energy sources	.3314
.41	Coal	.33141
.42	Gas	.33142
.43	Oil	.33143
.44	Electricity	.33144
.45	Nuclear	.33145
.46	*Others*	.33146
.5	Alternative energy sources	.332
.51	Solar power	.3321
.52	Tidal power	.3322
.53	Wind power	.3323
.59	*Others*	.3329
90	Water	.333
.1	Rivers, canals, watercourses	.3331
.2	Irrigation	.3332
.3	Drainage, flood control	.3333
.4	Foreshore, coast protection	.3334
.5	Public water supply, reservoirs	.3335
.6	Water conservation	.3336
91	Minerals, mining	.334
.1	Coal	.3341
.2	Iron	.3342
.3	Oil and gas	.3343
.31	Concessions	.33431
.32	Exploration	.33432

KN	**Common Law Treatises – Private Law**	347
91	Minerals, mining	.334
.33	Oil, oil industry	.33433
.333	Oil refineries	.334333
.336	Oil rigs and platforms	.334336
.34	Gas	.33434
.4	Radioactive minerals A–Z	.3344
.5	Precious minerals A–Z	.3345
.6	Non-ferrous metals A–Z e.g. .T5 Tin	.3346
.9	*Others*, A–Z	.3349
92	*Others*, A–Z, e.g. .A4 Airspace .S9 Subsidence .T7 Treasure trove	.335
94	Environmental law	.34
.1	Climate change	.341
.11	Carbon emissions	.3411
.12	Carbon taxes and accounting (If preferred, class carbon tax at KM337.9.E5/346.59.E5)	.3412
.13	Carbon trading	.3413
95	Environmental protection	.342
.1	Conservation	.3421
.11	Archaeological sites, ancient monuments	.34211
.12	Listed and historic buildings	.34212
.13	National parks, access to the countryside, footpaths, bridlepaths	.34213
.14	Nature reserves, SSSI	.34214
.3	Animals, birds	.3423
.31	Endangered species	.34231
.5	Ecology, environmental audit	.3425
.6	Plant and tree conservation	.3426
.7	Biodiversity	.3427
.8	Sustainable development	.3428
96	Planning	.343
.1	New towns, zoning	.3431
.15	Urban renewal	.34315

KN Common Law Treatises – Private Law 347

KN		347
96	Planning	.343
.2	Housing, inner cities	.3432
.22	Home improvement grants	.34322
.25	Demolition, slum clearance	.34325
.3	Compulsory purchase	.3433
.31	Compensation	.3434
.35	Land nationalisation	.34345
.4	Pipelines and cables	.3435
.5	Caravans, mobile homes	.3436
.51	Caravan sites	.3437
.54	Gipsy caravan sites	.3438
.7	Land development	.3447
.71	Land charges, betterment levy	.34471
.72	Land commissions etc.	.34472
.8	Planning control	.3448
.81	Planning permission	.34481
.82	Change of use	.34482
.9	Planning procedures	.3449
.91	Applications	.34491
.92	Appeals	.34492
.93	Enquiries	.34493
.96	Enforcements	.34496
.99	*Special industries* A–Z, e.g.	.34499
	.Q3 Quarrying	
97	Environmental health, public hygiene	.345
	(If preferred, class public health matters at KN185.3–4/347.4473-4479)	
.1	Building control, regulations	.3451
.11	Fire regulations	.3452
.3	Burials, cremation, exhumation	.346
.31	Cemeteries, crematoria	.3461
.4	Food hygiene and storage	.3462
.5	Sanitation	.3463
.6	Vermin control	.3464
.7	Pollution	.347
.71	Air pollution, clean air	.3471
.72	Noise pollution	.3472

KN	Common Law Treatises – Private Law	347
97	Environmental health, public hygiene	.345
.73	Water pollution	.3473
.74	Sea pollution	.3474
.75	Contaminated land, brownfield sites	.3475
.8	Hazardous substances	.348
.81	Pesticides, agricultural pollution	.3481
.82	Radioactive substances, radiation	.3482
.822	Nuclear reprocessing	.34822
.83	Toxic waste	.3483
.85	Waste disposal, litter	.3485
.87	Recycling	.3487
98	Agricultural law, farming	.35
.1	Agricultural tenancies	.3512
.12	Crofts	.3513
.14	Share-cropping	.3514
.2	*Special kinds of farms etc.*	.352
.21	Collective farms	.3521
.22	Agricultural co-operatives	.3522
.25	Smallholdings	.3525
.26	Market gardens	.3526
.27	Nurseries	.3527
.29	Allotments	.3529
.3	Finance, credit, subsidies	.353
.4	Soil conservation	.354
.5	Agricultural chemicals	.355
.51	Fertilisers	.3551
.53	Pesticides	.3553
.55	Fungicides	.3555
.6	Machinery	.3556
.7	Estate management	.3557
.8	Forestry	.3558
.9	Plant quarantine	.3559
99	Agricultural produce	.356
.1	Timber	.3561
.2	Crops	.3562
.3	Livestock	.3563
.35	Dairy produce	.35635

KN Common Law 347
Treatises – Private Law

KN		347
99	Agricultural produce	.356
.4	Game	.3564
100	Personal property	.36
102	*Classification*	.362
.1	Chattels	.3621
.2	Choses in action	.3622
.3	Choses in possession	.3623
104	Transfer inter vivos	.364
.1	Title	.3641
.2	Assignment	.3642
.3	Gifts	.3643
.4	Findings, flotsam and jetsam	.3644
.5	Accession	.3645
.6	Prescription	.3646
106	Bailment	.366
	(i.e. transfer of possession of chattels without transfer of title)	
.1	Loans	.3661
.2	Hire	.3662
.3	Liens	.3663
.4	Security	.3664
.5	Pledges	.3665
.6	Chattels mortgages, mortgage debentures	.3666
	(For pawnbroking *use* KN305.5/347.755)	
.7	Bailees' liability	.3667
	(For carriers *use* KN329/347.829)	
108	Actions, remedies (Table VI)	.368
	(For trover, conversion, detinue *use* KN38.7/347.276–8)	
.3	Delivery	.3683
.4	Declaration of title	.3684
110	*Special kinds of personal property*	.369
	(For negotiable instruments, stocks and shares etc. *use* KN304–6/347.73–7)	
111	Intellectual property	.37
.4	Innovation, invention	.3704

KN	Common Law Treatises – Private Law	347
112	Copyright	.371
.1	Literary works, books, etc.	.372
.15	Manuscripts	.3725
112	Copyright	.371
.2	Artistic works, illustrations, maps, photographs	.373
.3	Broadcasts, films	.374
.4	Plays, performing arts	.375
.5	Musical works, sound recordings	.3755
.6	Electronic works, Internet, multimedia etc.	.3756
.7	Computer software	.3757
.9	*Others*, A–Z, e.g.	.376
	.C8 Cultural heritage	
113	Moral rights	.3763
114	Industrial property	.377
.1	Patents	.3771
.12	Patent agents	.37715
.2	Trade marks, names	.3772
.3	Trade secrets, industrial espionage, commercial confidentiality	.3773
.4	Design right (unregistered designs)	.3774
.5	Registered designs	.3775
.6	Hallmarks	.3776
.7	Topography right	.3777
.8	Domain names	.3778
.9	*Others*, A–Z, e.g.	.3779
	.B5 Biotechnology	
	.I4 Image rights	
	.K6 Know-how	
115	Exclusive rights	.378
.1	Public Lending Right	.3781
.2	Rental rights	.3782
.3	Assignment	.3783
.4	Licensing	.3784
.41	Licensing schemes and bodies	.3785
.42	Copyright Tribunal	.3786
.43	Royalties	.3787
.5	Performing rights	.3788

KN	Common Law Treatises – Private Law	347
116	Infringement	.379
.1	Counterfeiting, piracy, bootlegging	.3791
.2	Passing off	.3792
117	Remedies	.3793
118	Permitted acts	.3794
.1	Fair dealing	.3795
120	Inheritance and succession	.38
125	Wills	.382
.1	Testator's capacity, undue influence	.3821
.2	Formation, validity	.3822
.3	Codicils	.3823
.4	Revocation	.3824
.5	Construction, interpretation	.3825
.6	Beneficiaries, family provision	.3826
.7	Legacies	.3827
.8	Testamentary freedom (For estate planning *use* KM337.35/346.555)	.3828
127	Probate	.384
.1	Presumption of death	.3841
.2	Revocation	.3842
130	Intestate succession	.385
131	Descent, heirs	.386
132	Partial intestacy	.387
133	Letters of administration	.388
140	Decedents' estates	.39
141	Devolution	.391
142	Administration of estates	.392
.1	Assets	.3921
.2	Debts	.3922
.3	Distribution, assents	.3923
143	Executors and administrators (For procedure against decedents' estates *use* KN377.D3/347.9377.D3)	.39

KN Common Law Treatises – Private Law 347

KN		347
	Person and Social Laws	
150	Persons	.4
.5	Names	.405
151–157	*Special classes of persons* (Table VII)	.411–7
	(Class here works on the general capacity and status of individuals and categories of natural persons. For method of linking persons to particular legal topics see the introduction) If necessary, modifications or extensions to Table VII may be made, e.g. under KN155.3	
	Insane persons 31 Proof of insanity	
	32 Mental health	
	33 Mental disability	
160	Legal personality	.418
161	Corporate personality	.4181
164	Meetings	.4184
168–9	*Special kinds of corporate persons* (Table VII)	.4188–9
170	Family law	.42
172	Marriage, husband and wife	.421
.1	Betrothal, marriage contracts, engagements	.4211
.2	Breach of promise	.4212
.3	Impediments	.4213
.32	Affinity	.42132
.4	Licences	.4214
.5	Ceremony of marriage, civil marriage, solemnisation	.4215
	(For registration of marriage *use* KM172.31/346.3131)	
.6	Maintenance	.4216
.7	Reproduction, fertility	.4217
.72	Contraception, birth control	.42172
.73	Abortion	.42173
	(For criminal abortion *use* KM542.6/346.8625)	
.74	Sterilisation, vasectomy	.42174
.79	*Others*, A–Z	.42179

KN	Common Law Treatises – Private Law	347
172	Marriage, husband and wife	.421
.8	Artificial reproductive techniques, infertility remedies	.4218
.82	Artificial insemination, *in vitro* fertilisation, embryo transfer	.42182
.85	Surrogate motherhood	.42185
.89	*Others*, A–Z, e.g.	.42189
	.C5 Cloning	
.9	*Special aspects of family law*, A–Z, e.g.	.422
	.A7 Arranged marriages	
	.C5 Civil partnerships	
	.C6 Common law marriage	
	.C7 Conjugal rights	
	.J3 Jactitation of marriage	
	.P6 Polygamy	
	.R4 Remarriage	
	(For matrimonial property *use* KN58.2/347.3052; for cohabitation *use* KN174/347.4259)	
173	Termination of marriage, matrimonial causes and proceedings	.423
.1	Divorce, grounds for divorce	.424
.11	Breakdown of marriage	.4241
.12	Matrimonial offences	.4242
.17	Undefended divorce	.42447
.18	Time restrictions	.42448
	(For matrimonial procedure *use* KN367/347.927)	
.2	Alimony, maintenance (*including* maintenance of children), financial consequences, financial relief	.4245
.29	*Other aspects of divorce*, A–Z, e.g.	.42459
	.A3 Divorce by agreement	
	.M4 Mediation	
.3	Separation, judicial separation	.425
.4	Nullity	.4254
.5	Decrees	.4255
.6	Counselling, reconciliation, conciliation	.4256
.62	Counselling organisations	.42562

KN Common Law Treatises – Private Law 347

173	Termination of marriage, matrimonial causes and proceedings	.423
.8	Custody of children, access	.4258
.82	Child abduction	.42582
174	Cohabitation, unmarried couples, de facto relationships	.4259
.1	Unmarried families	.42591
.5	One-parent families	.42595
175	Domestic violence	.42597
	Divide by table VII if required. (For assault *use* KM543/346.863)	
.2	Refuges	.425972
176	Children, young persons	.426
.1	Adoption	.4261
.2	Guardianship, fostering	.4262
.22	Children's guardians, guardians ad litem (US)	.42622
.23	Wards, wards of court	.42623
.26	Child minding, nannies etc.	.42626
.3	Illegitimacy, legitimation, paternity	.4263
.35	Paternity tests	.42635
	(class here: Blood tests, DNA profiling, etc.)	
.4	Child welfare	.4264
.41	Child abuse	.42641
	(For pederasty *use* KM544.7/346.8647; for incest *use* KM544.6/346.8646)	
.412	Interviews	.426412
.42	Children in care	.42642
	(class here: place of safety orders)	
.43	Administrative parent	.42643
	(i.e. local authority acting as parent)	
.44	Children's homes	.42644
.45	Punishment of children by parents or family	.42645
	(For punishments in school *use* KN184.25/347.44325)	
.5	Unborn children	.4265
.6	Parents, parental rights and responsibilities	.4266
.62	Maintenance of children	.42662
.65	Grandparent's rights	.42665

KN Common Law — Treatises – Private Law — 347

KN		347
176	Children, young persons	.426
.7	Step-children, step-parents	.4267
.8	Orphans	.4268
	(For age of majority *use* KN151.3/347.411.3)	
.9	*Other aspects*, A–Z, e.g.	.4269
	.D5 Effects of divorce on children	
180	Social laws, social services	.43
.5	Social work	.435
181	Social security, public welfare, social insurance	.44
.1	Older people	.4411
.2	Sickness, disablement, invalidity benefits	.4412
	(For private health insurance *use* KN292.3/347.685)	
.3	Unemployment	.4413
	(For redundancy *use* KN192.26/347.4636)	
.4	Family provision	.4414
.5	Widows	.4415
.6	Disaster relief	.4416
.7	Ex-service personnel, military pensions	.4417
.8	Public assistance	.4418
	e.g. grants and loans etc. to people in need, supplementary benefits	
.82	Poverty, poor law	.44182
.83	Means tests	.44183
.88	Housing benefits	.44188
.89	*Other benefits*, A–Z	.44189
.9	*Others*, (Table VII), e.g.	.4419
	.Q39.U5 Unmarried couples	
	.Q39.O5 One-parent families	
	.Q51.B5 Blind persons	
	.Q51.D4 Deaf persons	
182	Community care	.442
.1	Residential homes	.4421
.2	Homelessness	.4422
.22	Squatting	.44222
.23	Hostels	.44223
.3	Home-based services	.4423
.35	Care by families, informal carers	.44235

KN	Common Law Treatises – Private Law	347
182	Community care	.442
.4	Day centres	.4424
.45	Nurseries	.44245
184	Education	.443
.1	Compulsory education	.4431
.15	Curricula, National Curriculum	.44315
.2	Schools	.4432
.23	Teachers	.44323
.25	Discipline, punishments	.44325
.255	Bullying	.443255
.28	Governors	.44328
.29	Special educational needs	.44329
.3	Higher education, technical education	.444
.35	Grants, student loans	.4445
.36	Adult education, evening classes	.4446
.38	Arts, science, culture etc.	.4448
.4	Libraries, museums, galleries	.445
.5	Public records, archives (include here: Court records) (For registration of births, deaths and marriages *use* KM172.31/346.3131)	.4455
.6	Legal deposit (For copyright *use* KN112/347.371)	.4456
.7	Research	.4457
.8	Arts subsidies	.4458
185	Public health, medical law, mental health	.446
.1	Hospitals	.4461
.11	Patients	.44611
.112	Medical records	.446112
.12	Patients' rights	.44612
.122	Consent to medical care	.446122
.124	Discharge of patients	.446124
.129	*Type of patient* (Table VII), e.g. .Q11 Children	.446129
.13	Alternative, complementary medicine, *generally*, A–Z by type, e.g. .A3 Acupuncture	.44613

KN Common Law Treatises – Private Law 347

KN		347
185	Public health, medical law, mental health	.446
	.H6 Homeopathy	
	.R4 Reflexology	
.14	Life support, artificial prolongation	.44614
.15	Death, determination of death	.44615
	(For inquests *use* KM580.17/346.9117; for registration/certification of death *use* KM172.31/346.3131)	
.157	Living wills	.446157
.158	Voluntary euthanasia	.446158
	(For criminal law aspects *use* KM542.6/346.8628)	
.16	Health administration	.44616
	e.g. National Health Service (UK)	
.17	*Types of hospital*, A–Z, e.g.	.44617
	.C6 Convalescent homes	
	.M4 Mental hospitals	
	.N8 Nursing homes	
.18	Medical ethics, medical staff and professionals, A–Z, e.g.	.44618
	.D4 Dentists	
	.D6 Doctors	
	.H4 Health visitors	
	.M5 Midwives	
	.N8 Nurses	
	.O6 Opticians	
	.P5 Pharmacists	
	.P7 Psychiatrists	
	(For medical negligence *use* KN33.33.M4/347.2133.M4)	
.19	Medical organisations, *by name*, A–Z	.44619
.2	Food	.447
	(For hotels, restaurants, etc. *use* KN186.3/347.453)	
.22	Food hygiene and storage	.4472
	(If preferred, class at KN97.4/347.3462)	
.23	Food codes, packaging, labelling etc.	.44723

KN Common Law Treatises – Private Law 347

KN	Subject	347
185	Public health, medical law, mental health	.446
.24	Additives, preservatives, irradiation etc.	.44724
.27	Genetically modified foods	.44727
.28	Organisations administering food regulations etc., e.g. Food & Drug Administration (US)	.44728
.29	Slaughterhouses	.44729
	(Special note: KN185.3–.49/347.4473–.4479 is an alternative to KN97–97.85/347.345–.3484)	
.3	Public hygiene, pollution, environmental health	.4473
.31	Clean air, air pollution	.4474
.315	Noise pollution	.44745
.32	Water pollution	.4475
.322	Sea pollution	.44752
.33	Rubbish tips, waste disposal	.4476
.331	Hazardous substances	.44761
.332	Pesticides, agricultural pollution, nitrates in soil	.44762
.333	Radioactive substances, radiation	.44763
.3332	Nuclear reprocessing	.447632
.334	Toxic wastes	.44764
.337	Sanitation	.44767
.3375	Vermin control	.447675
.338	Litter	.44768
.4	Burial, cremation, exhumation	.4479
.41	Cemeteries, crematoria	.44791
.45	Building control, regulations	.44795
.451	Fire precautions	.447951
.5	Human tissues, transplant surgery, blood transfusion, surgery	.448
.51	Organ donation	.4481
.52	*Particular tests, operations, treatments,* A–Z, e.g.	.4482
	.A6 Amputation	
	.B5 Blood tests	
	.D6 DNA profiling	
	.S4 Shock treatment	

KN Common Law 347
Treatises – Private Law

KN		347
185	Public health, medical law, mental health	.446
.53	Human experimentation (include here use of foetuses)	.4483
.54	Genetic research/engineering, human genome	.4484
.545	Biotechnology, bioethics	.44845
.6	Quarantine, notifiable diseases, control of disease (For animal quarantine *use* KN186.8/347.458)	.4486
.62	Communicable diseases	.44862
.69	*Particular diseases, illnesses, etc.*, A–Z, e.g.	.44869
	.A4 AIDS	
	.L4 Legionnaire's disease	
	.T9 Typhoid	
.7	Preventive medicine	.4487
.8	Drugs	.4488
.81	Drug dependency, rehabilitation	.44881
.82	Proprietary medicines	.44882
.83	Prescriptions	.44883
.87	Cosmetics	.44887
186	*Control in the public interest*	.45
.1	Explosives, firearms, fireworks	.451
.2	Public holidays, Sundays, religious days	.452
.3	Hotels, restaurants (For food *use* KN185.2/347.447)	.453
.4	Alcohol, licensing	.454
.5	Gambling, lotteries	.455
.51	National lotteries	.4551
.6	Recreation, sport	.456
.61	Amusement arcades, fairgrounds	.4561
.615	Video games	.45615
.62	Circuses	.4562
.63	Hunting, blood sports	.4563
.632	Fishing	.45632
.639	*Others*, A–Z by animal, e.g.	.45639
	.B3 Badger baiting	
	.F6 Fox hunting	
	.H3 Hare coursing	

KN	Common Law Treatises – Private Law	347
186	*Control in the public interest*	.45
.64	Racing	.4564
.69	*Individual sports*, A-Z, e.g.	.4569
	.F6 Football	
.7	Parks, sports grounds	.457
.8	Veterinary medicine, animal quarantine, animals	.458
	(For human quarantine *use* KN185.6/347.4486)	
.82	Quarantine, animal passports	.4582
.84	Vivisection, laboratory animals	.4584
.9	*Others*, A–Z, e.g.	.459
	.D3 Dangerous things	
	.P6 Poisons	
	.T5 Time	
	.T6 Tobacco, smoking, passive smoking	
190	Industrial law and relations	.46
.5	*By types of person*, use Table VII	.4605
191	Right to work	.461
.1	Free choice of employment	.4611
.2	Discrimination	.4612
.3	Equal opportunities	.4613
.5	Forced labour	.4615
192	Employment	.462
.1	Employment contracts	.4621
.11	Appointment, probation, service agreements	.4622
.112	Selection procedures	.46222
.12	Qualifications	.4623
.13	Temporary employment	.4624
.14	Fixed-term contracts	.4625
.15	References	.4626
.16	Restraint of trade	.4627
.17	Breach of confidence	.4628
.18	Retirement	.4629
.2	Employment protection	.463
.21	Resignation	.4631
.22	Notice	.4632
.23	Suspension	.4633

KN Common Law Treatises – Private Law 347

192	Employment	.462
.24	Dismissal	.4634
.245	Unfair, wrongful, constructive dismissal	.46341
.25	Compensation for loss of office	.4635
.26	Redundancy	.4636
.27	Reinstatement	.4637
.28	Transfer of undertakings	.4638
.29	Public disclosure, e.g. whistle blowing	.4639
.3	Training, apprenticeship	.464
.33	Professional development, appraisal schemes	.4643
.35	Retraining	.465
.5	Discipline, rules	.4655
.51	Foremen	.46551
.57	Harassment, sexual harassment, bullying	.46557
.6	Part-time employment	.466
.65	Job-sharing	.4665
.7	Multiple employment, moonlighting	.467
.8	Industrial democracy, employee consultation	.468
.9	*By classes of person* (Table VII)	.469
193	Conditions of employment	.47
.1	Hours, shifts, overtime, working time regulations	.471
.2	Holidays, sick leave	.472
.25	Maternity/paternity rights	.4721
.255	Work life balance	.47215
.3	Welfare, canteen, sports facilities	.473
.4	Pensions	.474
.5	*Non-industrial employment*	.475
.51	Shops	.4751
.52	Offices	.4752
.53	Domestic, hotels, catering	.4753
.54	Hospitals, medical centres, etc.	.4754
.59	Home working	.4759
.6	*Industrial employment*	.476
.61	Factories, workshops	.4761
.62	Mines, quarries	.4762
.65	Dangerous occupations	.4765

KN	Common Law Treatises – Private Law	347
193	Conditions of employment	.47
.7	Hygiene	.477
	(For industrial health, *use* KN198/374.49)	
.8	Controversial terms, e.g. off-day working, onerous monitoring	.4778
.9	*Others,* A-Z, e.g.	.4779
	.C6 Control of internet use	
194	Remuneration	.478
.1	Earnings	.4781
.2	Non-wage payments, benefits in kind	.4782
.3	Bonuses, profit-sharing, co-ownership, employee share schemes etc.	.4783
.4	Productivity payments, commissions	.4784
.5	Tips	.4785
.6	Equal pay	.4786
.9	Deductions, attachment, assignment	.4789
	(For attachment as a remedy, *use* KN395.24)	
195	Trade unions, associations etc.	.48
.1	Formation, registration, immunities	.481
.11	Independent unions	.4811
.12	Company unions	.4812
.15	Federations	.4815
.18	Employers' associations	.4818
.19	Professional associations	.4819
.2	Membership, closed shop	.482
.3	Finance, accounts, welfare funds	.483
.4	Political funds	.4835
.5	Rules	.484
.53	Elections, voting	.4843
.55	Individuals' rights	.4845
.6	Officers, shop stewards	.4846
.7	Trade union recognition	.4847
.8	Inter-union relations	.485
196	Negotiations and disputes	.486
.1	Collective bargaining	.4861
.2	Grievance procedure, conciliation, arbitration	.4862
.25	Arbitration agencies	.48625

KN Common Law 347
Treatises – Private Law

196	Negotiations and disputes	.486
.3	Injunctions	.4863
.4	Strikes, lockouts	.4864
.5	Picketing	.4865
.6	Non-strike action, overtime bans, work-to-rule, boycotts	.4866
.9	Industrial tribunals	.4869
197	Unemployment	.487
.1	Employment services	.4871
.2	Employment agencies	.4872
.3	Job centres	.4873
.4	Enterprise zones	.4874
198	Health and safety	.49
.1	Employers' liability	.491
.2	Industrial safety, dangerous machinery	.492
.25	Fire precautions	.4925
.3	Industrial injuries, accidents	.493
.4	Diseases	.494
.5	Employment stress, hazards, A–Z, e.g. .N6 Noise	.495
.6	Insurance	.496
.8	Workers' compensation, disability evaluation	.498
.9	Survivors' benefits	.499

Equity

200	*General works* (For equity : common law *use* KL31/345.11)	.5
203	Equity : Roman law	.51
204	Maxims	.52
210	Trusts	.54
213	Creation of trusts	.541
.1	Capacity	.542
.2	Declaration	.543
.3	Precatory trusts	.544
.4	Volunteers	.545
.9	Variation	.549

KN	Common Law Treatises – Private Law	347
214	*Special kinds of trusts*	.55
.1	Constructive trusts	.551
.2	Resulting trusts	.552
.3	Statutory trusts	.553
.4	Secret trusts	.554
.5	Public policy, unlawful trusts	.555
	(For trusts for sale *use* KN64.13/347.3155)	
.6	Discretionary trusts	.5556
215	Charities	.556
.1	Mortmain	.5561
.3	Cy-prés doctrine	.5563
.8	Fundraising	.5568
.9	*Others, A–Z*	.5569
216	Trustees, fiduciaries	.56
.2	Liability	.562
.3	Powers, duties	.563
.4	Public trustees	.564
217	Beneficiaries	.57
.2	Breach of trust	.572
.3	Acquiescence, laches	.573
218	Trust funds, investment accounts	.578
221	Equitable interests	.58
	(i.e. other than trusts and interests in real property, for which *use* KN64.1/347.3151)	
.2	Elections, licences, liens	.582
222	Fraud, mistake	.585
230	Equitable remedies	.59
231	Specific performance	.591
.1	Part performance	.5911
.2	Specific restitution	.5912
232	Injunctions	.592
	(For labour injunctions *use* KN196.3/347.4863)	
.2	Freezing injunctions	.5922
233	Declaratory judgments	.593
234	Rectification	.594
235	Cancellation	.595

KN	Common Law Treatises – Private Law	347
	Commercial Law	
250	*General works*	.6
251	Stake holding (interests of a party in an organisation not fully recognised under commercial law)	.601
252	Interstate commerce (In federal jurisdictions, especially United States)	.605
253	Foreign trade	.61
.1	Exports, export credit guarantees	.611
.12	Export trade finance	.612
.13	Forfaiting	.613
253	Foreign trade	.61
.2	Imports, dumping	.614
.3	Countertrade	.615
.8	Commodities, A–Z, e.g. .C6 Coffee .M8 Munitions	.616
.9	*By jurisdiction* (Table IV)	.6174–9
254	Business contracts (General works only. For particular subjects *use* the number for the subject)	.618
255	Corporate governance (General works only. For works dealing with company officers *use* KN264.71/347.62671)	.6185
256	Commercial arbitration	.619
257	Contracting out	.6195
260	Business associations (For corporate personality *use* KN161/347.4181) (For unincorporated associations *use* KN169.4/347.41894)	.62
.1	Names (Generally; for company names *use* KN262.8/347.6248)	.621
.2	Small businesses, self-employed	.622
.3	Business Expansion Scheme	.6225
.5	Chambers of commerce	.623

KN	Common Law Treatises – Private Law	347
261	Company law	.624
.2	Company accounts	.6241
.5	Companies inspection and investigation	.62415
262	Incorporation	.6242
.1	Mergers, takeovers (For technical aspects only, otherwise *use* KN266.12/347.6312)	.62421
.2	Consortia, groups of companies	.62422
.22	Franchises	.62423
.25	Joint ventures	.62425
.3	Management buyouts	.6243
.4	Disincorporation	.6244
262	Incorporation	.6242
.5	Reorganisation	.6245
.6	Articles of association	.6246
.65	Tables A–F	.62465
.7	Memorandum of association	.6247
.75	Objects clauses, ultra vires	.62475
.8	Company names	.6248
.85	Prohibited names	.62485
.9	Companies House (UK)	.6249
.91	Company records	.62491
.92	Registered office	.62492
263	Capital	.625
.3	Venture capital	.6253
.4	Profits	.6254
.5	Shares (*see also* equities KN304.4/347.734)	.6255
.51	Allotment of shares	.62551
.54	Purchase of own shares	.62554
.59	*Types of shares*, A–Z, e.g.	.62559
	.N6 Non-voting shares	
	.P7 Preference shares	
.6	Share options	.6256
.61	Share sales and transfers	.62561
.62	Share issues	.62562
.63	Registration	.62563
.64	Dividends	.62564

KN Common Law Treatises – Private Law 347

263	Capital	.625
.7	Shareholders	.6257
.71	Disclosure of interests	.62571
.72	Majority shareholders	.62572
.73	Minority shareholders	.62573
.74	Nominees	.62574
.79	Types of shareholders, *use* Table VII	.62579
.8	Meetings	.6258
.81	Voting	.62581
264	Directors and other company officers	.626
.1	Remuneration	.6261
.3	Officers	.6263
.4	Shadow directors	.6264
.5	Non-executive directors	.6265
.6	Workers' directors	.6266
.7	Duties and liabilities	.6267
.71	Corporate governance (For general works *use* KN255/347.6185)	.62671
.72	Corporate social responsibility	.62672
.73	Conflict of interest (e.g. Chinese walls)	.62673
.75	Disclosure of interests	.62675
.8	Corporate crime, insider dealing, fraudulent trading, etc. (If preferred, for corporate crime *use* KM540.4/346.854; for insider dealing *use* KN304.9/347.739)	.6268
.9	Bribery and corruption	.6269
265	*Special kinds of companies*	.627
.1	Private companies	.6271
.15	Small and medium-sized enterprises	.62715
.16	Small businesses	.62716
.2	Multinational companies	.6272
.3	Holding companies	.6273
.4	Public companies	.6274
.45	Companies limited by guarantee	.62745
.5	Foreign companies	.6275

KN	Common Law Treatises – Private Law	347
265	*Special kinds of companies*	.627
.6	Nationalised industries	.6276
	(For nationalisation *use* KN56.6/347.3036)	
.65	Privatised industries	.62765
.7	Subsidiaries, subsidiary undertakings	.6277
.8	Statutory companies	.6278
.9	*Others*, A–Z, e.g.	.6279
	.C5 Close companies	
	.F3 Family companies	
266	Competition law	.63
.05	Fair trading	.6305
.1	Monopolies	.631
.12	Mergers, takeovers	.6312
.15	Enforcement, e.g. Competition Commission,	.6315
.17	Regulators, e.g. Office of Fair Trading	.6317
.2	Anti-competitive agreements, restraint of trade, Chapter 1 prohibition, horizontal agreements, vertical agreements	.632
.3	Retail price maintenance, price fixing	.633
.4	Unfair competition	.634
.5	Abuse of dominant position, Chapter II prohibition, anti-competitive practices, cartels	.6345
.6	State aids, subsidies	.6349
.7	Exemptions	.635
.71	Block exemption	.6351
.72	Individual exemption	.6352
267	Partnership	.636
.1	Professional partnerships	.6361
.2	Partners	.6362
.3	Limited liability partnerships	.6363
.4	Limited partnerships	.6364
.5	Joint ventures	.6365
.6	Third parties	.6366
.7	Dissolution	.6367
268	Co-operatives	.638
.1	Producers' co-operatives	.6381
.2	Wholesale co-operatives	.6382

KN	Common Law Treatises – Private Law	347
268	Co-operatives	.638
.3	Retail co-operatives	.6383
	(For co-operative banks *use* KN303.9.C6/347.729)	
.9	*Others*, A–Z, e.g.	.6389
	.H6 Housing co-operatives	
270	Industries	.64
	(General regulation of industries etc. For special aspects *use* subject, e.g. for productivity payments *use* KN194.4/347.4784)	
273	Research and development	.643
275	Particular industries, A–Z, e.g.	.645
	.C5 Chemical industry	
	.I7 Iron and steel industry	
	.P8 Public utilities	
279	Sale of business (as a going concern)	.649
280	Sale of goods	.65
282	*Special aspects*	.651
.1	Contract of sale	.652
.2	Bills of sale	.653
.3	Caveat emptor	.654
.4	Guarantees, warranties	.655
.5	Weights and measures	
283	Prices	.658
.1	Price control	.6581
.2	Reductions	.6582
284	Consumer protection	.66
.1	Advertising, trade descriptions, disclosure	.661
.2	Labelling	.662
.3	Quality control	.663
	(For control of quantities *use* KN282.5/347.655)	
.4	Consumer safety	.664
.5	Consumers' associations	.665
.6	Trading standards	.666
.7	Design standards (e.g. BSI)	.667

KN	Common Law Treatises – Private Law	347
285	*Special methods of selling*	.67
.1	Auctions	.671
.2	Markets	.672
.3	Mail order	.673
.4	Electronic commerce	.674
.43	Electronic signatures (For digital signatures *use* KN348.83/347.89783)	.6743
.5	Vending machines	.675
.6	Franchises	.676
.7	Pyramid selling	.677
.8	Ponzi schemes	.6778
.9	*Others*, A–Z, e.g.	.678
	.D6 Door-step selling	
	.I5 Internet sales	
	.S4 Second hand dealing	
	.S8 Street trading	
	.T4 Telephone sales	
	.U3 Unsolicited goods	
	.U8 Unsolicited services	
286	Retail trade, service industries A–Z, e.g.	.679
	.D3 Data processing	
	.L3 Laundries	
	.T6 Tourism	
287	Wholesaling	.6799
290	Insurance	.68
.2	Uberrimae fidei, utmost disclosure	.6802
.3	Insurance policies, contracts	.681
.6	Insurable interests	.68106
291	Insurance intermediaries	.6811
.2	Brokers	.6812
.4	Loss assessors	.6814
.5	Loss adjusters	.6815
292	Personal insurance	.682
.1	Life insurance	.683
.2	Annuities	.684

KN Common Law Treatises – Private Law 347

292	Personal insurance	.682
.3	Health insurance (private)	.685
.5	Burial insurance	.687
293	Group insurance	.689
	(General works only; for special subjects *use* the subject, e.g. Life insurance)	
294	Risks insurance, *by risk*, A–Z, e.g.	.694
	.A3 Accident	
	.A4 Air transport	
	.C3 Casualty	
	.C6 Consequential loss	
	(For employers' liability *use* KN198.6/347.496)	
	.F5 Fire	
	(For marine *use* KN335/347.835)	
295	Reinsurance	.695
297	Insurance industry supervision and regulation	.697
300	Finance, monetary system	.7
302	Money	.71
.1	Legal tender	.711
.2	Coinage, bank notes, mint	.712
.3	Foreign exchange, exchange rates	.713
.35	Currency markets	.7135
.4	Travellers' cheques	.714
303	Banking	.72
.1	Bank accounts	.7201
.11	Deposits	.721
.12	Withdrawals	.7212
.13	Cheque cards and other guarantee cards	.7213
	(For cheques *use* KN306.1/347.771)	
.14	Debit, credit and charge cards	.7214
	(If preferred, *use* KN305.45/347.762)	
.17	Automatic teller machines (ATMs)	.7217
.2	Electronic banking	.722
.21	Home banking	.7221
.3	Bank loans, overdrafts	.723

KN	Common Law Treatises – Private Law	347
303	Banking	.72
.4	*Other transactions*, A–Z, e.g.	.724
	.C6 Collection	
	.C7 Credit transfer	
	Special types of banks	
.5	Central banks	.725
.6	Commercial banks	.726
.61	Private banks	.7261
.62	Joint stock banks	.7262
.63	Merchant banks, investment banks	.7263
.65	Clearing houses	.7265
.7	Savings banks	.727
.8	Safe deposits	.728
.9	*Others*, A–Z, e.g.	.729
	.A3 Agricultural banks	
	.C6 Co-operative banks	
.95	Banking supervision and regulation	.7295
.955	Know Your Customer (KYC), due diligence	.72955
304	Investment, capital markets	.73
.1	Securities	.731
.11	Mortgage-backed securities	.7311
.2	Government securities, national savings	.732
.21	Municipal securities	.7325
.3	Debentures, preferred shares	.733
.31	Bonds	.7331
.315	Eurobonds	.73315
.32	Hybrid securities	.7332
.4	Equities (*see also* shares KN263.5/347.6255)	.734
.45	Equity warrants	.7345
.5	Collective investments	.735
.51	Unit trusts	.7351
.52	Investment trusts	.7352
.53	Open-ended investment companies (OEICs)	.7353
.54	Mutual funds	.7354
.58	Hedge funds	.7358

KN Common Law Treatises – Private Law 347

304	Investment, capital markets	.73
.6	Derivatives	.736
.63	Commodity futures	.7363
.65	Financial futures	.7365
.67	Options	.7367
.68	International Swaps and Derivatives Association	.7368
.7	*Others*, A–Z, e.g.	.737
	.I5 Individual Saving Accounts	
.8	Stock exchanges	.738
.81	Market makers (brokers etc.)	.7381
.82	Unlisted securities market	.7382
.83	Over-the-counter market, matched bargains	.7383
.84	Third Market	.7384
.86	*By name*, A–Z, e.g.	.7386
	.A4 Alternative Investment Market	
	.L6 London Stock Exchange	
.87	Electronic trading	.7387
.88	Clearing and settlement systems	.7388
.9	Speculation, insider dealing etc.	.739
	(If preferred, for insider dealing *use* KN264.8/347.6268)	
.92	Market abuse, market manipulation	.7392
.95	Investment supervision and regulation	.7395
	Organisations A–Z, e.g.	
	.F5 Financial Ombudsman	
	.F5 Financial Services Authority (FSA)	
	.P4 Pensions Ombudsman	
	(If preferred, *use* KN309.1/347.78691)	
.96	Industry bodies, A-Z, e.g.	.7396
	.E8 European Securities Markets Association	
	.I5 International Capital Market Association	
	.L6 Loan Market Association	
305	Credit, creditors	.75
.1	Debts	.751
.11	Factoring, debt collection	.7511
	(For suitors' cash *use* KN395/347.97)	

KN	Common Law Treatises – Private Law	347
305	Credit, creditors	.75
.15	Sovereign debt	.7515
.2	Moneylending, loans	.752
.21	Syndicated loans	.7521
.22	Venture capital (*see also* KN263.3/347.6253)	.7522
.23	Securitisation	.7523
.24	Project finance	.7524
.25	Company charges	.7525
.26	Asset-backed finance	.7526
.27	Islamic finance	.7527
.28	Real estate finance	.7528
.3	Interest, interest rates etc.	.753
.4	Hire purchase, consumer credit	.76
.45	Debit, credit and charge cards (If preferred, *use* KN303.14/347.7214)	.762
.5	Pawnbroking	.765
.6	Loan associations, credit unions	.766
.7	Building societies	.767
.8	Supervision and regulation	.768
306	Negotiable instruments	.77
.1	Cheques	.771
.2	Bills of exchange	.772
.3	Promissory notes	.773
.4	Commercial credits	.774
.42	Documentary credits	.7742
.44	Letters of credit	.7744
.5	Acceptances	.775
.6	Drafts	.776
.7	Commercial paper	.777
.8	Swap agreements	.778
.9	Security	.779
.91	Comfort letters	.7791
.92	Guarantees	.7792
.93	Liens	.7793
.94	Set-off	.7794

KN Common Law Treatises – Private Law 347

KN		347
307	Accountancy, accountants	.78
.1	Accounting, accounting systems	.781
.2	Accounts (*see also* company accounts KN261.2/347.6241)	.782
.3	Accounting standards	.783
.4	Balance sheets	.784
.5	Auditing, auditors' reports	.785
308	Financial services	.786
.1	Investor protection	.7861
.15	Churning	.78615
.2	Investment business, regulated activities	.7862
.3	Authorised persons, controlled functions (If preferred, *use* KN304.95)	.7863
.4	Exempt persons	.7864
.6	Financial promotion	.7866
.7	Market rigging	.7867
.8	Reciprocity	.7868
309	Regulation and compliance	.7869
.1	Regulatory bodies, A-Z, e.g.	.78691
	.F5 Financial Ombudsman	
	.F5 Financial Services Authority	
	.P4 Pensions Ombudsman	
	(If preferred, *use* KN304.95/347.7395)	
.2	Financial Services and Markets Tribunal	.78692
.3	Financial Services Compensation Scheme	.78693
310	Bankruptcy and insolvency	.79
312	Insolvency (use for companies)	.792
.1	Liquidators	.7921
.2	Administration	.7922
.25	Pre-pack administrations	.79225
.3	Insolvency practitioners	.7923
.4	Receivers, Official Receiver	.7924
.5	Winding up	.7925
.6	Dissolution	.7926
.7	Corporate rescue/recovery, restructuring	.7927
.71	Schemes of arrangement	.79271
.72	Company voluntary arrangements	.79272

KN	Common Law Treatises – Private Law	347
313	Bankruptcy (use for individuals) (Adapt subdivisions above as required, e.g. Individual voluntary arrangements KN313.72/347.79372)	.793
320	Transport (*other than marine*)	.8
321	*Mixed forms*, hovercraft	.811
322	Roads	.812
.1	Motorways	.8121
.15	Trunk roads, main roads	.81215
.2	Unadopted roads	.8122
.3	Private roads, privatisation	.8123
.4	Pedestrians, pedestrianisation (For footpaths *use* KN95.13/347.3414)	.8124
.5	Landscaping, verges	.8125
.55	Road works	.81255
.6	Road signs	.8126
.7	Lighting	.8127
.8	Bridges, tunnels, ferries	.8128
.9	Tolls	.8129
323	Road traffic	.813
.1	Motor vehicles	.8131
.11	Design	.8132
.12	Registration, licences	.8133
.13	Heavy goods vehicles	.81331
.14	Cars	.81332
.15	Motorcycles	.81335
.19	*Other motor vehicles*, A–Z	.81339
.2	Bicycles	.8134
.3	Animals	.81345
.5	Drivers, driving licences	.8135
.7	Traffic regulations	.8137
.73	Speed control, speed cameras	.81373
.75	Parking	.81375
.78	*Other regulations*, A–Z	.81378
.79	Enforcement, traffic wardens	.81379
.9	Accidents	.8139

KN Common Law Treatises – Private Law 347

324	Passenger traffic, public transport	.814
.1	Buses, coaches	.8141
.2	School buses	.8142
.3	Tramways	.8143
.4	Routes	.8144
.5	Taxis, minicabs	.8145
.6	Vehicle rental	.8146
	(For carriage of goods *use* KN328/347/828)	
325	Railways	.815
.1	Tracks	.8151
.2	Signalling	.8152
.25	Safety	.81525
.3	Rolling stock, wagons	.8153
.4	Routes	.8154
.5	Train crews, drivers, guards, conductors	.8155
.6	Underground railways	.8156
.7	*Others*, e.g. monorails	.8157
.9	Accidents	.8159
326	Inland waterways	.816
.1	Rivers	.8161
.2	Canals	.8162
327	Air transport	.82
	(Place here national rules only. For international air law *use* KC253–5/341.453–4)	
.1	Aircraft	.821
.15	Airships	.8215
.2	Airlines, flight crews	.822
.3	Routes	.823
.4	Airports	.824
.5	Flight control	.825
.6	Charter flights	.826
.9	Accidents	.829
328	Carriage of goods (*except maritime*)	.828
.1	Freight	.8281
.2	Charges	.8282
.4	Cash on delivery	.8284

KN Common Law Treatises – Private Law 347

328	Carriage of goods (*except maritime*)	.828
	By type of transport	
.5	Road freight	.8285
.6	Rail freight	.8286
.7	Canal freight	.8287
.8	Air freight	.8288
329	Carriers	.829
.2	Forwarding agents	.8292
330	Maritime law	.83
	(Place here works on national law only. For international maritime law *use* KC260–79/341.47–8)	
332	Shipping	.832
.1	Shipmasters, seamen, crews	.8321
.2	Shipowners	.8322
.3	Ships	.8323
.4	Submarines (commercial only; for military submarines *use* KC1381/341.8541)	.8324
.5	Shipbuilders, shipbuilding	.8325
.6	Shipyards	.8326
.7	Stowaways	.8327
.9	Shipping cartels, liner conferences	.8329
333	Navigation	.833
.1	Collisions	.8331
.2	Pilotage	.8332
.3	Lighthouses	.8333
.4	Shipping lanes	.8334
334	Salvage	.834
.1	Wrecks	.8341
.2	Towage	.8342
.3	Divers	.8343
335	Marine insurance	.835
.1	Average	.8351
.2	Hague Rules	.8352
.3	York-Antwerp Rules	.8353

KN Common Law Treatises – Private Law 347

336	Harbours, docks	.836
.1	Charges	.8361
.2	Harbourmasters	.8362
.3	Jetties	.8363
.4	Moorings	.8364
337	Carriage of goods by sea, Hamburg Rules, Rotterdam Rules, etc.	.837
.1	Freight, cargo	.8371
.2	CIF contracts, FOB contracts	.8372
.3	Bills of lading	.8373
.4	Charterparties, time charters	.8374
.5	Demurrage, laytime	.8375
.6	Liens	.8376
.7	Loading and unloading, stowage	.8377
.8	Cabotage	.8378
338	Fisheries (For sea pollution *use* KN97.74/185.322)	.838
.1	Conservation	.8381
.2	Fishing zones, inshore fisheries	.8382
.3	Fishing boats, factory ships	.8383
.4	Fishermen	.8384
.5	Fishery products	.8385
.6	Aquaculture	.8386
.9	*By type*, A–Z, e.g. .H4 Herring	.8389
340	Communications	.84
.5	Information age/society	.845
341	Mail, postal services	.85
.1	Rates	.851
.3	Air mail	.852
.4	Surface mail	.853
.5	Foreign mail	.854
.6	Private postal services	.855
342	Telecommunications	.86
.1	Telegraph	.861
.2	Telex	.862
.3	Telephone	.863

KN	Common Law Treatises – Private Law	347
342	Telecommunications	.86
.31	Broadband	.8631
.35	Mobile phones	.8635
.356	Smartphones	.86356
.4	Electronic mail	.864
.45	Spam	.8645
.5	Fax	.865
.6	Satellites	.866
343	Media law (*see also* copyright, privacy, freedom of the press)	.87
344	Broadcasting, entertainment	.871
.1	Transmitters, wavelengths, receivers	.8711
.15	Piracy	.8712
.2	Finance, licence fees, advertising, etc.	.8713
.3	Educational broadcasting	.8714
.4	Radio	.872
.45	CB radio, amateur radio	.8721
.5	Television	.873
.51	Cable television	.8731
.52	Satellite television	.8732
.53	Teletext	.8733
.7	Theatre	.874
.8	Cinema	.875
345	Publishing (For legal publishing *use* K105)	.88
.1	Books, bookselling	.881
.2	Journalism, press, newspapers	.882
.5	Electronic publishing	.885
347	Computer law, information technology (For computer contracts *use* Table VIII)	.89
.1	Computer applications (For software *use* KN348.4/347.8974; for computer applications in various subjects *use* Table VIII)	.891
.2	Information retrieval	.892
.3	Networks	.893
.4	Internet	.8935

KN Common Law 347
Treatises – Private Law

347	Computer law, information technology	.89
.41	Blogs	.89351
.43	Cloud computing	.89353
.46	Social media	.89356
.49	Wikis	.89359
.5	Office automation	.894
.55	Intranets	.8945
.56	Security of networks (e.g. firewalls)	.8946
.6	Data storage (e.g. CD-ROM, DVD)	.895
.9	Data protection	.896
	(If preferred, class with privacy at KM209 .P7)	
348	Computer technology	.897
.3	Hardware	.8973
.4	Software	.8974
	(For software licences *use* KN115.4/347.3784)	
.5	Computer bugs and viruses	.8975
.8	Encryption, data security	.8978
.83	Digital signatures	.89783
	(For electronic signatures *use* KN285.43/347.6743)	
349	Censorship	.898
.1	*By censor*, A–Z, e.g.	.8981
	.C3 Catholic Church	
	(If preferred, class at KD187.6/342.3976)	
.2	Self-censorship	.8982
.4	*Grounds for censorship*, A–Z, e.g.	.8983
	.N3 National security	
.9	*By form of presentation*	.899
.91	Mail	.8991
.92	Telecommunications	.8992
.93	Broadcasting, mass media	.8993
.94	Radio	.8994
.95	Television	.8995
.96	Theatre	.8996
.97	Film	.8997
.98	Print media	.8998
.99	Other forms	.8999

KN Common Law Treatises – Private Law 347

Procedure

(General matters and civil procedure. For criminal procedure *use* KM570–605/346.9)

350	*General works*	.9
351	*By common law jurisdiction (*Table IV)	.9094–9
353	Jurisdiction	.91
355	Limitation of actions	.915
357	Adjournment of actions	.917
359	Complex trials	.919
360	Court rules, forms, procedure	.92
361–9	*By court etc.* (Table V), e.g.	.921–9
	KN361 Appellate courts	.921
	KN372 Family courts	.927
370	Parties, *generally*	.93
.1	Litigants in person	.9301
.15	Non-legal representatives, e.g. friends	.93015
.2	Group actions, class actions	.9302
.3	Locus standi	.9303
371–9	Parties (Table VII, amplified if necessary) e.g.	.931–9
	KN377.D4 Decedents' estate	.937.D4
	KN378.3.C7 Crown immunities	.938.3.C7
	KN378.3.G6 Government actions	.938.3.G6
380	Preliminary proceedings	.94
381	*Methods of beginning proceedings*	.941
.1	Claim forms	.9411
.3	Motions	.9413
.4	Applications	.9414
.9	*Others*	.9419
383	Statements of case	.943
.1	Particulars	.9431
.2	Material facts	.9432
384	Defences	.944
.1	Accord and satisfaction	.9441
.2	Confession and avoidance	.9442
.3	Justification	.9443

KN Common Law Treatises – Private Law 347

384	Defences	.944
.4	Estoppel	.9444
.5	Res judicata	.9445
.8	Interpleader	.9448
.9	Set-off, counterclaim	.9449
.95	Disclosures in the public interest	.94495
.99	*Others*, A–Z	.94499
385	Reply	.945
.5	Rejoinder	.9455
386	Disclosure	.946
.5	Privilege	.9465
387	*Other matters*	.947
.1	Appearances	.9471
	(For judgment in default of appearance *use* KN395.5/347.973)	
.3	Interim relief	.9473
.5	Part 36 offer	.9475
.7	Consolidation of actions	.9477
.8	Interrogatories	.9478
388	Settlement	.95
.1	Discontinuance	.951
.3	Compromise	.953
389	Trial practice	.96
.1	Cause lists	.9601
.3	Non-jury list	.9603
.6	Juries	.9606
	(Civil only; for criminal juries *use* KM583/346.933)	
.61	Selection, summoning	.96061
.612	Exemption	.960612
.613	Conscientious objection	.960613
.62	Challenges	.96062
.64	Directions	.96064
.65	Unanimity, majority verdicts	.96065
.7	Jury instructions, summing up	.9607
.72	Verdicts	.96072

KN Common Law Treatises – Private Law 347

KN		347
389	Trial practice	.96
.8	Adversarial v. inquisitorial systems	.9608
.83	Opening remarks	.96083
	Evidence	
	(General matters and civil cases; for evidence in criminal cases *use* KM600–605/346.96)	
390	*General works*	.961
.1	Proof	.9611
.2	Presumptions, bad faith	.9612
.3	Judicial notice	.9613
.4	Suppression of evidence	.9614
	Forms of evidence	
391	Witnesses	.962
	(Class here competence and compellability)	
.1	Subpoena, summonses	.9621
.15	Payment, expenses	.96215
.2	Oaths, affirmations, statutory declarations	.9622
.3	Examination	.9623
.35	Hostile witnesses	.96235
.37	Video links	.96237
.4	*By type of person* (Table VII), e.g.	.9624
	.Q51 Physically disabled (deaf, blind etc.)	
.5	Expert evidence	.9625
.59	*By type of expert*, A–Z, e.g.	.96259
	.A3 Accountants	
	.M4 Medical expert witnesses	
.6	Opinions	.9626
.62	Character evidence, disposition	.96262
392	Documents, disclosure of information	.963
.1	Attestation	.9631
.2	Affidavits, depositions	.9632
.5	Sound, video recordings	.9635
.6	Electronic, computer records	.9636
.7	Exhibits, tangible objects, search orders	.9637

KN Common Law Treatises – Private Law 347

393	*Special aspects*	.964
.1	Relevance	.9641
.2	Credibility	.9642
.6	Direct evidence	.9646
.7	Circumstantial evidence	.9647
.8	Corroboration	.9648
394	Admissibility	.965
.1	Hearsay	.9651
.2	Dying declarations	.9652
.4	Illegally obtained evidence	.9654
.5	Computer evidence	.9655
.8	Privileged evidence	.9658
	(Class here Crown privilege)	
.9	Public policy	.9659
395	Judgments	.97
.1	Remedies	.971
	(General principles only. For remedies in relation to particular topics *use* the number for the topic and Table VI)	
.2	Execution	.972
.21	Orders	.9721
	Divide A–Z, if required, e.g.	
	.C5 Charging orders	
	.G8 Guardianship orders	
	.M3 Matrimonial orders	
.22	Writs	.9722
.24	Attachment, garnishment	.9724
.25	Sequestration	.9725
.27	Diligences	.9727
.3	Recognition of judgments	.9729
.5	Default judgments	.973
.6	Summary judgments	.9736
.8	Extraordinary remedies, prerogative orders	.974
.81	Certiorari	.9741
.82	Mandamus	.9742
.83	Prohibition	.9743
.84	Quo warranto	.9744

KN	Common Law Treatises – Private Law	347
397	Costs	.977
.2	Contentious costs	.9772
.3	Non-contentious costs	.9773
.7	Assessment of costs	.9777
.8	Conditional fee agreements	.9778
398	Arbitration	.98
	(For commercial arbitration *use* KN256/347.619)	
.1	Arbitrators	.981
.12	Appointment	.9812
.13	Powers and duties	.9813
.14	Proceedings before arbitrators	.9814
.2	Court-annexed arbitration	.982
.4	Conciliation, mediation and negotiation	.984
.5	Awards	.985
.6	Dispute resolution, minitrials	.986
	(class here: alternative dispute resolution)	
399	Legal aid	.99
.2	Judicare, group legal services, prepaid legal services	.992
.3	Financial eligibility, means tests etc.	.993
399	Legal aid	.99
.32	Green form scheme	.9932
.4	Franchising	.994
.6	Management	.996
.7	*By type of person requiring legal aid* (Table VII), e.g.	.997
	.Q42 Immigrants	
.8	*Organisations providing legal aid*, A–Z	.998
.9	Law centres	.999
400	Citizens advice bureaux, *other advice services*	.9991

KP Preferred Jurisdiction 348

Notes:

1. Class KP/348 has been set aside, as an optional alternative, for use by any library which finds that the provision in the main schedules for the law of its own country (or any other preferred jurisdiction) is unsuitable or inadequate.
2. A library using this class should compile its own schedule, preferably based on Tables I and II, according to local requirements.

KR Africa 349.6

Notes:
1. If using KR, arrange material for each jurisdiction by Tables I and II, sub-section A, B, C or D, as indicated.
2. If using 349.6, employ country numbers from the geographic table in the Dewey Decimal Classification and arrange material for each jurisdiction by Tables I and II, sub-section F.
3. For any jurisdiction allocated only a Cutter number use Tables I and II, sub-section F.

1–50 Africa as a whole (C)

51–100 **North Africa (C)**
101–150 Morocco (C)
151–170 French Morocco (to 1956) (D)
171–190 Spanish Morocco (to 1956) (D)
201–220 Tangier (i.e. International Zone, to 1956) (D)
251–300 Algeria (C)
301–350 Tunisia (C)
351–400 Libya (C)
401–420 Sahara (Spanish Sahara to 1975); Western Sahara (1976–) (D)

481–500 **North-East Africa (D)**
501–580 Egypt (B)
601–650 Sudan; South Sudan (2011–) (C)
651–700 Ethiopia (C)
701–720 Eritrea (D)
751–800 Somali Republic (i.e. Italian Somaliland to 1960) (C)
801–820 British Somaliland (to 1960) (D)
821–840 Djibouti (D)

951–1000 **Sub-Saharan Africa (C)**

1001–1050 **West Africa (C)**
1051–1100 Liberia (C)
1101–1150 British West Africa (to about 1957) (C)

KR Africa 349.6

1151–1200	Gambia (C)
1201–1250	Sierra Leone (C)
1251–1300	Ghana (i.e. Gold Coast to 1957) (C)
1321–1340	Ashanti (D)
1341–1360	Northern Territories (D)
1361–1380	British Togoland (D)
1401–1480	Nigeria (B)
1501	*States, regions etc.*, A–Z , e.g.
	.D4 Delta
	.K2 Kano
	.O9 Oyo
	(For other states, *see* Index of Jurisdictions)
1601–1650	French West Africa (to about 1960) (C)
1651–1700	Mauritania (C)
1701–1750	Senegal (to 1981, 1989–), Senegambia (1982–1989) (C)
1751–1800	Mali (C)
1801–1850	Guinea (C)
1851–1900	Côte d'Ivoire (C)
1901–1950	Burkina Faso (i.e. Upper Volta to 1984) (C)
1951–2000	Togo (C)
2001–2050	Benin (C)
2051–2100	Niger (C)
2161–2180	São Tomé and Principé (D)
2181–2200	Cape Verde (D)
2201–2220	Guinea–Bissau (D)
2261–2280	Equatorial Guinea (D)
2301–2350	French Equatorial Africa (to about 1960) (C)
2351–2400	Chad (C)
2401–2450	Cameroon (C)
2451–2500	Central African Republic (C)
2501–2550	Gabon (C)
2551–2600	Congo [Brazzaville] (C)
2651–2700	Congo, Democratic Republic (previously Zaïre) (C)
2701	*Provinces etc.*, A–Z
2841–2860	Ruanda-Urundi (to 1959) (D)
2861–2880	Rwanda (D)
2881–2900	Burundi (D)
2901–2950	Angola (C)

KR Africa 349.6

3001–3050 **East Africa (C)**
3051–3100 British East Africa (to about 1961) (C)
3101–3150 Kenya (C)
3151–3200 Uganda (C)
3201–3250 Tanzania (C)
3261–3280 Zanzibar (D)
3281–3300 Tanganyika (D)
3301–3320 Mauritius (D)
3321–3340 Seychelles (D)
3401–3450 Mozambique (C)
3481–3500 Comoros and Mayotte (D)
3501–3550 Madagascar (C)
3561–3580 Réunion (D)

3601–3650 **Central Africa (C)**
3651–3700 Rhodesia and Nyasaland (i.e. Federation, 1953–1963) (C)
3751–3800 Zambia (C)
3801–3850 Zimbabwe (C)
3851–3900 Malawi (C)

4001–4050 **Southern Africa (C)**
4151–4200 Namibia (C)
4201–4350 South African Republic (A)
4351–4400 Cape Province (C)
4401–4450 Kwazulu–Natal (C)
4451–4500 Free State (C)
4501–4550 Transvaal (C)
4551 ‘*Bantustans*’, A–Z, e.g.
.B6 Bophuthatswana
.C5 Ciskei
.T6 Transkei
.V3 Venda
New provinces, A–Z, e.g.
.G1 Gauteng
.W5 Western Cape

KR Africa 349.6

4600–4620	High Commission Territories (to about 1968) (D)
4651–4700	Lesotho (C)
4701–4750	Botswana (C)
4751–4800	Swaziland (C)
4901–4910	St. Helena (with Ascension and Tristan da Cunha) (D)

KS Latin America 349.8

Notes:
1. If using KS, arrange material for each jurisdiction by Tables I and II, sub-section A, B, C or D, as indicated
2. If using 349.8, employ country numbers from the geographic table in the Dewey Decimal Classificationand arrange material for each jurisdiction by Tables I and II, sub-section F.

1–80	**Central America (B)**
101–180	Mexico (B)
201–280	Guatemala (B)
301–380	Salvador (B)
401–480	Honduras (B)
501–580	Nicaragua (B)
601–680	Costa Rica (B)
701–780	Panama (B)
801–850	Panama Canal Zone (C)
901–980	Cuba (B)
1001–1050	Haiti (C)
1051–1100	Dominican Republic (C)
1101–1150	Puerto Rico (C)
1151–1200	Virgin Islands (U.S.) (C)
1201–1220	French West Indies (D)
1221–1240	St. Pierre and Miquelon (D)
1241–1260	Guadeloupe (D)
1261–1280	Martinique (D)
1301–1350	Netherlands Antilles (1948–2010); Dutch Caribbean (C)
1361–1380	Aruba (D)
1381–1400	Curaçao and St Maarten (D)

1401–1450	**South America (C)**
1501–1580	Colombia (B)
1601–1680	Venezuela (B)
1701–1750	Surinam (C)
1751–1800	Guyane (C)
1801–1880	Ecuador (B)
1901–1980	Peru (B)

KS Latin America 349.8

2001–2080	Brazil (B)
2101–2180	Bolivia (B)
2201–2280	Paraguay (B)
2301–2380	Uruguay (B)
2401–2480	Argentina (B)
2501–2580	Chile (B)
2601–2620	Falkland Islands (D)
2621–2640	Antarctica (D)
2681–2700	South Georgia and South Sandwich Islands (D)

KT Asia and Pacific 349.5

Notes:

1. If using KT, arrange material for each jurisdiction by Tables I and II, sub-section A, B, C or D, as indicated.
2. If using 349.5, employ country numbers from the geographic table in the Dewey Decimal Classification and arrange material for each jurisdiction by Tables I and II, sub-section F.
3. For any jurisdiction allocated only a Cutter number use Tables I and II, sub-section F.

1–50	Asia (as a whole) (C)

51–100	**Middle East (C)**
101–180	Palestine (to 1948) (B)
201–280	Israel (1948 onwards) (B)
301–380	West Bank (i.e. occupied territory. Use for any future Palestinian state) (B)
401–480	Lebanon (B)
501–580	Syria (B)
601–680	Jordan (B)
701–780	Iraq (B)
781–800	Arabia (as a whole) (D)
801–880	Saudi Arabia (B)
901–980	Yemen Arab Republic (B)
1001–1050	Aden (C)
1051–1100	Southern Yemen (C)
1101–1120	Oman (D)
1121–1140	United Arab Emirates (D)
1141–1160	Qatar (D)
1161–1180	Bahrain (D)
1181–1200	Kuwait (D)
1301–1380	Iran (B)

1381–1400	**Central Asia (D)**
1401–1480	Afghanistan (B)
1501–1650	India (A)

KT Asia and Pacific 349.5

1661–1680	Andhra Pradesh (D)
1681–1700	Assam (D)
1701–1720	Bihar (D)
1721–1740	Gujarat (D)
1741–1760	Kerala (D)
1761–1780	Madhya Pradesh (D)
1781–1800	Tamil Nadu (D)
1801–1820	Maharashtra (D)
1821–1840	Karnataka (D)
1841–1860	Orissa (D)
1861–1880	Punjab (D)
1881–1900	Rajasthan (D)
1901–1920	Uttar Pradesh (D)
1921–1940	West Bengal (D)
1941–1960	Delhi (D)
1961–1980	Himachal Pradesh (D)
1981–2000	Manipur (D)
2001–2020	Tripura (D)
2021–2040	Andaman Islands (D)
2041–2060	Nicobar Islands (D)
2061–2080	Lakshadweep (D)
2081–2100	Jammu and Kashmir (D)
2101–2120	Sikkim (D)
2121–2140	Goa (D)
2141–2160	Pondicherry (D)
2161	*Other states etc.* A–Z, e.g.
	.A69 Arunachal Pradesh
	.C45 Chandigarh
	.D12 Dadra and Nagar Haveli
	.H19 Haryana
	.M55 Meghalaya
	.M79 Mizoram
	.N12 Nagaland
2201–2280	Pakistan (B)
2301	*Provinces*, A–Z
2351–2400	Bangladesh (C)
2441–2460	Nepal (D)
2481–2500	Bhutan (D)

KT Asia and Pacific 349.5

2501–2580	Sri Lanka (B)
2601–2620	Maldives (D)
2621–2640	Cocos Islands (D)
2681–2700	**South-East Asia (D)**
2701–2780	Myanmar (i.e. Burma to 1989) (B)
2801–2880	Thailand (B)
2901–2950	Indo-China (C)
2951–3000	Laos (C)
3001–3080	Vietnam (B)
3101–3150	Cambodia (Kampuchea 1970-1993) (C)
3201–3280	Malaysia (B)
3301–3380	Malaya (B)
3401–3420	Johore (D)
3421–3440	Kedah (D)
3441–3460	Kelantan (D)
3461–3480	Malacca (D)
3481–3500	Negri Sembilan (D)
3501–3520	Pahang (D)
3521–3540	Penang (D)
3541–3560	Perak (D)
3561–3580	Perlis (D)
3581–3600	Selangor (D)
3601–3620	Trengganu (D)
3651–3700	Singapore (C)
3701–3720	Borneo (D)
3721–3740	Sabah (D)
3741–3760	Sarawak (D)
3761–3780	Brunei (D)
3801–3880	Indonesia (B)
3901	*Provinces, etc.*, A–Z, e.g.
	.K14 Kalimantan
	.L86 Loro Sae
	.W45 West Irian
3921–3940	East Timor (1975–2002); Timor-Leste (D)
3941–3960	Papua New Guinea (D)
4001–4080	Philippines (B)

KT Asia and Pacific 349.5

4081–4100 **East Asia (D)**
4101–4180 Mongolia (B)
4201–4280 China (B)
4281–4300 Tibet (D)
4301–4350 Taiwan (C)
4351–4400 Hong Kong (C)
4401–4420 Macao (D)
4451–4500 Korea (C)
4501–4550 North Korea (C)
4551–4600 South Korea (C)
4601–4680 Japan (B)

4701–4720 **Pacific (D)**
4721–4740 Pacific Islands Trust Territory (1947–1986); Federated States of Micronesia (1986–) (D)
4741–4760 North Mariana Islands (D)
4761–4780 Republic of Palau (D)
4781–4800 Marshall Islands (D)
4801–4850 *US territories* (C)
4861–4880 Ryukyu Islands (D)
4881–4900 Guam (D)
5001–5020 Wake, Midway, Johnston Atoll (D)
5021–5040 Eastern Samoa (D)
5041 *Others*, A–Z
5101–5150 Samoa (C)
5201–5250 *British territories* (C)
5251–5300 Western Pacific High Commission (C)
5301–5320 Gilbert and Ellice Islands (to 1975); Kiribati (D)
5321–5340 Solomon Islands (D)
5341–5360 Vanuatu (New Hebrides to 1980) (D)
5361–5380 Tuvalu (D)
5381–5400 South Pacific Commission (D)
5401–5420 Fiji Islands (D)
5421–5440 Pitcairn Islands (D)
5441–5460 Tonga (D)

KT Asia and Pacific 349.5

5501–5520	*Australian and New Zealand territories* (D)
5521–5540	Norfolk Island (*Austr.*) (D)
5541–5560	Nauru (*independent* 1968–) (D)
5561–5580	Christmas Island (*Austr.*) (D)
5581–5600	Cook Islands (*NZ*) (D)
5601–5620	Tokelau Islands (*NZ*) (D)
5621–5640	Niue Island (*NZ*) (D)
5701–5720	*French territories* (D)
5721–5740	New Caledonia (D)
5741–5760	Wallis and Fortuna (D)
5761–5780	French Polynesia (D)
5801	*Others*, A–Z

KV Europe 349.4

Notes:

1. If using KV, arrange material for each jurisdiction by Tables I and II, sub-section A, B, C or D, as indicated.
2. If using 349.4, employ country numbers from the geographic table in the Dewey Decimal Classification and arrange material for each jurisdiction by Tables I and II, sub-section F.
3. For any jurisdiction allocated only a Cutter number use Tables I and II, sub-section F.

1–50 Europe (as a whole) (C)
(May be used for the European Union, with Table B from KW, as an alternative to KC1001–35/341.68 or KW)

51–100 **Scandinavia (C)**
101–180 Norway (B)
181–200 Svalbard (D)
201–280 Sweden (B)
301–380 Denmark (B)
381–400 Faroe Islands (D)
401–420 Greenland (D)
421–500 Iceland (B)
501–580 Finland (B)

601–680 **Western Europe (B)**
701–780 Portugal (B)
781–800 Azores (D)
801–820 Madeira (D)
821–900 Spain (B)
901–920 Balearic Islands (D)
921–940 Canary Islands (D)
961–980 Andorra (D)
1001–1080 French Community (B)
1101–1250 France (A)
1301–1380 Belgium (B)
1401–1480 Netherlands (B)
1501–1580 Luxembourg (B)

KV Europe 349.4

1601–1750 Germany (A)
(Class here:
i. Germany, 1866–1949
ii. Federal Republic, 1949–1990
iii. Reunited Germany, 1990–)
1761–1780 Baden–Württemberg (D)
1781–1800 Bavaria (D)
1801–1820 Berlin (D)
(Class here: Berlin, 1866–1949 and 1990–
and West Berlin, 1949–1990)
1821–1840 Bremen (D)
1841–1860 Hamburg (D)
1861–1880 Hessen (D)
1881–1900 Lower Saxony (D)
1901–1920 North Rhine–Westphalia (D)
1921–1940 Rhineland–Palatinate (D)
1941–1960 Saarland (D)
1961–1980 Schleswig–Holstein (D)
1981 *Previous German states*, A–Z, e.g.
.H3 Hanover
.P7 Prussia
1991 *Eastern Länder*, A–Z, e.g.
.B7 Brandenburg
.M4 Mecklenburg-West Pomerania
.S2 Saxony
.S3 Saxony-Anhalt
.T5 Thuringia
2001–2050 German Democratic Republic (1949–1990) (C)
2101 *Local divisions*, A–Z, e.g.
.B4 Berlin (East)
2201–2280 Austria (B)
2281–2300 Liechtenstein (D)
2301–2380 Switzerland (B)
2381 *Cantons*, A–Z
2401–2480 Italy (B)
2481–2500 Monaco (D)
2501–2520 Vatican (state) (D)
2521–2540 San Marino (D)

2601–2650	**Eastern Europe (C)**
2651–2700	Baltic States (C) (Use for period up to 1940. For post-1940 Socialist Republics use KV3821–80)
2701–2780	Poland (B)
2801–2880	Czechoslovakia (1919–1992); Czech Republic (1993–) (B)
2881–2900	Slovakia (D)
2901–2980	Hungary (B)
3001–3080	Yugoslavia (1918–2003); Serbia (B)
	Successor states and provinces:
3081	Montenegro
3082	Kosovo and Metohija
3083	Vojvodina
3084	Bosnia–Herzegovina
3085	Croatia
3086	Macedonia
3087	Slovenia
3101–3180	Albania (B)
3201–3280	Bulgaria (B)
3301–3380	Romania (B)
3501–3650	Soviet Union (A)
	Successor states etc
3651–3700	RSFSR (Russia) (C)
3701–3750	Belarus (C)
3751–3800	Ukraine (C)
3801–3820	Moldova (D)
3821–3840	Estonia (D)
3841–3860	Latvia (D)
3861–3880	Lithuania (D)
3881–3900	Georgia (D)
3901–3920	Armenia (D)
3921–3940	Azerbaidzan (D)
3941–3960	Kazakhstan (D)
3961–3980	Turkmenistan (D)
3981–4000	Uzbekistan (D)
4001–4020	Tajikistan (D)
4021–4040	Kyrgyzstan (D)

KV Europe 349.4

4051 Russian Republics, A–Z, e.g.:
 .C5 Chechnya
 .K1 Karelia

4401–4450 **Mediterranean (C)**
4501–4550 Gibraltar (C)
4551–4600 Malta (C)
4601–4680 Greece (B)
 (Use for modern Greece. For ancient Greece use KE40–90/343.34–6)
4681–4700 Crete (D)
4701–4720 Aegean Islands (D)
4801–4880 Cyprus (B)
4881–4900 Turkish Republic of North Cyprus (D)
4901–4980 Turkey (B)

KW European Union Law

Notes:

1. The Treaty of Lisbon 2007 came into force on December 1, 2009, amending and streamlining the EU and EC Treaties and merging the European Community into the European Union.
2. The schedule for the European Union is printed here, rather than as one of the tables.
3. If one of the alternative class locations is to be used, the appropriate column of numbers on the right-hand side of the page should be used: for KV1-50, use column B, 50 numbers; for KC1001 or for 341.68, use column C, (1 number) inserting a decimal point after the second digit as necessary, e.g. KC1001.4 Official Journal.
4. Libraries which use the decimal notation, but do not wish to place the European Union in 341, are advised to use 349.4 with Table C from Class KW.
5. Care should be taken not to confuse European Union law with European law, either as a whole or the national law of individual EU member and non-member states.

	Constitution and Legislation	B 50 nos.	C 1 no.
1	Treaties of foundation, *by date* (Table III), e.g.	1	01
	.G07 Treaty of Lisbon 2007		
2	Treaties of accession	.5	011
3	Bilateral and multilateral agreements	.7	012
.5	Lomé Conventions	.75	0125
	(If preferred, *use* KC10–18)		
4	Charter of Fundamental Rights	.8	0128
	Legislation etc.		
5	Collections, codes, etc.	2	013
	By subject A–Z		
	(*If preferred, place with subject*)		
6	Official Journal (to 1969)	.1	014
.1	*L series*		
.3	*C series*		
.5	*Special edition*		
.7	*S series*		
.9	*Indexes and tables*	.15	0145

KW European Union Law

7	Glossaries, thesauri	.17	0147
8	Indexes and digests (*non-official*)	.2	015
9	Collections of national legislation applying EU rules	.9	019

Union Institutions

(*Use KW10–45 for publications of these institutions. Use KW88 et seq for publications of which they form the subject matter*)

10	Council of Ministers (*General publications only*)	3		02
15	European Commission	4		021
16	COM documents		.1	0211
17	SEC documents		.2	0212
18	*Other general documents* (*Place subject publications under subject*)		.3	0213
20	European Parliament	5		022
21	*Debates* (*OJ Annex*)		.1	0221
.1	*Minutes of Proceedings*		.15	02215
22	*Working/Session documents* (PE documents)		.2	0222
23	*Resolutions/Texts adopted*		.6	0226
.5	*Documents, research papers, etc.*		.7	0227
.7	*Symposia, meetings with other bodies, etc.*		.8	0228
24	Committees, A–Z		.9	0229
.5	Journals (*alternative to KW 65*)		.95	02295
25	Economic and Social Committee	6		023
26	*Documents*		.1	0231
27	*Opinions*		.2	0232
30	Committee of Permanent Representatives		.5	024
31	Court of Auditors		.8	025
32	European Investment Bank		.9	026
35	ACP–EU		.95	0265
.1	Council of Ministers		.96	0266
.2	Consultative Assembly		.97	0267
40	*Other bodies*, A–Z	7		029
42	European Coal and Steel Community		.2	0292
45	European Atomic Energy Community		.5	0295

KW European Union Law

Law Reports, etc.

50	Court of Justice of the European Communities	8	03
	Official series		
51	European Court Reports	.1	031
.2	Judgments or Orders of the Court	.12	0312
.4	Proceedings of the Court	.14	0314
.5	Information on the Court of Justice	.15	0315
.6	Synopsis of the Work of the Court	.16	0316
.8	*Other series*	.18	0318
52	*Non-official series*, A–Z, e.g.	.2	032
	.C6 Common Market Law Reports		
53	General Court (formerly Court of First Instance)	.3	033
54	*Other courts*, A–Z	.6	034
55	National courts' decisions concerning EU law	9	035
	Digests, indexes etc.		
60	*Official*	10	038
61	*Non-official*	.2	0382

Journals

	Official series		
65	*General by title*	11	041
66	Statistical	12	042
.1	By theme: General	.1	0421
.13	Regions	.13	04213
.15	ACP–EU	.15	04215
.2	Economy and finance	.2	0422
.3	Population and social conditions	.3	0423
.31	Employment and earnings	.31	04231
.33	Education and training	.33	04233
.35	Social protection	.35	04235
.4	Energy and industry	.4	0424
.5	Agriculture, forestry and fisheries	.5	0425
.6	Foreign trade	.6	0426
.65	ACP–EU	.65	04265
.67	Tariffs	.67	04267

KW European Union Law

66	Statistical	12	042
.7	Services and transport	.7	0427
.9	Miscellaneous	.9	0429
67	Bibliographies and indexes	13	043
	Non-official, by title		
68	Bibliographic	14	044
69	Other	.2	0442
	Treatises		
70	Encyclopaedias, reference works	.5	045
.1	Handbooks, guides etc.	.6	0454
.2	Directories	.7	0455
.3	Maps, atlases	.8	0457
71	Legal system as a whole	15	05
72	Philosophy, harmonisation, subsidiarity	.2	051
73	European integration	.3	052
74	Politics, public opinion	.4	053
75	International relations	16	054
76	Developing countries	.1	055
77	Economic relations, co-operation	.3	0551
.2	Humanitarian aid, food aid	.32	05512
.3	ACP-EU, Lomé Conventions	.33	05513
.4	European Development Fund (EDF)	.34	05514
.5	GSP – Generalised System of Preferences	.35	05515
78	External trade, commercial policy	.4	0552
.1	Single market and external trade	.41	05521
.2	Import quotas	.42	05522
.3	Dumping	.43	05523
79	Security, defence	.5	056
80	EU law : international law	17	057
81	EU relations with foreign states and groups	.2	058
.1	Europe	.21	0581
.12	Western Europe	.212	05812
.13	Eastern Europe	.213	05813
.2	*By country*, A–Z	.22	0582
.3	United States, Canada	.23	0583

KW European Union Law

81	EU relations with foreign states and groups		.2	058
.4	Latin America and Caribbean		.24	0584
	By country, A–Z			
.5	Middle East and North Africa		.25	0585
	By country, A–Z			
.6	Africa		.26	0586
	(ACP–EU *see* KW 77.3)			
	By country, A–Z			
.7	Asia and Pacific		.27	0587
	By country, A–Z			
.8	Australia and New Zealand		.28	0588
82	EU relations with other bodies, e.g. United Nations, A–Z		.3	059
83	Justice and home affairs		.4	0595
.1	Immigration, asylum, Schengen and other agreements		.42	0597
84	Constitutional law, institutional developments	18		06
85	Foundation treaties (For texts *use* KW1)	19		061
.5	Treaties of accession (For texts *use* KW2)		.3	0613
.6	Multilateral treaties (For texts *use* KW3)		.4	0614
86	EU and member states. Implementation and effect of EU law		.5	0615
	By member state, A–Z			
87	Membership, enlargement	20		062
	By individual state, A–Z			
88	Executive and consultative organs	21		063
89	Council of Ministers		.1	0631
90	Commission		.2	0632
91	Economic and Social Committee		.3	0633
92	*Others*, A–Z		.9	0639
93	Court of Justice		.93	06393
94	General Court (formerly Court of First Instance)		.95	06395
.5	Civil Service Tribunal		.955	063955
95	Parliament	22		064
96	Elections		.5	065
97	Parties and groups, A–Z		.7	0652
.5	Legislative procedures		.75	06525
.52	Opt outs, qualified majority voting (QMV)		.752	065252

KW European Union Law

97	Parties and groups, A–Z	.7	0652
.522	Emergency brake	.7522	0652522
98	Civil rights (divide by Table VII)	23	066
.5	European Citizens' Initiative	.5	0665
99	Administration, civil service	24	067
100	Finance	25	068
101	Budget	.1	0681
	EU budget and member states, A–Z		
.5	Eurozone, euro area	.15	06815
102	Balance of payments	.2	0682
103	Taxation	.3	0683
104	Economic and monetary policy	26	07
105	Free movement of capital	.1	071
106	Monetary integration	.2	072
.1	European monetary system	.21	0721
.2	European currency unit (Euro)	.22	0722
.3	European Central Bank	.23	0723
.4	Single Euro Payments Area	.24	0724
107	Banking	.3	073
108	Single market, competition	27	074
109	Free movement of goods, trade barriers	.1	0741
.2	Tariffs, customs union	.2	0742
.3	Price regulation	.3	0743
.4	Quotas, import licensing	.4	0744
.6	Public procurement	.6	0746
.7	Free movement of services	.7	0747
.8	Free movement of professions, harmonisation of qualifications (For free movement of workers *use* KW130.2)	.8	0748
110	Competition law	28	075
.1	State aids	.1	0751
.2	Merger control	.2	0752
.3	Effect on trade between Member States	.3	0753
.4	Anti-competitive agreements, horizontal agreements, vertical agreements	.4	0754
.5	Concerted practices, abuse of dominant position, price fixing, cartels	.5	0755
.6	Monopolies	.6	0756

KW European Union Law

110	Competition law	28	075
.7	Distribution, licensing, franchising	.7	0757
.8	Exemptions	.8	0758
.82	Block exemption	.82	07582
.84	Individual exemption	.84	07584
.9	Enforcement	.9	0759
.92	EU courts etc.	.92	07592
.94	National courts	.94	07594
111	Company law	29	076
112	Consumer law	30	077
.1	Product safety/liability	.1	0771
.2	Advertising	.2	0772
.3	Consumer credit	.3	0773
.4	Food issues	.4	0774
.5	Labelling	.5	0775
.6	Dangerous products, accidents	.6	0776
113	Agriculture, common agricultural policy	31	08
.1	CAP and regions. Less-favoured areas	.1	0801
.2	Reform, surpluses etc.	.2	0802
.4	CAP and world agriculture	.4	0804
114	Prices, incomes	32	081
.3	Farm accounts	.3	0813
.6	Farming methods. Fertilisers and pesticides, biotechnology	.6	0816
.7	Animals – treatment, slaughter, transport	.7	0817
115	Marketing	33	082
116	Intervention purchasing	34	083
117	Fisheries	35	084
.2	Forestry	.2	0842
.3	Specific CAP sectors, A–Z, e.g.	.25	0845
	.B4 Beef and veal		
	.C4 Cereals		
	.D3 Dairy		
	.F7 Fruit		
	.H6 Horticulture		
	.O5 Oils and fats		
	.P5 Pigs		
	.P6 Poultry		

KW	European Union Law		
.3	Specific CAP sectors, A–Z, e.g. .S5 Sheep .S9 Sugar .W4 Wine	.25	0845
118	Business, industry, commerce, contracts	36	085
.1	European Economic Interest Grouping	.1	0851
.2	Small and medium-sized enterprises	.2	0852
.3	Multinational companies	.3	0853
119	Industries	.5	0855
.1	Service industries (banking, financial services, insurance, retailing)	.51	08551
.2	Steel	.52	08552
.3	Shipbuilding	.53	08553
.4	Textiles, clothing, footwear	.54	08554
.5	Food and drink	.55	08555
.6	Communication industries, information technology, electronics	.56	08556
.7	Transport industries (e.g. car manufacture) (*see also* KW135)	.57	08557
.8	Engineering, manufacturing, chemical, construction industries	.58	08558
.9	Others	.59	08559
120	Standards	37	086
121	Technology	.5	0865
122	Energy policy	38	087
.1	Energy market	.1	0871
.2	Nuclear power	.2	0872
.4	Coal	.4	0874
.6	Oil and gas	.6	0876
.7	Electricity	.7	0877
.8	Alternative energy sources	.8	0878
.9	Renewable energy, efficiency and savings	.9	0879
123	Regional policy, structural policy, subsidies, regional aid, Committee of the Regions	39	088
.1	Structural funds	.1	0881
.2	European Regional Development Fund	.2	0882
.5	By region or country, A–Z	.5	0885

KW European Union Law

124	European Investment Bank	.8	0888
125	Environment	40	089
.1	Action programmes	.1	0891
.15	Sustainable development	.15	08915
.2	Rural environment, the countryside	.2	0892
.3	Wildlife conservation	.3	0893
.4	Atmospheric pollution	.4	0894
.5	Aquatic environment, water, beaches	.5	0895
.6	Noise pollution	.6	0896
.7	Waste disposal, recycling	.7	0897
.8	Hazardous materials	.8	0898
.9	Climate change	.85	08985
126	Population, demography	.9	0899
127	Social policy	41	09
	(*see also* public health policy KW149)		
.2	European Social Fund	.2	0901
.4	Poverty	.4	0904
.5	Community development schemes	.45	0905
128	Social security, social services	.5	091
.2	Family	.22	09112
.3	Children, child care	.23	09113
.5	Health	.25	09115
.6	Housing	.26	09116
129	Special groups	.3	0912
.1	Women	.31	09121
.2	Young persons	.32	09122
.3	Older people	.5	09125
.4	Disabled	.6	09126
.5	Migrants	.7	09127
.8	Others	.8	09128
130	Labour and employment	42	092
	(For individual industries and sectors *use* KW118–9)		
.1	Incomes, income distribution	.1	0921
.2	Freedom of movement of workers	.2	09213
.3	Equal opportunities	.3	09215
.4	Apprenticeship	.4	09217

KW	European Union Law		
.5	Unemployment	.5	0922
130	Labour and employment	42	092
.6	Job creation, local employment initiatives	.51	09224
.7	Co-operatives	.52	09226
131	Conditions of work	.6	0925
.1	Hours (flexibility, work sharing, part-time work, etc.)	.61	09251
.2	Health and safety	.62	09252
.3	Social impact of technology	.63	09253
.5	Management, industrial relations	.65	0926
.6	Trade unions	.66	09261
.7	Industrial disputes	.67	09262
132	European Foundation for the Improvement of Living and Working Conditions	.7	0927
133	Criminal law	.8	0928
.1	Crimes, A–Z	.81	09281
.3	Law enforcement. European Police Office (Europol)	.83	09283
.5	Criminal procedure, evidence	.85	09285
.6	Judicial co-operation, Eurojust	.86	09286
135	Transport policy	43	093
.1	Rail	.1	0931
.2	Road	.2	0932
.3	Inland waterways	.3	0933
.4	Sea, ships, ports	.4	0934
.5	Air	.5	0935
136	Tourism	.6	0936
140	Science and technology, R&D	44	094
.1	By programme, agency, etc., A–Z	.1	0941
.2	Joint Research Centre	.2	0942
141	Information technology By programme, A–Z	45	0943
142	Intellectual property, trade marks, patents	46	096
143	Education and training	47	097
.2	Higher education	.2	0972
.3	European University Institute	.3	0973
.5	Other sectors	.4	0974

KW European Union Law

.6	Teachers, teacher training	.45	09745
.7	Literacy	.46	09746
144	Vocational training	.5	0975
.1	Training of trainers	.51	09751
.2	Special groups (Table VII)	.52	09752
.3	Culture	.6	0976
.4	Language	.65	09765
.5	Communication, broadcasting	.7	0977
.7	Sport, leisure, recreation	.8	0978
145	Information, documentation	48	098
146	Press, publishing	.2	0982
.2	Commission Library	.3	0983
147	Databases	.4	0984
148	EU publications catalogues etc.	.5	0985
149	Public health policy (*see also* social policy KW127)	49	099
.1	Disease prevention	.1	0991
.3	Mental health	.3	0993
.5	Co-operation in health matters	.5	0995

KZ Non-Legal Subjects

Notes:

1. Class KZ should be used, if at all, by specialist law libraries only.
2. A library using the 340-9 notation should not use KZ but should instead use the appropriate numbers from the Dewey Decimal Classification.
3. General libraries should use the non-legal classes of the scheme used for the remainder of the library, e.g. Library of Congress, Dewey Decimal Classification.
4. A library using class KZ should compile its own schedule, based on local requirements. One recommendation is that numbers from the DDC should be added to KZ, e.g.

KZ320 Political science
KZ390 Social anthropology

Appendix – Criminology

Note: This schedule can be used in KA (KA100-199), KB (KB300-399), or KM (KM700-799).

00	*General works*
01	History
02	Statistical studies
05	The criminal
06	*By kind of person* (Table VII), e.g.
	.06 Dangerous offenders
07	First offenders
.5	Single offenders
09	Recidivism
10	Causes of crime
11	Heredity, physiological causes, chromosome abnormality criminal anthropology
12	Psychological
13	Social conditions, economic factors
14	War, rebellion etc.
15	Minority problems, racial conflict
16	Alcohol, drugs
17	Films, television, video recordings
.5	Pornography
19	*Others*, A-Z
20	Prevention of crime
21	Potential offenders
22	Counselling, psychiatric treatment
23	Welfare services
24	Preventive policing
29	*Others*, A–Z, e.g.
	.B4 Behaviour alteration
	.E5 Environmental improvement
40	Treatment of offenders, sentencing policy
50	Theory of punishment and reform
.2	Aims, purpose of punishment
.22	Deterrence
.23	Reformation, correction
.24	Atonement

Appendix – Criminology

50		Theory of punishment and reform
	.25	Retribution
	.29	*Others*
51–59		*By kind of offender* (Table VII) (By crime *use* KM540–65/346.85–89 or country number and Table II)
60		Types of punishment
61		Capital punishment
	.9	*Particular forms*, A–Z, e.g.
		.E4 Electric chair
		.H3 Hanging
62		Corporal punishment
	.2	Torture
	.7	Public display, pillory, stocks
63		Transportation, deportation
64		Imprisonment, detention
65		Preventive detention
66		Indeterminate sentence
67		Suspended sentence
68		Partial detention (e.g. weekends only)
69		Non-custodial sentences, alternatives to imprisonment, community service
	.2	House arrest
	.3	Curfew
	.4	Electronic tagging
	.5	Reporting to police
	.6	Training centres, compulsory training
	.8	Withholding passports
70		Probation
71		Conditional discharge, binding over
72		Cautions, absolute discharge
73		Fines, enforcement of payment
74		Automatic fines, fixed penalties (e.g. traffic offences)
75		*Others*, A-Z, e.g.
		.C3 Castration
		.F6 Forfeiture
		.S8 Sterilisation

Appendix – Criminology

76 Discharge from prison, release
(If preferred, *use* KM685-90/346.988)
77 Free pardon, amnesty
78 Reductions for good behaviour
.2 Remission
.5 Parole
79 Treatment of discharged prisoners, after-care, rehabilitation of offenders
80 Penal institutions
Class individual institutions either at 81 *By jurisdiction*, A–Z, then A–Z by institution if required, or add 01 to a specific number at 83–99 and divide A–Z if required, e.g.
Brixton Prison 81.E65.B7
or 84.5.01B7
Overcrowding in Brixton Prison 88.2.01.B7
81 *By jurisdiction*, A-Z
82 Prisons
83 *By degree of security*
.2 Open prisons
.3 Special security units
84 *By purpose*, e.g. 'short sharp shock', classification, remand, pre-release, e.g. type of penal establishment
.2 Borstals, reformatories, approved schools
.5 Remand prisons
.9 *Others*, A–Z, e.g.
.A8 Attendance centres
85 *By type of inmate* (Table VII) e.g.
85.Q22 Women's prisons
85.Q53 Criminally insane
86 Political prisoners
87 Military prisoners
88 Management
.2 Prison population, overcrowding
.6 Prison staff, officers
(For the relationship between staff and prisoners *use* 94.32)
.8 Prison inspection
89 Architecture, equipment, building etc.

Appendix – Criminology

92 Discipline and security
(If preferred, *use* KM661–71/346.9872–4)
.2 Security regulations
.22 Rules
.23 Inspection
.3 Disciplinary regulations
.4 Disciplinary proceedings, punishments
.42 Fines
.43 Loss of rights
.44 Loss of remission
.45 Solitary confinement
.49 *Others*
.5 Offences
.52 Assault
.53 Riots, disturbances
.59 *Others*
.7 Prison work
.72 Workshops
.73 Remuneration
93 Prisoners' rights and privileges
(If preferred, *use* KM680–1/346.9875–6)
.2 Complaints, requests
.3 Welfare, conditions
.31 Self-injury (include here suicides by prisoners)
.32 Alcoholism
.33 Drug abuse
.4 Recreation
.5 Visits
.6 Education, libraries
94 Prison life
.2 Psychological effect of prison on prisoners
.3 Prison relationships
.32 Prisoner–staff
.33 Prisoner–prisoner
.4 Homosexuality
.8 Prisoners' families

Appendix – Criminology

95	Famous prisoners, escapes etc.
98	Privatisation of prisons and other penal institutions
99	Prison reform

Tables

Table I – Primary Materials

	A	B	C	D	E	F
	60 nos.	20 nos.	10 nos.	8 nos.	class 344	class 349
Official gazettes	1	1	1	1	01	01
Parliamentary publications	2	2	2	.1	015	011
Upper House	3	.1	.1	.2	016	0111
Journal	4	.2	.15	.22	0162	0112
Debates	5	.3	.2	.23	0163	0113
Bills	6	.4	.3	.24	0164	0114
Committees, A–Z	7	.5	.4	.25	0165	0115
Lower House	9	3	.5	.3	017	0116
Journal	10	.1	.55	.32	0172	01165
Debates	11	.2	.6	.33	0173	0117
Bills	12	.3	.7	.34	0174	0118
Committees, A–Z	13	.4	.8	.35	0175	0119
Legislation						
Constitutions	14	.9	.9	.9	02	012
Statutes						
Collections, by date	15	4	3.1	2.1	021	0121
Annual, sessional	16	5	.2	.2	022	0122
Private, local, personal	17	.3	.3	.3	0223	01223
Emergency legislation	.4	.4	.4	.4	0224	01224
Indexes, tables	18	6	.6	.6	023	0123
Subordinate legislation						
Collections, by date	20	7	4.1	3.1	03	013
Annual, sessional	21	8	.2	.2	032	0132
Indexes, tables	22	9	.3	.3	033	0133
Codes (annotated codes codes may be placed with the subject, using Table II)						
Collections	24	10	5	4	04	014
Civil	25	.1	.1	.1	041	0141
Civil procedure	26	.2	.2	.2	042	0142
Commercial	27	.3	.3	.3	043	0143
Criminal, penal	28	.4	.4	.4	044	0144
Administrative	29	.5	.5	.5	045	0145
Social, labour etc.	30	.6	.6	.6	046	0146
Financial, taxation etc.	31	.7	.7	.7	047	0147
Others, by subject, A–Z	32	.8	.8	.8	048	0148
Local legislation						
Counties, departments etc., A–Z	34	12	6	.9	05	015
Cities, towns etc., A–Z	35	.5	.5	.95	055	0155

	A	B	C	D	E	F
	60 nos.	20 nos.	10 nos.	8 nos.	class 344	class 349
Administrative and executive publications					060	016
Attorney-General etc.	36	13.1	7.1	5.1	061	0161
Other government departments, A–Z	37	.2	.2	.2	062	0162
Ad hoc commissions, committees, etc.	38	.3	.3	.3	063	0163
Law reports					07	02
Early reports (dates vary with jurisdiction)	40	14	8.1	6.1	071	0201
Modern reports						
All, or several courts, by title, A–Z	41	15	.2	.2	072	0202
Single courts, or special subjects, by title, A–Z	42	.2	.25	.25	073	0203
State trials	43	.3	.3	.3	074	0204
Individual cases (for arrangement see note at KF72)	45	16	.5	.5	075	021
Administrative decisions					08	022
Collections	47	17.1	9.1	7.1	081	0221
By department, A–Z	48	.2	.2	.2	082	0222
Digests etc.						
(Place material relating to a particular series of reports with the reports)						
Historical digests	50	18	10	8	09	025
Modern digests	51	19	.5	.5	095	026
Treaties (texts) (alternative to KC12)	(59)	(.8)	(.8)	(.8)	(098)	(028)
Journals (alternative to K1)	(60)	(20)	(10.9)	(8.9)	(099)	(029)

Table II – Subjects of Law

	A	B	C	D	F
	90 nos.	60 nos.	40 nos.	12 nos.	class 349
Primary materials *see* Table I	1–60	1–20	1–10	1–8	01–02
Legal system	61	21	11	9	03
Bibliography (alternative to K30–76)	(61.1)	(21.1)	(11.6)	(9.01)	(0301)
Customary law	62	22	12	.1	0302
By tribe, etc., A–Z	.5	.5	.5	.2	0303
Special subjects, A–Z	.9	.9	.9	.29	0305
Legal dictionaries	63	23	13	.3	0307
Legal profession	64	24	14	.4	031
Law offices, business organisation	.5	.5	.3	.45	0315
Associations	.8	.8	.4	.48	0317
Legal education	65	25	.5	.5	0318
Legal research, law reform	66	26	.9	.9	0319
Administration of justice	68	27	15	10	032
Courts	69	.2	.2	.2	0322
Court management	.2	.22	.22	.22	03222
Judiciary	.5	.25	.25	.25	03225
Legal officers	.7	.27	.27	.27	03227
Juries	70	.4	.4	.4	0324
Legal aid	71	.6	.6	.6	033
Statistics	72	28	16	.8	034
Legal history	74	29	17	11	035
Special subjects, A–Z	75	30	18	.5	038
Constitutional law	77	31	19	12	04
Special aspects, A–Z	.5	.1	.1	.05	0405
Executive	78	.2	.2	.1	041
Legislature	79	.4	.4	.2	042
Nationality	80	.6	.6	.3	043
Civil rights	81	.8	.8	.4	044
Equal opportunities	.5	.85	.85	.45	0445
Administrative law	82	32	20	.5	045
Government	83	.2	.2	.6	046
Government departments, public administration	.2	.22	.22	.62	0462
Civil service	.3	.23	.23	.63	0463
Public finance	84	.4	.4	.7	047
Taxation	.5	.5	.5	.72	0472
Other government regulations	85	.6	.6	.75	0475
Local government	86	.8	.8	.8	048
Military law	87	.9	.9	.9	049

	A	B	C	D	F
	90	60	40	12	class
	nos.	nos.	nos.	nos.	349
Criminal law and procedure	90	33	21	13	05
Classification of crimes	.2	.2	.2	.02	0502
Criminal liability	.3	.3	.3	.03	0503
Crimes, A–Z	91	34	22	.2	052
Law enforcement	92	35	.5	.5	055
Police	.2	.2	.52	.52	0552
Criminal records	.4	.4	.54	.54	0554
Criminal procedure	93	36	23	.9	059
Sentences	.2	.2	.2	.92	0592
Evidence	.4	.4	.4	.94	0594
Witnesses	.5	.5	.5	.95	0595
Prison law (alternative to Appendix)	(94)	(.9)	(.9)	(.99)	(0599)
Private (i.e. civil) law	95	37	24	14	06
Conflict of laws (alternative to KC2010–45/341.9)	(95.5)	(37.5)	(24.5)	(14.5)	(061)
Obligations	96	38	25	15	062
Contract	97	39	26	.2	063
Special aspects	98	.2	.2	.22	
Agency	99	40	.4	.4	064
Tort, delict	100	41	27	.6	065
Negligence	.5	.1	.1	.7	066
Special aspects	101	.2	.2	.9	069
Property	103	42	28	16	07
Real property	104	43	29	.2	071
Land tenure, conveyancing	105	.2	.2	.3	0711
Construction law	.5	.5	.25	.31	07115
Landlord and tenant	106	.6	.4	.32	0712
Natural resources, energy	107	44	.6	.33	0713
Environmental law, climate change	.2	.2	.7	.34	07142
Planning	.25	.25	.71	.35	0715
Environmental health, pollution	.4	.4	.8	.36	0716
Agricultural law	.6	.6	.9	.38	0718
Personal property	108	45	30	.4	072
Intellectual property	109	46	.2	.5	0725
Inheritance and succession	110	47	31	.6	073
Persons and social laws	112	48	32	17	075
Persons, names	113	49	.2	.1	0751
Corporate personality	114	50	33	.2	0752

	A	B	C	D	F
	90	60	40	12	class
	nos.	nos.	nos.	nos.	349
Family law	116	52	35	.4	076
Marriage	117	53	.2	.42	0762
Reproduction, fertility	.2	.2	.22	.43	0763
Special aspects A–Z	.3	.3	.23	.44	0764
Divorce etc.	.4	.4	.24	.45	0765
Cohabitation etc.	.6	.6	.26	.46	0766
Domestic violence	.7	.7	.27	.47	0767
Children, young persons	118	54	.4	.48	0768
Child welfare	.5	.5	.45	.49	0769
Social laws	120	56	36	.5	077
Social services, social security	121	.2	.2	.52	0772
Community care, homelessness	.5	.5	.3	.53	0773
Education	122	57	.4	.54	0774
Libraries, public records etc	.5	.5	.5	.55	0775
Public health, medical law	123	58	.6	.56	0776
Food	.3	.3	.63	.563	07763
Industrial law	124	59	37	.6	078
Equity, trusts	126	60	38	18	079
Commercial law	127	61	39	19	08
Company law	128	62	40	.1	081
Partnership	129	.2	.2	.15	0815
Directors	.3	.3	.3	.153	08153
Shares, shareholders	.5	.5	.5	.155	08155
Monopolies, competition	130	63	.6	.2	082
Industries, A–Z	131	64	.8	.3	083
Sale of goods, consumer protection	132	65	41	.4	084
Insurance (except marine)	133	66	42	.5	085
Finance, banking	134	67	43	.6	086
Investment, capital markets	.3	.3	.3	.63	0863
Financial services	.5	.5	.5	.65	0865
Accountancy	.7	.7	.7	.67	0867
Bankruptcy, insolvency	135	68	.9	.69	0869
Transport					
Roads, railways	136	69	44	.7	087
Air law	137	70	.5	.75	0875
Maritime law	138	71	45	.8	088
Salvage, marine insurance	139	72	.2	.82	0882
Fisheries	140	73	.4	.84	0884
Communications	141	74	46	.9	089
Telecommunications	.5	.5	.2	.91	0891
Media law, censorship	142	75	.5	.92	0892

	A	B	C	D	F
	90 nos.	60 nos.	40 nos.	12 nos.	class 349
Computer law	143	.5	.7	.95	0895
Internet	.5	.55	.75	.955	08955
Procedure (general and civil)	144	76	47	20	09
Special aspects, A–Z	145	.2	.2	.1	091
Statements of case	146	.4	.4	.2	092
Evidence	147	77	48	.3	093
Witnesses	.3	.3	.3	.33	0933
Special aspects, A–Z	.9	.9		.39	0939
Arbitration	148	78	49	.4	094
Judgments	.9	.9	.9	.49	0949
Remedies	149	79	50	.5	095
Execution	.5	.9			0955
Costs	150	80	.9	.6	096

Table III – Dates

Notes:

1. This table provides a system of 'Cutter' numbers for arranging material by date. It should be used where specified, and may be used elsewhere if desired. It can be used for any materials produced after 1400 AD. If it is necessary to arrange earlier works by date, the full date should be used instead of a 'Cutter' number.
2. Each date symbol consists of a letter, representing the century, and the last two digits of the actual year, e.g.

1642	is shown as	.C42
1800	is shown as	.E00
1909	is shown as	.F09

.A00–.A99	represents	AD 1400–1499
.B00–.B99	"	AD 1500–1599
.C00–.C99	"	AD 1600–1699
.D00–.D99	"	AD 1700–1799
.E00–.E99	"	AD 1800–1899
.F00–.F99	"	AD 1900–1999
.G00–.G99	"	AD 2000–2100

Table IV – Common Law Jurisdictions

19 nos.	1 no. or Cutter no.	
1	.A1	England
1.5	.A15	Wales
2	.B2	Scotland
3	.C3	Ireland (as a whole)
4	.C4	Northern Ireland
5	.C5	Republic of Ireland
6	.D1	Isle of Man
7	.E1	Channel Islands
8	.E2	Jersey
9	.E3	Guernsey
10	.F1	Canada
11	.F2	Provinces, A–Z
11.5	.F3	North America (i.e. USA and Canada)
12	.G1	United States
13	.G2	States, A–Z
14	.H1	West Indies, A–Z
16	.K1	Australia
17	.K2	States, A–Z
17.5	.K3	Australia and New Zealand
18	.L1	New Zealand
19	.M1	Commonwealth generally

Optional number for use in common law jurisdictions:

19.5	.N1	European Union

Table V – Courts

Examples, both historic and current, are given for the British Isles. Other jurisdictions will need to insert their own courts as required.

10 nos.	1 no.	
1	.X1	Supreme courts, appeal courts
		Superior courts
		Court of Appeal Civil Division
		Court of Appeal Criminal Division
		Court of Criminal Appeal
		Court of Session (Scotland)
		High Court of Justiciary (Scotland)
		House of Lords
		Judicial Committee of the Privy Council
		Supreme Court
2	.X2	Constitutional courts
.5	.X25	Administrative courts
		Crown Office
3	.X3	Courts with both criminal and civil jurisdiction
		Queen's Bench Division
		Sheriff Court (Scotland)
4	.X4	Criminal courts
.1	.X41	Higher
		Queen's Bench Divisional Court
.2	.X42	Lower
		Crown Courts
		Circuit Court (Ireland)
.3	.X43	Summary jurisdiction
		Magistrates' Courts
		District Courts (Scotland, Ireland)
		(class here general works on Magistrates' Courts)
.4	.X44	Traffic courts
.9	.X49	*Other special*, A–Z
5	.X5	Civil courts
.1	.X51	Higher
		High Court
		District Registries
		Queen's Bench Division
.2	.X52	Lower
		County Courts
		Circuit Court (Ireland)
.3	.X53	Magistrates' Courts etc.

10 nos.	1 no.	
.9	.X59	*Others*, A–Z, e.g.
		.C6 Common Pleas
6	.X6	Equity courts, chancery courts
		Chancery Division
7	.X7	Family courts
		Family Division
		Divorce Division
.1	.X71	Youth courts
.6	.X76	Probate courts
.8	.X78	Court of Protection
8	.X8	Commercial courts
		Technology and Construction Court
.1	.X81	Admiralty courts, prize courts
		High Court of Admiralty
.3	.X83	Bankruptcy courts
.6	.X86	Industrial courts
9	.X9	*Others, by key word*, A–Z, e.g.
		.C6 Coroners Court
		.P2 Patents County Court
		.S5 Small claims courts

Table VI – Special Legal Forms and Topics

.Z1	Sources, texts
.Z11	Legislative bills
.Z12	Legislative proceedings
.Z14	Statutes
.Z16	Codes
.Z18	Subordinate legislation
.Z2	Casebooks
.Z25	Citation manuals
.Z3	Forms, precedents
.Z4	Jurisdiction
.Z43	Capacity
.Z45	Liability
.Z5	Formation (of agreements etc.)
.Z53	Amendments, alteration, revision, reform
.Z55	Termination
.Z6	Parties
.Z61	Prosecutors, claimants
.Z62	Defendants, defence lawyers
.Z63	Personal representatives
.Z64	Joint parties
.Z65	Third parties
.Z66	Government, etc.
.Z7	Actions
.Z71	Procedure, trial practice, litigation
.Z72	Court Rules
.Z75	Arbitration
.Z8	Remedies, damages, etc.
.Z9	Sentences, decisions, compensation
.Z92	Enforcement, compliance

Table VII – Persons

Note: This table may be used for legal capacity, liability, etc. of natural or corporate persons at any place in the schedules, whether specified or not.

10 nos.	1 no.	
		Natural persons
1	.Q1	By age
.1	.Q11	Children
.2	.Q12	Young persons
.3	.Q13	Age of responsibility, age of majority
.4	.Q14	Adults
.6	.Q16	Older people, retirement age
2	.Q2	By sex, sexual orientation
.1	.Q21	Males
.2	.Q22	Females
.3	.Q23	Homosexuals
.4	.Q24	Transsexuals
3	.Q3	By family relationships
.1	.Q31	Single persons
.2	.Q32	Married persons
.3	.Q33	Separated, divorced
.4	.Q34	Widowed
.5	.Q35	Remarried
.6	.Q36	Parents, grandparents, ancestors
.7	.Q37	Descendants
.8	.Q38	Siblings
.9	.Q39	*Others*, A–Z, e.g.
		.G8 Guardians
		.S8 Step-parents/children
		.W3 Wards
4	.Q4	Minorities, special groups
.1	.Q41	National groups
.2	.Q42	Immigrants, refugees
.3	.Q43	Races, aboriginals
.4	.Q44	Linguistic, cultural
.5	.Q45	Religious groups
.9	.Q49	Others
5	.Q5	Disadvantaged persons, disabled persons
.1	.Q51	Physically disabled, e.g.
		.D4 Deaf persons
.2	.Q52	Mentally disabled, mental patients
.3	.Q53	Insane, mentally ill persons
.4	.Q54	Addicts
.5	.Q55	Economically handicapped
5	.Q5	Disadvantaged persons, disabled persons

10 nos.	1 no.	
.6	.Q56	Illiterates
.8	.Q58	Slaves
6	.Q6	By occupation, profession etc., A–Z, e.g. .A1 Accountants .N8 Nurses .T4 Teachers
7	.Q7	*Others*, A–Z, e.g. .E9 Ex-service personnel .P4 Peers
		Corporate persons
8	.Q8	Official bodies
.1	.Q81	International bodies
.3	.Q83	Governments, government departments
9	.Q9	Non-official bodies
.2	.Q92	Business associations
.4	.Q94	Other associations, e.g. unincorporated associations
.5	.Q95	Clubs, friendly societies
.6	.Q96	Voluntary organisations
.7	.Q97	Trade unions, trade associations
.8	.Q98	Professional associations (For legal profession *use* KL50-120 *or* Table IA: 64)
.9	.Q99	Others, e.g. Freemasons

Table VIII – Non-Legal Forms and Treatments

.001	Journals
.002	Reference books
.0021	Bibliographies
.0022	Directories
.0023	Dictionaries, encyclopedias
.0024	Statistics
.003	Associations
.004	Conferences, symposia, collections, festschriften
.005	Research etc.
.0051	Drafts, working papers
.0052	Reports (not Law reports)
.0055	Theses
.006	Biography
.007	Historical treatment
.008	Comparative treatment
.0085	Elementary treatment, e.g. school textbooks
.009	Non-printed material
.0091	Manuscripts
.0095	Microforms
.0098	Audio-visual materials
.0099	Computer applications and methodology

Indexes

Index of Jurisdictions

	K number	Cutter number
Abia (state)	KR1501.A2	A10
Abuja (state)	KR1501.A25	A105
Abyssinia *see* Ethiopia		
Adamawa (state)	KR1501.A3	A11
Aden	KT1001–50	A12
Aegean Islands	KV4701–20	A16
Afars and Issas *see* Djibouti		
Afghanistan	KT1401–80	A22
Africa	KR	A26
Akwa Ibom (state)	KR1501.A4	A28
Alabama	KG401–20	A31
Alaska	KG421–40	A32
Albania	KV3101–80	A33
Alberta	KG61–80	A34
Alderney	KF541–50	A35
Algeria	KR251–300	A36
American Samoa *see* Eastern Samoa		
Anambra	KR1501.A5	A41
Andaman Islands	KT2021–40	A43
Andhra Pradesh	KT1661–80	A44
Andorra	KV961–80	A46
Angola	KR2901–50	A52
Anguilla	KG1561–70	A53
Antarctica	KS2621–40	A57
Antigua and Barbuda	KG1541–50	A58
Arabia	KT781–800	A61
Argentina	KS2401–80	A63
Arizona	KG441–60	A64
Arkansas	KG461–80	A65
Armenia	KV3901–20	A66
Aruba	KS1361–80	A68
Arunachal Pradesh	KT2161.A69	A69
Ascension	KR4901–20	A72
Ashanti	KR1321–40	A74
Asia	KT1–50	A75
Assam	KT1681–700	A78
Australasia	KH	A81
Australia	KH1–60	A82
Australian Capital Territory	KH201–20	A83
Australian New Guinea *see* Papua New Guinea		
Australian Pacific territories	KT5501–20	A85
Austria	KV2201–80	A86
Azerbaidzan	KV3921–40	A93
Azores	KV781–800	A96

	K number	Cutter number
Baden-Württemberg	KV1761–80	B12
Bahamas	KG1681–1700	B14
Bahrain	KT1161–80	B15
Balearic Islands	KV901–20	B17
Baltic States *see also* Estonia; Latvia; Lithuania	KV2651–700	B18
Bandundu	KR2701	B22
Bangladesh *see also* East Pakistan	KT2351–400	B23
Bantustans	KR4551	B24
Barbados	KG1521–30	B26
Barbuda	KG1541–50	B265
Basutoland *see* Lesotho		
Bas-Zaïre	KR2701	B27
Bauchi (state)	KR1501.B3	B28
Bavaria	KV1781–800	B29
Bayelsa (state)	KR1501.B35	B30
Bear Island *see* Svalbard		
Bechuanaland *see* Botswana		
Belarus	KV3701–50	B31
Belgian Congo *see* Congo, Democratic Republic		
Belgium	KV1301–80	B32
Belize	KG1741–60	B33
Bendel	KR1501	B35
Benin (country)	KR2001–50	B36
Benue (state)	KR1501.B4	B41
Benue-Plateau	KR1501	B42
Berlin	KV1801–20	B45
Berlin (East)	KV2101.B4	B46
Bermuda	KG1701–20	B48
Bhutan	KT2481–500	B52
Biafra *see* Eastern Nigeria		
Bihar	KT1701–20	B57
Bolivia	KS2101–80	B62
Bombay (state) *see* Gujarat; Maharashtra		
Bophuthatswana	KR4551.B6	B63
Borneo (Indonesia) *see* Kalimantan		
Borneo (island) *see also* Brunei; Kalimantan; Sabah; Sarawak	KT3701–20	B64
Borno (state)	KR1501.B6	B65
Bosnia-Herzegovina	KV3084	B67
Botswana	KR4701–50	B68
Brandenburg	KV1991.B7	B70
Brazil	KS2001–80	B71
Bremen	KV1821–40	B73
British Columbia	KG81–100	B75
British East Africa	KR3051–100	B76

	K number	Cutter number
British Guiana *see* Guyana		
British Honduras *see* Belize		
British Isles	KF	B81
British Pacific territories	KT5201–50	B82
British Somaliland *see also* Somali Republic	KR801–20	B83
British Togoland	KR1361–80	B84
British Virgin Islands *see* Virgin Islands (British)		
British West Africa	KR1101–50	B86
British West Indies *see* Commonwealth Caribbean		
Brunei	KT3761–80	B89
Bulgaria	KV3201–80	B92
Burkina Faso	KR1901–50	B93
Burma *see* Myanmar		
Burundi *see also* Ruanda-Urundi	KR2881–900	B96
Byelorussia *see* Belarus		
Caicos Islands *see* Turks and Caicos Islands		
California	KG481–500	C12
Cambodia	KT3101–50	C13
Cameroon *see also* Southern Cameroons	KR2401–50	C14
Canada	KG1–60	C16
Canary Islands	KV921–40	C18
Canberra *see* Australian Capital Territory		
Cape Province	KR4351–400	C21
Cape Verde	KR2181–200	C22
Caribbean *see also* Central America	KG1501–1760	C24
Cayman Islands	KG1791–800	C29
Central Africa	KR3601–50	C32
Central African Republic	KR2451–500	C33
Central America *see also* Caribbean	KS1–80	C35
Central Asia	KT1381–400	C37
Central Australia *see* Northern Territory (Australia)		
Ceylon *see* Sri Lanka		
Chad	KR2351–400	C42
Chandigarh	KT2161.C45	C45
Channel Islands	KF511–20	C47
Chechnya	KV4051.C5	C49
Chile	KS2501–80	C52
China	KT4201–80	C54
Christmas Island	KT5561–80	C57
Ciskei	KR4551.C5	C58
Cocos Islands	KT2621–40	C62
Colombia	KS1501–80	C65

	K number	Cutter number
Colorado	KG501–20	C66
Commonwealth Caribbean	KG1501–20	C67
Comoros and Mayotte	KR3481–500	C68
Congo (Brazzaville)	KR2551–600	C72
Congo, Democratic Republic	KR2651–2700	C73
Connecticut	KG521–40	C74
Cook Islands	KT5581–600	C76
Costa Rica	KS601–80	C78
Côte d'Ivoire	KR1851–900	C79
Crete	KV4681–700	C83
Croatia	KV3085	C85
Cross River (state)	KR1501.C7	C87
Cuba	KS901–80	C92
Curaçao	KS1381–400	C95
Cyprus *see also* Turkish Republic of North Cyprus	KV4801–80	C96
Czechoslovakia *see also* Slovakia	KV2801–80	C99
Czech Republic (1993–)	KV2801–80	C99
Dadra and Nagar Haveli	KT2161.D12	D12
Dahomey *see* Benin		
Daman *see* Goa		
Delaware	KG541–60	D22
Delhi (state)	KT1941–60	D26
Delta (state)	KR1501.D4	D30
Denmark	KV301–80	D31
District of Columbia	KG1401–20	D47
Diu *see* Goa		
Djibouti	KR821–40	D48
Dominica	KG1591–600	D64
Dominican Republic	KS1051–100	D66
Dutch Caribbean	KS1301–50	D69
East Africa	KR3001–50	E11
East Asia	KT4081–100	E12
East Central Nigeria	KR1501	E14
East Germany *see* German Democratic Republic		
East Pakistan *see also* Bangladesh; Pakistan		
East Timor *see* Timor-Leste		
Eastern Europe	KV2601–50	E21
Eastern New Guinea *see* Papua New Guinea		
Eastern Nigeria	KR1501	E25
Eastern Samoa	KT5021–40	E28
Ebonyi (state)	KR1501.E2	E30
Ecuador	KS1801–80	E38
Edo (state)	KR1501.E3	E40
Egypt	KR501–80	E49
Eire *see* Irish Republic		
Ekiti (state)	KR1501.E4	E51

	K number	Cutter number
El Salvador *see* Salvador		
Ellice Islands *see* Gilbert and Ellice Islands; Tuvalu		
England	KF1–99	E65
Enugu	KR1501.E5	E69
Equateur (province)	KR2701	E73
Equatorial Guinea	KR2261–80	E75
Eritrea	KR701–20	E82
Estonia *see also* Baltic states	KV3821–40	E87
Ethiopia	KR651–700	E93
Europe	KV1–50	E95
Falkland Islands	KS2601–20	F13
Far East *see* East Asia		
Faroe islands	KV381–400	F17
Federal Republic of Germany *see* Germany		
Federated Malay States *see* Malaya		
Federated State of Micronesia	KT4721–40	F25
Federation of the West Indies *see* West Indies Federation		
Fernando Po *see* Equatorial Guinea		
Fiji Islands	KT5401–20	F44
Finland	KV501–80	F46
Florida	KG561–80	F55
Formosa *see* Taiwan		
Fortuna *see* Wallis and Fortuna		
France	KV1101–250	F72
Free State (S.Africa)	KR4451–500	O71
French Community	KV1001–80	F74
French Equatorial Africa	KR2301–50	F75
French Guiana *see* Guyana		
French India *see* Pondicherry		
French Morocco *see also* Morocco	KR151–70	F78
French Pacific territories	KT5701–20	F80
French Polynesia	KT5761–80	F82
French Somaliland *see* Djibouti		
French West Africa	KR1601–50	F87
French West Indies	KS1201–20	F89
Friendly Islands *see* Tonga		
Gabon	KR2501–50	G12
Gambia *see also* Senegambia	KR1151–200	G16
Gauteng	KR4551.G1	G18
Gaza *see* West Bank (Palestine)		
Georgia (former USSR)	KV3881–900	G25
Georgia (US)	KG581–600	G24
German Democratic Republic	KV2001–50	G27
Germany	KV1601–750	G28
Ghana	KR1251–300	G44

	K number	Cutter number
Gibraltar	KV4501–50	G52
Gilbert and Ellice Islands *see also* Kiribati; Tuvalu	KT5301–20	G55
Gilbert Islands *see* Kiribati		
Goa	KT2121–40	G61
Gold Coast *see* Ghana		
Gobi (state)	KR1501.G6	G62
Gondola	KR1501	G66
Greece	KV4601–80	G72
Greenland	KV401–20	G73
Grenada (West Indies)	KG1601–10	G77
Griqualand East *see* Natal		
Griqualand West *see* Cape Province		
Guadeloupe	KS1241–60	G81
Guam	KT4881–900	G83
Guatemala	KS201–80	G85
Guernsey	KF531–40	G87
Guinea	KR1801–50	G92
Guinea-Bissau	KR2201–20	G93
Gujarat	KT1721–40	G94
Guyana	KG1721–40	G98
Guyane	KS1751–800	G99
Haiti	KS1001–50	H13
Hamburg	KV1841–60	H16
Hanover	KV1981.H3	H17
Haryana	KT2161.H19	H19
Haute-Zaïre	KR2701	H23
Hawaii	KG601–20	H28
Hessen	KV1861–80	H45
High Commission Territories *see also* Botswana; Lesotho; Swaziland	KR4600–20	H63
Himachal Pradesh	KT1961–80	H66
Holland *see* Netherlands		
Honduras	KS401–80	H84
Hong Kong	KT4351–400	H86
Hungary	KV2901–80	H95
Hyderabad (state) *see* Andhra Pradesh		
Iceland	KV421–500	I12
Idaho	KG621–40	I16
Ifni *see* Sahara		
Illinois	KG641–60	I24
Imo (state)	KR1501.I4	I27
India	KT1501–1650	I32
Indiana	KG661–80	I34
Indo-China	KT2901–50	I36
Indonesia	KT3801–80	I37
Iowa	KG681–700	I48

	K number	Cutter number
Iran	KT1301–80	I52
Iraq	KT701–80	I54
Ireland *see also* Irish Republic; Northern Ireland	KF201–60	I56
Irish Republic	KF401–60	I57
Isle of Man	KF501–10	I64
Israel *see also* Palestine	KT201–80	I67
Italian Somaliland *see also* Somali Republic	KR751–800	I72
Italy	KV2401–80	I73
Ivory Coast *see* Côte d'Ivoire		
Jamaica	KG1641–60	J14
Jammu and Kashmir	KT2081–100	J15
Japan	KT4601–80	J17
Jersey	KF521–30	J25
Jibuti *see* Djibouti		
Jigawa (state)	KR1501.J5	J34
Johnston Atoll *see* Wake and Midway		
Johore	KT3401–20	J44
Jordan	KT601–80	J47
Jugoslavia *see* Yugoslavia		
Kaduna (state)	KR1501.K1	K12
Kalimantan	KT3901.K14	K14
Kampuchea *see* Cambodia		
Kano (state)	KR1501.K2	K17
Kansas	KG701–20	K18
Karelia (Russia)	KV4051.K1	K20
Karnataka	KT1821–40	K22
Kasai	KR2701	K25
Kashmir *see* Jammu and Kashmir		
Katanga	KR2701	K27
Katsuna (state)	KR1501.K3	K28
Kazakhstan	KV3941–60	K29
Kebbi (state)	KR1501.K4	K31
Kedah	KT3421–40	K32
Keeling Islands *see* Cocos Islands		
Kelantan	KT3441–60	K36
Kentucky	KG721–40	K44
Kenya	KR3101–50	K45
Kerala	KT1741–60	K48
Kinshasa (province)	KR2701	K64
Kirghizistan *see* Kyrgyzstan		
Kiribati *see also* Gilbert and Ellice Islands	KT5301–20	K66
Kivu	KR2701	K69
Kogi (state)	KR1501.K6	K75
Korea *see also* North Korea; South Korea	KT4451–500	K86
Kosovo	KV3082	K88
Kuwait	KT1181–200	K94

	K number	Cutter number
Kwara (state)	KR1501.K9	K97
Kwazulu-Natal	KR4401–50	N18
Kyrgyzstan	KV4021–40	K65
Labrador *see* Newfoundland		
Lubuan *see* Sabah		
Laccadive Islands *see* Lakshadweep		
Lagos (state)	KR1501.L3	L13
Lakshadweep	KT2061–80	L15
Laos	KT2951–3000	L21
Latin America	KS	L26
Latvia *see also* Baltic states	KV3841–60	L28
Lebanon	KT401–80	L32
Leeward Islands	KG1531–40	L34
Lesotho	KR4651–700	L38
Liberia	KR1051–1100	L52
Libya	KR351–400	L53
Liechtenstein	KV2281–300	L56
Lithuania *see also* Baltic states	KV3861–80	L68
Loro Sae	KT3901.L86	L86
Louisiana	KG741–60	L87
Lower Saxony	KV1881–900	L88
Loyalty Islands *see* New Caledonia		
Luxembourg	KV1501–80	L98
Macao	KT4401–20	M12
Macedonia	KV3086	M125
Madagascar	KR3501–50	M13
Madeira	KV801–20	M14
Madhya Pradesh	KT1761–80	M15
Madras (state) *see* Tamil Nadu		
Maharashtra	KT1801–20	M17
Maine	KG761–80	M18
Malacca	KT3461–80	M21
Malagasy Republic *see* Madagascar		
Malawi	KR3851–900	M22
Malaya	KT3301–80	M23
Malaysia	KT3201–80	M24
Maldives	KT2601–20	M26
Mali	KR1751–800	M27
Malta	KV4551–600	M29
Manipur	KT1981–2000	M33
Manitoba	KG101–20	M34
Marshall Islands	KT4781–800	M38
Martinique	KS1261–80	M41
Maryland	KG781–800	M42
Massachusetts	KG801–20	M45
Mauritania	KR1651–700	M47

	K number	Cutter number
Mauritius	KR3301–20	M48
Mayotte	KR3481–90	M49
Mecklenburg-West Pomerania	KV1991.M4	M51
Mediterranean	KV4401–50	M52
Meghalaya	KT2161.M55	M55
Metohija *see* Kosovo		
Mexico	KS101–80	M58
Michigan	KG821–40	M62
Micronesia	KT4721–40	M63
Middle Congo *see* Congo (Brazzaville)		
Middle East	KT51–100	M64
Midway Island *see* Wake and Midway		
Mid-Western Nigeria	KR1501	M65
Minnesota	KG841–60	M68
Miquelon *see* St. Pierre and Miquelon		
Mississippi	KG861–80	M74
Missouri	KG881–900	M75
Mizoram	KT2161.M79	M79
Moldova	KV3801–20	M83
Monaco	KV2481–500	M84
Mongolia	KT4101–80	M85
Montana	KG901–20	M86
Montenegro	KV3081	M865
Montserrat	KG1551–60	M87
Morocco *see also* French Morocco; Spanish Morocco; Tangier	KR101–50	M89
Mozambique	KR3401–50	M92
Muscat and Oman *see* Oman		
Myanmar	KT2701–80	M98
Mysore *see* Karnataka		
Nagaland	KT2161.N12	N12
Namibia	KR4151–200	N15
Nasawara (state)	KR1501.N3	N17
Natal	KR4401–50	N18
Nauru	KT5541–60	N19
Nebraska	KG921–40	N21
Negri Sembilan	KT3481–500	N23
Nepal	KT2441–60	N25
Netherlands	KV1401–80	N28
Netherlands Antilles *see* Dutch Caribbean		
Netherlands East Indies *see* Indonesia		
Netherlands Guiana *see* Surinam		
Netherlands New Guinea *see* West Irian		
Netherlands West Indies *see* Dutch Caribbean		
Nevada	KG941–60	N31
Nevis *see* St. Christopher and Nevis		

	K number	Cutter number
New Brunswick	KG121–40	N32
New Caledonia	KT5721–40	N33
New Guinea *see* Papua New Guinea; West Irian		
New Hampshire	KG961–80	N36
New Hebrides *see* Vanuatu		
New Jersey	KG981–1000	N39
New Mexico	KG1001–20	N41
New South Wales	KH61–80	N44
New York (state)	KG1021–40	N46
New Zealand	KH301–60	N47
Newfoundland	KG141–60	N49
New Zealand Pacific territories	KT5501–20	N50
Nicaragua	KS501–80	N52
Nicobar Islands	KT2041–60	N53
Niger (country)	KR2051–100	N59
Niger (state)	KR1501.N5	N61
Nigeria	KR1401–80	N63
Niue Island	KT5621–40	N68
Norfolk Island	KT5521–40	N72
North Africa	KR51–100	N73
North Borneo *see* Sabah		
North Carolina	KG1041–60	N74
North Central Nigeria	KR1501	N75
North Dakota	KG 1061–80	N76
North East Frontier Agency (India) *see* Arunachal Pradesh		
North Korea	KT4501–50	N78
North Mariana Islands	KT4741–60	N785
North Rhine-Westphalia	KV1901–20	N79
North Vietnam *see* Vietnam		
North-East Africa	KR481–500	N81
North-Eastern Nigeria	KR1501	N82
North-Western Nigeria	KR1501	N92
Northern Ireland *see also* Ireland	KF301–60	N84
Northern Nigeria	KR1501	N85
Northern Rhodesia *see* Zambia		
Northern Territories (Ghana)	KR1341–60	N89
Northern Territory (Australia)	KH181–200	N91
Northwest Territories (Canada)	KG271–80	N88
Norway	KV101–80	N96
Nova Scotia	KG161–80	N98
Nyasaland *see* Malawi		
Ogun (state)	KR1501.O35	O27
Ohio	KG1081–100	O35
Oklahoma	KG1101–20	O45
Oman	KT1101–20	O51

	K number	Cutter number
Ondo (state)	KR1501.O5	O62
Ontario	KG181–200	O68
Orange Free State	KR4451–500	O71
Oregon	KG1121–40	O73
Orissa	KT1841–60	O75
Osun (state)	KR1501.O8	O78
Outer Mongolia *see* Mongolian People's Republic		
Oyo (state)	KR1501.O9	O96
Pacific	KT4701–20	P12
Pacific Islands Trust Territory	KT4721–40	P13
Pahang	KT3501–20	P17
Pakistan *see also* Bangladesh	KT2201–80	P22
Palau, Republic of	KT4761–80	P24
Palestine *see also* Israel; West Bank (Palestine)	KT101–80	P25
Panama	KS701–80	P29
Panama Canal Zone	KS801–50	P31
Papua New Guinea	KT3941–60	P34
Paraguay	KS2201–80	P37
Pemba *see* Zanzibar		
Penang	KT3521–40	P44
Pennsylvania	KG1141–60	P46
People's Democratic Republic of Yemen *see* Southern Yemen		
Perak	KT3541–60	P53
Perlis	KT3561–80	P55
Persia *see* Iran		
Peru	KS1901–80	P59
Philippines	KT4001–80	P62
Pitcairn Island	KT5421–40	P65
Plateau (state)	KR1501.P55	P68
Poland	KV2701–80	P72
Pondicherry	KT2141–60	P75
Portugal	KV701–80	P78
Portuguese East Africa *see* Mozambique		
Portuguese Guinea *see* Guinea-Bissau		
Portuguese India *see* Goa		
Portuguese Timor *see* Loro Sae		
Portuguese West Africa *see* Angola		
Prince Edward Island	KG201–20	P85
Principé *see* São Thomé and Principé		
Prussia	KV1981.P7	P90
Puerto Rico	KS1101–50	P93
Punjab (India)	KT1861–80	P95
Qatar	KT1141–60	Q1
Quebec	KG221–40	Q2
Queensland	KH81–100	Q3

	K number	Cutter number
Rajasthan	KT1881–900	R14
Réunion	KR3561–80	R29
Rhineland-Palatinate	KV1921–40	R43
Rhode Island	KG1161–80	R45
Rhodesia *see* Rhodesia and Nyasaland; Zambia; Zimbabwe		
Rhodesia and Nyasaland (Federation)	KR3651–700	R47
Rio de Oro *see* Sahara		
Rio Muni *see* Equatorial Guinea		
Rivers (state)	KR1501.R5	R55
Romania	KV3301–80	R66
Ruanda-Urundi (to 1959) *see also* Burundi; Rwanda	KR2841–60	B96
Russia	KV3651–700	R11
Rwanda *see also* Ruanda-Urundi	KR2861–80	R82
Ryukyu Islands	KT4861–80	R98
Saarland	KV1941–60	S11
Sabah	KT3721–40	S12
Sahara	KR401–20	S13
St Christopher and Nevis *see also* Anguilla	KG1561–70	S14
St Helena *see also* Ascension; Tristan da Cunha	KR4901–20	S15
St Kitts *see* St. Christopher and Nevis		
St Lucia	KG1611–20	S16
St Maarten	KS1381–1400	S17
St Pierre and Miquelon	KS1221–40	S18
St Vincent	KG1621–30	S19
Salvador	KS301–80	S21
Samoa *see also* Eastern Samoa	KT5101–50	W68
San Marino	KV2521–40	S23
Santo Domingo *see* Dominican Republic		
São Tomé and Principé	KR2161–80	S24
Sarawak	KT3741–60	S26
Sark	KF551–60	S27
Saskatchewan	KG241–60	S28
Saudi Arabia	KT801–80	S29
Saxony	KV1991.S2	S301
Saxony-Anhalt	KV1991.S3	S302
Scandinavia	KV51–100	S31
Schleswig-Holstein	KV1961–80	S33
Scotland	KF101–60	S35
Selangor	KT3581–600	S36
Senegal *see also* Senegambia	KR1701–50	S38
Senegambia	KRI701–50	S39
Serbia	KV3001–80	S40
Seychelles	KR3321–40	S42
Shaba	KR2701	S44
Siam *see* Thailand		

	K number	Cutter number
Siberia *see* Russia		
Sierra Leone	KR1201–50	S46
Sikkim	KT2101–20	S47
Singapore	KT3651–700	S48
Slovakia	KV2881–900	S50
Slovenia	KV3087	S51
Sokoto (state)	KR1501.S6	S52
Solomon Islands	KT5321–40	S53
Somali Republic *see also* British Somaliland; Italian Somaliland	KR751–800	S54
Somaliland *see* British Somaliland; Italian Somaliland; Djibouti; Somali Republic		
Soudan *see* Mali		
South African Republic	KR4201–350	S57
South America	KS1401–50	S58
South Arabian Federation *see* Southern Yemen		
South Australia	KH101–20	S62
South Carolina	KG1181–200	S63
South Dakota	KG1201–20	S64
South Georgia	KS2681–700	S751
South Korea	KT4551–600	S66
South Pacific Commission	KT5381–400	S68
South Sandwich Islands	KS2681–700	S752
South Sudan *see* Sudan		
South Vietnam *see* Vietnam		
South-East Asia	KT2681–700	S71
South-East Nigeria	KR1501	S72
South-West Africa *see* Namibia		
Southern Africa	KR4001–50	S73
Southern Cameroons *see also* Cameroon	KR1501	S74
Southern Rhodesia *see* Zimbabwe		
Southern Yemen	KT1051–100	S76
Soviet Union	KV3501–650	S78
Spain	KV821–900	S81
Spanish Guinea *see* Equatorial Guinea		
Spanish Morocco *see also* Morocco	KR171–90	S82
Spanish Sahara *see* Sahara		
Spitsbergen *see* Svalbard		
Sri Lanka	KT2501–80	S84
Sub-Saharan Africa	KR951–1000	S86
Sudan	KR601–50	S87
Sudanese Republic *see* Mali		
Surinam	KS1701–50	S89
Svalbard	KV181–200	S91
Swaziland	KR4751–800	S93
Sweden	KV201–80	S95

	K number	Cutter number
Switzerland	KV2301–80	S97
Syria	KT501–80	S99
Tahiti *see* French Polynesia		
Taiwan	KT4301–50	T14
Tajikistan	KV4001–20	T12
Tamil Nadu	KT1781–800	T16
Tanganyika *see also* Tanzania; Zanzibar	KR3281–300	T18
Tangier *see also* Morocco	KR201–20	T21
Tanzania *see also* Tanganyika; Zanzibar	KR3201–50	T24
Taraba (state)	KR1501.T3	T26
Tasmania	KH121–40	T27
Tennessee	KG1221–40	T34
Texas	KG1241–60	T38
Thailand	KT2801–80	T42
Thuringia	KV1991.T5	T44
Tibet	KT4281–300	T46
Timor *see* Loro Sae		
Timor-Leste	KT3921–40	T47
Tobago *see* Trinidad and Tobago		
Togo	KR1951–2000	T53
Togoland *see* British Togoland	Togo	
Tokelau Islands	KT5601–20	T55
Tonga	KT5441–60	T57
Transjordan *see* Jordan		
Transkei	KR4551.T6	T62
Transvaal	KR4501–50	T63
Trengganu	KT3601–20	T66
Trinidad and Tobago	KG1661–80	T72
Tripura	KT2001–20	T75
Tristan da Cunha *see also* St. Helena	KR4901–20	T78
Trucial States *see* United Arab Emirates		
Tunisia	KR301–50	T83
Turkey	KV4901–80	T86
Turkish Republic of North Cyprus	KV4881–90	T865
Turkmenistan	KV3961–80	T87
Turks and Caicos Islands *see also* Jamaica	KG1781–90	T91
Tuvalu *see also* Gilbert and Ellice Islands	KT5361–80	T98
U.S.A. *see* United States		
U.S.S.R. *see* Soviet Union		
Ubangi-Shari *see* Central African Republic		
Uganda	KR3151–200	U21
Ukraine	KV3751–800	U34
Ulster *see* Northern Ireland		
Union of Soviet Socialist Republics *see* Soviet Union		
United Arab Emirates	KT1121–40	U41
United Arab Republic *see* Egypt		

	K number	Cutter number
United Kingdom	KF1–99	U45
United States	KG301–1420	U48
United States Pacific territories	KT4801–50	U50
Upper Volta *see* Burkina Faso		
Uruguay	KS2301–80	U68
Utah	KG1261–80	U81
Uttar Pradesh	KT1901–20	U88
Uzbekistan	KV3981–4000	U92
Vanuatu	KT5341–60	V11
Vatican (state)	KV2501–20	V17
Venda	KR4551.V3	V23
Venezuela	KS1601–80	V25
Vermont	KG1281–300	V28
Victoria (Australia)	KH141–60	V32
Vietnam	KT3001–80	V35
Virgin Islands (British)	KG1571–80	V42
Virgin Islands (US)	KS1151–200	V43
Virginia	KG1301–20	V45
Vojvodina	KV3083	V47
Voltaic Republic *see* Burkina Faso		
Wake and Midway	KT5001–20	W14
Wales	KF161–80	W19
Wallis and Fortuna	KT5741–60	W21
Washington (state)	KG1321–40	W27
Washington, D.C. *see* District of Columbia		
West Africa	KR1001–50	W32
West Bank (Palestine) *see also* Palestine	KT301–80	W34
West Bengal	KT1921–40	W36
West Germany *see* Germany		
West Indies Associated states	KG1631–40	W41
West Indies Federation (1958–62)	KG1501–20	W42
West Irian	KT3901.W45	W45
West Pakistan *see* Pakistan		
West Pomerania *see* Mecklenberg		
West Virginia	KG1341–60	W51
Western Australia	KH161–80	W54
Western Cape	KR4551.W5	W55
Western Europe	KV601–80	W56
Western New Guinea *see* West Irian		
Western Nigeria	KR1501	W63
Western Pacific High Commission	KT5251–300	W65
Western Sahara	KR401–20	S13
Western Samoa *see* Samoa		
White Russia *see* Belarus		
Windward Islands	KG1581–90	W75
Wisconsin	KG1361–80	W78

	K number	Cutter number
Wyoming	KG1381–400	W98
Yemen, People's Democratic Republic *see* Southern Yemen		
Yemen Arab Republic	KT901–80	Y3
Yobe (state)	KR1501.Y6	Y6
Yugoslavia	KV3001–80	Y7
Yukon	KG261–70	Y8
Zaïre *see* Congo, Democratic Republic		
Zambia	KR3751–800	Z2
Zamfaraa (state)	KR1501.Z3	Z25
Zanzibar *see also* Tanzania	KR3261–80	Z3
Zimbabwe	KR3801–50	Z6

How to Use the Index-Thesaurus

This is not a full-scale thesaurus as broader and narrower terms have been deliberately excluded. Anyone requiring either of them can find them by consulting the schedules. Included are all specific terms in the schedules, the Appendix and Tables, together with some synonyms.

Preferred terms

Terms recommended for use are printed in **bold type**.

Conventional thesaurus abbreviations:

UF	*use for*: used under the preferred term referring to non-recommended term(s).
RT	*related term*: terms which might usefully be consulted by researchers in addition to the preferred term.
SN	*scope note*: explaining the context content or limits of the term.
USE	directs the researcher from a term not used to the preferred term.

Colon and plus signs

In both the schedules and the Index-Thesaurus a colon is used to indicate that two terms are considered in relation to each other, e.g.

Common law : Civil law

can be used to classify books in which the inter-relationship of the two systems is studied.

In the Index-Thesaurus the different aspects of a preferred term are indicated by the use of a **plus** sign followed by appropriate delimiting terms e.g.

films + causes of crime films + censorship
films + criminal evidence films + intellectual property
films + taxation

Order of entries

It should be noted that hyphenated words are treated as if they were two separate words so that:

co-operation comes between **CND** and **coaches.**

Finding entries

For space reasons only a limited number of entries could be made for a particular class number. For example:

1. Reference is normally made only to the first of a group of numbers covering various aspects of the subject. The schedules should **always** be consulted before any classification or cataloguing decision is taken.

2. Where instructions are given in the schedules to classify topics A-Z only the examples actually cited are included in the index. Users should add their own alphabetical sub-divisions both to the schedules and the index in their own copies.

3. Where optional alternatives are provided in the schedules only the preferred alternative is indexed. Users who prefer the alternative place should annotate their copies accordingly.

4. Countries and other jurisdictions are indexed separately in the Index of Jurisdictions to be found on pages 235–250.

If the term sought is not found quickly users should try one or more of the following:

1. If the total subject is made up of two or more topics, e.g. **evidence + previous convictions,** try looking up **previous convictions + evidence**.

2. If the subject is not found under the singular form try the plural and vice versa.

3. Try alternative spellings, e.g. enquiry or inquiry.

4. Try omitting an initial adjective, e.g. **presumptions** instead of **irrefutable presumptions.**

5. Try omitting other words which precede the main topic, e.g. **perpetuities** instead of **rule against perpetuities.**

Use in compiling catalogue entries

In using the thesaurus as an aid to compiling subject catalogues or indexes terms may be combined as required. In addition to the preferred terms there are a number of terms which are designated for use as sub-divisions only. For convenience they are listed here:

agreements
appointments
apportionment
bias
cases
cessation
civil codes
clauses
commercial codes
criminal codes
effects
handbooks
manuals
pamphlets
powers
prospectuses
reports
tenders
textbooks
texts
translations
variation
waiver

The vast majority of terms are those in use in one or more parts of the United Kingdom many of which are used throughout the common law world. A few terms specific to Australia, Canada, New Zealand or the United States have also been

included. Users in these or any other jurisdictions are invited to contact their local Users Group representatives with suggestions for further local terms which could be added to future editions.

Index-Thesaurus

abandonment + real property KN79.1; 347.32311

abattoirs
USE: slaughterhouses KN185.29; 347.44729

abbreviations K110; 340.07

abdication KM112.9; 346.259
UF: resignation + executive

abduction
USE: kidnapping KM543.4; 346.8634

abetting suicide
USE: aiding suicide KM542.3; 346.8623

abolition of slavery
USE: slavery KM208.58; 346.3658

aboriginal law
USE: customary law KL8; 345.08; [Table IIA: 62]

aboriginal reserves KN72.4; 347.32175
UF: reserves for aboriginals

aboriginals [Table VII: 4.3]
UF: indigenous peoples
RT: customary law KL8; 345.08; [Table IIA: 62]

aboriginals + America KE530; 343.94
UF: Indians of North America
UF: North American Indians

aboriginals + Australia KE540.A8; 343.99.A8

aboriginals + minorities KM208.431; 346.36431; [Table VII: 4.3]

aboriginals + treaty rights KM208.432; 346.36432

abortion + crime KM542.5; 346.8625

abortion + family law KN172.73; 347.42173
UF: termination + pregnancy
RT: birth control KN172.72; 347.42172
RT: foetuses + experimentation KN185.53; 347.4483

abridgments + UK KF80

absolute discharge [App: 72]

absolute liability
USE: strict liability + criminal law KM505.9; 346.828
USE: strict liability + tort KN33.4; 347.214

abstract of title KN72.1; 347.3215

abstracts K28; 340.019

abuse of children
USE: child abuse KN176.41; 347.42641

abuse of dominant position KN266.5; 347.6345
UF: Chapter II prohibition
UF: dominance + competition
UF: restrictive trade practices
RT: anti-competitive practices KN266.5; 347.6345

abuse of dominant position + EU KW110.5

abuse of legal procedure KN38.3; 347.25

academic freedom KM209.A2; 346.368.A2

academic libraries
USE: libraries KN184.4; 347.445; [Table IIA: 122.5]

acceptance + contract KN13.2; 347.112

acceptances + negotiable instruments KN306.5; 347.775

access + children KN173.8; 347.4258
UF: parental access

access + countryside KN95.13; 347.34213
RT: national parks KN95.13; 347.34213

access + neighbouring land KN65.125; 347.31735
RT: neighbours KN72.15; 347.32155

access courses + legal education KL131–149 [Table: .43]; 345.1794–9 [Table: 43]

accession + personal property KN104.5; 347.3645

accessories KM508; 346.84
UF: accomplices
UF: principal and accessory

accident KN33.1; 347.211

accidental damage KN39.A3; 347.29.A3
UF: damage + accidents

accidents + air law KN327.9; 347.829
UF: air accidents

accidents + consumer law + EU KW112.6

accidents + industrial law KN198.3; 347.493

accidents + insurance KN294.69.A3; 347.694.A3

accidents + railways KN325.9; 347.8159

accidents + roads KN323.9; 347.8139
UF: road accidents
UF: traffic accidents

accommodation + courts KL230.7; 345.37
UF: court accommodation

accommodation + libraries K84.5; 340.0545

accommodation + Parliament KM87.1; 346.2481
UF: legislatures + accommodation
UF: parliamentary accommodation

accomplices
USE: accessories KM508; 346.84

accord and satisfaction KN384.1; 347.9441
UF: satisfaction

accountability
USE: liability [Table VI: .Z45]

accountability + criminal
USE: criminal liability KM505; 346.82; [Table IIA: 90.3]

accountancy KN307; 347.78; [Table IIA: 134.7]
UF: bookkeeping

accountants KN307; 347.78 [Table VII: 6.A1]

accountants + expert evidence KN391.69.A3; 347.96259.A3

accountants + expert evidence + criminal procedure KM604.94.A2; 346.9674.A2

accounting KN307.1; 347.781

accounting + standards KN307.3; 347.783

accounts KN307.2; 347.782

accounts + courts KL230.14; 345.314
UF: court accounts
RT: financial management + courts KL230.14; 345.314

accounts + trade unions KN195.3; 347.483
UF: trade unions + accounts

accretion + international law KC142.1; 341.2521
RT: artificial islands KC145.1; 341.2551

accretion + real property KN76.A2; 347.323.A2
UF: land reclamation
UF: polders

accumulations
USE: perpetuities KN64.241; 347.31641

accumulations + real property KN64.242; 347.31642

accusatorial system
USE: adversarial systems KN389.8; 347.9608

accused persons
USE: defendants KM579; 346.905; [Table VI: .Z62]

ACP-EU + external relations KW77.3
UF: ACP-EEC

ACP-EU + publications KW35
UF: African-Caribbean-Pacific nations:EU
RT: Lomé Conventions + texts KW2.5

ACP-EU + statistics + journals KW66.15

ACP-EU + trade + statistics + journals KW66.65

acquiescence KN217.3; 347.573

acquired immune deficiency syndrome
USE: AIDS KN185.69.A4; 347.44869.A4

acquisition + nationality
USE: nationality + international law KC190; 341.31

acquisition + territory
USE: national territory KC142; 341.252

acquittal KM586.1; 346.9361

ACT
USE: advance corporation tax + UK KM337.23; 346.543

act of state KC151.1; 341.2611

Acta Apostolicae Sedis KD161; 342.371

actions [Table VI: .Z7]

actions + personal property KN108; 347.368

actions and defences
USE: procedure KN350; 347.9; [Table IIA: 144]; [Table VI: .Z71]

acts
USE: statutes + texts [Table IA: 15]; [Table VI: .Z140]

Acts of Congress
USE: legislation (texts) [Table IA: 15]

Acts of Parliament
USE: legislation (texts) [Table IA: 15]

actual bodily harm KM543.1; 346.8631
UF: bodily harm
RT: grievous bodily harm KM543.1; 346.8631

actuarial tables KN37.15; 347.2315

actus reus KM505.1; 346.821

acupuncture KN185.13.A3; 347.44613.A3

ad hoc regions KM366.3; 346.663

added value + taxation KM336.32; 346.5232

addicts [Table VII: 5.4]

additives + food KN185.24; 347.44724
UF: food additives

adjective law
USE: procedure KN350; 347.9; [Table IIA: 144]; [Table VI: .Z71]

adjournments + actions KN357; 347.917

administration + chambers KL96.1; 345.1761

administration + insolvency KN312.2; 347.7922

administration of estates KN142; 347.392

administration of justice KL200; 345.2; [Table IIA: 68]

administrative agencies
UF: government departments KM235; 346.38; [Table IIA: 83.2]; [Table VII: 8.3]

administrative courts [Table V: 2.5]
RT: administrative tribunals KM303; 346.43

administrative decisions + England and Wales KF75

administrative decisions + US KG376

administrative law KM300; 346.4; [Table IIA: 82]

administrative law + EU KW99

administrative law + procedure KM304; 346.44
RT: procedure KN350; 347.9; [Table IIA: 144]; [Table VI: .Z71]

administrative law + remedies KM305; 346.45

administrative legislation
USE: subordinate legislation KM302; 346.42; [Table IA: 20]

administrative parent KN176.43; 347.42643

administrative publications + England and Wales KF45

administrative tribunals KM303; 346.43
UF: boards + administration
UF: tribunals
RT: administrative courts [Table V: 2.5]
RT: industrial tribunals KN196.9; 347.4869

administrators + government
USE: civil service KM237; 346.382; [Table IIA: 83.3]

administrators + probate KN143; 347.39
RT: executors KN143; 347.39
RT: personal representatives KN143; 347.39; [Table VI: .Z63]

Admiralty Court
USE: High Court of Admiralty [Table V: 8.1]

admiralty courts [Table V: 8.1]

admiralty law
USE: maritime law KN330; 347.83; [Table IIA: 138]

admissibility + evidence KN394; 347.965

admissibility + evidence + criminal procedure KM603; 346.963
RT: Judges' Rules KM603.1; 346.9631

admission to the Bar KL83; 345.1703
UF: bar + admissions
UF: disbarment
RT: licensing + lawyers KL83; 345.1703

adolescents
USE: young persons KN176; 347.426; [Table IIA: 118]; [Table VII: 1.2]

adoption KN176.1; 347.4261

adult education KN184.36; 347.4446
RT: evening classes KN184.36; 347.4446

adults [Table VII: 1.4]
RT: age of majority KN151.3; 347.4113; [Table VII: 1.3]

advance corporation tax + UK KM337.23; 346.543
UF: ACT

adversarial systems KN389.8; 347.9608
UF: accusatorial system
RT: inquisitorial systems KN389.8; 347.9608

adverse possession KN76.A3; 347.323.A3

advertising + consumer protection KN284.1; 347.661

advertising + consumer protection + EU KW112.2

advertising + legal profession KL98; 345.1768
RT: marketing + legal profession KL98; 345.1768

advertising revenue + broadcasting KN344.2; 347.8713
UF: broadcasting + advertising revenue

advice services KN400; 347.9991
UF: tips + advice
RT: legal aid KN399; 347.99; [Table IIA: 71]

advocacy KL93; 345.1723

advocates KL86; 345.1711
RT: barristers KL86; 345.1711

advowsons KD484; 342.684

aerial warfare KC1375; 341.852
UF: war in the air

aerodromes
USE: airports KN327.4; 347.824

aeronautics
USE: air law KN327; 347.82; [Table IIA: 137]

affidavits KN392.2; 347.9632

affidavits + criminal evidence KM605.4; 346.974

affiliation
USE: paternity KN176.3; 347.4263

affinity KN172.32; 347.42132
RT: marriage + impediments KN172.3; 347.4213

affirmations KN391.2; 347.9622
RT: oaths KN391.2; 347.9622

affirmations + criminal procedure KM605.12; 346.9712

affray KM562.1; 346.8831

affreightment
USE: freight KN328.1; 347.8281

Africa + international relations KC302; 341.512

Africa : European Union KW81.6
UF: European Union : Africa

African Commission on Human and Peoples' Rights KC716; 341.6516

African-Caribbean-Pacific nations: EU
USE: ACP-EU + publications KW35

aftercare + prisoners KM690; 346.9885; [App: 79)

age discrimination KM208.1; 346.361
RT: older people [Table VII: 1.6]

age of consent + sexual activity
USE: capacity + consent + sexual activity KM544.01; 346.86401

age of criminal responsibility KM507.Q13; 346.83.Q13
UF: children + criminal liability

age of majority KN151.3; 347.4113; [Table VII: 1.3]
UF: majority + children
RT: adults [Table VII: 1.4]

age of retirement
USE: retirement age [Table VII: 1.6]

agency KN25; 347.18; [Table IIA: 99]
UF: principal and agent

agents + contract KN25.1; 347.181

agents + conveyancing
USE: conveyancing agents KN74.9; 347.3228

agents + diplomacy KC327; 341.554

agents provocateurs
USE: entrapment KM580.15; 346.9115

aggravated assault KM543.1; 346.8631

aggravated circumstances
USE: criminal liability KM505; 346.82; [Table IIA: 90.3]

aggravated damages KN37.1; 347.231

aggregates levy KM337.9.A35; 346.59.A35

aggression KC1355.1; 341.821

agreements
SN: use as subdivision only

agricultural banks KN303.9.A3; 347.729.A3

agricultural chemicals KN98.5; 347.355
RT: fungicides + agriculture KN98.55; 347.3555
RT: poisons KN186.9.P6; 347.459.P6

agricultural co-operatives KN98.22; 347.3522

agricultural credit
USE: credit + agriculture KN98.3; 347.353

agricultural law KN98; 347.35; [Table IIA: 107.6]
UF: cultivation of land

agricultural machinery
USE: machinery + agriculture KN98.6; 347.3556

agricultural pollution KN97.81; 347.3481
UF: pollution + agriculture

agricultural prices + EU
USE: prices + agriculture + EU KW114

agricultural produce KN99; 347.356
UF: farm produce

agricultural reform + EU KW113.2

agricultural tenancies KN98.1; 347.3512
UF: farm tenancies

agriculture + EU KW113
RT: common agricultural policy + EU KW113

agriculture + EU + statistics + journals KW66.5

agriculture + finance KN98.3; 347.353

agriculture + taxation KM336.68.A3; 346.5268.A3

AID + family law
USE: artificial insemination KN172.82; 347.42182

aid to developing countries
USE: development + international law KC228; 341.4154

aiding suicide KM542.3; 346.8623
UF: abetting suicide
UF: assisted suicide

AIDS KN185.69.A4; 347.44869.A4
UF: acquired immune deficiency syndrome
UF: HIV

AIM
USE: Alternative Investment Market KN304.86.A4; 347.7386.A4

aims of punishment
USE: purpose of punishment [App: 50.2]

air + easements
USE: light and air + easements KN65.11; 347.3172

air accidents
USE: accidents + air law KN327.9; 347.829

air charter
USE: charter flights KN327.6; 347.826

air crew
USE: flight crews KN327.2; 347.822

air force law KM412; 346.77
RT: military law KM400; 346.7; [Table IIA: 87]

air freight KN328.8; 347.8288
UF: freight + air law

air law KN327; 347.82; [Table IIA: 137]
UF: aeronautics
UF: aviation
UF: civil aviation
RT: air transport KN327; 347.82

air law + international law KC253; 341.453

air mail KN341.3; 347.852

air passenger duty KM337.765; 346.5865

air piracy
USE: crime + aircraft KC213.3; 341.3533

air pollution KN97.71; 347.3471
UF: atmospheric pollution
UF: greenhouse effect
UF: ozone levels
RT: clean air KN97.71; 347.3471

air pollution + EU KW125.4

air routes
USE: routes + air transport KN327.3; 347.823

air rule of the road
USE: flight control KN327.5; 347.825

air stewards
USE: flight crews KN327.2; 347.822

air traffic control
USE: flight control KN327.5; 347.825

air transport KN327; 347.82

air transport + EU KW135.5

air transport + insurance KN294.A4; 347.694.A4

aircraft KN327.1; 347.821
UF: airworthiness

aircraft + hijacking KC213.3; 341.3533
RT: crime + aircraft KC213.3; 341.3533

aircraft + international law KC253.5; 341.4535
UF: nationality + aircraft
UF: state aircraft

aircraft + security + international law KC255.5; 341.4549
UF: security of aircraft

aircraft + servicing + international law KC255.4; 341.4548

airlines KN327.2; 347.822

airmen
USE: flight crews KN327.2; 347.822

airports KN327.4; 347.824
UF: aerodromes

airships KN327.15; 347.8215

airspace KN92.A4; 347.335.A4

airspace + international law KC253.2; 341.4532
UF: freedom of the air
UF: sovereignty + airspace

airworthiness
USE: aircraft KN327.1; 347.821

alcohol KN186.4; 347.454
UF: beer
UF: distilling
UF: licensing + alcohol
UF: liquor
UF: moonshine

UF: prohibition + US
UF: spirits
UF: temperance
UF: wine
RT: brewing KN186.4; 347.454
RT: drugs + offences KM565.D7; 346.89.D7

alcohol + causes of crime [App: 16]

alcohol + criminal liability KM505.4; 346.824

alcohol + excise duties KM337.762; 346.5862

alcohol + wine + EU KW117.3.W4

alcoholism + prison KM681.32; 346.987632; [App: 93.32]

aliases
USE: names + persons KN150.5; 347.405; [Table IIA: 113]

alibis KM584.3; 346.9343

alien property KN58.6; 347.3056
UF: foreign property

alienation + real property
UF: restraints on alienation KN71.2; 347.321

aliens KM177; 346.336
UF: foreign nationals

aliens + international law KC197; 341.317

aliens + tax liability KM336.12; 346.5212

alimony KN173.2; 347.4245
RT: divorce KN173.1; 347.424; [Table IIA: 117.4]

All England Law Reports KF60.A5

all party groups
USE: parliamentary groups KM83.8; 346.228

allegations against police
USE: police + complaints KM615.7; 346.9857

allegiance KM172.3; 346.313
UF: loyalty

alliances KC316; 341.536

allotment + shares KN263.51; 347.62551

allotments + smallholdings KN98.29; 347.3529

allowances + legislators KM83.9; 346.229

allowances + taxation KM336.6; 346.526
UF: personal allowances + taxation
UF: rates of allowances + taxation
UF: tax allowances

almshouses
USE: residential homes KN182.1; 347.4421

alterations
USE: amendments [Table VI: .Z53]

alternative counts
USE: indictments KM582.2; 346.931

alternative dispute resolution
USE: dispute resolution KN398.6; 347.986

alternative energy sources KN89.5; 347.332

alternative energy sources + EU KW122.8

Alternative Investment Market KN304.86.A4; 347.7386.A4
UF: AIM

alternative medicine KN185.13; 347.44613
RT: complementary medicine KN185.13; 347.44613

alternative procedure KN381.2; 347.9312
UF: originating summons

alternative verdicts
USE: verdicts KN389.72; 347.96072

amalgamations
USE: mergers + competition KN266.12; 347.6312
USE: takeovers + competition KN266.12; 347.6312
USE: takeovers + incorporation KN262.1; 347.62421

amateur radio KN344.45; 347.8721

ambassadors KC324; 341.551

ambulance service KM234; 346.3739

amendments [Table VI: .Z53]
UF: alterations
UF: revisions

amendments + constitutional law KM53; 346.133
UF: constitutional amendments

amendments + treaties KC333.5; 341.5615
UF: revision of treaties

America + international relations KC306; 341.516

America + organisations KC750; 341.657

American aboriginals KE530; 343.94
UF: American Indians
UF: Red Indians

American Indians
USE: American aboriginals KE530; 343.94

amicus curiae
USE: friends + civil procedure KN370.15; 347.93015

amnesty [App: 77]

amortisation + debts KN305.1; 347.751

amputation KN185.52.A6; 347.4482.A6

Amsterdam Treaty
USE: Treaty of Amsterdam (1997) KW1.F97

amusement arcades KN186.61; 347.4561

amusements
USE: recreation KN186.6; 347.456

analgesics
USE: drugs + medicine KN185.8; 347.4488

analytical jurisprudence KA20; 340.12

ancestors [Table VII: 3.6]

ancient law KE; 343

ancient law : modern law KB125; 340.57
UF: modern law : ancient law

ancient monuments KN95.11; 347.34211
UF: national monuments

ancient Near East KE21; 343.2

ancillary relief
USE: remedies KN395.1; 347.971; [Table IIA: 149]; [Table VI: .Z8]

anecdotes
USE: humorous writings KB34; 340.374

Anglican churches KD450; 342.6
RT: Church of England KD450; 342.6

Anglo-Saxon law KL401.2; 345.9422

animal passports
USE: passports + animals KN186.82; 347.4582

animal rights KA66; 340.156

animals + control KN186.8; 347.458
UF: bulls
UF: domestic animals
UF: ferae naturae
UF: wild animals
RT: game KN99.4; 347.3564
RT: hunting KN186.63; 347.4563
RT: livestock KN99.3; 347.3563
RT: veterinary medicine KN186.8; 347.458

animals + cruelty
USE: offences against animals KM565.A5; 346.89.A5

animals + diseases
USE: veterinary medicine KN186.8; 347.458

animals + environmental protection KN95.3; 347.3423

animals + EU KW114.7

animals + experiments
USE: laboratory animals KN186.84; 347.4584

animals + quarantine KN186.82; 347.4582
UF: rabies
RT: quarantine KN185.6; 347.4486

animals + road traffic KN323.3; 347.81345

animals + slaughter
USE: slaughterhouses KN185.29; 347.44729

animals + tort KN39.A5; 347.29.A5

annexation + national territory KC142.6; 341.2526

annotations
USE: citation manuals K114; 340.074

annuities + insurance KN292.2; 347.684

annuities + taxation KM336.34; 346.5234

annulment
USE: nullity KN173.4; 347.4254

Antarctic + international relations
USE: polar regions + international relations KC308; 341.518

anti-avoidance + taxation KM336.7; 346.527

anti-competitive agreements KN266.2; 347.632
UF: Chapter I prohibition
UF: horizontal agreements + competition
UF: restrictive trade practices
UF: vertical agreements + competition

anti-competitive agreements + EU KW110.4

anti-competitive practices KN266.5; 347.6345
RT: abuse of dominant position KN266.5; 347.6345

anti-discrimination
USE: discrimination + industrial law KN191.2; 347.4612

anti-dumping
USE: dumping KN253.2; 347.614

anti-dumping + taxes KM337.72; 346.582

anti-paedophile crimes
USE: hate crimes KM540.15; 346.8515

anti-pollution laws
USE: pollution KN97.7; 347.347; [Table IIA: 107.4]

anti-slavery laws
USE: slavery KM208.58; 346.3658

anti-trust laws
USE: competition KN266; 347.63; [Table IIA: 130]

antique dealers
USE: second hand dealing KN285.S4; 347.679.S4

Anton Piller orders
USE: search orders KN392.7; 347.9637

antonyms K123; 340.083

Anzus Pact KC881; 341.6691

apartheid
USE: racial discrimination KM208.43; 346.3643; [Table IIA: 81.5]

apartments
USE: flats KN83.1; 347.3251

apology KN38.28; 347.2488

appeal courts KL221; 345.301; [Table V: 1]
UF: appellate courts

appeal papers (individual cases) KF72.A5

appeals + criminal law
USE: criminal appeals KM595; 346.95

appeals + planning
USE: planning + appeals KN96.92; 347.34492

appeals + procedure
USE: appellate procedure KN361; 347.921

appeals + taxation
USE: taxation + appeals KM336.87; 346.5287

appearance + default
USE: default judgments KN395.5; 347.973

appearances KN387.1; 347.9471

appellate courts
USE: appeal courts [Table V: 1]

appellate procedure KN361; 347.921
UF: appeals + procedure

applications + procedure KN381.4; 347.9414

appointed legislators
USE: non-elected legislators KM83.7; 346.227

appointments
SN: use as subdivision only

apportionment
SN: use as subdivision only

appraisal schemes + employment KN192.33; 347.4643

apprenticeship KN192.3; 347.464

apprenticeship + EU KW130.4

appropriation accounts KM331.7; 346.507

aquaculture KN338.6; 347.8386

aquatic environment + EU KW125.5

Arab League KC801; 341.661

arbitral awards + conflict of laws
USE: foreign arbitral awards KC2085; 341.98

arbitral awards + international law KC1256; 341.736

arbitration KN398; 347.98; [Table IIA: 148]; [Table VI: .Z75]
RT: commercial arbitration KN256; 347.619

arbitration + conflict of laws KC2086; 341.985

arbitration + industrial law KN196.2; 347.4862

arbitration + international law
USE: international arbitration KC1250; 341.73

arbitration agencies KN196.25; 347.48625

arbitration courts + international law KC1260; 341.74

arbitration proceedings KN398.14; 347.9814

arbitrators KN398.1; 347.981

arbitrators + appointment KN398.12; 347.9812

archaeological sites KN95.11; 347.34211

archipelagos
USE: islands KC145; 341.255

architects + law
USE: law for architects KL30.A7; 345.1.A7

archives KN184.5; 347.4455
UF: documents + history
UF: historical documents

archives + courts
USE: public records KN184.5; 347.4455; [Table IIA: 122.5]

Arctic + international relations
USE: polar regions + international relations KC308; 341.518

armaments + treaties
USE: arms limitation + treaties KC336.1; 341.581

armed conflict KC1350; 341.8

armed crimes KM540.2; 346.852

armed forces
USE: military law KM400; 346.7; [Table IIA: 87]

armed robbery
USE: robbery KM546.2; 346.8712

armistice KC1422; 341.892

arms + police KM615.3; 346.9853
UF: guns + police
UF: weapons + police

arms limitation + international law KC313.5; 341.5335
UF: nuclear disarmament
RT: disarmament + international law KC313; 341.533

arms limitation + treaties KC336.1; 341.581
UF: armaments + treaties
UF: disarmament + treaties
RT: non-proliferation + treaties KC336.1; 341.581

army law KM411; 346.76
UF: soldiers
RT: military law KM400; 346.7; [Table IIA: 87]

arraignment
USE: indictments KM582.2; 346.931

arranged marriages KN172.9.A7; 347.422.A7

array + challenges
USE: challenges + juries + criminal procedure KM583.2; 346.9332
USE: juries + challenges

arrest KM580.3; 346.913
UF: warrants + arrest

arrest + ships + international law KC272.5; 341.4755

arrestable offences KM503.4; 346.8154

arson KM548; 346.873

art + trade + international law KC231.9.A7; 341.4219.A7

art : law KA70.A7; 340.16.A7

art galleries
USE: galleries KN184.4; 347.445

art works + war KC1357.2; 341.8282
UF: cultural property + war

articled clerks KL87.1; 345.171341
RT: trainee solicitors KL87.1; 345.171341

articles of association KN262.6; 347.6246

articles of war
USE: military law KM400; 346.7; [Table IIA: 87]

artificial insemination KN172.82; 347.42182
UF: AID + family law

artificial intelligence K103; 340.063

artificial islands KC145.1; 341.2551
RT: accretion + international law KC142.1; 341.2521

artificial prolongation of life
USE: life + artificial prolongation KN185.14; 347.44614

artistic works + intellectual property KN112.2; 347.373

arts + subsidies KN184.8; 347.4458
UF: Arts Council
UF: music + subsidies
UF: subsidies to the arts
UF: theatre + subsidies

Arts Council
USE: arts + subsidies KN184.8; 347.4458

asbestosis KN198.4; 347.494

ASEAN
USE: Association of South East Asian Nations KC861; 341.665

Asia + international organisations KC800; 341.66

Asia + international relations KC303; 341.513

Asia : EU KW81.7
UF: European Union : Asia

asphyxiating gas
USE: poison gas KC1395; 341.8652

assassination
USE: murder KM542.1; 346.8621

assault KM543; 346.863
RT: battery KM543.3; 346.8633
RT: common assault KM543.2; 346.8623
RT: domestic violence KN175; 347.42597; [Table IIA: 117.7]

assault + prisons [App: 92.52]

assault + tort KN38.12; 347.242

assemblies (legislative)
USE: legislatures KM82; 346.21; [Table IIA: 79]

Assembly Cabinet [Wales] KM113.A15; 346.26.A15
SN: Welsh name is Cabinet y Cynulliad

Assembly Cabinet [Wales] + publications KF173.1

assents + administration of estates KN142.3; 347.3923

assessment + damages KN37.1; 347.331
UF: quantum of damages

assessment + taxation KM336.8; 346.528
UF: computation + taxation
UF: procedure + assessment + taxation
UF: taxation + procedure

assessment of costs KN397.7; 347.9777
UF: taxation of costs

assessors + judiciary KL244; 345.49
UF: law assessors

asset-backed finance KN305.26; 347.7526

assets + administration of estates KN142.1; 347.3921

assets + transfers abroad + taxation KM336.74; 346.5274

assignment + contract KN14.2; 347.122

assignment + copyright KN112; 347.371

assignment + industrial law KN194.9; 347.4789

assignment + intellectual property KN115.3; 347.3783

assignment + personal property KN104.2; 347.3642

assisted suicide
USE: aiding suicide KM542.3; 346.8623

associated states KC154.8; 341.2648

Association of South East Asian Nations KC861; 341.665
UF: ASEAN

associations KN169.4; 347.41894; [Table VII: 9.4]; [Table VIII: .003]
UF: legal societies
UF: societies
RT: business associations KN260; 347.62; [Table VII: 9.2]
RT: clubs KN169.Q95; 347.4189.Q95; [Table VII: 9.5]
RT: employers' associations KN195.18; 347.4818
RT: friendly societies KN169.5; 347.41895; [Table VII: 9.5]
RT: professional associations [Table VII: 9.8]
RT: trade unions KN195; 347.48; [Table IIA: 124]; [Table VII: 9.7]

associations + comparative law KB110; 340.52

associations + industrial law KN195; 347.48

associations + law libraries K81; 340.051

associations + legal profession KL100; 345.177; [Table IIA: 64.8]
UF: bar + associations
UF: law societies
UF: legal associations
UF: legal societies

associations + legal profession + comparative law KB111; 340.521

associations + legal profession + directories K160; 340.092

associations + taxation KM336.495; 346.52495

assurance
USE: insurance KN290; 347.68; [Table IIA: 133]

assured tenancies KN87.71; 347.32971

Assyro-Babylonian law KE23; 343.23

astronautics
USE: outer space KC280; 341.49

asylum + EU KW83.1

asylum + international law KC206; 341.336
UF: right of asylum
UF: sanctuary + international law

asylum seekers KM177.7; 346.3375

asylum seekers + international law KC206; 341.336

athletics
USE: sport KN186.6; 347.456

atlases K200; 340.099

atmospheric pollution
USE: air pollution KN97.71; 347.3471

ATMs
USE: automatic teller machines KN303.17; 347.7217

atomic energy
USE: nuclear energy KN89.45; 347.33145

atomic weapons
USE: nuclear weapons + international law KC1392; 341.862

atonement [App: 50.24]

attachés (diplomats) KC325; 341.552

attachment + industrial law KN194.9; 347.4789

attachment + remedies KN395.24; 347.9724

attempts + criminal law KM509; 346.842

attendance centres KM654.9.A8; 346.987149.A8; [App: 84.9.A8]

attestation KN392.1; 347.9631

attorney and client
USE: lawyer-client relationship KL82.2; 345.17022

Attorney-General KL251; 345.51
RT: legal officers KL250; 345.5

attorneys
USE: lawyers KL85; 345.171

auctions KN285.1; 347.671
RT: second hand dealing KN285.S4; 347.679.S4

audio-visual materials [Table VIII: 0098]

audit areas + courts KL230.16; 345.316

auditing KN307.5; 347.785

auditors' reports KN307.5; 347.785

audits + courts KL230.16; 345.316

Australia + aboriginals KE540.A8; 343.99.A8

Australia + international relations KC307; 341.517

Australia : EU KW81.8

authentication + contract KN13.9; 347.119

authorised persons + financial services KN308.3; 347.7863

authorship + lawyers K105.2; 340.0652

autobiography KB15; 340.33

autobuses
USE: buses KN324.1; 347.8141

automatic fines [App: 74]

automatic penalties KM588.1; 346.941

automatic teller machines KN303.17; 347.7217
UF: ATMs
UF: holes in the wall

automation + law offices
USE: computers + law offices KL96.2; 345.1762

automation + legal research
USE: computers + legal research KL157; 345.192

automation + libraries
USE: computers in libraries K86; 340.056

automation + offices KN347.5; 347.894

automatism KM506.4; 346.8294

automobiles
USE: cars KN323.14; 347.81332

autonomic legislation KL36.9; 345.167

autopsies
USE: post mortems KM608.4; 346.9794

autrefois acquit
USE: pleas + criminal procedure KM582.3; 346.9315

autrefois convict
USE: pleas + criminal procedure KM582.3; 346.9315

autumn statements (budget) KM331.22; 346.5022
UF: pre-budget report
RT: budget KM332; 346.51

average + marine insurance KN335.1; 347.8351

aviation
USE: air law KN327; 347.82; [Table IIA: 137]

aviation routes
USE: routes + air transport KN327.3; 347.823

avoidance
USE: confession and avoidance KN384.2; 347.9442

avoidance of contracts
USE: void contracts KN15.2; 347.132

awards + arbitration KN398.5; 347.985

awards + arbitration + international law KC1256; 341.736

awards of honour
USE: honours KM114.5; 346.275

Babylonian law KE23; 343.23

backbenchers
USE: legislators KM83; 346.22

bacteriological weapons + international law KC1395.5; 341.8655
RT: disarmament + international law KC313; 341.533

bad faith + evidence KN390.2; 347.9612

badger baiting KN186.639.B3; 347.45639.B3

bail KM580.6; 346.916
UF: recognisances

bailees + liability KN106.7; 347.3667

bailiffs KN88.13; 347.329913

bailment KN106; 347.366

balance of payments + EU KW102

balance of probabilities
USE: burden of proof KN390.1; 347.9611

balance sheets KN307.4; 347.784

ballistics
USE: firearms KN186.1; 347.451

ballots
USE: voting + elections + legislatures KM83.45; 346.2245

bank holidays
USE: public holidays KN186.2; 347.452

bank loans KN303.3; 347.723

bank notes KN302.2; 347.712
RT: coinage KN302.2; 347.712

Bank Rate
USE: interest rates KN305.3; 347.753

banking KN303; 347.72; [Table IIA: 134]

banking + EU KW107

banking + international law
USE: international banks KC226; 341.414

banking + service industries + EU KW119.1

banking + supervision KN303.95; 347.7295

Banking Ombudsman
USE: Financial Ombudsman KN304.95.F5; 347.7395.F5

bankruptcy KN313; 347.793; [Table IIA: 135]
RT: insolvency KN312; 347.792; [Table IIA: 135]

bankruptcy + courts [Table V: 8.3]

bankruptcy + land tenure KN76.B3; 347.323.B3

banks + international law
USE: international banks KC226; 341.414

banns
USE: marriage + impediments KN172.3; 347.4213

Baptist Church KD540; 342.6914

bar + admissions
USE: admission to the Bar KL83; 345.1703

bar + associations
USE: associations + legal profession KL100; 345.177; [Table IIA: 64.8]

Bar Council KL101.1; 345.177421
UF: General Council of the Bar

bar libraries
USE: law libraries K80; 340.05

barristers KL86; 345.1711
UF: counsel
RT: advocates KL86; 345.1711
RT: duty to accept work KL82.5; 345.17025
RT: lawyers KL85; 345.171

barristers + complaints
USE: complaints + legal profession KL95; 345.174

barristers + direct access KL94; 345.173
UF: direct access to barristers

barristers + pupillage
USE: pupillage + barristers KL86.8; 345.1713

barristers + remuneration KL89.2; 345.17142

barristers' clerks KL86.9; 345.17132

Basilica KE256; 343.52

bastardy
USE: illegitimacy KN176.3; 347.4263

battered wives
USE: domestic violence KN175; 347.42597; [Table IIA: 117.7]

battery KM543.3; 346.8633
RT: assault KM543; 346.863

bays + international law KC265; 341.472
UF: gulfs

beef + EU KW117.3.B4

beer
USE: alcohol KN186.4; 347.454

begging KM562.5; 346.8835

behaviour alteration [App: 29.B4]

belligerent occupation
USE: military occupation KC1400; 341.87

belligerent rights KC1355.4; 341.824

benefices KD482; 342.682

beneficial interests + land
USE: equitable interests + land KN64.1; 347.3151

beneficiaries + trusts KN217; 347.57
UF: cestui que trust

beneficiaries + wills KN125.6; 347.3826

benefits in kind + employment KN194.2; 347.4782
UF: fringe benefits
UF: non-wage payments
UF: perquisites

benefits in kind + taxation KM336.31; 346.5231
UF: car benefits
UF: company cars
UF: fringe benefits
UF: non-wage payments
UF: perquisites

Benelux KC961; 341.677

bequests
USE: legacies KN125.7; 347.3827

Berne Convention KC236.1; 341.431
RT: copyright + international law KC236.1; 341.431

BES
USE: Business Expansion Scheme KN260.3; 347.6225

betrothal KN172.1; 347.4211

better title KN72.5; 347.3218

betterment levy KN96.71; 347.34471

betting
USE: gambling KN186.5; 347.455

BIALL K81.9.B5; 340.0519.B5
UF: British and Irish Association of Law Librarians

bias
SN: use as subdivision only

bibliographical research
USE: research + bibliography K32; 340.023

bibliographies K29; 340.02; [Table VIII: 0021]
RT: legal bibliographies K30; 340.021

bibliographies + international law KC71; 341.171

bicameral legislatures KM82.2; 346.212

bicycles KN323.2; 347.8134
UF: cycling

bigamy KM544.3; 346.8643
RT: polygamy KN172.9.P6; 347.422.P6

Bijnkershoek KE420; 343.85

bilateral treaties KC18; 341.128

bilateral treaties + EU KW3

bill of particulars
USE: particulars KN383.1; 347.9431

bill of rights KM201.2; 346.3502

bills + legislation
USE: legislative bills [Table IA: 6; 12]; [Table VI: .Z11]

bills of exchange KN306.2; 347.772

bills of lading KN337.3; 347.8373

bills of sale KN282.2; 347.652

binding over [App: 71]

biodiversity + environmental protection KN95.7; 347.3427

biodiversity + international law KC243.2; 341.4442

bioethics KN185.545; 347.44845

biographies KB10; 340.31; [Table VIII: 006]
UF: legal biographies

biological warfare
USE: prohibited weapons + international law KC1395; 341.865

biotechnology + EU KW114.6

biotechnology + patents KN114.9.B5; 347.3779.B5

biotechnology + public health KN185.545; 347.44845

birds KN95.3; 347.3423

birth + nationality KM172.4; 346.314
UF: nationality by birth

birth control KN172.72; 347.42172
UF: contraception
UF: family planning
RT: abortion + family law KN172.73; 347.42173

births + registration
USE: registration + births KM172.31; 346.3131

black market KM562.9.B5; 346.884.B5

blackmail KM552; 346.877

blasphemy KM565.B5; 346.89.B5; [KD Table: 6]

blind persons KN181.9.Q51.B5; 347.4419.Q51.B5
RT: disabled persons [Table VII: 5]

blind persons + allowances + taxation KM336.61; 346.5261

block exemption + competition law KN266.71; 347.6351

block exemption + competition law + EU KW110.82

blockade KC1385; 341.8545
RT: maritime warfare KC1380; 341.854
RT: pacific blockade KC1313; 341.793

blogs KN347.41; 347.89351

blood + samples
USE: pathological samples + identification KM604.33; 346.9646

blood sports KN186.63; 347.4563
RT: fishing + sport KN186.632; 347.45632
RT: hunting KN186.63; 347.4563

blood tests KN185.52.B5; 347.4482.B5
RT: paternity tests KN176.35; 347.42635

blood transfusion KN185.5; 347.448

blue laws
USE: Sundays KN186.2; 347.452

blue sky law
USE: securities + finance KN304.1; 347.731

boarding houses
USE: hotels KN186.3; 347.453

boards + administration
USE: administrative tribunals KM303; 346.43

boats
USE: ships KN332.3; 347.8323

bodies
USE: burials KN97.3; 347.346

bodily harm
USE: actual bodily harm KM543.1; 346.8631
USE: grievous bodily harm KM543.1; 346.8631

bomb threats KM562.25; 346.88325
UF: hoaxes + terrorists

bona vacantia KN79.1; 347.32311

bond stores KM337.763; 346.5863
RT: warehouses KN83.3; 347.3253

bond washing KN304.9; 347.739
UF: dividend stripping

bond washing + taxation KM336.72; 346.5272

bonds KN304.31; 347.7331

bonuses KN194.3; 347.4783
RT: earnings KN194.1; 347.4781

bonuses + taxation KM336.31; 346.5231

bookkeeping
USE: accountancy KN307; 347.78

books + intellectual property KN112.1; 347.372

books + publishing KN345.1; 347.881

booksellers + directories K107; 340.067

booksellers + law books
USE: law booksellers K105.9; 340.0659

bookselling KN345.1; 347.881

bootlegging + intellectual property KN116.1; 347.3791

boroughs
USE: towns + local government KM365.2; 346.653

borrowing
USE: loans KN305.2; 347.752

Borstals KM654.2; 346.987142; [App: 84.2]

boundaries + constituencies
USE: constituencies KM83.2; 346.222

boundaries + international law
USE: frontiers KC143; 341.253

boundaries + real property KN72.13; 347.32153

boycotts + industrial law KN196.6; 347.4866

boycotts + international law
USE: embargoes + international disputes KC1311; 341.791

brain damage
USE: personal injuries KN38.1; 347.24

brain death
USE: death KN185.15; 347.44615

brand names
USE: trade names KN114.2; 347.3772

breach of confidence + industrial law KN192.17; 347.4628

breach of confidence + tort KN38.9; 347.289

breach of contract + remedies KN17; 347.148

breach of duty KN33.31; 347.2131

breach of promise + marriage KN172.2; 347.4212

breach of the peace KM562.3; 346.8833

breach of treaty KC338.4; 341.594
UF: treaties + breaches
RT: treaties + supervision KC338.4; 341.594

breach of trust KN217.2; 347.572

breakdown of marriage
USE: marriage breakdown KN173.11; 347.4241

breaking and entering
USE: burglary KM546.1; 346.8711

Brethren (sect) KD590.B7; 342.6919.B7

brewing KN186.4; 347.454
RT: alcohol KN186.4; 347.454

brewing + crime
USE: excise offences KM564.4; 346.8864

bribery
USE: corruption KM563.6; 346.8856

bribery + company law KN264.9; 347.6269

bridges KN322.8; 347.8128

bridges + international law KC252; 341.452

bridle paths KN95.13; 347.34213
RT: footpaths KN95.13; 347.34213
RT: rights of way KN65.12; 347.3073

briefs KL92; 345.1722
UF: case preparation

British and Irish Association of Law Librarians
USE: BIALL K81.9.B5; 340.0519.B5

British Constitution
USE: constitution + UK KM61; 346.14

British Standard Time
USE: time KN186.9.T5; 347.459.T5

British Summer Time
USE: time KN186.9.T5; 347.459.T5

broadband KN342.31; 347.8631

broadcasting KN344; 347.871
RT: radio KN344.4; 347.872
RT: television KN344.5; 347.873

broadcasting + advertising revenue
USE: advertising revenue + broadcasting KN344.2; 347.8713

broadcasting + censorship KN349.93; 347.8993

broadcasting + EU KW144.5

broadcasting + finance KN344.2; 347.8713

broadcasting + international law KC258; 341.464

broadcasting + licences + fees KN344.2; 347.8713
UF: licence fees + broadcasting

broadcasting + parliamentary procedure KM84.8; 346.23485

broadcasts + intellectual property KN112.3; 347.374

brokers + insurance
USE: insurance brokers KN291.2; 347.6812

brothels KM544.1; 346.8641

brothers
USE: siblings [Table VII: 3.8]

brownfield sites KN97.75; 347.3475

Buddhist law KD800; 342.91

budget KM332; 346.51
RT: autumn statements (budget) KM331.22; 346.5022
RT: estimates + public expenditure KM331.5; 346.505

budget + EU KW101

buffer states + international relations KC309.7; 341.5197

buggery
USE: sodomy KM544.2; 346.8642

bugging
USE: wire tapping KM604.52; 346.9662

bugs + computers KN348.5; 347.8975
UF: millennium bug
UF: YK2 bug

building contracts
USE: construction contracts KN84.4; 347.3264

building control KN84.1; 347.3261

building regulations KN84.1; 347.3261

building societies KN305.7; 347.767

buildings KN83; 347.325
UF: premises

buildings + courts KL230.72; 345.372
UF: court buildings

buildings + heritage sites
USE: listed buildings KN95.12; 347.34212

buildings + law libraries
USE: law libraries + accommodation K84.5; 340.0545

buildings + libraries
USE: libraries + accommodation K84.5; 340.0545

buildings + Parliament KM87.1; 346.2481

buildings + prisons KM659; 346.98719; [App: 89]

bullets
USE: firearms KN186.1; 347.451

bulls
USE: animals + control KN186.8; 347.458

bullying + employment KN192.57; 347.46557

bullying + schools KN184.255; 347.443255

burden of proof KN390.1; 347.9611
UF: balance of probabilities
UF: onus of proof
UF: proof
UF: standard of proof

burden of proof + criminal procedure KM 602; 346.962
UF: proof + criminal procedure

bureaucracy
USE: civil service KM237; 346.382; [Table IIA: 83.3]
USE: government KM231; 346.37; [Table IIA: 83]

bureaucracy + local officials
USE: officers + local government KM370; 346.680

Bureaux Internationaux Réunis pour la Protection de la Propriété Intellectuelle
USE: World Intellectual Property Organisation KC648; 341.6458

burglary KM546.1; 346.8711
UF: breaking and entering
UF: housebreaking

Burgundian law KE320.1; 343.621

burial KN97.3; 347.346
UF: bodies
UF: human bodies
UF: mortuary law
RT: cemeteries KN97.31; 347.3461
RT: cremation KN97.3; 347.346

burial insurance KN292.5; 347.687

bus routes
USE: routes + road transport KN324.4; 347.8144

buses KN324.1; 347.8141
UF: autobuses
UF: omnibuses
UF: trolley-buses
RT: coaches KN324.1; 347.8141

business + courts + management KL230.4; 345.34

business assets + taxation KM337.153; 346.5353

business associations KN260; 347.62; [Table VII: 9.2]
RT: associations KN169.4; 347.41894; [Table VII: 9.4]; [Table VIII: .003]

business contracts KN254; 347.618

Business Expansion Scheme KN260.3; 347.6225
UF: BES

Business Expansion Scheme + taxation KM336.65; 346.5265

business law
USE: commercial law KN250; 347.6; [Table IIA: 127]

business names
USE: names + commercial law KN260.1; 347.621; [Table IIA: 114]
USE: trade names KN114.2; 347.3772

business organisation + legal profession KL97; 345.1767; [Table IIA: 64.5]
RT: law firms KL97; 345.1767
RT: partnerships + legal profession KL97; 345.1767

business rating (taxation) KM337.65; 346.575
UF: council tax + businesses
UF: rates + businesses

business restructuring
USE: restructuring + companies KN312.7; 347.7927

business secrets
USE: commercial confidentiality KN114.3; 347.3773

business tenancies KN87.6; 347.3296
UF: commercial leases

business turnaround
USE: corporate rescue KN312.7; 347.7927

businesses + sale KN279; 347.649
UF: sale of businesses

busking
USE: street trading KN285.9.S8; 347.678.S8

buyouts
USE: management buyouts KN262.3; 347.6243

by-laws KF41; [Table IA: 34]
RT: local government KM361; 346.6; [Table IIA: 86]
RT: local legislation (texts) KF41; [Table IA: 34]

Byzantine law KE251; 343.5
UF: Eastern Empire (600 AD to 1453 AD)

cab rank rule
USE: duty to accept work KL82.5; 345.17025

cabinet KM113; 346.26
UF: Council of Ministers + UK

Cabinet y Cynulliad KM113.A15; 346.26.A15
SN: English name is Assembly Cabinet [Wales]

cable television KN344.51; 347.8731

cable television + international law KC259.1; 341.4661

cables + planning KN96.4; 347.3435

cables + real property KN65.4; 347.3184

cabotage + international air law KC255.1; 341.4546

cabotage + maritime law KN337.8; 347.8378

cabs
USE: taxis KN324.5; 347.8145

cafes
USE: restaurants KN186.3; 347.453

Calderbank offer
USE: part 36 offer KN387.5; 347.9475

Calvinist churches KD420; 342.52

Calvo clause KC233.1; 341.4231

Campaign for Nuclear Disarmament KC312.2.C2; 341.532.C3
UF: CND

Canada : EU KW81.3

canals KN90.1; 347.3331

canals + freight KN328.7; 347.8287

canals + international law KC267; 341.473

canals + transport KN326.2; 347.8162
RT: inland waterways KN326; 347.816

cancellation + contracts KN16.2; 347.142

cancellation + equitable remedies KN235; 347.595

canon law : common law KD477; 342.67

canons + Church of England KD450; 342.6

canteens + industrial law KN193.3; 347.473

capacity [Table VI: .Z43]
UF: legal capacity

capacity + consent + sexual activity KM544.01; 346.86401
UF: age of consent + sexual activity

capacity + contract KN14; 347.12

capacity + sexual activity KM544.01; 346.86401
UF: sexual capacity

capacity + tort KN34; 347.22

capacity + trusts KN213.1; 347.542

capital + company law KN263; 347.625

capital allowances + taxation KM337.155; 346.5355

capital gains tax KM337.151; 346.5351

capital markets KN304; 347.73; [Table IIA: 134.3]
UF: gearing

capital movements + international law KC222; 341.41

capital punishment [App: 61]
RT: execution (punishment) [App: 61]

capital taxes KM337.15; 346.535

capitulation
USE: surrender + war KC1421; 341.891

capitulations
USE: concessions + international law KC172; 341.282

car benefits
USE: benefits in kind + taxation KM336.31; 346.5231

car hire
USE: motor vehicles + rental KN324.6; 347.8146

car parking
USE: parking + regulations KN323.75; 347.81375

car taxes
USE: motor vehicles + taxation KM337.9.M6; 346.59.M6

caravan sites KN96.51; 347.3437
RT: gipsy caravan sites KN96.54; 347.3438

caravans KN96.5; 347.3436

carbon emissions KN94.11; 347.3411

carbon taxes KN94.12; 347.3412

carbon trading KN94.13; 347.3413

care in the community
USE: community care KN182; 347.442; [Table IIA: 121.5]

careless driving KM565.D7; 346.89.D7
RT: dangerous driving KM565.D7; 346.89.D7
RT: reckless driving KM565.D7; 346.89.D7

carers + families KN182.35; 347.44235

cargo KN337.1; 347.8371

Caribbean : EU KW81.4

Caribbean Community KC770; 341.659
UF: CARICOM

Caribbean Court of Justice KC1235; 341.7235

Carnegie Endowment for International Peace KC312.1; 341.531

carriage of goods KN328; 347.828

carriage of goods + air transport KN328.8; 347.8288

carriage of goods + air transport + international law KC253.8; 341.4538

carriage of goods + inland waterways KN328.7; 347.8287

carriage of goods + international law KC250.5; 341.4501

carriage of goods + international maritime law KC272.8; 341.4758

carriage of goods + maritime law KN337; 347.837
UF: carriage of goods by sea

carriage of goods + railways KN328.6; 347.8286

carriage of goods + road transport KN328.5; 347.8285

carriage of goods + road transport + international law KC252.8; 341.4528

carriage of goods by sea
USE: carriage of goods + maritime law KN337; 347.837

carriages + railways KN325.3; 347.8153
UF: rolling stock
RT: wagons + railways KN325.3; 347.8153

carriers KN329; 347.829

carry-back + taxation KM336.86; 346.5286

carry-forward + taxation KM336.86; 346.5286

cars KN323.14; 347.81332
UF: automobiles

cars + police
USE: police + equipment KM615.4; 346.9854

cartels + competition law KN266.55; 347.6345

cartels + EU KW110.5
RT: concerted practices + competition + EU KW110.5

cartels + international law KC234; 341.424
RT: monopolies KN266.1; 347.631; [Table IIA: 130]

cartels + shipping KN332.9; 347.8329
UF: liner conferences

cartoons KB35; 340.375
RT: pictures KB35; 340.375

case listing KL230.47; 345.347
RT: judicial time KL230.48; 345.348

case load + courts KL230.42; 345.342

case management KL230.422; 345.3422
UF: flow management

case preparation
USE: briefs KL92; 345.1722

case reports
USE: law reports [Table IA: 40–48]

casebooks [Table VI: .Z2]

cases
SN: use as subdivision only

cash limits + public expenditure KM331.52; 346.5053

cash on delivery KN328.4; 347.8284
UF: COD

casinos
USE: gambling KN186.5; 347.455

caste KD749.5; 342.82907515

castration + punishment [App: 75.C3]

casualty insurance KN294.C3; 347.694.C3

cataloguing + law libraries K85.C3; 340.055.C3

catering KN193.53; 347.4753

cathedrals
USE: church property [KD Table: 4]

Catholic Church
USE: Roman Catholic Church KD110; 342.31

Catholicism + international law KC124.C3; 341.224.C3

cattle passports
USE: passports + animals KN186.82; 347.4582

causation KA26; 340.126
UF: chain of events

cause lists KN389.1; 347.9601
UF: setting down

causes of crime [App: 10]

cautions [App: 72]

caveat emptor KN282.3; 347.653

CB radio KN344.45; 347.8721
UF: citizen's band

cellular phones
USE: mobile phones KN342.35; 347.8635

Celtic law (ancient) KE330; 343.65

cemeteries KN97.31; 347.3461
RT: burials KN97.3; 347.346

censorship KN349; 347.898; [Table IIA: 142]
RT: freedom of the press KM207; 346.357

censorship + Roman Catholic Church KN349.1.C3; 347.8981.C3

census KM172.32; 346.3132
RT: population KM172.32; 346.3132

central banks KN303.5; 347.725
UF: federal banks
UF: national banks

Central Criminal Court
USE: Old Bailey KL230.721.O4; 345.3721.O4

Central Treaty Organisation KC821; 341.662

cereals + EU KW117.3.C4

ceremony of marriage
USE: marriage + ceremony KN172.5; 347.4215

certainty
USE: material facts KN383.2; 347.9432

certiorari KN395.81; 347.9741

cessation
SN: use as a subdivision only

cestui que trust
USE: beneficiaries + trusts KN217; 347.57

chain of events
USE: causation KA26; 340.126

chains + conveyancing KN74.6; 347.3226

challenges + juries KN389.62; 347.96062

challenges + juries + criminal procedure KM583.2; 346.9332
UF: array + challenges

chambers + law offices KL96; 345.176

chambers of commerce KN260.5; 347.623

champerty KN38.31; 347.251

Chancery courts [Table V: 6]

change of use + planning control KN96.82; 347.34482

Channel Tunnel KC251.2; 341.4512

chanting abuse + sports grounds
USE: sports grounds + offences KM562.13; 346.88313

Chapter I prohibition
USE: anti-competitive agreements KN266.2; 347.632

Chapter II prohibition
USE: abuse of dominant position KN266.5; 347.6345

character evidence KN391.62; 347.96262

character evidence + criminal procedure KM604.952; 346.96752

characterisation + conflict of laws KC2055; 341.925
UF: classification + conflict of laws

charge cards KN303.14; 347.7214

charges + criminal procedure KM580.4; 346.914
UF: holding charges
UF: police charges

charges + freight KN328.2; 347.8282
UF: freight charges
UF: tare + freight
UF: tariffs (charges)

charges + harbours KN336.1; 347.8361

charges + property KN56.5; 347.3035

charging orders KN395.21.C5; 347.9721.C5

charities KN215; 347.556

charities + reliefs + taxation KM336.64; 346.5264

charities + taxation KM336.496; 346.52496

charter flights KN327.6; 347.826
UF: air charter

charter flights + international law KC254.3; 341.4542

Charter of Fundamental Rights KW4

charterparties KN337.4; 347.8374
UF: ship chartering

charters + local government KM363; 346.63

chattel mortgages KN106.6; 347.3666

chattels KN102.1; 347.3621

chemical industry KN275.C5; 347.645.C5

chemical industry + EU KW119.8

chemical weapons + international law KC1395.1; 341.8651
RT: disarmament + international law KC313; 341.533

cheque cards KN303.13; 347.7213

cheques KN306.1; 347.771

chief executives + company law KN264; 347.626

chief executives + constitutional law
USE: heads of government KM112; 346.251

child abduction KN173.82; 347.42582

child abduction + criminal law KM543.42; 346.86342

child abuse KN176.41; 347.42641
UF: abuse of children
RT: incest KM544.6; 346.8646
RT: pederasty KM544.7; 346.8646

child abuse + victims + interviews KN176.412; 347.426412

child allowances + taxation KM336.61; 346.5261

child minding KN176.26; 347.42626

child soldiers KC1355.6; 341.8256

children KN176; 347.426; [Table IIA: 118]; [Table VII: 1.1]
UF: infants
UF: minors
UF: parent and child

children + criminal liability
USE: age of criminal responsibility KM507.Q13; 346.83.Q13

children + criminal procedure KM590.Q11; 346.945.Q11

children + effect of divorce
USE: divorce + effect on children KN176.9.D5; 347.4269.D5

children + patients KN185.129.Q11; 347.446129.Q11

children + religious laws KD30.86; 342.1986

children + social policy + EU KW128.3

children + welfare KN176.4; 347.4264; [Table IIA: 118.5]

children in care KN176.42; 347.42642

children's allowances
USE: family provision + social security KN181.4; 347.4414

children's courts
USE: youth courts KL227.1; 345.3071; [Table V: 7.1]

children's guardians KN176.22; 347.42622
UF: guardians ad litem

children's homes KN176.44; 347.42644

Chinese walls KN264.73; 347.62673

choice of domicile
USE: domicile + choice KC2067; 341.952

choice of law KC2058; 341.93

choses in action KN102.2; 347.3622

choses in possession KN102.3; 347.3623

Christian churches KD100; 342.3

chromosome abnormality [App: 11]

church + government [KD Table: 1]

church + organisation [KD Table: 1]

church and state KM58; 346.138
UF: established church
UF: state and church
RT: freedom of religion KM206; 346.356

Church Assembly Measures (UK) KD465; 342.63

church desecration
USE: sacrilege KM550; 346.875

Church of England KD450; 342.6
RT: Anglican churches KD450; 342.6

church property [KD Table: 4]
UF: cathedrals
UF: tithes

churning + investments KN308.15; 347.78615

CIF contracts KN337.2; 347.8372
UF: cost insurance and freight

cinema KN344.8; 347.875

Circuit Court + Ireland [Table V: 4.2; 5.2]

Circuit Judges + UK KL241.3; 345.463

circuits + court management KL230.3; 345.33
RT: districts + court management KL230.32; 345.332

circumstantial evidence KN393.7; 347.9647

circumstantial evidence + criminal procedure KM602.3; 346.9623

circuses KN186.62; 347.4562

citation manuals K114; 340.074; [Table VI: .Z25]
UF: annotations
UF: legal citations
RT: legal abbreviations K112; 340.072

cities KM365.3; 346.653

citizens KM171; 346.3
UF: subjects (citizens)
RT: individuals [Table VII]

citizens abroad + protection
USE: diplomatic protection KC196; 341.316

citizens advice bureaux KN400; 347.9991

citizens' band
USE: CB radio KN344.45; 347.8721

citizenship
USE: nationality KM172; 346.31; [Table IIA: 80]

city planning
USE: planning KN96; 347.343; [Table IIA: 107.25]

city regions
USE: conurbations KM365.2; 346.652

civil aviation
USE: air law KN327; 347.82; [Table IIA: 137]

civil codes
SN: use as a subdivision only

civil courts [Table V: 5]
UF: common law courts

civil defence KM233.2; 346.3732

civil disobedience KA65; 340.155
UF: disobedience
UF: opposition to immoral laws

Civil Division + Court of Appeal
USE: Court of Appeal Civil Division [Table V: 1]

civil engineering + contracts
USE: construction contracts KN84.4; 347.3264

civil judicial statistics
USE: statistics KL300; 345.7; [Table IIA: 72]; [Table VIII: .0024]

civil law : common law KB120; 340.54
UF: common law : civil law

civil law systems KB121; 340.55

civil liberties
USE: civil rights KM201; 346.35; [Table IIA: 81]

civil partnerships KN172.9.C5; 347.422.C5

civil procedure
USE: procedure KN350; 347.9; [Table IIA: 144]; [Table VI: .Z71]

civil rights KM201; 346.35; [Table IIA: 81]
UF: civil liberties
UF: fundamental rights
UF: liberties
UF: Petition of Right
UF: political rights
RT: human rights KM201; 346.35; [Table IIA: 81]

civil rights + EU KW98

civil rights + international law
USE: human rights + international law KC200; 341.33

civil rights + jurisprudence KA64; 340.154

civil salvage
USE: salvage KN334; 347.834; [Table IIA: 139]

civil servants + international organisations
USE: international officials KC346; 341.614

civil service KM237; 346.382; [Table IIA: 83.3]
UF: administrators + government
UF: bureaucracy
UF: employees + state
UF: officials + public service
UF: public officials

civil service + local government
USE: local civil servants KM370; 346.68

Civil Service Tribunal KW94.5

civil trials + popular accounts KB66; 340.46

civil war + international law KC1365; 341.84

civil wrongs
USE: tort KN30; 347.2; [Table IIA: 100]

civilians + military occupation KC1403; 341.873
UF: protection + civilians

claim forms KN381.1; 347.9411
UF: writs

claimants [Table VI: .Z61]
UF: plaintiffs

claims + international arbitration KC1254; 341.734
UF: private claims + international law

claims + statements
USE: statements of case KN383; 347.943; [Table IIA: 146]

claims commissions + law reports KC48; 341.143

class actions
USE: group actions KN370.2; 347.9302

classification + conflict of laws
USE: characterisation + conflict of laws KC2055; 341.925

classification + criminals [App: 06]

classification + libraries K85.C5; 340.055.C5

classified information
USE: official secrets KM233.7; 346.3737

clauses
SN: use as subdivision only

clean air KN97.71; 347.3471
RT: air pollution KN97.91; 347.3471

clearing banks KN303.65; 347.7265

clearing systems KN304.8; 347.7388

clemency KM587.3; 346.9373
UF: mercy

clergy KD32; 342.192
UF: religious personnel

clerks of the court
USE: court officials KL255; 345.55

client affairs KL99; 345.1769

client-lawyer relationship
USE: lawyer-client relationship KL82.2; 345.17022

clients + interviewing KL91; 345.1721

clients + money
USE: management + clients' money KL99; 345.1769

climate change KN94.1; 347.341; [Table IIA: 107.2]
UF: global warming

climate change + EU KW125.9

climate change + international law KC243.5; 341.4445

climate change levy KM337.9.C5; 346.59.C5

clinics
USE: hospitals KN185.1; 347.4461

cloning KN172.89.C5; 347.42189.C5

close companies KN265.9C5; 347.6279.C5
RT: companies KN261; 347.624; [Table IIA: 128]

close companies + taxation KM336.491; 346.52491

closed shop + industrial law KN195.2; 347.482

closing speeches + criminal procedure KM585; 346.935

clothing industry + EU KW119.4

cloud computing KN347.43; 347.89353

clubs KN169.Q95; 347.4189.Q95; [Table VII: 9.5]
RT: associations KN169.4; 347.41894; [Table VII: 9.4]; [Table VIII: 003]

CND
USE: Campaign for Nuclear Disarmament KC312.2.C3; 341.531.C3

co-operation + public health + EU KW149.5

co-operative banks KN303.9.C6; 347.729.C6

co-operatives KN268; 347.6382

co-operatives + EU KW130.7

co-ownership + industrial law KN194.3; 347.4783

co-ownership + property KN54.5; 347.3025
UF: collective ownership + property

co-tenancy
USE: joint tenancy KN92.2; 347.3312

coaches KN324.1; 347.8141
RT: buses KN324.1; 347.8141

coal + energy policy + EU KW122.4

coal + mining KN91.1; 347.3341

coal + natural resources KN89.41; 347.33141

coal + seabed resources KC277.2; 341.4822

coalitions KM113.1; 346.261

Coast Guard + US KM413.C6; 346.78.C6

coast protection KN90.4; 347.3334

COD
USE: cash on delivery KN328.4; 347.8284

Code of Federal Regulations KG331

codes [Table VI: .Z16]

codes + England and Wales KF40

Codex (Corpus Juris Civilis) KE153; 343.474

Codex Juris Canonici KD150; 342.36

Codex Theodosianus KE140; 343.46

codicils KN125.3; 347.3823

codification KL160; 345.197
UF: uniform laws
RT: unification of private law KB115; 340.53

codification + international law KC130; 341.231

coercion
USE: duress + criminal liability KM505.3; 346.823

coffee + foreign trade KN253.8.C6; 347.616.C6

cohabitation KN174; 347.4259; [Table IIA: 117.6]
RT: common law marriage KN172.9.C6; 347.422.C6
RT: de facto relationships KN174; 347.4259
RT: unmarried couples KN174; 347.4259

coinage KN302.2; 347.712
UF: coins
RT: bank notes KN302.2; 347.712
RT: legal tender KN302.1; 347.711

coining
USE: counterfeiting + crime KM564.1; 346.8861

coins
USE: coinage KN302.2; 347.712

cold calling
USE: doorstep selling KN285.9.D6; 347.678.D6
USE: telephone sales KN285.9.T4; 347.678.T4

cold storage KN83.7.C6; 347.3257.C6

cold war
USE: international relations KC300; 341.5

collaboration with the enemy
USE: treason KM561.1; 346.8811

collection + banking KN303.4.C6; 347.724.C6

collections [Table VIII: 004]
UF: Festschriften
UF: symposia

collective bargaining KN196.1; 347.4861

collective farms KN98.21; 347.3521

collective investments KN304.5; 347.735

collective ownership + property
USE: co-ownership + property KN54.5; 347.3025

college libraries
USE: libraries KN184.4; 347.445; [Table IIA: 122.5]

College of Law (London) KL131.8.C3; 345.179428.C3

colleges
USE: higher education KN184.3; 347.444

collisions + international law KC274.1; 341.4781
UF: marine accidents
RT: wrecks + international law KC275; 341.479

collisions + maritime law KN333.1; 347.8331
RT: pilotage KN333.2; 347.8332

collusion
USE: conspiracy + criminal law KM565.C6; 346.89.C6

Colombo Plan KC831; 341.663

coloni KE213; 343.490751

colonial governors
USE: governors KM112.4; 346.255

colonial law + comparative law KB141; 340.591

colonial law + UK KL29; 345.09.A–Z
RT: imperial law KM57; 346.137

colonies + international law KC154.1; 341.2641

colonisation + international law KC142.5; 341.2525

COM documents + EU KW16

Comecon KC1121; 341.6892
UF: Council for Mutual Economic Assistance

comfort letters KN306.91; 347.7791

Cominform
USE: Communist Information Bureau KC1101; 341.689

coming into force + legislation
USE: commencement + legislation KL36; 345.16

command : law KA42; 340.142
UF: imperative theory of law
UF: law + command
UF: law as command

command papers (UK) KF17

commencement + legislation KL36; 345.16
UF: coming into force + legislation
UF: entry into force + legislation

commerce
USE: commercial law KN250; 347.6; [Table IIA: 127]

commerce + maritime law
USE: maritime law KN330; 347.83; [Table IIA: 138]

commercial agreements + international law KC231; 341.421
UF: trade agreements
UF: treaties + commerce
UF: treaties + trade

commercial agreements + reciprocity
USE: reciprocity + trade KC231.1; 341.4211

commercial arbitration KN256; 347.619
RT: arbitration KN398; 347.98; [Table IIA: 148]; [Table VI: .Z75]

commercial banks KN303.6; 347.726

commercial codes
SN: use as a subdivision only

commercial confidentiality KN114.3; 347.3773
UF: business secrets
UF: confidentiality + commercial law

commercial courts [Table V: 8]

commercial credits KN306.4; 347.774

commercial law KN250; 347.6; [Table IIA: 127]
UF: business law
UF: commerce

commercial law + EU KW118

commercial law + international law
USE: international economic law KC220; 341.4

commercial leases
USE: business tenancies KN87.6; 347.3296

commercial organisations + international law
USE: international economic organisations KC349.E2; 341.619.E2

commercial paper KN306.7; 347.777

commercial property KN58.3; 347.3053

Commission of the EU
USE: European Commission KW90

commissioners (judiciary) KL242; 345.47

commissions + payments KN194.4; 347.4784

commissions of enquiry KM238; 346.383

committal KM581.2; 346.922

Committee of Permanent Representatives + EU KW92.P4

Committee of Permanent Representatives + EU + publications KW30

Committee of the Regions + EU KW123

committees + government KM238; 346.383

committees + legislatures KM86.3; 346.243

commodities KN253.8; 347.616

commodity futures KN304.63; 347.7363
UF: futures + commodities

common agricultural policy + EU KW113
RT: agriculture + EU KW113

common assault KM543.2; 346.8623
RT: assault KM543; 346.863

common land
USE: commons KN65.5; 347.3185

common law : canon law KD477; 342.67

common law : civil law
USE: civil law : common law KB120; 340.54

common law : equity KL31; 345.11
UF: equity : common law

common law courts
USE: civil courts [Table V: 5]

common law marriage KN172.9.C6; 347.422.C6
UF: marriage + common law
RT: cohabitation KN174; 347.4259; [Table IIA: 117.6]
RT: de facto relationships KN174; 347.4259
RT: unmarried couples KN174; 347.4259

Common Pleas Court
USE: Court of Common Pleas [Table V: 5.9.C6]

commonhold KN63.3; 347.3143

commons KN65.5; 347.3185
UF: common land

Commonwealth + international law KC153.1; 341.2631

communicable diseases KN185.62; 347.44862

communications KN340; 347.84; [Table IIA: 141]

communications + EU KW144.5

communications + international law KC256; 341.46

communications + Parliament KM87.2; 346.2482

communications industries + EU KW119.6

communications satellites
USE: satellites + communications KN342.6; 347.866

communications satellites + space law
USE: satellites + communications + space law KC284.2; 341.4942

communism + international law KC122; 341.222

Communist bloc + international relations KC309.1; 341.5191

Communist Information Bureau KC1101; 341.689
UF: Cominform

communist jurisprudence KA48; 340.146

community care KN182; 347.442; [Table IIA: 121.5]
UF: care in the community
RT: district nurses KN182.3; 347.4423

community charge (UK) KM337.14; 346.534
RT: local taxation KM337.8; 346.589

community development schemes + EU KW127.5

community relations
USE: racial discrimination KM208.43; 346.3643; [Table IIA: 81.5]

community service [App: 69]

community titles KN72.4; 347.32184

companies KN261; 347.624; [Table IIA: 128]
RT: close companies KN265.9.C5; 347.6279.C5
RT: company groups KN262.2; 347.62422
RT: company law KN261; 347.624; [Table IIA: 128]
RT: family companies KN265.9.F3; 347.6279.F3
RT: foreign companies KN265.5; 347.6275
RT: subsidiaries KN265.7; 347.6277

companies + accounts KN261.2; 347.6241

companies + crimes
USE: corporate crime KN264.8; 347.6268

companies + directors
USE: company directors KN264; 347.626; [Table IIA: 129.3]

companies + inspections KN261.5; 347.62415
UF: company investigations

companies + names KN262.8; 347.6248

companies + officers
USE: company officers KN264.3; 347.6263

companies + purchase of own shares
USE: purchase of own shares KN263.54; 347.62554

companies + records KN262.91; 347.62491

companies + taxation KM336.492; 346.52492
SN: theory of company taxation
RT: company taxes KM337.2; 346.54

Companies House (UK) KN262.9; 347.6249

companies limited by guarantee KN265.45; 347.62745

company cars
USE: benefits in kind + taxation KM336.31; 346.5231

company charges KN305.25; 347.7525

company directors KN264; 347.626; [Table IIA: 129.3]
UF: companies + directors
UF: directors of companies

company directors + disclosure of interests
USE: disclosure of interests + company directors KN264.75; 347.62675

company directors + remuneration KN264.1; 347.6261

company distributions
USE: dividends KN263.64; 347.62564

company groups KN262.2; 347.62422
UF: groups of companies
RT: companies KN261; 347.624; [Table IIA: 128]

company groups + taxation KM336.493; 346.52493

company investigations
USE: companies + inspections KN261.5; 347.62415

company law KN261; 347.624; [Table IIA: 128]
UF: corporation law
RT: companies KN261; 347.623; [Table IIA: 128]
RT: memorandum of association KN262.7; 347.6247

company law + EU KW111

company law + reorganisation KN262.5; 347.6245

company officers KN264.3; 347.6263
UF: companies + officers
UF: officers + companies

company taxes KM337.2; 346.54
UF: corporation taxes
RT: companies + taxation KM336.492; 346.52492

company unions KN195.12; 347.4812

company voluntary arrangements KN312.72; 347.79272

comparative treatment [Table VIII: 008]

compellability + witnesses KN391; 347.962
RT: competence + witnesses KN391; 347.962

compellability + witnesses + criminal procedure KM605; 346.97

compensation [Table VI: .Z9]
UF: lump sum payments

compensation + loss of office KN192.25; 347.4635

compensation + miscarriage of justice KM597.9; 346.9579

compensation + planning KN96.31; 347.3434

compensation + tort KN37.1; 347.231

compensation + victims of crime KM594; 346.948

competence + witnesses KN391; 347.962
RT: compellability + witnesses KN391; 347.962

competence + witnesses + criminal procedure KM605; 346.97

competition KN266; 347.63; [Table IIA: 130]
UF: anti-trust laws
RT: fair trading KN266.05; 347.6305

competition + EU KW110

Competition Commission KN266.15; 347.6315

complaints + legal profession KL95; 345.174
UF: barristers + complaints
UF: lawyers + complaints
UF: solicitors + complaints

complaints + prisoners KM680.2; 346.98752; [App: 93.2]

complaints against police
USE: police + complaints KM615.7; 346.9857

complementary medicine KN185.13; 347.44613
RT: alternative medicine KN185.13; 347.44613

completion KN74.4; 347.32234

complex trials KN359; 347.919

compliance + financial services KN309; 347.7869
RT: enforcement [Table VI: .Z92]

compliance + international law KC133; 341.233

compliance + treaties KC334.1; 341.571

composition + documents
USE: drafting + documents KL34.2; 345.142; [Table VIII: .0051]

comprehensive education
USE: schools KN184.2; 347.4432

compromise KN388.3; 347.953

compromise + international disputes KC1290.2; 341.762

compulsion
USE: duress + criminal liability KM505.3; 346.823

compulsory education KN184.1; 347.4431

compulsory military service
USE: conscription KM402; 346.715

compulsory purchase KN96.3; 347.3433
RT: expropriation KN56.6; 347.3036

compulsory training [App: 69.6]

computation + taxation
USE: assessment + taxation KM336.8; 346.528

computer applications KN347.1; 347.891; [Table VIII: 0099]
RT: software KN348.4; 347.8974

computer crime KM565.C6; 346.89.C6
UF: hacking

computer evidence KN394.5; 347.9655

computer evidence + criminal procedure KM603.7; 346.9637

computer law KN347; 347.89; [Table IIA: 143]

computer programs
USE: software KN348.4; 347.8974; [Table VIII: 0099]

computer records + court documents KN392.6; 347.9636

computer software + intellectual property KN112.7; 347.3757

computer technology KN348; 347.897

computers KN347; 347.89; [Table IIA: 143]
RT: information technology KN347; 347.89

computers + courts KL230.61; 345.361
UF: courts + computers

computers + law offices KL96.2; 345.1762
UF: use of computers + law offices

computers + law reporting KL33.1; 345.131

computers + legal research KL157; 345.192

computers + libraries K86; 340.056

computers + Parliament KM87.3; 346.2483

computers in libraries K86; 340.056
UF: automation + libraries

concealment of birth KM542.4; 346.8624
RT: infanticide KM542.4; 346.8624

concepts of law
USE: legal concepts KA21; 340.121

concerted practices + competition + EU KW110.5
RT: cartels + EU KW110.5

concessions + international law KC172; 341.282
UF: capitulations

concessions + mining KN91.31; 347.33431

conciliation + arbitration KN398.4; 347.984

conciliation + family law KN173.6; 347.4256
UF: mediation + family law

conciliation + industrial law KN196.2; 347.4862

conciliation + international disputes KC1290.3; 341.763
UF: mediation + international disputes

concordats
USE: treaties KC330; 341.56

concurrent interests KN64.5; 347.3168

concurrent jurisdiction + competition KN266.17; 347.6317

conditional discharge [App: 71]

conditional fee agreements KN397.8; 347.9778

conditions + employment KN193; 347.47
UF: working conditions

conditions + employment + EU KW131

conditions + employment + police KM615.9; 346.9859

condominiums KN63.9.C6; 347.3149.C6
UF: horizontal property

condominiums + international law KC154.6; 341.2646

conduct + judiciary KL240.3; 345.43
UF: judicial conduct

conduct + legal profession KL81; 345.17011
UF: legal professional conduct

conductors + trains KN325.5; 347.8155

Conference on Security and Co-operation in Europe KC1136; 341.6895
UF: CSCE

conferences [Table VIII: 004]

conferences + comparative law KB105; 340.51

conferences + international law KC60; 341.161
UF: international conferences
UF: international law + conferences

conferences + international relations KC300.4; 341.504

confession and avoidance KN384.2; 347.9442
UF: avoidance

confessions KM603.2; 346.9632

confidentiality
USE: privacy KM209.P7; 346.368.P7

confidentiality + commercial law
USE: commercial confidentiality KN114.3; 347.3773

confiscation KM594.7; 346.9487

confiscations + international law
USE: expropriation + international law KC238; 341.438

conflict of interest + businesses KN264.73; 347.62673

conflict of interest + criminal law KM563.5; 346.8855

conflict of interest + legal profession KL82.9; 345.17029

conflict of interest + legislators KM83.92; 346.2292

conflict of laws KC2000; 341.9
UF: private international law
RT: international law KC; 341

Confucian law KD900; 342.95

congestion + court management KL230.42; 345.342
UF: courts + congestion

Congregational Church KD530; 342.6913

Congress (US) KM82; 346.21
RT: legislatures KM82; 346.21; [Table IIA: 79]

congresses + constitutional law KM52; 346.132
UF: constitutional congresses
UF: conventions (meetings) + constitutional law

Congressional investigations
USE: legislative investigations KM86.2; 346.242

Congressional publications (US) KG301–17

Congressmen
USE: legislators KM83; 346.22

conjugal rights KN172.9.C7; 347.422.C7

conquest KC142.7; 341.2527
RT: military occupation KC1400; 341.87

consanguinity
USE: incest KM544.6; 346.8646

conscientious objection + human rights KM206.346; 346.356

conscientious objection + jurors KN389.613; 347.960613

conscientious objection + military law KM403; 346.72

conscientious objection + taxation KM336.79; 346.5279

conscription KM402; 346.715
UF: compulsory military service
UF: draft (US)
UF: military service (compulsory)
UF: selective service

consent + international law KC132; 341.232

consent + medical care KN185.122; 347.446122
UF: informed consent + medical care

consent + sexual activity KM544.01; 346.86401

consequential loss insurance KN294.C6; 347.694.C6

conservation KN95.1; 347.3421
RT: environmental law KN94; 347.34; [Table IIA: 107.2]

conservation + fisheries KN338.1; 347.8381

conservation + historical sites + international law KC243.3; 341.4443

conservation + plants KN95.6; 347.3426
UF: plant conservation

conservation of resources
USE: resources + conservation + international law KC243.4; 341.4444

consideration KN13.3; 347.113

consistory courts KD489; 342.689

consolidation of actions KN387.7; 347.9477

consortia KN262.2; 347.62422

conspiracy + criminal law KM565.C6; 346.89.C6
UF: collusion

conspiracy + tort KN38.5; 347.265

constables
USE: police KM615; 346.985; [Table IIA: 92.2]

constituencies KM83.2; 346.222
UF: boundaries + constituencies
UF: delimitation + electoral districts
UF: electoral districts
UF: gerrymandering
UF: legislative districts

Constitutio Antoniniana KE135; 343.45

constitution + UK KM61; 346.14
UF: British Constitution

Constitution + US (texts) KG318

constitutional amendments
USE: amendments + constitutional law KM53; 346.133

constitutional congresses
USE: congresses + constitutional law KM52; 346.132

constitutional conventions KM38; 346.12345
UF: conventions (constitutional)
UF: habits (constitutional)

constitutional courts [Table V: 2]

constitutional history KL431; 346.1007

constitutional law KM31; 346.1; [Table IIA: 77]

constitutional law + EU KW84

constitutional monarchy
USE: monarchy KM41; 346.125

constitutional principles KM33; 346.12

constitutional protection + evidence KM603.1; 346.9631

constitutional reform KM37; 346.1234

constitutions (texts) [Table IA: 14]

constitutions (theory) KM32; 346.11
UF: written constitutions

construction + statutes KL35; 345.15
UF: statutory construction
RT: interpretation KL35; 345.15

construction + wills KN125.5; 347.3825

construction contracts KN84.4; 347.3264
UF: building contracts
UF: civil engineering + contracts

construction industries + EU KW119.8

construction industry KN84.2; 347.3262

construction law KN84; 347.326; [Table IIA: 105.5]

construction projects KN84.3; 347.3263

constructive dismissal KN192.245; 347.46341

constructive trusts KN214.1; 347.551

consular courts KC326.1; 341.5531

consuls KC326; 341.553

consumer credit KN305.4; 347.76

consumer credit + EU KW112.3

consumer protection KN284; 347.66; [Table IIA: 132]

consumer protection + EU KW112

consumer safety KN284.4; 347.664

consumers + associations KN284.5; 347.665

contaminated land KN97.75; 347.3475
UF: soil + pollution
RT: pollution KN97.7; 347.347; [Table IIA: 107.4]

contempt of Congress
USE: contempt of Parliament KM85.1; 346.2351

contempt of court KM563.3; 346.8853

contempt of Parliament KM85.1; 346.2351
UF: contempt of Congress

content of law KA22; 340.122

contentious costs KN397.2; 347.9772

continental shelf KC144.2; 341.2542
UF: submerged lands
RT: seabed + resources KC277; 341.482
RT: territorial sea KC144.1; 341.2541

contingency fees KL89.5; 345.17145

continuing legal education KL131–149 [Table: .46]; 345.1794–9 [Table: 46]

contraband KC1385; 341.8545
RT: smuggling KM564.3; 346.8863

contraception
USE: birth control KN172.72; 347.42172

contract KN10; 347.1; [Table IIA: 97]

contract + agreements KN13.1; 347.111

contract + EU KW118

contract + privacy KN14; 347.12

contract + sale KN282.1; 347.651
UF: sale + contract

contract + sale + land KN73; 347.322

contracting out + commercial law KN257; 347.6195
UF: outsourcing + commercial law

contracting out + government KM236.4; 346.3814

contracting out + local services KM361.15; 346.6115

contracting out + office services (legal) KL96.15; 345.17615

contracts + international trade KC233; 341.423
UF: international contracts

contracts of marriage
USE: marriage + contracts KN172.1; 347.4211

contributory negligence KN33.32; 347.2132
UF: negligence + claimant

control of disease
USE: disease + control KN185.6; 347.4486

control of public expenditure
USE: public expenditure + control KM331.3; 346.503

controlled drugs
USE: drugs + offences KM565.D7; 346.89.D7

controlled foreign companies + taxation KM336.494; 346.52494

controlled functions + financial services KN308.3; 347.7863

conurbations KM365.2; 346.652
UF: city regions
UF: county boroughs
UF: metropolitan areas

convalescent homes KN185.17.C6; 347.44176.C6
UF: sanatoria

conventional energy sources
USE: energy + conventional sources KN89.4; 347.3314

conventional weapons
USE: explosives + war KC1391; 341.861
USE: firearms + international law KC1391; 341.861

conventions (constitutional)
USE: constitutional conventions KM38; 346.12345

conventions (meetings)
USE: meetings KN164; 347.4184

conventions (meetings) + constitutional law
USE: congresses + constitutional law KM52; 346.132

conventions (treaties)
USE: treaties KC330; 341.56

conversations KB15; 340.33
UF: table talk

conversion + currency
USE: exchange rates KN302.3; 347.713

conversion + tort KN38.71; 347.276

converts [KD Table: 3]

conveyancing KN74; 347.3223; [Table IIA: 105]

conveyancing + ecclesiastical law KN75.E3; 347.3229.E3

conveyancing agents KN74.9; 347.3228
UF: agents + conveyancing
RT: licensed conveyancers KN74.9; 347.3228

convicted persons
USE: offenders KM587.1; 346.9371

conviction KM586.3; 346.9363

convictions + quashing KM597.3; 346.9573
UF: quashing convictions

convictions + review KM596; 346.956
UF: review of convictions

cooling off period
USE: hire purchase KN305.4; 347.76
USE: sale of goods KN280; 347.65; [Table IIA: 132]

Coptic Church KD220.C6; 342.44.C6

copy editing K105.3; 340.0653

copyright KN112; 347.371
RT: design right KN114.4; 347.3774
RT: fair dealing KN118.1; 347.3795
RT: legal deposit KN184.6; 347.4456

copyright + international law KC236.1; 341.431
RT: Berne Convention KC236.1; 341.431

copyright + taxation KM336.37; 346.5237

Copyright Tribunal KN115.42; 347.3786
UF: tribunals

coroners KL254; 345.54
RT: inquests KM580.17; 346.9117

Coroners Court [Table V: 9.C6]

corporal punishment [App: 62]

corporate crime KN264.8; 347.6268
UF: companies + crimes
UF: corporations + crimes
UF: crimes + companies

corporate governance KN255; 347.6185

corporate governance + company officers KN264.71; 347.62671

corporate personality KN161; 347.4181; [Table IIA: 114]
RT: legal personality KN160; 347.418

corporate rescue KN312.7; 347.7927
UF: business turnaround
UF: corporate recovery

corporate social responsibility KN264.72; 347.62672

corporation law
USE: company law KN261; 347.624; [Table IIA: 128]

corporation taxes
USE: company taxes KM337.2; 346.54

corporations + crimes
USE: corporate crime KN264.8; 347.6268

Corpus Juris Canonici KD130; 342.34

Corpus Juris Civilis KE150; 343.471
RT: Justinian KE145; 343.47

correction (punishment) [App: 50.23]
SN: use for purpose of punishment

corroboration KN393.8; 347.9648

corroboration + criminal procedure KM602.1; 346.9621

corruption KM563.6; 346.8856
UF: bribery
UF: graft

corruption + company law KN264.8; 347.6268

cosmetics KN185.87; 347.44887

cost insurance and freight
USE: CIF contracts KN337.2; 347.8372

costs KN397; 347.977; [Table IIA: 150]
UF: disbursements
UF: fees
RT: taxation of costs KN397.7; 347.9777

costs + accused + acquittal KM586.12; 346.93612

costs + conveyancing KN74.3; 347.32233

costs + criminal procedure KM599.4; 346.9594

costume + legal profession
USE: legal dress KL81; 345.17011

Council for Mutual Economic Assistance
USE: Comecon KC1121; 341.6892

Council of Europe KC921; 341.673

Council of Legal Education KL131.8.C5; 345.188.C5

Council of Ministers + EU KW89

Council of Ministers + EU + publications KW10

Council of Ministers + UK
USE: cabinet KM113; 346.26

council tax KM337.65; 346.575
UF: rating + property
RT: local taxation KM337.8; 346.589

council tax + businesses
USE: business rating (taxation) KM337.65; 346.575

councillors + local government
USE: local councillors KM367; 346.667

counsel
USE: barristers KL86; 345.1711

counselling + crime prevention [App: 22]

counselling + marriage KN173.6; 347.4256
UF: marriage guidance

counter-espionage
USE: intelligence services KM233.8; 346.3738

counterclaim KN384.9; 347.9449

counterfeiting + crime KM564.1; 346.8861
UF: coining
UF: currency + forgery
UF: false coinage
UF: forgery + coinage

counterfeiting + intellectual property KN116.1; 347.3791

countertrade KN253.3; 347.615

counties KM365.1; 346.651
RT: local legislation (texts) KF41; [Table IA: 34]

countryside + EU KW125.2

counts in indictments
USE: indictments KM582.2; 346.931

county boroughs
USE: conurbations KM365.2; 346.652

county courts [Table V: 5.2]

coursework + legal education KL130–149 [Table: .2]; 345.1794–9 [Table: 2]

court accommodation
USE: accommodation + courts KL230.7; 345.37

court accounts
USE: accounts + courts KL230.14; 345.314

court administration
USE: court management KL230; 345.3; [Table IIA: 69.2]

court administrators KL230.17; 345.317

court archives
USE: public records KN184.5; 347.4455; [Table IIA: 122.5]

court buildings
USE: buildings + courts KL230.72; 345.372

court dress
USE: legal dress KL81; 345.17011

court forms
USE: forms KN360; 347.92; [Table VI: .Z3]

court governance KL230.11; 345.311

court hand
USE: palaeography K102; 340.062

court management KL230; 345.3; [Table IIA: 69.2]
UF: court administration
UF: management + courts
RT: court techniques KL230; 345.3

Court of Appeal Civil Division [Table V: 1]
UF: Civil Division + Court of Appeal

Court of Appeal Criminal Division [Table V: 1]
UF: Criminal Division + Court of Appeal
RT: Court of Criminal Appeal [Table V:1]

Court of Auditors + EU + publications KW31

Court of Common Pleas [Table V: 5.9.C6]
UF: Common Pleas Court

Court of Criminal Appeal [Table V:1]
RT: Court of Appeal Criminal Division [Table V: 1]

Court of First Instance
USE: General Court KW94

Court of Justice of the EU
USE: European Court of Justice KC1240; 341.724; KW93

Court of Protection [Table V: 7.8]

Court of Session [Table V: 1]
UF: Scotland + Court of Session

court officials KL255; 345.55
UF: clerks of the court

court practice
USE: trial practice KN389; 347.96

court records
USE: public records KN184.5; 347.4455; [Table IIA: 122.5]

court reporting
USE: law reporting KL33; 345.13

court rolls KF51

court rules KN360; 347.92; [Table VI: .Z72]
UF: rules of court

court rules + criminal procedure KM571; 346.9.Z72

court techniques KL230; 345.3
RT: court management KL230; 345.3; [Table IIA: 69.2]

court-annexed arbitration KN398.2; 347.982

courts KL220; 345.3; [Table IIA: 69]; [Table V]
UF: law courts

courts + computers
USE: computers + courts KL230.61; 345.361

courts + congestion
USE: congestion + court management KL230.42; 345.342

courts + facilities KL230.74; 345.374

courts + interpreters
USE: interpreters + courts KL230.5; 345.35

courts + reorganisation KL230.2; 345.32

courts + vacations
USE: vacations KL230.18; 345.318

courts-martial KM405; 346.74
UF: military courts
UF: naval courts

covenants + contract KN13.4; 347.114

covenants + leases KN87.4; 347.3294

covenants + taxation KM336.69.C6; 346.5269.C6

CPS
USE: Crown Prosecution Service KL253; 345.53

creation of leases
USE: leases + creation KN87.1; 347.3291

creation of trusts
USE: trusts + creation KN213; 347.541

credibility KN393.2; 347.9642

credibility + criminal evidence KM602.5; 346.9625

credit KN305; 347.75
UF: creditors

credit + agriculture KN98.3; 347.353
UF: agricultural credit

credit + international law KC226; 341.414

credit cards KN303.14; 347.7214
RT: debit cards KN303.14; 347.7214

credit transfers KN303.4.C7; 347.724.C7

credit unions KN305.6; 347.766

creditors
USE: credit KN305; 347.75

cremation KN97.3; 347.346

crematoria KN97.31; 347.3461

Cretan law (ancient) KE29.C7; 343.29.C7

crews + international maritime law KC273; 341.476

crews + shipping KN332.1; 347.8321

crime + aircraft KC213.3; 341.3533
UF: air piracy
UF: hijacking + aircraft
RT: aircraft + hijacking KC213.3; 341.3533

crime + high seas KC213.2; 341.3532
RT: piracy + international law KC213.2; 341.3532

crime + outer space KC213.4; 341.3534

crime + victims KM593; 346.947
UF: victims of crime

crime prevention KM612; 346.982; [App: 20]
UF: prevention of crime

crimes KM540; 346.85; [Table IIA: 91]
UF: wrongs

crimes + companies
USE: corporate crime KN264.8; 347.6268

crimes + international law KC215; 341.36
UF: international crimes
RT: international criminal courts KC219; 341.39

crimes against humanity KC215; 341.36

crimes without victims
USE: victimless crime KM540.8; 346.858

criminal anthropology [App: 11]

criminal appeals KM595; 346.95
UF: appeals + criminal law

criminal codes
SN: use as a subdivision only

criminal courts [Table V: 4]

criminal courts + international law KC219; 341.39

criminal damage KM549; 346.874
UF: damage + criminal law
UF: malicious damage
RT: vandalism KM549; 346.874

Criminal Division + Court of Appeal
USE: Court of Appeal Criminal Division [Table V: 1]

Criminal Injuries Compensation Board KM594.8; 346.9488

criminal intent
USE: mens rea KM505.1; 346.821

criminal investigation
USE: investigation + criminal law KM580.1; 346.911

criminal jurisdiction KM573; 346.901

criminal jurisdiction + international law KC212; 341.352

criminal law KM500; 346.8; [Table IIA: 90]
UF: penal law

criminal law + EU KW133

criminal law + international law KC210; 341.35
UF: international criminal law

criminal law + religious law [KD Table: 6]

criminal law : morality KM504; 346.818
UF: enforcement of morality
UF: law : morality
UF: morality : criminal law
UF: purpose of criminal law

criminal law : tort KM502; 346.81
UF: tort : criminal law

criminal liability KM505; 346.82; [Table IIA: 90.3]
UF: accountability + criminal
UF: aggravated circumstances
UF: extenuation
UF: liability for crime

criminal libel
USE: libel + criminal law KM541.4; 346.8612

criminal negligence
USE: negligence + criminal law KM505.6; 346.826

criminal procedure KM570; 346.9; [Table IIA: 93]
RT: procedure KN350; 347.9; [Table IIA: 144]; [Table VI: .Z71]

criminal procedure + EU KW133.5

criminal records KM617; 346.986; [Table IIA: 92.4]

criminal records + evidence KM603.5; 346.9635

criminal statistics KM620; 346.9865
UF: statistics of crime
RT: statistics KL300; 345.7; [Table IIA: 72]; [Table VIII: .0024]

criminal trials + popular accounts KB65; 340.45

criminally insane + prisons KM655.Q53; 346.98715.Q53; [App: 85.Q53]

criminals [App: 05]

criminology [App]

criminology + history [App: 01]

criminology + statistics [App: 02]

crisis management + international disputes KC1202; 341.702
UF: international crises

critical legal studies KA59; 340.149

crofts KN98.12; 347.3513
RT: farms KN98; 347.35

crops KN99.2; 347.3562

cross examination
USE: examination + witnesses KN391.3; 347.9623

crowd control + sports grounds KM562.13; 346.88313
UF: pitch invasions
RT: sports grounds + offences KM562.13; 346.88313

Crown
USE: government KM231; 346.37; [Table IIA: 83]
USE: monarchy KM41; 346.125
USE: state KM31; 346.1

Crown + succession
USE: royal succession KM112.1; 346.252

crown courts [Table V: 4.2]

crown courts + criminal procedure KM571.42; 346.90042

Crown immunities + civil procedure KN378.3.C7; 347.938.3.C7

Crown immunities + criminal law KM114.9; 346.279
UF: immunities + Crown

Crown Office (England & Wales) [Table V: 2.5]

Crown privilege KN394.8; 347.9658

crown proceedings
USE: government actions KN378.3.G6; 347.938.3.G6

Crown Prosecution Service KL253; 345.53
UF: CPS

cruelty + animals
USE: offences against animals KM565.A5; 346.89.A5

cruelty + marriage
USE: matrimonial offences KN173.12; 347.4242

CSCE
USE: Conference on Security and Co-operation in Europe KC1136; 341.6895

cultivation of land
USE: agricultural law KN98; 347.35; [Table IIA: 107.6]

cultural defences + administration of justice KM584.9.C8; 346.9349.C8

cultural groups [Table VII: 4.4]

cultural heritage + intellectual property KN112.9.C8; 347.376.C8

cultural organisations
USE: heritage organisations [Table VII: 9.6]

cultural property + international law KC236.4; 341.434

cultural property + war
USE: art works + war KC1357.2; 341.8282

cultural rights KM201.5; 346.3505

culture + EU KW144.3

culture + treaties KC336.5; 341.585

Cuneiform laws KE22; 343.22

curfews + punishment [App: 69.3]

Curia Regis rolls KF51.C9

curiosities
USE: humorous writings KB34; 340.374

currency + conversion
USE: exchange rates KN302.3; 347.713

currency + forgery
USE: counterfeiting + crime KM564.1; 346.8861

currency + integration + EU
USE: single currency + EU KW106

currency markets KN302.35; 347.7135
UF: foreign currency + markets

Current Law KF85.C9

curriculum + education KN184.15; 347.44315

curriculum + legal education KL131–149 [Table: .3]; 345.1794–9 [Table: 3]

custody + children KN173.8; 347.4258

custody + police KM580.35; 346.9135
UF: police custody

customary law KL8; 345.08; [Table IIA: 62]
UF: aboriginal law
UF: law and custom
UF: native law
UF: time immemorial
UF: tribal law
UF: usage and custom
RT: aboriginals [Table VII: 4.3]

customary law + comparative law KB130; 340.58

customary law + international law
USE: international custom KC82.1; 341.193

Customs and Excise
USE: Revenue and Customs KM235.R4; 346.38.R4

customs duties KM337.71; 346.581
UF: import duties
UF: tariffs (customs duties)
RT: smuggling KM564.3; 346.8863

customs duties + EU KW109.2

customs duties + international law KC225; 341.413

customs unions KC225.1; 341.4131

customs unions + EU KW109.2

cy-pres doctrine KN215.3; 347.5563

cybercrime KM540.7; 346.857

cycling
USE: bicycles KN323.2; 347.8134

Cynulliad Cenedlaethol Cymru KM82.A15; 346.21.A15
SN: English name is National Assembly for Wales

dairy produce KN99.35; 347.35635

dairy produce + EU KW117.3.D3

damage + accidents
USE: accidental damage KN39.A3; 347.29.A3

damage + criminal law
USE: criminal damage KM549; 346.874

damage + latency
USE: latent damage KN33.3; 347.213

damage + military occupation KC1404; 341.874
UF: military occupation + damage

damages KN37.1; 347.231; [Table VI: .Z8]

dams
USE: flood control KN90.3; 347.3333

dangerous chemicals
USE: dangerous things KN186.9.D3; 347.459.D3

dangerous driving KM565.D7; 346.89.D7
RT: careless driving KM565.D7; 346.89.D7
RT: reckless driving KM565.D7; 346.89.D7

dangerous drugs
USE: drugs + offences KM565.D7; 346.89.D7

dangerous machinery KN198.2; 347.492

dangerous occupations KN193.65; 347.4765

dangerous offenders [App: 06.06]

dangerous products + EU KW112.6

dangerous things KN186.9.D3; 347.459.D3
UF: dangerous chemicals
UF: flammable goods
UF: inflammable goods
RT: hazardous substances KN97.8; 347.348
RT: labelling KN284.2; 347.662
RT: poisons KN186.9.P6; 347.459.P6
RT: toxic waste KN97.83; 347.3483

dangerous things + tort KN39.D3; 347.29.D3

dangerous waste
USE: toxic waste KN97.83; 347.3483

Danube Commission KC1131; 341.6893

data + processing KN286.D3; 347.679.D3

data + protection + computing KN347.9; 347.896

data + protection + human rights KM209.P7; 346.368.P7

data + security + computers
UF: encryption + computers KN348.8; 347.8978

data + storage + computers KN347.6; 347.895

databases + EU KW147

date due + payment of tax KM336.912; 346.52912

day centres KN182.4; 347.4424

day release
USE: technical education KN184.3; 347.444

Dayabhaga KD712; 342.812

daylight saving
USE: time KN186.9.T5; 347.459.T5

de facto recognition
USE: recognition + international law KC164; 341.274

de facto relationships KN174; 347.4259
RT: cohabitation KN174; 347.4259; [Table IIA: 117.6]
RT: common law marriage KN172.9.C6; 347.422.C6
RT: unmarried couples KN174; 347.4259

de jure recognition
USE: recognition + international law KC164; 341.274

de-alignment + international relations KC317; 341.537

deaf persons KN181.9.Q51.D4; 347.4419.Q51.D4; [Table VII: .Q51.D4]
RT: disabled persons [Table VII: 5]

death KN185.15; 347.44615
UF: brain death
UF: determination of death
RT: inquests KM580.17; 346.9117
RT: presumption of death KN127.1; 347.3841
RT: registration + deaths KM172.31; 346.3131

death + custody KM615.75; 346.98575

death + registration
USE: registration + deaths KM172.31; 346.3131

death duties
USE: inheritance taxes KM337.33; 346.553

debates + international organisations [Table before KC351: 2]
UF: international organisations + debates

debentures KN304.3; 347.733

debit cards KN303.14; 347.7214
RT: credit cards KN303.14; 347.7214

debt collection KN305.11; 347.7511

debtors
USE: credit KN305; 347.75

debts KN305.1; 347.751

debts + administration of estates KN142.2; 347.3922

debts + international law KC223; 341.411

debts + land tenure KN76.D4; 347.323.D4

decedents' estates KN140; 347.39
RT: probate KN127; 347.384

decedents' estates + procedure KN377.D4; 347.937.D4

deceit
USE: deception + criminal law KM547.2; 346.8722

deception + criminal law KM547.2; 346.8722
UF: deceit
UF: trickery

deception + tort KN38.4; 347.26

decision making KM141.4; 346.284

decisions [Table VI: .Z9]

declaration + trusts KN213.2; 347.543

declaration of title KN108.4; 347.3684

declaration of war KC1355.2; 341.822
UF: war + declaration

declaratory judgments KN233; 347.593

decorations (medals)
USE: honours KM114.5; 346.275

decorations + landlord and tenant KN88.5; 347.32995

decrees + divorce KN173.5; 347.4255

decriminalisation KM503.8; 346.8158

deductions + earnings KN194.9; 347.4789

deductions + taxation KM336.6; 346.526
UF: tax deductions

deeds KN72.1; 347.3215

defamation KN38.2; 347.248

default judgments KN395.5; 347.973
UF: default of appearance

defence + EU KW79

defence + information
USE: official secrets KM233.7; 346.3737

defence + military action KM233.1; 346.3731

defence information
USE: official secrets KM233.7; 346.3737

defence lawyers [Table VI: .Z62]

defence secrets
USE: espionage KM561.3; 346.8813
USE: espionage + war + international law KC1355.5; 341.825
USE: official secrets KM233.7; 346.3737

defences + civil procedure KN384; 347.944

defences + criminal procedure KM584; 346.934

defendants KM579; 346.905; [Table VI: .Z62]
UF: accused persons
RT: offenders KM587.1; 346.9371

definitions by judges
USE: judicial definitions KL41; 345.1691

delays + court management KL230.42; 345.342

delegated legislation
USE: subordinate legislation KM302; 346.42; [Table IA: 20]

delegation of powers KM302; 346.42

delimitation + electoral districts
USE: constituencies KM83.2; 346.222

delivery KN108.3; 347.3683

demergers + taxation
USE: mergers + taxation KM336.493; 346.52493

demilitarised zones KC174; 341.284

democracy KM39; 346.1235

demography + EU KW126

demolition KN96.25; 347.34325

demurrage KN337.5; 347.8375

denaturalisation KM174.5; 346.325

denaturalisation + international law KC192; 341.312
UF: deprivation of nationality
UF: loss of citizenship
RT: naturalisation KM174; 346.32

dentists KN185.18.D4; 347.44618.D4

Department for Work and Pensions KM235.W6; 346.38.W6

dependants [Table VII: 3]

dependent states KC154; 341.264

deportation KM177.5; 346.337
UF: repatriation

deportation + international law KC197; 341.317

deportation + punishment [App: 63]

depositions KN392.2; 347.9632

depositions + criminal procedure KM605.4; 346.974

depository libraries
USE: legal deposit KN184.6; 347.4456

deposits + banking KN303.11; 347.7211

deposits + conveyancing KN74.3; 347.32233

depravity
USE: obscenity KM565.O2; 346.89.O2

deprivation of nationality
USE: denaturalisation + international law KC192; 341.312

deregulation KM301; 346.41

derivatives + investment KN304.6; 347.736

descendants [Table VII: 3.7]

descent KN131; 347.386

desecration
USE: sacrilege KM550; 346.875

deserters + international law KC1355.7; 341.826

desertion + armed forces
USE: military crimes KM409; 346.749

desertion + marriage
USE: matrimonial offences KN173.12; 347.4242

design + court buildings KL230.73; 345.373

design + motor vehicles KN323.11; 347.8132

design + standards KN284.7; 347.667

design right KN114.4; 347.3774
RT: copyright KN112; 347.371

designs + international law KC236.5; 341.435

desktop publishing K105.1; 340.0651
UF: DTP
RT: electronic publishing K105.1; 340.0651

detection
USE: investigation + criminal law KM580.1; 346.911

detention [App: 64]

detention centres + illegal immigrants KM177.35; 346.33655

determinable interests KN64.3; 347.3166

determination of death
USE: death KN185.15; 347.44615

deterrence + punishment [App: 50.22]

detinue KN38.72; 347.277

devaluation KN302.2; 347.712
RT: exchange rates KN302.3; 347.713

developing countries + EU KW76

developing countries + international relations KC309.5; 341.5195
UF: third world
UF: underdeveloped countries
RT: development : law KA70.D4; 340.16.D4

development
USE: research (academic) KN184.7; 347.4457

development + EU KW77.2

development + international law KC228; 341.4154
UF: aid to developing countries
UF: development aid

development : law KA70.D4; 340.16.D4
UF: development aid
RT: developing countries + international relations KC309.5; 341.5195

development aid
USE: development + international law KC228; 341.4154
USE: development : law KA70.D4; 340.16.D4

development gains + taxation KM337.68; 346.578

development grants KM334; 346.518
UF: government development grants
UF: regional employment premiums

devolution + constitutional law KM366; 346.66

devolution + probate KN141; 347.391

diaries KB15; 340.33

dictators KM112.7; 346.257

dictionaries K120; 340.08; [Table VIII: 0023]
RT: legal dictionaries K120; 340.08; [Table IIA: 63]

dictionaries + Latin K122.L3; 340.082.L3
UF: Latin dictionaries K122.L3; 340.082.L3

dictionaries + polyglot K121; 340.081
UF: polyglot dictionaries

Digesta (Corpus Juris Civilis) KE152; 343.473

digests [Table IA: 50; 51]

digests + Australia (federal) KH50

digests + Canada (federal) KG50

digests + England and Wales KF80

digests + EU KW8

digests + international law KC50; 341.15

digests + US (federal) KG380

digital forensics KM608.3.D5; 346.9793.D5

digital signatures KN348.83; 347.89783
RT: electronic signatures KN285.43; 347.6743

dilapidations KN88.4; 347.32994

diligences KN395.27; 347.9727

diminished responsibility KM506.3; 346.8293

diplomacy KC320; 341.54
RT: negotiation + international disputes KC1290.1; 341.761

diplomatic districts
USE: diplomatic quarters KC322.2; 341.5422

diplomatic immunities KC322; 341.542
UF: immunities + diplomats

diplomatic information services KC328; 341.555

diplomatic negotiations
USE: negotiation + international disputes KC1290.1; 341.761

diplomatic privileges KC322; 341.542
UF: privileges + diplomacy

diplomatic protection KC196; 341.316
UF: citizens abroad + protection
UF: protection of citizens abroad

diplomatic quarters KC322.2; 341.5422
UF: diplomatic districts
UF: embassies
RT: legations + buildings KC322.1; 341.5421

diplomatic recognition
USE: recognition + international law KC164; 341.274

diplomatic relations + suspension
USE: suspension + diplomatic relations KC1304; 341.784

diplomats KC323; 341.55

diplomats + directories KC75; 341.175

direct access to barristers
USE: barristers + direct access KL94; 345.173

direct evidence KN393.6; 347.9646

direct evidence + criminal procedure KM602.6; 346.9626

direct legislation
USE: referendums KM56; 346.136

direct taxation KM336.19; 346.5219

directions + juries KN389.64; 347.96064
UF: judges + directions to juries

directions + juries + criminal procedure KM583.4; 346.9334
UF: judges + directions to juries + criminal procedure

directories K150; 340.09; [Table VIII: 0022]
UF: law lists

directories (non-legal) K180; 340.098

directors + disclosure of interests
USE: disclosure of interests + company directors KN264.75; 347.62675

directors of companies
USE: company directors KN264; 347.626; [Table IIA: 129.3]

disability + evaluation + industrial law KN198.8; 347.498

disability + pensions
USE: disabled persons + pensions KN181.2; 347.4412

disabled legislators KM87.5; 346.2485

disabled persons [Table VII: 5]
UF: handicapped persons
RT: blind persons KN181.9.Q51.B5; 347.4419.Q51.B5
RT: deaf persons KN181.9.Q51.D4; 347.4419.Q51.D4; [Table VII: .Q51.D4]

disabled persons + allowances + taxation KM336.61; 346.5261

disabled persons + EU KW129.4

disabled persons + pensions KN181.2; 347.4412
UF: disability + pensions
RT: mobility allowances KN181.2; 347.4412

disabled persons + social security KN181.2; 347.4412
UF: invalidity benefits

disabled persons + transport KN181.2; 347.4412
UF: invalid carriages
UF: motability

disappearances + crimes + international law KC218.D5; 341.369.D5
UF: secret killing + international law

disarmament + international law KC313; 341.533
RT: arms limitation + international law KC313.5; 341.5335
RT: bacteriological weapons + international law KC1395.5; 341.8655
RT: chemical weapons + international law KC1395.1; 341.8651
RT: firearms + international law KC1391; 341.861
RT: nuclear weapons + international law KC1392; 341.862

disarmament + treaties
USE: arms limitation + treaties KC336.1; 341.581

Disarmament Commission KC448; 341.627

disaster relief **KN181.6;** **347.4416**
UF: emergency relief
UF: natural disasters

disbarment
USE: admission to the Bar KL83; 345.1703
USE: licensing + lawyers KL83; 345.1703

disbursements
USE: costs KN397; 347.977; [Table IIA: 150]

discharge + contracts **KN16;** **347.14**

discharge + patients **KN185.124;** **347.446124**

discharge + prisons **KM685;** **346.988;** **[App: 76]**
UF: prison discharges

discharged prisoners **KM690;** **346.9885;** **[App: 79]**
UF: prisoners + discharge

discipline + industrial law **KN192.5;** **347.4655**
UF: employment + discipline
UF: rules + employment

discipline + judiciary **KL240.3;** **345.43**
UF: judicial discipline
UF: judiciary + discipline

discipline + legislators **KM84.7;** **346.2347**
UF: parliamentary discipline

discipline + police **KM615.8;** **346.9858**
UF: police discipline

discipline + prisons **KM670;** **346.9873**
UF: prison discipline

discipline + prisons + regulations **KM662;** **346.9873;** **[App: 92.3]**

discipline + schools KN184.25; 347.44325
UF: school discipline

disclosure KN386; 347.946
UF: discovery
UF: notice to admit

disclosure + consumer protection KN284.1; 347.661

disclosure + contracts KN15.7; 347.137

disclosure + criminal procedure KM581.4; 346.924

disclosure + public interest KN384.95; 347.94495

disclosure of information KN392; 347.963
UF: information + disclosure

disclosure of information + employment KN192.29; 347.4639
UF: public disclosure + employment
UF: whistle-blowing

disclosure of interests + company directors KN264.75; 347.62675
UF: company directors + disclosure of interests
UF: directors + disclosure of interests

disclosure of interests + shareholders KN263.71; 347.62571
UF: shareholders + disclosure of interests

disclosure of tax avoidance schemes KM336.77; 346.5277

disclosures + public interest + criminal procedure KM584.4; 346.9344

discontinuance KN388.1; 347.951
UF: withdrawal of actions

discontinuance + criminal procedure
USE: nolle prosequi KM582.5; 346.9325

discovery
USE: disclosure KN386; 347.946

discovery + criminal procedure
USE: disclosure + criminal procedure KM581.4; 346.924

discovery + territory KC142.2; 341.2522

discretionary trusts KN214.6; 347.5556

discrimination KM208; 346.36

discrimination + industrial law KN191.2; 347.4612
UF: anti-discrimination
RT: minorities KM208; 346.36; [Table VII: 4]

discrimination + international law KC204; 341.334

disease + control KN185.6; 347.4486
UF: control of disease

disease + reporting
USE: notifiable diseases KN185.6; 347.4486

disease prevention + EU KW149.1

disease transmission + crimes KM565.D5; 346.89.D5

diseases + industrial law KN198.4; 347.494
UF: industrial diseases

disincorporation KN262.4; 347.6244

dismantling of nations
USE: transfer of sovereignty KC161; 341.271

dismissal + employment law KN192.24; 347.4634

disobedience
USE: civil disobedience KA65; 340.155

dispensations + marriage
USE: marriage + impediments KN172.3; 347.4213

displaced persons + international law KC205; 341.335

disposal rates + court management KL230.421; 345.3421

disposition + criminal evidence KM604.952; 346.96752

disposition + evidence KN391.62; 347.96262

dispute resolution KN398.6; 347.986
UF: alternative dispute resolution

dispute resolution + international law KC1205; 341.705

disputes + industrial law KN196; 347.486

disqualification + judges KL240.3; 345.43

disqualification + legislators KM83.1; 346.221
UF: legislative disqualification

dissolution + insolvency KN312.6; 347.7926

dissolution + legislatures KM84.4; 346.234
UF: parliamentary dissolution

dissolution + partnerships KN267.7; 347.6367
UF: partnerships + dissolution

distance learning + legal education KL131–149 [Table: .47]; 345.1794–9 [Table: 47]

distilling
USE: alcohol KN186.4; 347.454

distilling + crime
USE: excise offences KM564.4; 346.8864

distinguishment KL32.5; 345.125

distress + landlord and tenant KN88.13; 347.329913
RT: rent KN88.1; 347.32991

distress + social services
USE: public welfare KN181; 347.44

distribution + competition + EU KW110.7

distribution + probate KN142.3; 347.3923

distribution of business + court management KL230.43; 345.343

distributions + companies
USE: dividends KN263.64; 347.62564

District Attorneys + US KL253; 345.53
RT: public prosecutors KL253; 345.53

District Courts [Table V: 4.3]

District Judges + UK KL241.32; 345.4632

district nurses KN182.3; 347.4423
RT: community care KN182; 347.442; [Table IIA: 121.5]
RT: home-based services KN182.3; 347.4423

District Registrars KL241.21; 345.4621

District Registries [Table V: 5.1]

districts + court management KL230.32; 345.332
RT: circuits + court management KL230.3; 345.33

districts + local government KM365.5; 346.655
UF: local government districts
UF: rural districts
UF: urban districts

disturbances + prisons KM671.3; 346.9874993; [App: 92.53]

divers KN334.3; 347.8343

diversity + judiciary KL240.12; 345.412

divided profession
USE: legal profession + structure KL84; 345.1704

dividend stripping
USE: bond washing KN304.9; 347.739

dividends KN263.64; 347.62564
UF: company distributions
UF: distributions + companies

dividends + tax deducted at source KM336.94; 346.5294

dividends + taxation KM336.35; 346.5235
SN: covers theory and principles

dividends + taxes KM337.24; 346.544

division of states KC163; 341.273

divorce KN173.1; 347.424; [Table IIA: 117.4]
RT: alimony KN173.2; 347.4245

divorce + effect on children KN176.9.D5; 347.4269.D5
UF: children + effect of divorce

divorce + financial consequences KN173.2; 347.4245

divorce + financial relief KN173.2; 347.4245

divorce + religious laws KD30.84; 342.1884

divorce by agreement KN173.29.A3; 347.42459.A3

divorce courts [Table V: 7]

divorced persons [Table VII: 3.3]

DNA profiling KN185.52.D6; 347.4482.D6

DNA profiling + criminal procedure KM604.333; 346.96463

DNA profiling + paternity
USE: paternity tests KN176.35; 347.42635

dock briefs KM599.1; 346.9591

docks KN336; 347.836

doctors KN185.18.D6; 347.44618.D6
UF: physicians
UF: surgeons

doctrine + religious laws [KD Table: 5]

documentary credits KN306.42; 347.7742

documentary films
USE: films + intellectual property KN112.3; 347.374

documents + criminal evidence KM604.4; 346.965

documents + drafting
USE: drafting + documents KL34.2; 345.142; [Table VIII: .0051]

documents + evidence KN392; 347.963
RT: disclosure KN386; 347.946

documents + history
USE: archives KN184.5; 347.4455

documents + interpretation KL35.2; 345.152
UF: legal instruments + interpretation

documents + privilege KN386.5; 347.9465
UF: privileged documents

dog racing
USE: racing KN186.64; 347.4564

dole
USE: unemployment + social security KN181.3; 347.4413

domain names KN114.8; 347.3778

Domesday Book KL401.3; 345.9423

domestic animals
USE: animals + control KN186.8; 347.458

domestic employment KN193.53; 347.4753

domestic relations
USE: family law KN170; 347.42; [Table IIA: 116]

domestic violence KN175; 347.42597; [Table IIA: 117.7]
UF: battered wives
UF: family violence
RT: assault KM543; 346.863
RT: matrimonial offences KN173.12; 347.4242
RT: refuges + domestic violence KN175.2; 347.425972

domicile + choice KC2067; 341.952
UF: choice of domicile

domicile + conflict of laws KC2065; 341.95
UF: residence + conflict of laws

domicile + taxation KM336.12; 346.5212
RT: residence + taxation KM336.12; 346.5212

dominance + competition
USE: abuse of dominant position KN266.5; 347.6345

donations + personal property
USE: gifts + personal property KN104.3; 347.3643

donations + taxation
USE: gifts + taxation KM337.31; 346.551

doorstep selling KN285.9.D6; 347.678.D6
UF: cold calling

double jeopardy KM579.2; 346.907
UF: former jeopardy

double nationality
USE: dual nationality KM178; 346.338

double summer time
USE: time KN186.9.T5; 347.459.T5

double taxation KM336.15; 346.5215

double taxation + international law KC224.1; 341.4121

dowry KN58.2; 347.3052
RT: marriage settlements KN58.2; 347.3052

draft (US)
USE: conscription KM402; 346.715

drafting + documents KL34.2; 345.142; [Table VIII: .0051]
UF: composition + documents
UF: documents + drafting
UF: draftsmanship
UF: legal drafting
RT: legal composition K101; 340.061

drafting + legislation KL34.1; 345.141
UF: legislative drafting

drafts + negotiable instruments KN306.6; 347.776

draftsmanship
USE: drafting + documents KL34.2; 345.142; [Table VIII: .0051]

Drago doctrine KC223.1; 341.4111

drainage + land resources KN90.3; 347.3333

drainage basins KC144.5; 341.2545
UF: international drainage basins
RT: rivers KN90.1; 347.3331

drama KB32; 340.372
RT: fiction (novels) KB33; 340.373
RT: legal writing K100; 340.06
RT: poetry KB32; 340.372

drawings KB35; 340.375
RT: illustrations + intellectual property KN112.2; 347.373

drivers KN323.5; 347.8135
RT: driving licences KN323.5; 347.8135

drivers + railways
USE: train drivers KN325.5; 347.8155

driving licences KN323.5; 347.8135
UF: licences + drivers
RT: drivers KN323.5; 347.8135

driving offences KM565.D7; 346.89.D7
RT: traffic offences KM565.T7; 346.89.T7

dropping litter
USE: litter KN97.85; 347.3485

drug offences + prisons KM681.33; 346.987633; [App: 93.33]

drugs + causes of crime [App: 16]

drugs + criminal liability KM505.4; 346.824

drugs + dependency KN185.81; 347.44881
RT: rehabilitation + drugs KN185.81; 347.44881

drugs + international law KC241.1; 341.4411

drugs + medicine KN185.8; 347.4488
UF: analgesics
UF: medicines
UF: pharmaceutical drugs

drugs + offences KM565.D7; 346.89.D7
UF: controlled drugs
UF: dangerous drugs
UF: narcotics
UF: prohibited drugs
RT: alcohol KN186.4; 347.454

drunken driving KM565.D7; 346.89.D7

drunkenness KM562.4; 346.8834
UF: intoxication

DTP
USE: desktop publishing K105.1; 340.0651

dual nationality KM178; 346.338
UF: double nationality
UF: plural nationality

dual nationality + international law KC193; 341.313

due diligence + banks KN303.955; 347.72955

due process of law
USE: rule of law KM34; 346.121

duelling KM543.9; 346.8639

dumping KN253.2; 347.614
UF: anti-dumping

dumping + EU KW78.3

dumping + international law KC235; 341.425

duress + contract KN15.6; 347.136

duress + criminal liability KM505.3; 346.823
UF: coercion
UF: compulsion
UF: force majeure
UF: threats

duties + arbitrators KN398.13; 347.9813

duties + company directors KN264.7; 347.6267

duties + trustees KN216.3; 347.563

duty of care KN33.31; 347.2131

duty solicitors scheme KM599.2; 346.9592

duty to accept work KL82.5; 345.17025
UF: cab rank rule
RT: barristers KL86; 345.1711

duty-free importation KM337.73; 346.583

dying declarations KN394.2; 347.9652

dying declarations + criminal evidence KM605.7; 346.977

e-commerce
USE: electronic commerce KN285.4; 347.674

e-mail
USE: electronic mail KN342.4; 347.864

earnings KN194.1; 347.4781
SN: actual amounts earned
UF: emoluments
UF: salaries

UF: wages
RT: bonuses KN194.3; 347.4783
RT: remuneration KN194; 347.478

earnings + civil service KM237.5; 346.3825

earnings + EU + statistics + journals KW66.31

earnings + tax deducted at source KM336.93; 346.5293

earnings + taxation KM336.31; 346.5231

earnings abroad
USE: foreign earnings + taxation KM336.33; 346.5233

easements KN65.1; 347.3171
UF: encumbrances

East Asia + international relations KC303.1; 341.5131
UF: Far East + international relations

Eastern Empire (600 AD to 1453 AD)
USE: Byzantine law KE251; 343.5

Eastern Europe + international relations KC305.1; 341.5151

Eastern Europe : EU KW81.13

eastern law : western law KB122; 340.56
UF: western law : eastern law

Eastern non-orthodox churches KD200; 342.4

EC
USE: European Union KC1001; 341.68; KW

EC Treaty
USE: Treaty of Rome (1971) KW1.F71

ecclesiastical courts
USE: religious courts [KD Table: 9]

ecology KN95.5; 347.3425

Economic and Social Committee + EU KW91

Economic and Social Committee + EU + publications KW25

Economic and Social Council + United Nations KC431; 341.625

economic development + international law KC237; 341.437

economic factors + causes of crime [App: 13]

economic organisations + international law
USE: international economic law KC220; 341.4
USE: international economic organisations KC349.E2; 341.619.E2

economic policy KM331.2; 346.502
UF: monetary control
UF: monetary policy

economic policy + EU KW104

economic torts KN39.E3; 347.29.E3

economic zones + national waters KC144.3; 341.2543
UF: exclusive economic zones + national waters

economics + dictionaries K126.E2; 340.086.E2

economics : law KA70.E2; 340.16.E2

economy + EU + statistics + journals KW66.2

ECSC
USE: European Coal and Steel Community KC1021; 341.68; KW42

ECU
USE: European Currency Unit KW106.2

ecumenical movement KD109.1; 342.3091

EDF
USE: European Development Fund KW77.4

EDI
USE: electronic data interchange KC257.6; 341.4626

education KN184; 347.443; [Table IIA: 122]
RT: legal education KL130; 345.18; [Table IIA: 65]
RT: training KN184; 347.443

education + comparative law KB222; 340.60774

education + EU KW143

education + EU + statistics + journals KW66.33

education + judiciary KL240.5; 345.45
RT: legal education KL130; 345.18; [Table IIA: 65]
RT: training + judiciary KL240.5; 345.45

education + prisoners KM681.6; 346.98766; [App: 93.6]

education : law KA70.E3; 340.16.E3

educational broadcasting KN344.3; 347.8714

EEIG
USE: European Economic Interest Grouping KW118.1

effects
SN: use as subdivision only

Egyptian law (pre-Hellenistic) KE27; 343.27
UF: pre-Hellenistic Egyptian law

eighteenth century European law
USE: European law + 18th century KE380; 343.78

elderly
USE: older people [Table VII: 1.6]

elected representatives + local government KM367; 346.667
RT: local councillors KM367; 346.667

election + equity KN221.2; 347.582

election + heads of state KM112.8; 346.258

elections + legislatures KM83.4; 346.224
UF: national elections
UF: parliamentary elections

elections + local government KM369; 346.679
UF: local elections

elections + trade unions KN195.53; 347.4843
UF: trade union elections

electoral districts
USE: constituencies KM83.2; 346.222

electorate
USE: suffrage KM83.2; 346.223

electric chair [App: 61.9.E4]

electricity KN89.44; 347.33144
UF: power stations
RT: public utilities KN275.P8; 347.645.P8

electricity + EU KW122.7

electronic banking KN303.2; 347.722

electronic commerce KN285.4; 347.674
UF: e-commerce

electronic conveyancing KN75.E4; 347.3229.E4

electronic data interchange KC257.6; 341.4626
UF: EDI

electronic filing systems + courts KL230.69.E4; 345.369.E4

electronic mail KN342.4; 347.864
UF: e-mail
UF: email
RT: internet + international law KC257.7; 341.4627

electronic mail + evidence KM604.43; 346.9653

electronic mail + international law KC257.7; 341.4627

electronic publishing K105.1; 340.0651
RT: desktop publishing K105.1; 340.0651

electronic publishing + communications KN345.5; 347.885

electronic publishing + copyright KN112.6; 347.3756

electronic records + court documents KN392.6; 347.9636

electronic signatures KN285.43; 347.6743
RT: digital signatures KN348.83; 347.89783

electronic tagging [App: 69.4]

electronics industry + EU KW119.6

elementary treatment [Table VIII: 0085]

email
USE: electronic mail KN342.4; 347.864

embargoes + international disputes KC1311; 341.791
UF: boycotts + international law
RT: sanctions + international disputes KC1312; 341.792

embassies
USE: diplomatic quarters KC322.2; 341.5422

embezzlement KM547.1; 346.8721
UF: fraudulent conversion

embryo transfer KN172.82; 347.42182

emergencies KM233.3; 346.3733
SN: political and economic emergencies

emergency brake + EU KW97.522

emergency relief
USE: disaster relief KN181.6; 347.4416

emergency services KM234; 346.3739
RT: police KM615; 346.985; [Table IIA: 92.2]
RT: rescue services KM234; 346.3739

emigration
USE: migration KM176; 346.33

emigration + international law
USE: migration + international law KC199; 341.319

eminent domain
USE: expropriation KN56.6; 347.3036

emoluments
USE: earnings KN194.1; 347.4781

employee consultation KN192.8; 347.468

employee share schemes KN194.3; 347.4783

employee share schemes + taxation KM336.69.E4; 346.5269.E4

employees + state
USE: civil service KM237; 346.382; [Table IIA: 83.3]

employees + tied accommodation
USE: tied accommodation KN88.25; 347.329925

employers' associations KN195.18; 347.4818
RT: associations KN169.4; 347.41894; [Table VII: 9.4]; [Table VIII: .003]

employers' liability KN198.1; 347.491
RT: strict liability + criminal law KM505.9; 346.828

employment KN192; 347.462

employment + appointment KN192.11; 347.4622

employment + discipline
USE: discipline + industrial law KN192.5; 347.4655

employment + EU KW130

employment + EU + statistics + journals KW66.31

employment + onerous terms KN193.8; 347.4775
UF: off-day working
UF: onerous monitoring + employment
UF: working on days off

employment agencies KN197.2; 347.4872

employment contracts KN192.1; 347.4621

employment protection KN192.2; 347.463
UF: security of employment

employment services KN197.1; 347.4871

EMS
USE: European Monetary System KW106.1

encryption + computers KN348.8; 347.8978
USE: data + security + computers

encumbrances
USE: easements KN65.1; 347.3171

encyclopedias K140; 340.089; [Table VIII: 0023]
UF: legal encyclopedias

encyclopedias + common law KL42; 345.1692

encyclopedias + EU law KW70

encyclopedias + international law KC73; 341.173

endangered species KN95.31; 347.34231

endangering + criminal liability KM505.6; 346.826

endowment KN56.3; 347.3033

enduring power of attorney KN25.2; 347.182
RT: power of attorney KN25.2; 347.182

enemy aliens + international law KC1355.8; 341.8261

enemy property KN58.7; 347.3057

energy KN89; 347.33; [Table IIA: 107]
UF: fuel

energy + conservation KN89.3; 347.3313

energy + conventional sources KN89.4; 347.3314
UF: conventional energy sources

energy + EU + statistics + journals KW66.4

energy market + EU KW122.1

energy policy KN89.1; 347.331

energy policy + EU KW122

enforcement [Table VI: .Z92]
RT: compliance + financial services KN309; 347.7869

enforcement + competition law KN266.15; 347.6315

enforcement + competition law + EU KW110.9

enforcement + foreign judgments KC2082; 341.975

enforcement + international arbitral awards KC1258; 341.738

enforcement + judgments + international courts KC1218; 341.718

enforcement + payment + fines [App: 73]

enforcement + traffic regulations KN323.79; 347.81379

enforcement of judgments + common law
USE: execution of judgments KN395.2; 347.972; [Table IIA: 149.5]

enforcement of law
USE: law enforcement KM610; 346.98; [Table IIA: 92]

enforcement of morality
USE: criminal law : morality KM504; 346.818

enfranchisement + leases KN87.9; 347.32989

engagement + marriage KN172.1; 347.4211

engineering + industries + EU KW119.8

England and Wales + legal history KL401; 345.942

English dictionaries **K120;** **340.08**

English legal system **KL11;** **345.0942**

English Reports **KF53.E6**

enjoyment + property **KN54.4;** **347.3024**

enlistment
USE: recruitment + armed forces KM401; 346.71

enquiries + conveyancing **KN74.2;** **347.32232**
UF: inquiries + conveyancing

enterprise investment scheme + taxation **KM336.69.E5;** **346.5269.E5**

enterprise zones **KN197.4;** **347.4874**

entertainment **KN344;** **347.871**

enticement **KN38.13;** **347.243**

entomology + forensic science **KM608.3.E5;** **346.9793.E5**

entrapment **KM580.15;** **346.9115**
UF: agents provocateurs

entrepreneurs' relief **KM336.69.E5;** **346.5269.E5**

entries + pleadings
USE: pleadings KN383; 347.943; [Table IIA: 146]

entry into force + legislation
USE: commencement + legislation KL36; 345.16

entry into force + treaties **KC333.4;** **341.5614**

environmental audit **KN95.5;** **347.3425**

environmental crimes **KM565.E5;** **346.89.E5**

environmental health KN97; 347.345; [Table IIA: 107.4]
RT: pollution KN97.7; 347.347; [Table IIA: 107.4]

environmental improvement + crime prevention [App: 29.E5]

environmental law KN94; 347.34; [Table IIA: 107.2]
RT: conservation KN95.1; 347.3411

environmental law + EU KW125

environmental law + international law KC243; 341.444

environmental law + treaties KC336.6; 341.586

environmental protection KN95; 347.342

environmental taxes KM337.9.E5; 346.59.E5

Episcopalian churches KD500; 342.69

equal opportunities KM208; 346.36; [Table IIA: 81.5]
UF: equality of treatment
RT: equal pay KN194.6; 347.4786
RT: minorities KM208; 346.36; [Table VII: 4]
RT: women KN152.2; 347.4122; [Table VII: 2.2]

equal opportunities + EU KW130.3

equal opportunities + industrial law KN191.3; 347.4613

equal pay KN194.6; 347.4786
RT: equal opportunities KM208; 346.36; [Table IIA: 81.5]

equal pay + EU KW130.1

equal protection of the law
USE: equality before the law KA30.E6; 340.1295.E6

equality before the law KA30.E6; 340.1295.E6
UF: equal protection of the law
RT: rule of law KM34; 346.36

equality of states + international law KC152; 341.262

equality of treatment
USE: equal opportunities KM208; 346.36; [Table IIA: 81.5]

equipment + forensic medicine KM608.5; 346.9795

equipment + libraries K84.6; 340.0546

equitable interests KN221; 347.58

equitable interests + land KN64.1; 347.3151
UF: beneficial interests + land

equitable remedies KN230; 347.59
RT: remedies KN395.1; 347.971; [Table IIA: 149]; [Table VI: .Z8]

equities KN304.4; 347.734

equity KN200; 347.5; [Table IIA: 126]

equity : common law
USE: common law : equity KL31; 345.11

equity : Roman law KN203; 347.51
UF: Roman law : equity

equity courts [Table V: 6]

equity release KN67; 347.3191

equity warrants KN304.45; 347.7345

ERDF
USE: European Regional Development Fund KW123.2

errors + criminal justice
USE: miscarriage of justice KM597; 346.957

escapes + prisons [App: 95]

escheat KN64.12; 347.3154

escrows KN74.5; 347.3225

espionage KM561.3; 346.8813
UF: defence secrets
RT: intelligence services KM233.8; 346.3739

espionage + international law KC1306; 341.7845
UF: peaceful espionage
RT: industrial espionage KN114.3; 347.3773
RT: spy satellites KC1306; 341.7845

espionage + war + international law KC1355.5; 341.825
UF: defence secrets
UF: spies
UF: spying

essays KB30; 340.37

established church
USE: church and state KM58; 346.138

estate agents KN74.8; 347.32275
UF: real estate agents

estate duty
USE: inheritance taxes KM337.33; 346.553

estate management KN98.7; 347.3557

estates KN63; 347.312
UF: landed estates

estimates + public expenditure KM331.5; 346.505
RT: budget KM332; 346.51

estoppel + leases
USE: leases + creation KN72.1; 347.3311

estoppel + procedure KN384.4; 347.9444

ethical jurisprudence
USE: justice KA35; 340.13

ethics + judiciary KL240.3; 345.43
UF: judicial ethics

ethics + legal profession
USE: legal ethics KL82; 345.1702

ethics + medical profession KN185.18; 347.44618
UF: medical ethics

ethics : law KA70.E8; 340.16.E8
UF: law : ethics

ethnic cleansing KC216; 341.361

ethnic groups
USE: multiculturalism KA67; 340.157

ethnic minorities + civil rights KM208; 346.36

etiquette + legal profession KL81; 345.17011
UF: legal etiquette

Euratom
USE: European Atomic Energy Community KC1031; 341.683; KW45

Eurobonds KN304.315; 347.73315

Eurojust KW133.6

Europe + international relations **KC305;** **341.515**

European Atomic Energy Community **KC1031;** **341.683;** **KW45**
UF: Euratom

European Central Bank **KW106.3**

European Central Inland Transport Organisation **KC931;** **341.674**

European Citizens' Initiative **KW98.5**

European Coal and Steel Community **KC1021;** **341.68;** **KW42**
SN: expired 2002
UF: ECSC

European Coal and Steel Community Treaty
USE: Treaty of Paris (1951) KW1.F51

European Commission **KW90**
UF: Commission of the EU

European Commission + publications **KW15**

European Commission of Human Rights **KC928;** **341.6733**

European Commission of Human Rights + law reports **KC30;** **341.1355**

European Communities
USE: European Union KC1001; 341.68; KW

European Communities Treaty
USE: Treaty of Rome (1971) KW1.F71

European Court of First Instance
USE: General Court KW94

European Court of Human Rights **KC1245;** **341.725**

European Court of Human Rights + law reports **KC29;** **341.135**

European Court of Justice KC1240; 341.724; KW93
UF: Court of Justice of the EU

European Court of Justice + law reports KC28; 341.134; KW51

European Court Reports KW51

European Currency Unit KW106.2
UF: ECU
UF: Euros

European Development Fund KW77.4
UF: EDF

European Economic Community
USE: European Union KC1001; 341.68; KW

European Economic Interest Grouping KW118.1
UF: EEIG

European elections KW96

European Foundation for the Improvement of Living and Working Conditions KW132

European Free Trade Association KC981; 341.678

European integration KW73

European Investment Bank KW124

European Investment Bank + publications KW32

European law (600–1499)
USE: European law + medieval period (600–1499) KE355; 343.72

European law + 16th century KE360; 343.77

European law + 17th century KE370; 343.78

European law + 18th century KE380; 343.79
UF: eighteenth century European law

European law + medieval period (600–1499) KE355; 343.72
UF: European law (600–1499)

European Monetary System KW106.1
UF: EMS

European Movement KC1156; 341.692

European Parliament KW95

European Parliament + publications KW20

European Police Office KW133.3
UF: Europol

European Regional Development Fund KW123.2
UF: ERDF

European Securities Markets Association (ESMA) KN304.96.E8; 347.7396.E8

European Social Fund KW127.2

European Trade Union Confederation KC1176; 341.696

European Union KC1001; 341.68; KW
UF: EC
UF: European Communities
UF: European Economic Community

European Union + atlases KW70.3

European Union + directories KW70.2

European Union + enlargement
USE: European Union + membership KW87

European Union + executive organs KW88

European Union + external relations KW75

European Union + external trade KW78

European Union + home affairs KW83

European Union + justice KW83

European Union + legal system KW71

European Union + legislation KW5

European Union + membership KW87
UF: European Union + enlargement

European Union : Africa
USE: Africa : EU KW81.6

European Union : Asia
USE: Asia : EU KW81.7

European Union : international law KW80

European University Institute KW143.3

Europol
USE: European Police Office KW133.3

Euros
USE: European Currency Unit KW106.2

eurozone KW101.5

euthanasia + criminal law KM542.6; 346.8626
UF: mercy killing

euthanasia + medical law KN185.158; 347.446158
UF: right to die

evening classes KN184.36; 347.4446
RT: adult education KN184.36; 347.4446

eviction KN88.14; 347.329914

evidence KN390; 347.961; [Table IIA: 147]
UF: eyewitnesses
UF: oral evidence
UF: testimony

evidence + criminal procedure KM600; 346.96; [Table IIA: 93.4]

evidence + criminal procedure + European courts KW133.5

evidence + international courts KC1214; 341.714

evidence + privilege
USE: privilege + evidence KN394.8; 347.9658

ex post facto laws
USE: retroactive legislation KL36.4; 345.164

ex-service personnel [Table VII: 7.E9]
UF: veterans

ex-service personnel + public welfare KN181.7; 347.4417

examination + witnesses KN391.3; 347.9623
UF: cross examination
UF: leading questions
RT: re-examination + witnesses KN391.3; 347.9623

examination + witnesses + criminal procedure KM605.1; 346.971

examinations + legal education KL131–149 [Table: .2]; 345.1794–9 [Table: 2]

exchange programmes + legal education KL131–149 [Table: .5]; 345.1794–9 [Table: 5]

exchange rates KN302.3; 347.713
UF: conversion + currency
UF: currency + conversion
RT: devaluation KN302.2; 347.712

excise duties KM337.76; 346.586

excise offences KM564.4; 346.8864
UF: brewing + crime
UF: distilling + crime
UF: illegal stills
UF: stills + alcohol

exclusion clauses KN13.4; 347.114

exclusive economic zones + national waters
USE: economic zones + national waters KC144.3; 341.2543

exclusive rights KN115; 347.378

excommunication KD186; 342.396

execution (punishment) [App: 61]
RT: capital punishment [App: 61]

execution of judgments KN395.2; 347.972; [Table IIA: 149.5]
UF: enforcement of judgments + common law

executive [Table IIA: 78]

executive agencies
USE: government departments KM235; 346.38; [Table IIA: 83.2]; [Table VII: 8.3]

executive agreements + international law
USE: treaties KC330; 341.56

executive power KM111; 346.25

executive prerogatives KM114; 346.27
UF: royal prerogatives

executors KN143; 347.39
RT: administrators + probate KN143; 347.393
RT: personal representatives KN143; 347.39; [Table VI: .Z63]

executory interests KN64.23; 347.3163

exempt persons + financial services KN308.4; 347.7864

exemption + juries KN389.612; 347.960612

exemption + juries + criminal KM583.12; 346.93312

exemption + taxation KM336.6; 346.526
UF: tax exemptions

exemptions + competition law KN266.7; 347.635

exemptions + competition law + EU KW110.8

exhibitionism KM544.5; 346.8645
UF: indecent exposure

exhibits + evidence KN392.7; 347.9637
UF: objects + evidence
UF: tangible objects + evidence

exhumation KN97.3; 347.346

exiles
USE: refugees + international law KC205; 341.335

exit permits KM176.6; 346.334

expatriation
USE: statelessness KC194; 341.314

expenditure + courts KL230.14; 345.314
RT: financial management + courts KL230.14; 345.314

expenditure plans KM331.22; 346.5022

expenses + allowances + taxation KM336.63; 346.5263

expenses + legislators KM83.9; 346.229

expenses + witnesses KN391.15; 347.96215

expert evidence KN391.5; 347.9625
UF: medical witnesses

expert evidence + criminal procedure KM604.9; 346.967
UF: medical witnesses + criminal procedure

exploration + mining KN91.32; 347.33432

explosives + control KN186.1; 347.451

explosives + crimes KM562.2; 346.8832

explosives + war KC1391; 341.861
UF: conventional weapons

export credit guarantees KN253.1; 347.611

export duties KM337.74; 346.584

export trade + finance KN253.12; 347.612

exports KN253.1; 347.611

expropriation KN56.6; 347.3036
UF: eminent domain
RT: compulsory purchase KN96.3; 347.3433
RT: nationalisation KN56.6; 347.3036

expropriation + international law KC238; 341.438
UF: confiscations + international law
UF: nationalisation + alien property

extenuation
USE: criminal liability KM505; 346.82; [Table IIA: 90.3]

external financing limits KM331.52; 346.5053

external relations + EU
USE: international relations + EU KW75

external trade + EU KW78
RT: trade + EU KW108

extinction of estates and interests KN79; 347.3231

extortion KM552; 346.877
UF: blackmail

extradition + international law KC214; 341.354

extraordinary remedies KN395.8; 347.974

extraterritorial crimes KC213; 341.353

extraterritoriality KC171; 341.281

eyewitnesses
USE: evidence KN390; 347.961; [Table IIA: 147]

facsimile transmission
USE: fax KN342.5; 347.865

factories + hygiene
USE: hygiene + industrial law KN193.7; 347.477

factories + industrial law KN193.61; 347.476

factories + land usage KN83.3; 347.3253

factoring + contract KN25.3; 347.183

factoring + credit KN305.11; 347.7511

factory ships KN338.3; 347.8383
UF: freezer ships
RT: fishing boats KN338.3; 347.8383

facts
USE: material facts KN383.2; 347.9432

fair comment KN38.27; 347.2487

fair dealing KN118.1; 347.3795
RT: copyright KN112; 347.371

fair trading KN266.05; 347.6305
RT: competition KN266; 347.63; [Table IIA: 130]

fairgrounds KN186.61; 347.4561

false accounting KM547.4; 346.8724

false arrest
USE: wrongful arrest KM543.6; 346.8636

false coinage
USE: counterfeiting + crime KM564.1; 346.8861

false imprisonment + criminal law KM543.6; 346.8636

false imprisonment + tort KN38.33; 347.253

false pretences KM547.3; 346.8723
UF: imposture

families + single parent KN174.5; 347.42595
UF: one-parent families
UF: single parent families

families + single parent + welfare KN181.9.Q39.O5; 347.4419.Q3.O5

family companies KN265.9.F3; 347.6279.F3
RT: companies KN261; 347.623; [Table IIA: 128]

family companies + taxation KM336.491; 346.52491

family courts [Table V: 7]

family courts + procedure KN367; 347.927

Family Division [Table V: 7]

family law KN170; 347.42; [Table IIA: 116]
UF: domestic relations

family law + EU KW128.2

family law + religious laws [KD Table: 8]

family planning
USE: birth control KN172.72; 347.42172

family provision + social security KN181.4; 347.4414
UF: children's allowances

family provision + wills KN125.6; 347.3826

family settlements KN58.1; 347.3051

family violence
USE: domestic violence KN175; 347.42597

famous prisoners [App: 95]

FAO
USE: Food and Agriculture Organisation KC521; 341.633

Far East + international relations
USE: East Asia + international relations KC303.1; 341.5131

fares + international air law KC255.3; 341.4547

farm accounts + EU KW114.3

farm law
USE: agricultural law KN98; 347.35; [Table IIA: 107.6]

farm produce
USE: agricultural produce KN99; 347.356

farm tenancies
USE: agricultural tenancies KN98.1; 347.3512

farming KN98; 347.35
RT: crofts KN98.12; 347.3513

farming methods + EU KW114.6

fascism + international law KC121; 341.221

fascism + political systems KM39; 346.1235

fascist jurisprudence KA47; 340.145
UF: national socialism
UF: Nazi jurisprudence

fatal injuries + tort KN38.11; 347.241

fathers
USE: parents KN176.6; 347.4266; [Table VII: 3.6]

fault + tort KN33.1; 347.211

favoured nation clauses KC231.2; 341.4212
UF: most favoured nation clauses

fax KN342.5; 347.865
UF: facsimile transmission

fax + courts KL230.69.F2; 345.369.F2

fax + international law KC257.2; 341.4622

feature films
USE: films + intellectual property KN112.3; 347.374

federal banks
USE: central banks KN303.5; 347.725

Federal District Judges + US KL241.3; 345.463

Federal Register KG330

federations + constitutional law KM44; 346.128
UF: states' rights

federations + industrial law KN195.15; 347.4815

federations + international law KC153.2; 341.2632

fee simple KN63.11; 347.3131

fee tail KN63.12; 347.3132

fees
USE: costs KN397; 347.977; [Table IIA: 150]

felonies KM503.2; 346.8152

females [Table VII: 2.2]

feminism KA49.F4; 340.147.F4

fences + boundaries KN72.13; 347.32153

ferae naturae
USE: animals + control KN186.8; 347.458

ferries KN322.8; 347.8128

fertility KN172.7; 347.4217; [Table IIA: 117.2]

fertilisers KN98.51; 347.3551

fertilisers + EU KW114.6

Festschriften
USE: collections [Table VIII: 004]

feudal law + England and Wales KL401.6; 345.9426
UF: feudal tenure
UF: land tenure + feudal law
RT: medieval law + England and Wales KL401.6; 345.9426

feudal law + Europe KE356; 343.74

feudal tenure
USE: feudal law + England and Wales KL401.6; 345.9426

fiction (novels) KB33; 340.373
UF: novels
UF: short stories
RT: drama KB32; 340.372
RT: legal writing K100; 340.06
RT: poetry KB32; 340.372

fiduciaries KN216; 347.56

films + causes of crime [App: 17]

films + censorship KN349.97; 347.8997

films + criminal evidence KM604.55; 346.9665
RT: video recordings + criminal evidence KM604.55; 346.9665

films + intellectual property KN112.3; 347.374
UF: documentary films
UF: feature films

films + taxation KM336.68.F5; 346.5268.F5

finance KN300; 347.7; [Table IIA: 134]

finance + EU KW100

finance + EU + statistics + journals KW66.2

finance + international law KC222; 341.41

financial eligibility for legal aid
USE: legal aid + eligibility KN399.3; 347.933

financial futures KN304.65; 347.7365
UF: futures + finance
UF: hedging + finance

financial institutions KN303; 347.72

financial institutions + international law KC226; 341.414

financial management KN307; 347.78

financial management + courts KL230.14; 345.314
RT: accounts + courts KL230.14; 345.314
RT: expenditure + courts KL230.14; 345.314

financial management + law offices KL96.5; 345.1765

Financial Ombudsman KN304.95.F5; 347.7395.F5

financial promotion KN308.6; 347.7866
UF: investment advertisements

financial services KN308; 347.786; [Table IIA: 134.5]

financial services + EU KW119.1

Financial Services and Markets Tribunal KN309.2; 347.78692

Financial Services Authority KN304.95.F5; 347.7395.F5
UF: FSA

Financial Services Compensation Scheme KN309.3; 347.78693

findings + personal property KN104.4; 347.3644

fines KM670.2; 346.98742; [App: 73; 92.42]

fingerprints KM604.32; 346.9645
RT: footprints KM604.32; 346.9645

fire insurance KN294.F5; 347.694.F5

fire precautions + industrial law KN198.25; 347.4925

fire regulations KN84.15; 347.32615

fire service KM234; 346.3739

firearms KN186.1; 347.451
UF: ballistics
UF: bullets
UF: guns
UF: rifles
RT: munitions + trade KN253.8.M8; 347.616.M8

firearms + criminal law KM562.2; 346.8832

firearms + international law KC1391; 341.861
UF: conventional weapons
RT: disarmament + international law KC313; 341.533

firewalls + networks
USE: security + networks KN347.56; 347.8946

fireworks KN186.1; 347.451

first offenders [App: 07]
RT: offenders KM587.1; 346.9371

fiscal evasion
USE: tax evasion KM564.2; 346.8862

fisheries KN338; 347.838; [Table IIA: 140]

fisheries + EU KW117

fisheries + international law KC276.1; 341.481

fishermen KN338.4; 347.8384

fishery products KN338.5; 347.8385

fishing + sport KN186.632; 347.45632
RT: blood sports KN186.63; 347.4563

fishing boats KN338.3; 347.8383
UF: trawlers
RT: factory ships KN338.3; 347.8383

fishing rights
USE: sporting rights KN65.9.S6; 347.3189.S6

fishing zones KN338.2; 347.8382

fitness for purpose + sale of goods
USE: trading standards KN284.6; 347.666

fixed penalties [App: 74]

fixed-term contracts KN192.14; 347.4625

fixing prices
USE: prices KN283; 347.658

fixtures + landlord and tenant KN88.3; 347.32993

flag KM59; 346.139

flag of truce
USE: truce KC1422; 341.892

flags of convenience KC272.2; 341.4752

flammable goods
USE: dangerous things KN186.9.D3; 347.459.D3

flat-rate taxes
USE: poll taxes KM337.14; 346.5314

flats KN83.1; 347.3251
UF: apartments

flight control KN327.5; 347.825
UF: air rule of the road
UF: air traffic control

flight control + international law KC253.4; 341.4534

flight crews KN327.2; 347.822
UF: air crew
UF: air stewards
UF: airmen
UF: pilots (air)

flight crews + international law KC253.6; 341.4536

flights + international law KC254; 341.454

flood control KN90.3; 347.3333
UF: dams
UF: weirs

flotsam and jetsam KN104.4; 347.3644
UF: jetsam

flow management
USE: case management KL230.422; 345.3422

fluoridation KN185.7; 347.4487
RT: preventive medicine KN185.7; 347.4487

FOB contracts KN337.2; 347.8372
UF: free on board

foetuses
USE: unborn children KN176.5; 347.4265

foetuses + experimentation KN185.53; 347.4483
RT: abortion + family law KN172.73; 347.42173

food KN185.2; 347.447; [Table IIA: 123.3]
RT: hotels KN186.3; 347.453
RT: restaurants KN186.3; 347.453

food + EU KW112.4

food + hygiene KN97.4; 347.3462
UF: hygiene + food

food + labelling KN185.23; 347.44723
UF: labelling + food

food + packaging KN185.23; 347.44723
UF: packaging + food

food + preservatives KN185.24; 347.44724
UF: preservatives in food

food + regulatory bodies KN185.28; 347.44728

food + storage KN97.4; 347.3462
UF: storage of food

food additives
USE: additives + food KN185.24; 347.44724

Food and Agriculture Organisation KC521; 341.633
UF: FAO
UF: United Nations Food and Agriculture Organisation

Food and Drug Administration (US) KN185.28; 347.44728

food codes KN185.23; 347.44723

food industry + EU KW119.5

football KN186.69.F6; 347.4569.F6

football grounds
USE: sports grounds KN186.7; 347.457

footpaths KN95.13; 347.34213
RT: bridle paths KN95.13; 347.3414
RT: rights of way KN65.12; 347.3173

footprints KM604.32; 346.9645
RT: fingerprints KM604.32; 346.9645

footwear industry + EU KW119.4

force + war
USE: legality + war KC1353; 341.81

force : law KA29; 340.129
UF: law : force

force majeure
USE: duress + criminal liability KM505.3; 346.823

forced labour KN191.5; 347.4615

foreign arbitral awards KC2085; 341.98
UF: arbitral awards + conflict of laws

foreign companies KN265.5; 347.627

foreign companies + taxation KM336.494; 346.52494

foreign court theory KC2061; 341.945

foreign currency + markets
USE: currency markets KN302.35; 347.7135

foreign earnings + taxation KM336.33; 346.5233
UF: earnings abroad
UF: overseas earnings

foreign enlistment KM561.5; 346.8815
UF: mercenaries

foreign exchange KN302.3; 347.713

foreign governments + taxation KM336.488; 346.52488

foreign investment + international law KC227.1; 341.4151

foreign judgments KC2080; 341.97

foreign law + conflict of laws KC2070; 341.96

foreign law + proof KC2071; 341.961
UF: proof of foreign law

foreign mail KN341.5; 347.854

foreign nationals
USE: aliens KM177; 346.336

foreign property
USE: alien property KN58.6; 347.3056

foreign relations
USE: international relations KC300; 341.5

foreign sovereigns
USE: heads of state KC189.H4; 341.299.H4

foreign subsidiary companies + taxation KM336.494; 346.52494
RT: subsidiaries + taxation KM336.493; 346.52493

foreign trade KN253; 347.61

foreign trade + EU + statistics + journals KW66.6

foremen KN192.51; 347.46551

forensic laboratories KM608.5; 346.9795

forensic pathology KM608; 346.979
UF: forensic medicine

forensic physicians KM608.8; 346.9798

forensic psychiatry KM506.2; 346.8292

forensic science KM607; 346.9788

foreshore KN90.4; 347.3334

forestry KN98.8; 347.3558

forestry + EU KW117.2

forfaiting KN253.13; 347.613

forfeiture [App: 75.F6]

forgery KM551; 346.876

forgery + coinage
USE: counterfeiting + crime KM564.1; 346.8861

formation [Table VI: .Z5]

formation + contracts KN13; 347.11

formation + trade unions KN195.1; 347.481

formation + treaties KC333; 341.561
UF: treaties + formation

formation + wills KN125.2; 347.3822

former jeopardy
USE: double jeopardy KM579.2; 346.907

forms KN360; 347.92; [Table VI: .Z3]
UF: court forms
UF: precedents

forms + criminal procedure KM571; 346.9.Z72

forms + taxation KM336.81; 346.5281

forms and precedents + drafting KL34.2; 345.142

Forum Fisheries KC886.F6; 341.6695.F6

forum shopping KC2050; 341.92

forward averaging KM336.86; 346.5286
SN: used in Canada

forwarding agents KN329.2; 347.8292

fostering KN176.2; 347.4262

foundation treaties + EU KW85

foundation treaties + EU + texts KW1

fox hunting KN186.639.F6; 347.45639.F6

fragmentation of ownership KN54.2; 347.3022

franchise (elections)
USE: suffrage KM83.2; 346.223

franchises + company law KN262.22; 347.62423

franchises + EU KW110.7

franchises + sale of goods KN285.6; 347.676

franchising + legal aid KN399.4; 347.994

Frankish law KE320.2; 343.622
UF: Salic law

fraud + contract KN15.4; 347.134

fraud + criminal law KM547; 346.872
UF: misrepresentation
UF: statute of frauds
UF: swindling

fraud + equity KN222; 347.585

fraudulent conversion
USE: embezzlement KM547.1; 346.8721

fraudulent trading KN264.8; 347.6268

free choice of employment KN191.1; 347.4611

free churches KD510; 342.691

free movement KC199; 341.319
UF: freedom of movement
RT: migration KM176; 346.33
RT: migration + international law KC199; 341.319

free movement + capital + EU KW105

free movement + goods + EU KW109

free movement + professions + EU KW109.8

free movement + services + EU KW109.7

free movement + workers + EU KW130.2

free on board
USE: FOB contracts KN337.2; 347.8372

free pardon KM597.8; 346.9578; [App: 77]
UF: pardon

free ports
USE: free zones + international law KC173; 341.283

free trade KC225.8; 341.4138

free zones + international law KC173; 341.283
UF: free ports

freedom + international law
USE: human rights + international law KC200; 341.33

freedom of assembly KM205; 346.355

freedom of conscience KM206; 346.356

freedom of expression
USE: freedom of speech KM204; 346.354

freedom of information KM209.I6; 346.368.I6

freedom of movement
USE: free movement KC199; 341.319

freedom of property
USE: right to own property KM209.P8; 346.368.P8

freedom of religion KM206; 346.356
RT: church and state KM58; 346.138

freedom of speech KM204; 346.354
UF: freedom of expression

freedom of the air
USE: airspace + international law KC253.2; 341.4532

freedom of the press KM207; 346.357
UF: press freedom
RT: censorship KN349; 347.898; [Table IIA: 142]

freedom of the seas
USE: high seas KC264; 341.4715

freehold KN63.1; 347.313

Freemasons [Table VII: 9.9]

freeways
USE: motorways KN322.1; 347.8121

freezer ships
USE: factory ships KN338.3; 347.8383

freezing injunctions KN232.2; 347.5922
UF: Mareva injunctions

freight KN328.1; 347.8281
UF: affreightment

freight + air law
USE: air freight KN328.8; 347.8288

freight + maritime law KN337.1; 347.8371

freight + railways KN328.6; 347.8286
UF: rail freight

freight + roads KN328.5; 347.8285
UF: road freight

freight charges
USE: charges + freight KN328.2; 347.8282

friendly military personnel KC186; 341.292

friendly societies KN169.5; 347.41895; [Table VII: 9.5]
RT: associations KN169.4; 347.41894; [Table VII: 9.4]; [Table VIII: .003]

friendly societies + taxation KM336.495; 346.52495

friends + civil procedure
USE: non-legal representatives + civil procedure KN370.15; 347.9

friends + criminal procedure
USE: non-legal representatives + criminal procedure KM579.3;

Friesian law (ancient) KE320.3; 343.623

fright KN38.12; 347.242

fringe benefits
USE: benefits in kind + taxation KM336.31; 346.5231

fringe benefits tax + Australia KM337.9.F7; 346.59.F7

frontiers KC143; 341.253
UF: boundaries + international law
UF: international boundaries

frontiers + treaties KC336.3; 341.583

fruit + EU KW117.3.F7

frustration + contracts KN16.4; 347.144

FSA
USE: Financial Services Authority KN304.95.F5; 347.7395.F5

fuel
USE: energy KN89; 347.33; [Table IIA: 107]

fugitive offenders + international law KC214; 341.354
UF: hot pursuit
RT: offenders KM587.1; 346.9371

fundamental rights
USE: civil rights KM201; 346.35; [Table IIA: 81]
USE: human rights + international law KC200; 341.33

funding + political parties KM232.5; 346.3725

fundraising + charities KN215.8; 347.5568

funds + trade unions
RT: political funds + trade unions KN195.4; 347.4835

funerals KN185.4; 347.4479

fungicides + agriculture KN98.55; 347.3555
RT: agricultural chemicals KN98.5; 347.355

furniture + law libraries K84.6; 340.0546
UF: libraries + furniture

further education KN184.3; 347.444
RT: higher education KN184.3; 347.444
RT: technical education KN184.3; 347.444

fused profession
USE: legal profession + structure KL84; 345.1704

future interests KN64.2; 347.316

futures + commodities
USE: commodity futures KN304.63; 347.7363

futures + finance
USE: financial futures KN304.65; 347.7365

Gaius KE130; 343.44

galleries KN184.4; 347.445
UF: art galleries

gambling KN186.5; 347.455
UF: betting
UF: casinos
UF: gaming
UF: wagering

gambling + taxation KM337.9.G3; 346.59.G3
UF: pools betting levy

game KN99.4; 347.3564
RT: animals + control KN186.8; 347.458
RT: hunting KN186.63; 347.4563

gaming
USE: gambling KN186.5; 347.455

gangs
USE: organised crime KM540.5; 346.855

garbage disposal
USE: waste disposal KN97.85; 347.3485

gardens KN83.17; 347.32517

garnishment KN395.24; 347.9724

gas + energy KN89.42; 347.33142
RT: public utilities KN275.P8; 347.645.P8

gas + EU KW122.6

gas + mining KN91.34; 347.33434

gas + natural resources KN89.42; 347.33142
UF: natural gas

GATS
USE: General Agreement on Trade in Services KC641; 341.645

GATT
USE: General Agreement on Tariffs and Trade KC641; 341.645

gazumping KN74.1; 347.32231

gazundering KN74.1; 347.32231

GBH
USE: grievous bodily harm KM543.1; 346.8631

gearing
USE: capital markets KN304; 347.73

Gemara KD68.2; 342.232

genealogy KB21; 340.34

General Agreement on Tariffs and Trade KC641; 341.645
UF: GATT

General Agreement on Trade in Services KC641; 341.645
UF: GATS

General Assembly (UN) KC406; 341.623

general average
USE: marine insurance KN335; 347.835; [Table IIA: 139]

General Council of the Bar
USE: Bar Council KL101.1; 345.177421

General Court KW94
UF: Court of First Instance

General Court + law reports KW53

General Synod Measures (texts) KD465; 342.63

generalised system of preferences + EU KW77.5
UF: GSP

genetic engineering KN185.54; 347.4484
UF: plant variety rights

genetic modification + patents KN114.1; 347.3771
UF: patented genes

genetic modification + patents + international law KC236.9.G4; 341.436.G4

genetic research KN185.54; 347.4484

genetically modified foods KN185.27; 347.44727

Geneva conventions KC1411; 341.881

genocide KC216; 341.361

Gentoo KD726.G4; 342.8229.G4

geography : law KA70.G4; 340.16.G4

Germanic law (ancient) KE320; 343.62

gerrymandering
USE: constituencies KM83.2; 346.222

gifts + personal property KN104.3; 347.3643
UF: donations + personal property

gifts + property KN56.3; 347.3033

gifts + taxation KM337.31; 346.551
UF: donations + taxation

gilt-edged securities
USE: government securities KN304.2; 347.732

gipsy caravan sites KN96.54; 347.3438
RT: caravan sites KN96.51; 347.3437

global warming
USE: climate change KN94.1; 347.341

glossaries + EU KW7

going equipped for stealing
USE: housebreaking tools **KM546.7; 346.8717**

gold clause KC226.1; 341.4141

good behaviour + prisoners
USE: reductions + sentences + good behaviour KM686; 346.9881; [App:78]

goods and services tax KM337.45; 346.565
UF: GST
RT: value added tax KM337.45; 346.565

goods vehicles + taxation
USE: motor vehicles + taxation KM337.9.M6; 346.59.M6

goodwill KN279; 347.649

Gothic law KE320.4; 343.624

government KM231; 346.37; [Table IIA: 83]
UF: bureaucracy
UF: Crown

government + military occupation KC1401; 341.871
UF: military government

government actions KN378.3.G6; 347.938.3.G6
UF: crown proceedings

government departments KM235; 346.38; [Table IIA: 83.2]; [Table VII: 8.3]
UF: administrative agencies
UF: executive agencies
UF: ministries

government departments + publications KF46

government development grants
USE: development grants KM334; 346.518

government liability
USE: public liability KN33.5; 347.215

government liability + international law
USE: states + responsibility + international law KC180; 341.29

government purchasing KM236.5; 346.3815

government securities KN304.2; 347.732
UF: gilt-edged securities

government ships KC272.3; 341.4753
UF: state ships

governments [Table VI: .Z66]; [Table VII: 8.3]

governments + taxation KM336.483; 346.52483

governments in exile KC189.G6; 341.299.G6
UF: refugee governments

governors KM112.4; 346.255
UF: colonial governors
UF: state governors + US

governors + schools
USE: school governors KN184.28; 347.44328

graft
USE: corruption KM563.6; 346.8856

grand juries KM581.1; 346.921
RT: juries + criminal procedure KM583; 346.933

grandparents [Table VII: 3.6]

grandparents + rights KN176.65; 347.42665

grants to students
USE: student grants KN184.35; 347.4445

gratuities
USE: tips + employment KN194.5; 347.4785

graves + desecration
USE: sacrilege KM550; 346.875

Gray's Inn KL101.2; 345.177422

Greater London Council
USE: London + local government KM391.L6; 346.69.L6

Greek law (Hellenistic) KE40; 343.34

Greek law (pre-Hellenistic) KE26; 343.26
UF: pre-Hellenistic Greek law
RT: Hellenistic law KE30; 343.3

Greek Orthodox Church KD308.G7; 342.458.G7

green form scheme KN399.32; 347.9932

greenhouse effect
USE: air pollution KN97.71; 347.3471

Greenwich Mean Time
USE: time KN186.9.T5; 347.459.T5

greyhound racing
USE: racing KN186.64; 347.4564

grievance procedure + industrial law KN196.2; 347.4862

grievous bodily harm KM543.1; 346.8631
UF: bodily harm
UF: GBH
RT: actual bodily harm KM543.1; 346.8631

Grotius + international law KC105; 341.213

Grotius + Roman-Dutch law KE412; 343.83

ground rent KN88.11; 347.329911

grounds for divorce KN173.1; 347.424

group actions KN370.2; 347.9302
UF: class actions
UF: representative actions

group insurance KN293; 347.689

group legal services KN399.2; 347.992

group relief + taxation KM336.66; 346.5266

groups of companies
USE: company groups KN262.2; 347.62422

GSP
USE: generalised system of preferences + EU KW77.5

GST
USE: goods and services tax KM337.45; 346.565

guarantee cards KN303.13; 347.7213

guarantees + sale of goods KN282.4; 347.654
UF: warranties

guarantees + security (finance) KN306.92; 347.7792

guardians [Table VII: 3.9.G8]
RT: wards [Table VII: 3.9.W1]

guardians ad litem
USE: children's guardians KN176.22; 347.42622

guardianship KN176.2; 347.4262

guardianship orders KN395.21.G8; 347.9721.G8

guards + trains KN325.5; 347.8155
RT: train drivers KN325.5; 347.8155

guerrilla warfare KC1368; 341.845
UF: partisans + war

guest houses
USE: hotels KN186.3; 347.453

guilty pleas
USE: pleas + criminal procedure KM582.3; 346.9315

Gulf Co-operation Council KC811; 341.6613

gulfs
USE: bays + international law KC265; 341.472

guns
USE: firearms KN186.1; 347.451

guns + police
USE: arms + police KM615.3; 346.9853

habeas corpus KM203; 346.353

habits (constitutional)
USE: constitutional conventions KM38; 346.12345

hacking
USE: computer crime KM565.C6; 346.89.C6

hagiographa **KD66.3;** **342.223**

Hague Rules **KN335.2;** **347.8352**

Hague-Visby Rules **KN337;** **347.837**

Halakha **KD68.3;** **342.233**

hallmarks **KN114.6;** **347.3776**

Hamburg Rules **KN337;** **347.837**

Hamburg Rules + international law **KC272.8;** **341.4758**

handbooks
SN: use as subdivision only

handicapped persons
USE: disabled persons [Table VII: 5]

handwriting + criminal evidence **KM604.41;** **346.9651**
RT: palaeography K102; 340.062

hanging **[App: 61.9.H3]**

Hansard **KM84.8;** **346.2348**

Hansard + House of Commons **KF11**

Hansard + House of Lords **KF5**

harassment + criminal law **KM544.9.H3;** **346.8649.H3**

harassment + employment **KN192.57;** **347.46557**

harbourmasters **KN336.2;** **347.8362**

harbours **KN336;** **347.836**
UF: ports

harbours + EU KW135.4

hardware + computers KN348.3; 347.8973

hare coursing KN186.639.H3; 347.45639.H3

harmonisation + qualifications + EU KW109.8
RT: single market + EU KW108

hate crimes KM540.15; 346.8515
UF: anti-paedophile crimes
UF: homophobic crimes

hate propaganda KM561.2; 346.8812

hazardous substances KN97.8; 347.348
RT: dangerous things KN186.9.D3; 347.459.D3

hazardous substances + consumer law + EU KW112.6

hazardous substances + environmental law + EU KW125.8

hazardous waste
USE: toxic waste KN97.83; 347.3483

hazards + employment KN198.5; 347.495

headnotes + drafting KL33.9; 345.139

heads of government KM112; 346.251
UF: chief executives

heads of state KC189.H4; 341.299.H4
UF: foreign sovereigns
RT: monarchs KM112.1; 346.252

health + EU KW128.5

health administration KN185.16; 347.44616

health and safety KN198; 347.49
UF: industrial health
UF: occupational health
UF: safety and health
RT: industrial safety KN198.2; 347.492

health and safety + EU KW131.2

health care
USE: public health KN185; 347.446

health insurance (private) KN292.3; 347.685
UF: medical insurance (private
UF: sickness insurance (private)
RT: sickness + social security KN181.2; 347.4412

health visitors KN185.18.H4; 347.44618.H4

hearsay KN394.1; 347.9651

hearsay + criminal evidence KM603.6; 346.9636

heavy goods vehicles KN323.13; 347.81331
UF: lorries
UF: trucks + road transport
RT: motor vehicles KN323.1; 347.8131

hedge funds KN304.58; 347.7358

hedges KN72.13; 347.32153

hedging + finance
USE: financial futures KN304.65; 347.7365

heirs KN131; 347.386

Hellenistic law KE30; 343.3
RT: Greek law (pre-Hellenistic) KE26; 343.26

heraldry KB22; 340.35

hereditary legislators
USE: non-elected legislators KM83.7; 346.227

heredity + causes of crime [App: 11]

heritage organisations [Table VII: 9.6]
UF: cultural organisations

heritage organisations + taxation KM336.496; 346.52496

herring fisheries KN338.9.H4; 347.8389.H4

Hexabiblos KE257; 343.53

High Commission for Refugees KC456; 341.6292
UF: United Nations High Commission for Refugees

High Court [Table V: 5.1]

High Court judges KL241.2; 345.462
UF: puisne judges

High Court Masters KL241.21; 345.4621

High Court of Admiralty [Table V: 8.1]
UF: Admiralty Court

High Court of Justiciary (Scotland) [Table V: 1]

high seas KC264; 341.4715
UF: freedom of the seas

High Sheriffs (England and Wales) KL252; 345.52

high treason
USE: treason KM561.1; 346.8811

higher civil courts [Table V: 5.1]

higher criminal courts [Table V: 4.1]

higher education KN184.3; 347.444
UF: colleges
UF: polytechnics
RT: further education KN184.3; 347.444
RT: universities KN184.3; 347.444

higher education + directories K165; 340.095

higher education + EU KW143.2

highway code
USE: traffic regulations KN323.7; 347.8137

highways
USE: roads KN322; 347.812; [Table IIA: 136]

hijacking + aircraft
USE: crime + aircraft KC213.3; 341.3533

hijacking + motor vehicles
USE: motor vehicles + hijacking KM546.3; 346.8713

Hindu law KD700; 342.8

hire KN106.2; 347.3662
RT: leasing KN18.6; 347.156

hire purchase KN305.4; 347.76
UF: cooling off period

hired cars
USE: motor vehicles + rental KN324.6; 347.8146

historic buildings KN95.12; 347.34212
UF: sites of historic interest

historic sites + conservation KN95.11; 347.34211
UF: sites of historic interest

historic sites + international conservation KC243.3; 341.4443

historical documents
USE: archives KN184.5; 347.4455

historical jurisprudence KA19; 340.12007

history [Table VIII: 007]
RT: legal history KL400; 345.8 [Table IIA: 74]

history + legal profession KL80; 345.17005

history : law KA70.H5; 340.16.H5

Hittite law KE29.H5; 343.29.H5

HIV
USE: AIDS KN185.69.A4; 347.44869.A4

hoaxes + terrorists
USE: bomb threats KM562.25; 346.88325

holding charges
USE: charges + criminal procedure KM580.4; 346.914

holding companies KN265.3; 347.6273

holes in the wall
USE: automatic teller machines KN303.17; 347.7217

holidays KN193.2; 347.472
UF: leave of absence
RT: public holidays KN186.2; 347.452

holocaust denial KM565.H6; 346.89.H6

home affairs + EU KW83

home banking KN303.21; 347.7221

home duties + magistrates KL243.5; 345.485

home helps
USE: home-based services KN182.3; 347.4423

home improvement grants KN96.22; 347.34322

home improvements KN88.5 347.32995

home working KN193.59; 347.4759

Home Office (UK) KM235.H6; 346.38.H6

home-based services KN182.3; 347.4423
UF: home helps
UF: meals on wheels
RT: district nurses KN182.3; 347.4423

homelessness KN182.2; 347.4422; [Table IIA: 121.5]

homeopathy KN185.13.H6; 347.44613.H6

homesteads KN82; 347.3242

homicide KM542; 346.862
UF: killing
UF: unlawful killing

homophobic crimes
USE: hate crimes KM540.15; 346.8515

homosexuality + prisons KM683.4; 346.9876954; [App: 94.4]

homosexuals [Table VII: 2.3]
UF: lesbians

honours KM114.5; 346.275
UF: awards of honour
UF: decorations (medals)
UF: medals

hooliganism KM562.12; 346.88312

horizontal agreements + competition
USE: anti-competitive agreements KN266.2; 347.632

horizontal property
USE: condominiums KN63.9.C6; 347.3149.C6

horse racing
USE: racing KN186.64; 347.4564

horticulture + EU KW117.3.H6
RT: market gardens KN98.26; 347.3526

hospital ships KC1416.5; 341.8865

hospitals KN185.1; 347.4461
UF: clinics
UF: infirmaries

hospitals + employment KN193.54; 347.4754

hospitals + international humanitarian law KC1416; 341.886

hostage-taking KM543.5; 346.8635
UF: ransom

hostages + international humanitarian law KC1414; 341.884

hostels + homelessness KN182.23; 347.44223

hostile witnesses KN391.35; 347.96235

hostile witnesses + criminal evidence KM605.3; 346.973

hostilities
USE: war KC1350; 341.8

hot pursuit
USE: fugitive offenders + international law KC214; 341.354
USE: invasion KC1355.1; 341.821

hotels KN186.3; 347.453
UF: boarding houses
UF: guest houses
UF: inns
UF: motels
RT: food KN185.2; 347.447; [Table IIA: 123.3]

hotels + industrial law KN193.53; 347.4753

hours of work KN193.1; 347.471

hours of work + EU KW131.1

house arrest [App: 69.2]

house detectives
USE: private detectives KM614.2; 346.9842

House of Commons (UK) KM82.4; 346.214

House of Commons (UK) + bills
USE: legislative bills + House of Commons [texts] KF12

House of Commons (UK) + publications KF9

House of Lords (UK) KM82.3; 346.213
RT: non-elected legislators KM83.7; 346.227

House of Lords (UK) + bills
USE: legislative bills + House of Lords [texts] KF6

House of Lords (UK) + courts [Table V: 1]

House of Representatives (US) KM82.4; 346.214

House of Representatives (US) + publications KG312

housebreaking
USE: burglary KM546.1; 346.8711

housebreaking tools KM546.7; 346.8717
UF: going equipped for stealing

houses + land usage KN83.1; 347.3251

housing + planning KN96.2; 347.3432
RT: slum clearance KN96.25; 347.34325

housing + EU KW128.6

housing associations KN86.3; 347.3283

housing benefits KN181.88; 347.44188

housing co-operatives KN268.9.H6; 347.6389.H6

hovercraft KN321; 347.811

human bodies
USE: burial KN97.3; 347.346
USE: human tissues KN185.5; 347.448

human experimentation KN185.53; 347.4483

human genome KN185.54; 347.4484

human reproduction
USE: reproduction + family law KN172.7; 347.4217

human rights KM201; 346.35

human rights + international law KC200; 341.33
UF: civil rights + international law
UF: freedom + international law
UF: fundamental rights
RT: minorities + international law KC204; 341.334

human rights + international protection KC203; 341.333

human tissues KN185.5; 347.448
UF: human bodies
RT: transplant surgery KN185.5; 347.448

human trafficking KC208; 341.338
UF: white-slave traffic

humorous writings KB34; 340.374
UF: anecdotes
UF: curiosities
UF: legal humour
UF: wit and humour

hunting KN186.63; 347.4563
RT: animals + control KN186.8; 347.458
RT: blood sports KN186.63; 347.4563
RT: game KN99.4; 347.3564
RT: sporting rights KN65.9.S6; 347.3189.S6

hunting rights
USE: sporting rights KN65.9.S6; 347.3189.S6

husband and wife
USE: marriage KN172; 347.421; [Table IIA: 117]

hybrid securities KN304.32; 347.7332

hygiene + food
USE: food + hygiene KN97.4; 347.3462

hygiene + industrial law KN193.7; 347.477
UF: factories + hygiene
UF: workplaces + hygiene

IAEA
USE: International Atomic Energy Agency KC551; 341.636

IATA
USE: International Air Transport Association KC1193; 341.698

IBRD
USE: International Bank for Reconstruction and Development KC601; 341.64

ICAO
USE: International Civil Aviation Organisation KC561; 341.637

ICJ
USE: International Court of Justice KC1225; 341.722

IDA
USE: International Development Association KC631; 341.644

idealism KA43; 340.143

identification KM604.3; 346.9643

identity cards KM175.1; 346.3281

identity parades KM604.31; 346.9644

IFC
USE: International Finance Corporation KC621; 341.643

ignorance + criminal liability KM505.6; 346.826

Ijma KD623; 342.723

illegal assembly
USE: unlawful assembly KM562.1; 346.8831

illegal contracts KN15.1; 347.131

illegal immigrants KM177.3; 346.3365

illegal stills
USE: excise offences KM564.4; 346.8864

illegal trusts
USE: unlawful trusts KN214.5; 347.555

illegally obtained evidence KN394.4; 347.9654
RT: searches + criminal investigation KM580.2; 346.912
RT: seizure KM580.2; 346.912

illegally obtained evidence + criminal evidence KM603.4; 346.9634

illegitimacy KN176.3; 347.4263
UF: bastardy

illiterates [Table VII: 5.6]

illustrations + intellectual property KN112.2; 347.373
UF: paintings + intellectual property
RT: drawings KB35; 340.375
RT: photographs + intellectual property KN112.2; 347.373

ILO
USE: International Labour Organisation KC511; 341.632

image rights KN114.9.I5; 347.3779.I5

IMCO
SN: now renamed International Maritime Organisation
USE: International Maritime Consultative Organisation KC591; 341.639

IMF
USE: International Monetary Fund KC611; 341.642

immigrants [Table VII: 4.2]

immigrants + legal aid KN399.7.Q42; 347.997.Q42

immigration
USE: migration KM176; 346.33

immigration + international law
USE: migration + international law KC199; 341.319

immoral art, literature, etc.
USE: obscenity KM565.O2; 346.89.O2

immoral earnings
USE: prostitution KM544.1; 346.8641

immoral laws KA65; 340.155

immoveable property
USE: real property KN60; 347.31; [Table IIA: 104]

immunities + Crown
USE: Crown immunities + criminal law KM114.9; 346.279

immunities + diplomats
USE: diplomatic immunities KC322; 341.542

immunities + international organisations KC344; 341.612

immunities + judges
USE: judicial immunity KL240.35; 345.435

immunities + ships KC272.3; 341.4753

immunities + trade unions KN195.1; 347.481

IMO
USE: International Maritime Organisation KC591; 341.639

impeachment KM112.9; 346.259
UF: trial by impeachment

impeachment + judiciary KL240.3; 345.43

impediments to marriage
USE: marriage + impediments KN172.3; 347.4213

imperative theory of law
USE: command : law KA42; 340.142

imperial law KM57; 346.137
SN: Present status of pre-independence laws
RT: colonial law + UK KL29; 345.09

implied contracts KN20.1; 347.161

import duties
USE: customs duties KM337.71; 346.581

imports KN253.2; 347.614

imports + licensing + EU KW109.4

imports + quotas + EU KW78.2

impossibility of performance KN16.4; 347.144
UF: performance + impossibility

imposture
USE: false pretences KM547.3; 346.8723

imprisonment [App: 64]

imprisonment + alternatives [App: 69]

improvements + landlord and tenant KN88.5; 347.32995

imputation (Australia) KM337.24; 346.544

in vitro fertilisation KN172.82; 347.42182
UF: IVF
UF: test tube babies
RT: infertility + treatment KN172.8; 347.4218

incest KM544.6; 346.8646
UF: consanguinity
RT: child abuse KN176.41; 347.42641

incitement KM508.5; 346.841

income KN194; 347.478
RT: remuneration KN194; 347.478

income + agriculture + EU KW114

income + business + taxation KM336.32; 346.5232

income + industry + EU KW130.1

income splitting + taxation KM336.71; 346.5271

income taxation (theory) KM336.3; 346.523

income taxes KM337.11; 346.5311

incorporation KN262; 347.6242

incorporeal hereditaments KN65; 347.317

incursion
USE: invasion KC1355.1; 341.821

indecent assault KM544.4; 346.8644

indecent exposure
USE: exhibitionism KM544.5; 346.8645

indemnity insurance + legal profession KL95.8; 345.1748

independence + judiciary KM141.2; 346.282
UF: judicial independence

independent unions KN195.11; 347.4811

indeterminate sentences [App: 66]

indexes + EU KW8

indexing K105.8; 340.0658
UF: law indexing
UF: legal indexing

Indians of North America
USE: aboriginals + America KE530; 343.94

indictable offences KM503.1; 346.8151

indictments KM582.2; 346.931
UF: alternative counts
UF: arraignment
UF: counts in indictments

indigenous peoples
USE: aboriginals [Table VII: 4.3]

indirect taxation KM336.19; 346.5219

indirect taxes KM337.4; 346.56

individual exemption + competition KN266.72; 347.6352

individual exemption + competition + EU KW110.84

individual reporters
UF: named reporters

individual savings accounts KN304.7.I5; 347.737.I5
UF: ISAs

individual voluntary arrangements KN313.72; 347.79372

individuals [Table VII]
RT: citizens KM171; 346.3

individuals + international law KC135; 341.235

individuals + trade unions KN195.55; 347.4845
UF: rights + individuals + trade unions

indorsement
USE: writs + preliminary proceedings KN381.1; 347.4411

industrial courts [Table V: 8.6]
UF: labour courts
RT: industrial tribunals KN196.9; 347.4869

industrial democracy KN192.8; 347.468
UF: workers + participation
UF: works councils

industrial diseases
USE: diseases + industrial law KN198.4; 347.494

industrial disputes KN196; 347.486

industrial disputes + EU KW131.7

industrial espionage KN114.3; 347.3773
RT: espionage + international law KC1306; 341.7845

industrial espionage + international law KC239.E8; 341.439.E8

industrial health
USE: health and safety KN198; 347.49

industrial injuries KN198.3; 347.493
UF: repetitive strain injury

industrial law KN190; 347.46; [Table IIA: 124]
UF: labour law
UF: master and servant

industrial law + bibliography K57.6; 340.0378

industrial law + EU KW130

industrial law + international law KC242; 341.442
UF: international labour law
UF: labour law + international law

industrial property KN114; 347.377

industrial property + EU KW142

industrial property + international law KC236; 341.43

industrial relations KN190; 347.46
UF: labour relations

industrial relations + EU KW131.5

industrial safety KN198.2; 347.492
RT: health and safety KN198; 347.49

industrial tribunals KN196.9; 347.4869
UF: tribunals
RT: administrative tribunals KM303; 346.43
RT: industrial courts [Table V: 8.6]

industries KN270; 347.64; [Table IIA: 131]

industries + EU KW118

infanticide KM542.4; 346.8624
RT: concealment of birth KM542.4; 346.8624

infants
USE: children KN176; 347.426; [Table IIA: 118]; [Table VII: 1.1]

infertility + treatment KN172.8; 347.4218
RT: in vitro fertilisation KN172.82; 347.42182

infirmaries
USE: hospitals KN185.1; 347.4461

inflammable goods
USE: dangerous things KN186.9.D3; 347.459.D3

informal carers KN182.35; 347.44235

information + disclosure
USE: disclosure of information KN392; 347.963

information + EU KW145

information + industry + EU KW119.6

information + secrecy
USE: official secrets KM233.7; 346.3737

information + taxation
USE: tax returns KM336.81; 346.5281

information age KN340.5; 347.845
UF: information society

information retrieval + computers KN347.2; 347.892

information science K80; 340.05

information society
USE: information age KN340.5; 347.845

information technology KN347; 347.89
RT: computers KN347; 347.89; [Table IIA: 143]

information technology + EU KW141

information work + law libraries K85.I5; 340.055.I5

informed consent + medical care
USE: consent + medical care KN185.122; 347.446122

informers + evidence KM603.8; 346.9638
UF: supergrasses

infringement + intellectual property KN116; 347.379

inheritance KN120; 347.38; [Table IIA: 110]
RT: succession KN120; 347.38; [Table IIA: 110]

inheritance + religious laws [KD Table: 7.4]

inheritance taxes KM337.33; 346.553
UF: death duties
UF: estate duty

injunctions KN232; 347.592

injunctions + industrial law KN196.3; 347.4863
UF: labour injunctions

injuries
USE: personal injuries KN38.1; 347.24

Inland Revenue
USE: Revenue and Customs KM235.R4; 346.38.R4

inland transport
USE: transport KN320; 347.8

inland waterways KN326; 347.816
RT: canals + transport KN326.2; 347.8162

inland waterways + EU KW135.4

inner cities KN96.2; 347.3432

Inner Temple KL101.3; 345.177423

innocence + presumption
USE: presumption of innocence KM579.1; 346.906

innocent dissemination KN38.26; 347.2486

innocent passage KC1386; 341.8546

innovation KN111.4; 347.3704

inns
USE: hotels KN186.3; 347.453

Inns of Chancery KL101.6; 345.177426

Inns of Court KL101.1; 345.177421

Inns of Court + legal education KL131.9.I5; 345.17942.I5

inoculations
USE: preventive medicine KN185.7; 347.4487

inquests KM580.17; 346.9117
RT: coroners KL254; 345.54
RT: death KN185.15; 347.44615

inquiries + conveyancing
USE: enquiries + conveyancing KN74.2; 347.32232

inquisitorial systems KN389.8; 347.9608
RT: adversarial systems KN389.8; 347.9608

insane persons KN155.3; 347.4153; [Table VII: 5.3]; [App: 55.3]
RT: mental patients KN155.2; 347.4152; [Table VII: 5.2]

insane persons + criminal liability KM506; 346.829

inshore fisheries KN338.2; 347.8382

insider dealing + company law KN264.8; 347.6268

insider dealing + investment KN304.9; 347.739

insolvency KN312; 347.792; [Table IIA: 135]
RT: bankruptcy KN313; 347.793; [Table IIA: 135]

insolvency practitioners KN312.3; 347.7923
RT: receivers + insolvency KN312.4; 347.7924

Institutiones + Corpus Juris Civilis KE151; 343.472

instructions to juries
USE: jury instructions KN389.7; 347.9607

insurable interests KN290.6; 347.68106

insurance KN290; 347.68; [Table IIA: 133]
UF: assurance
UF: underwriting
RT: social insurance KN181; 347.44

insurance + EU KW119.1

insurance + industrial law KN198.6; 347.496

insurance + maritime law
USE: marine insurance KN335; 347.835; [Table IIA: 139]

insurance brokers KN291.2; 347.6812
UF: brokers + insurance

insurance companies + taxation KM336.4929.I5; 346.524929.I5

insurance contracts KN290.3; 347.681

insurance intermediaries KN291; 347.6811

insurance policies KN290.3; 347.681
UF: policies + insurance

insurance premium tax KM337.46; 346.566

insurrection
USE: rebellion KM561.1; 346.8811

integration + currency + EU
USE: single currency + EU KW106

intellectual property KN111; 347.37; [Table IIA: 109]

intellectual property + EU KW142

intellectual property + international law KC236; 341.43

intellectual property + remedies KN117; 347.3793

intelligence services KM233.8; 346.3738
UF: counter-espionage
RT: espionage KM561.3; 346.8813
RT: official secrets KM233.7; 346.3737

intention + contract KN13.1; 347.111

intention + criminal law
USE: mens rea KM505.1; 346.821

Inter-American Conference KC756; 341.6581

Inter-American Court of Justice KC1230; 341.723

Inter-American Court of Justice + law reports KC27; 341.133

inter-continental relations
USE: international relations KC300; 341.5

Inter-Parliamentary Union KC1151; 341.691

inter-union relations KN195.8; 347.485

interest + credit KN305.3; 347.753

interest + overdue tax
USE: overdue tax + interest KM336.914; 346.52914

interest + taxation KM336.35; 346.5235

interest + taxation + allowances KM336.63; 346.5263

interest rates KN305.3; 347.753
UF: Bank Rate
UF: rates of interest

interests + property KN54.2; 347.3022

interests upon condition KN64.4; 347.3167

Intergovernmental Bureau for Informatics KC586; 341.6386

interim relief KN387.3; 347.9473
UF: interlocutory relief

interlocutory relief
USE: interim relief KN387.3; 347.9473

international agencies
USE: international organisations KC340; 341.6; [Table VII: 8.1]

international agreements
USE: treaties KC330; 341.56

international air routes
USE: routes + international air law KC255.1; 341.4546

International Air Transport Association KC1193; 341.698
UF: IATA

international arbitration KC1250; 341.73
UF: arbitration + international law

international arbitration + cases KC40; 341.14
UF: law reports + international arbitration

international arbitration + courts KC1260; 341.74

international arbitration + procedure KC1255; 341.735

International Atomic Energy Agency KC551; 341.636
UF: IAEA

International Bank for Reconstruction and Development KC601; 341.64
UF: IBRD
UF: World Bank

international banks KC226; 341.414
UF: banking + international law
UF: banks + international law

international boundaries
USE: frontiers KC143; 341.253

International Capital Market Association KN304.96.I5; 347.7396.I5

International Chamber of Commerce KC1181; 341.6965

International Civil Aviation Organisation KC561; 341.637
UF: ICAO

international commerce
USE: international economic law KC220; 341.4

International Confederation of Free Trade Unions KC1166; 341.694

international conferences
USE: conferences + international law KC60; 341.161

international contracts
USE: contracts + international trade KC233; 341.423

International Court of Justice KC1225; 341.722
UF: ICJ

International Court of Justice + law reports KC23; 341.132

international courts KC1210; 341.71
RT: international criminal courts KC219; 341.39
RT: law reports + international law KC20; 341.13

international courts + jurisdiction
USE: jurisdiction + international courts KC1212; 341.712

international courts + procedure
USE: procedure + international courts KC1214; 341.714

international crimes
USE: crimes + international law KC215; 341.36

International Criminal Court KC219.I5; 341.391.I5

international criminal courts KC219; 341.39
RT: crimes + international law KC215; 341.36
RT: international courts KC1210; 341.71

international criminal law
USE: criminal law + international law KC210; 341.35

International Criminal Tribunal for Rwanda KC219.1.R9; 341.391.R9

International Criminal Tribunal for the former Yugoslavia KC219.1.Y8; 341.391.Y8

international crises
USE: crisis management + international disputes KC1202; 341.702

international custom KC82.1; 341.193
UF: customary law + international law

International Development Association KC631; 341.644
UF: IDA

international disputes KC1200; 341.7
UF: peaceful settlement of international disputes

international drainage basins
USE: drainage basins KC144.5; 341.2545

international economic law KC220; 341.4
UF: commercial law + international law
UF: economic organisations + international law
UF: international commerce

international economic organisations KC349.E2; 341.619.E2
UF: commercial organisations + international law
UF: economic organisations + international law

International Finance Corporation KC621; 341.643
UF: IFC

international forces KC1280; 341.75
UF: multinational forces + international law

international humanitarian law KC1410; 341.88

international labour law
USE: industrial law + international law KC242; 341.442

International Labour Organisation KC511; 341.632
UF: ILO

international law KC; 341
UF: public international law
RT: conflict of laws KC2000; 341.9

international law + conferences
USE: conferences + international law KC60; 341.161

international law + dictionaries KC72; 341.172

international law + encyclopedias KC73; 341.173

international law + history KC102; 341.21
UF: legal history + international law

international law : municipal law KC86; 341.196
UF: municipal law : international law

International Law Commission KC450; 341.628
UF: United Nations International Law Commission

International Maritime Consultative Organisation KC591; 341.639
SN: now renamed International Maritime Organisation
UF: IMCO

international maritime law KC260; 341.47
UF: maritime law + international law
RT: maritime law KN330; 347.83; [Table IIA: 138]

International Maritime Organisation KC591; 341.639
UF: IMO

international migration
USE: migration + international law KC199; 341.319

International Military Tribunal + law reports KC35.N8; 341.136.N8
UF: Nuremberg Tribunal
RT: war crimes KC217; 341.362

International Monetary Fund KC611; 341.642
UF: IMF

International Narcotics Control Board KC536; 341.6345

international officials KC346; 341.614
UF: civil servants + international organisations

international organisations KC340; 341.6; [Table VII: 8.1]
UF: international agencies

international organisations + debates
USE: debates + international organisations [Table before KC351: 2]

international organisations + internal regulation KC345; 341.613

international organisations + privileges KC344; 341.612
UF: privileges + international organisations

international organisations + taxation KM336.481; 346.52481

international police KC1280; 341.75
UF: police + international law
RT: peace-keeping forces KC1280; 341.75

international protection + human rights KC203; 341.333

international relations KC300; 341.5
UF: cold war
UF: foreign relations

UF: inter-continental relations
UF: peaceful coexistence
UF: power politics

international relations + EU KW75
UF: external relations + EU

international sanitary regulations
USE: public health + international law KC241; 341.441

International Seabed Authority KC597; 341.6397

international social law KC240; 341.44

International Swaps and Derivatives Association (ISDA) KN304.68; 347.7368

International Telecommunications Union KC581; 341.6385

international trade KC230; 341.42
UF: trade + international law

international travel regulation
USE: passports + international law KC195; 341.315

international trusteeships
USE: trust territories KC154.4; 341.2644

international waters KC263; 341.471

international zones KC154.7; 341.2647

internees + international humanitarian law KC1413; 341.883

internet KN347.4; 347.8935; [Table IIA: 143.5]
UF: web sites
UF: world wide web
UF: WWW

internet + copyright KN112.6; 347.3756

internet + international law KC257.7; 341.4627
UF: world wide web
RT: electronic mail KN342.4; 347.864

internet + law reporting KL33.5; 345.135

internet + legal research KL157; 345.192

internet sales KN285.9.I5; 347.678.I5

internet use + employment KN193.9.C6; 347.4779.C6

interpleader KN384.8; 347.9448

interpretation KL35; 345.15
RT: construction + statutes KL35; 345.15

interpreters + courts KL230.5; 345.35
UF: courts + interpreters
UF: translators + courts

interrogation + criminal investigation KM580.12; 346.9112
UF: police + questioning
UF: questioning
RT: tape-recording + criminal investigation KM580.12; 346.9112

interrogatories KN387.8; 347.9478

interstate commerce + federations KN252; 347.605
RT: single market + EU KW108

interstate relations + federations KM45; 346.1285

intervention + international disputes KC1302; 341.782

intervention purchasing + EU KW116

intestate succession KN130; 347.385

intimidation of witnesses KM563.7; 346.8857

intoxication KM562.4; 346.8834

intoxication + criminal liability KM505.4; 346.824

intranets KN347.55; 347.8945

invalid carriages
USE: disabled persons + transport KN181.2; 347.4412

invalidity benefits
USE: disabled persons + social security KN181.2; 347.4412

invasion KC1355.1; 341.821
UF: hot pursuit
UF: incursion

invention KN111.4; 347.3704

investigation + criminal law KM580.1; 346.911
UF: criminal investigation
UF: detection

investigation + real property KN72.1; 347.3215

investment KN304; 347.73; [Table IIA: 134.3]

investment + advertising
USE: financial promotion KN308.6; 347.7866

investment + international law KC227; 341.415
UF: loans + international law

investment + real property KN81; 347.3241
UF: property development
UF: property investment

investment + supervision KN304.95; 347.7395

investment accounts KN218; 347.578

investment banks KN303.63; 347.7263

investment business KN308.2; 347.7862

investment reliefs + taxation KM336.65; 346.5265

investment trusts KN304.52; 347.7352

investments + electronic trading KN304.87; 347.7387

investor protection KN308.1; 347.7861

iron KN91.2; 347.3342

iron and steel industry KN275.I7; 347.645.I7

irradiation + food KN185.24; 347.44724

irrelevant evidence
USE: relevance + evidence KN393.1; 347.9641

irrigation KN90.2; 347.3332

ISAs
USE: individual savings accounts KN304.7.I5; 347.737.I5

Islam + international law KC124.I8; 341.224.I8

Islamic finance KN305.27; 347.7527

Islamic law KD600; 342.7
UF: Muhammadan law
UF: Muslim law

islands + international law KC145; 341.255
UF: archipelagos

IVF
USE: in vitro fertilisation KN172.82; 347.42182

jactitation of marriage KN172.9.J3; 347.422.J3

Jain law KD820; 342.92

JCT Standard Forms of Building Contract KN84.45; 347.32645

jetties KN336.3; 347.8363

jetsam
USE: flotsam and jetsam KN104.4; 347.3644

Jewish law KD60; 342.2

job centres KN197.3; 347.4873

job creation + EU KW130.6

job security
USE: employment protection KN192.2; 347.463

job sharing KN192.65; 347.4665

job sharing + EU KW131.1

jobs
USE: occupations KN156; 347.416; [Table VII: 6]

joinder and severance KM582.6; 346.9326
UF: severance

joint contracts KN18.3; 347.153

joint parties [Table VI: .Z64]

Joint Research Centre (EU) KW140.2

joint stock banks KN303.62; 347.7263

joint tenancy KN87.2; 347.3292
UF: co-tenancy

joint ventures + incorporation KN262.25; 347.62425

joint ventures + partnership KN267.5; 347.6365

journalism KN345.2; 347.882

journals K1; 340.01; [Table VIII: 001]
UF: magazines
UF: periodicals
UF: serial publications

journals + bibliographies K31; 340.022

journals + censorship KN349.98; 347.8998

journals + EU KW65

journals + indexes K28; 340.019

Judge-Advocates KM406; 346.745
UF: military legal officers

judge-made law KL32; 345.12
UF: judicial legislation

judges KL241; 345.46
RT: judiciary KL240; 345.4; [Table IIA: 69.5]

judges + directions to juries
USE: directions + juries KN389.64; 347.96064

judges + directions to juries + criminal procedure
USE: directions + juries + criminal procedure KM583.4; 346.9334

Judges' Rules KM603.1; 346.9631
RT: admissibility + evidence + criminal procedure KM603; 346.963

judgments KN395; 347.97; [Table IIA: 148.9]
SN: use for theory only; for texts of judgments use law reports

judgments + international courts
USE: law reports + international law KC20; 341.13

judicare KN399.2; 347.992

judicial co-operation + EU KW133.6

Judicial Committee of the Privy Council [Table V: 1]
UF: Privy Council Judicial Committee

judicial conduct
USE: conduct + judiciary KL240.3; 345.43

Judicial Councils KL230.12; 345.312
RT: judiciary KL240; 345.4; [Table IIA: 69.5]

judicial definitions KL41; 345.1691
UF: definitions by judges
UF: words and phrases judicially defined

judicial discipline
USE: discipline + judiciary KL240.3; 345.43

judicial discretion + sentencing KM587.3; 346.9373

judicial error
USE: miscarriage of justice KM597; 346.957

judicial ethics
USE: ethics + judiciary KL240.3; 345.43

judicial immunity KL240.35; 345.435
UF: immunities + judges

judicial independence
USE: independence + judiciary KM141.2; 346.282

judicial legislation
USE: judge-made law KL32; 345.12

judicial notice KN390.3; 347.9613

judicial notice + criminal procedure KM601.2; 346.9612

judicial pensions
USE: pensions + judiciary KL240.4; 345.44

judicial power KM141; 346.28
UF: judiciary + constitutional law
RT: judiciary KL240; 345.4; [Table IIA: 69.5]

judicial precedent
USE: precedent KL32; 345.12

judicial process KA28; 340.128

judicial review KM36; 346.123

judicial review + administrative law KM306; 346.46

judicial separation
USE: separation + marriage KN173.3; 347.425

judicial statistics
USE: statistics KL300; 345.7; [Table IIA: 72]; [Table VIII: .0024]

judicial time KL230.48; 345.348
UF: use of judicial time
RT: case listing KL230.47; 345.347

judiciary KL240; 345.4; [Table IIA: 69.5]
RT: judges KL241; 345.46
RT: Judicial Councils KL230.12; 345.312
RT: judicial power KM141; 346.28

judiciary + appointment KL240.1; 345.41

judiciary + constitutional law
USE: judicial power KM141; 346.28

judiciary + discipline
USE: discipline + judiciary KL240.3; 345.43

judiciary + remuneration KL240.2; 345.42

judiciary + retirement
USE: retirement + judiciary KL240.4; 345.44

judiciary + training
USE: training + judiciary KL240.5; 345.45

juries KN389.6; 347.9606; [Table IIA: 70]
UF: petty jury
UF: trial by jury

juries + challenges
UF: array + challenges

juries + criminal procedure KM583; 346.933
RT: grand juries KM581.1; 346.921

jurimetrics KL156; 345.191

jurisdiction KN353; 347.91; [Table VI: .Z4]
UF: venue

jurisdiction + conflict of laws KC2050; 341.92

jurisdiction + international courts KC1212; 341.712
UF: international courts + jurisdiction

jurisprudence KA; 340.1
UF: legal theory
UF: philosophy of law
UF: science of law
UF: theory of law
RT: philosophy : law KA70.P4; 340.16.P4

juristic persons
USE: legal personality KN160; 347.418

jurors + crimes KM563.4; 346.8854
UF: offences by jurors

jurors + victims
USE: offences against jurors KM563.4; 346.8854

jury instructions KN389.7; 347.9607
UF: instructions to juries
UF: misdirection + juries

jury instructions + criminal procedure KM585; 346.935

jus ad bellum KC1353; 341.81

jus cogens KC338.7; 341.597

justice KA35; 340.13
UF: ethical jurisprudence

justice + EU KW83

justice : law KA37; 340.132
UF: law : justice

justice : morality KA38; 340.134
UF: morality : justice
UF: sanctity of life

Justices of the Peace
USE: magistrates KL243; 345.48

Justices of the Supreme Court KL241.1; 345.461

justification KN383.3; 347.9443

justification + criminal law KM584.2; 346.9342

Justinian KE145; 343.47
RT: Corpus Juris Civilis KE150; 343.471

juvenile courts
USE: youth courts KL227.1; 345.3071; [Table V: 7.1]

juvenile delinquents KM507.Q12; 346.83.Q12

kidnapping KM543.4; 346.8634
UF: abduction
UF: ransom

kidnapping + international law KC218.D4; 341.369.D4

killing
USE: homicide KM542; 346.862
USE: manslaughter KM542.2; 346.8622
USE: murder KM542.1; 346.8621

King's Bench Division
USE: Queen's Bench Division [Table V: 3; 5.1]

kings
USE: monarchs KM112.1; 346.252

kiosks KL230.69.K5; 345.369.K5

know how + industrial property KN114.9.K6; 347.3779.K6

Know Your Customer (KYC) KN303.955; 347.72955

knowledge management + legal profession KL96.3; 345.1763

Koran KD621; 342.721

labelling KN284.2; 347.662
RT: dangerous things KN186.9.D3; 347.459.D3

labelling + EU KW112.5

labelling + food
USE: food + labelling KN185.23; 347.44723

laboratory animals KN186.84; 347.4584
UF: animals + experiments

labour courts
USE: industrial courts [Table V: 8.6]

labour injunctions
USE: injunctions + industrial law KN196.3; 347.4863

labour law
USE: industrial law KN190; 347.46; [Table IIA: 124]

labour law + international law
USE: industrial law + international law KC242; 341.442

labour relations
USE: industrial relations KN190; 347.46

laches KN217.3; 347.573

Lamaism KD940; 342.97

land + development KN96.7; 347.3447

land + nationalisation KN96.35; 347.34345

land + registration KN72.2; 347.3216
RT: Torrens system KN72.3; 347.3217

land charges KN96.71; 347.34471

land claims + aboriginals KM208.433; 346.36433

land commissions KN96.72; 347.34472

land grants KN82; 347.3242

land law
USE: real property KN60; 347.31; [Table IIA: 104]

land reclamation
USE: accretion + real property KN76.A3; 347.323.A3

Land Registry KN72.2; 347.3216

land taxes
USE: real property + taxes KM337.6; 346.57

land tenure KN62; 347.311; [Table IIA: 105]
UF: tenure + land

land tenure + feudal law
USE: feudal law + England and Wales KL401.6; 345.9426

land titles KN72; 347.3214
UF: title + real property

land use KN80; 347.324

land warfare KC1370; 341.85
UF: war on land

landed estates
USE: estates KN63; 347.312

landfill tax KM337.9.L3; 346.59.L3

landlocked states KC146; 341.256

landlord and tenant KN85; 347.327; [Table IIA: 106]
UF: tenant and landlord
RT: private landlords KN86.1; 347.3281

landscaping + roads
USE: roads + landscaping KN322.5; 347.8125

language + civil rights KM208.44; 346.3644
RT: official languages KM208.44; 346.3644

language + education + EU KW144.4

language groups
USE: linguistic groups KM208.44; 346.3644; [Table VII: 4.4]

language of law
USE: legal language K100; 340.06

larceny
USE: theft KM546; 346.871

latent damage KN33.3; 347.213
UF: damage + latency

Latin America + international relations KC306.3; 341.5163

Latin America : EU KW81.4

Latin dictionaries K122.L1; 340.082.L1
USE: dictionaries + Latin K122.L3; 340.082.L3

laundering money
USE: money laundering KM540.6; 346.856

laundries KN286.L3; 347.679.L3

law + command
USE: command : law KA42; 340.142

law + language
USE: legal language K100; 340.06

law : ethics
USE: ethics : law KA70.E8; 340.16.E8

law : force
USE: force : law KA29; 340.129

law : justice
USE: justice : law KA37; 340.132

law : morality
USE: criminal law : morality KM504; 346.818

law : state KA27; 340.127
UF: state and law

law and custom
USE: customary law KL8; 345.08; [Table IIA: 62]
USE: sources of law KA23; 340.123; [Table VI: .Z1]

law and order
USE: law enforcement KM610; 346.98; [Table IIA: 92]

law as a profession KA90; 340.19
RT: legal profession KL50; 345.17; [Table IIA: 64]

law as command
USE: command : law KA42; 340.142

law assessors
USE: assessors + judiciary KL244; 345.49

law booksellers K105.9; 340.0659
UF: booksellers + law books

law centres KN399.9; 347.999

Law Commission KL161; 345.19842

law courts
USE: courts KL220; 345.3; [Table IIA: 69]; [Table V]

law enforcement KM610; 346.98; [Table IIA: 92]
UF: enforcement of law
UF: law and order

law enforcement + EU KW133.3

law firms KL97; 345.1767
RT: business organisation + legal profession KL97; 345.1767; [Table IIA: 64.5]
RT: partnerships + legal profession KL97; 345.1767

law for architects KL30.A7; 345.1.A7
UF: architects + law

law for motorists KL30.M6; 345.1.M6
UF: motorists + law

law for social workers KL30.S6; 345.1.S6
UF: social workers + law

Law French KL44; 345.1694

law indexing
USE: indexing K105.8; 340.0658

Law Latin KL43; 345.1693

law librarians K84.4; 340.0544

law librarians + directories K82; 340.052

law libraries K80; 340.05
UF: bar libraries
UF: libraries + legal profession
RT: librarianship K80; 340.05
RT: libraries KN184.4; 347.445; [Table IIA: 122.5]

law libraries + accommodation K84.5; 340.0545
UF: buildings + law libraries

law libraries + directories K82; 340.052

law libraries + equipment K84.6; 340.0546

law libraries + finance K84.2; 340.0542

law libraries + government K84.1; 340.0541

law libraries + staff K84.4; 340.0544

law lists
USE: directories K150; 340.09; [Table VIII: 0022]

law of the sea
USE: maritime law KN330; 347.83

law of the sea + international law KC260; 341.47

Law Officers of the Crown
USE: legal officers KL250; 345.5

law offices KL96; 345.176; [Table IIA: 64.5]

law publishing K105; 340.065
UF: legal publishing
RT: publishing KN345; 347.88

law reform KL160; 345.197; [Table IIA: 66]; [Table VI: .Z53]
UF: law revision
UF: reform of law
UF: revision of law
RT: statute law reform KL36; 345.16

Law Reform Committee KL161; 345.19842

law reporting KL33; 345.13
UF: court reporting
UF: law reports + theory
RT: legal composition K101; 340.061
RT: sound recordings + law reporting KL33.2; 345.132

law reports [Table IA: 40–48]
UF: case reports

Law Reports (texts) KF55

law reports + Australia + federal courts KH40

law reports + Canada + federal courts KG40

law reports + England and Wales KF50

law reports + EU KW50

Law Reports + indexes KF55.Z1

law reports + international arbitration
USE: international arbitration + cases KC40; 341.14

law reports + international law KC20; 341.13
UF: judgments + international courts
RT: international courts KC1210; 341.71

law reports + Permanent Court of Arbitration KC41; 341.141

law reports + Permanent Court of International Justice KC21; 341.131

law reports + theory
USE: law reporting KL33; 345.13

law reports + United States + federal courts KG361

law revision
USE: law reform KL160; 345.197; [Table IIA: 66]; [Table VI: .Z53]

law schools KL131–149 [Table: .1]; 345.1794–9 [Table: 1]

law schools + directories K165; 340.095

law societies
USE: associations + legal profession KL100; 345.177; [Table IIA: 64.8]

Law Society KL101.7; 345.177427

law suits
USE: litigation [Table VI: .Z71]

law teachers KL131–149 [Table: .6]; 345.1794–9 [Table: 6]
UF: teachers of law

Law Times Reports KF60.L4

lawyer-client relationship KL82.2; 345.17022
UF: attorney and client
UF: client-lawyer relationship

lawyers KL85; 345.171
UF: attorneys
RT: barristers KL86; 345.1711
RT: solicitors KL87; 345.17134

lawyers + complaints
USE: complaints + legal profession KL95; 345.174

lawyers + directories K150; 340.09

lay magistrates
USE: magistrates KL243; 345.48

laymen + religious laws [KD Table: 3]

laytime KN337.5; 347.8375

leading questions
USE: examination + witnesses KN391.3; 347.9623

League of Nations KC351; 341.62

leased territories KC154.5; 341.2645

leasehold KN63.2; 347.314

leases KN87; 347.329
UF: letting

leases + creation KN72.1; 347.3311
UF: creation of leases
UF: estoppel + leases

leases + termination KN87.8; 347.3298

leasing KN18.6; 347.156
RT: hire KN106.2; 347.3662

leave of absence
USE: holidays KN193.2; 347.472

legacies KN125.7; 347.3827
UF: bequests

legal abbreviations K112; 340.072
RT: citation manuals K114; 340.074; [Table VI: .Z25]

legal advice
USE: legal aid KN399; 347.99; [Table IIA: 71]

legal aid KN399; 347.99; [Table IIA: 71]
UF: legal advice
RT: advice services KN400; 347.9991

legal aid + criminal procedure KM599; 346.959

legal aid + eligibility KN399.3; 347.933
UF: financial eligibility for legal aid
UF: means tests + legal aid

legal argument
USE: legal logic KA55; 340.148

legal associations
USE: associations + legal profession KL100; 345.177; [Table IIA: 64.8]

legal bibliographies K30; 340.021
RT: bibliographies K29; 340.02; [Table VIII: 0021]

legal bibliographies + Commonwealth K61; 340.044–9 [DDC Table 2]

legal bibliographies + England and Wales K62; 340.044–9 [DDC Table 2]

legal bibliographies + Ireland K64; 340.044–9 [DDC Table 2]

legal bibliographies + Scotland K63; 340.044–9 [DDC Table 2]

legal bibliographies + United States K71; 340.044–9 [DDC Table 2]

legal biographies
USE: biographies KB10; 340.31; [Table VIII: 006]

legal capacity
USE: capacity [Table VI: .Z43]

legal citations
USE: citation manuals K114; 340.074; [Table VI: .Z25]

legal composition K101; 340.061
UF: techniques + legal writing
UF: writing + law
RT: drafting + documents KL34.2; 345.142; [Table VIII: .0051]
RT: law reporting KL33; 345.13

legal concepts KA21; 340.121
UF: concepts of law
UF: nature of law

legal deposit KN184.6; 347.4456
UF: depository libraries
RT: copyright KN112; 347.371

legal dictionaries K120; 340.08; [Table IIA: 63]
UF: legal phrases
UF: legal vocabulary
UF: phrases and terms
UF: terms and phrases

UF: vocabulary of law
UF: words and phrases
RT: dictionaries K120; 340.08; [Table VIII: 0023]

legal dictionaries + common law KL40; 345.169

legal drafting
USE: drafting + documents KL34.2; 345.142; [Table VIII: .0051]

legal dress KL81; 345.17011
UF: costume + legal profession
UF: court dress
UF: robes + lawyers

legal education KL130; 345.178; [Table IIA: 65]
UF: legal training
RT: education KN184; 347.443; [Table IIA: 122]
RT: education + judiciary KL240.5; 345.45

legal education + finance KL131–149 [Table: .7]; 345.1794–9 [Table: 7]

legal encyclopedias + common law KL42; 345.1692
RT: encyclopedias K140; 340.089; [Table VIII: 0023]

legal ethics KL82; 345.1702
UF: ethics + legal profession

legal etiquette
USE: etiquette + legal profession KL81; 345.17011

legal executives KL87.2; 345.171342
RT: paralegals KL87.2; 345.171342

legal fictions KL35.5; 345.155

legal history KL400; 345.8; [Table IIA: 74]
RT: history [Table VIII: 007]

legal history + international law
USE: international law + history KC102; 341.21

legal humour
USE: humorous writings KB34; 340.374

legal indexing
USE: indexing K105.8; 340.0658

legal instruments + interpretation
USE: documents + interpretation KL35.2; 345.152

legal language K100; 340.06
UF: language of law
UF: law + language
UF: legal style
UF: style + legal language

legal liability
USE: liability [Table VI: .Z45]

legal logic KA55; 340.148
UF: legal argument
UF: legal method
UF: legal reasoning
UF: logic
UF: reasoning + law

legal maxims K124; 340.084

legal method
USE: legal logic KA55; 340.148

legal miscellany KB30; 340.37

legal obligations
USE: obligations [Table IIA: 96]

legal officers KL250; 345.5
UF: Law Officers of the Crown
RT: Attorney-General KL251; 345.51

Legal Ombudsman KL95; 345.1741
UF: Legal Services Ombudsman

legal personality KN160; 347.418
UF: juristic persons
UF: personality
RT: corporate personality KN161; 347.4181; [Table IIA: 114]

legal personality + jurisprudence KA24; 340.124

legal phrases
USE: legal dictionaries K120; 340.08; [Table IIA: 63]

legal pluralism KB140; 340.59
UF: mixed legal systems
UF: plural systems

legal positivism
USE: positivism KA44; 340.144

legal profession KL50; 345.17; [Table IIA: 64]
UF: practice of law
UF: profession of law
RT: law as a profession KA90; 340.19
RT: professions KN156; 347.416; [Table VII: 6]

legal profession + bibliography K49.4; 340.0331

legal profession + comparative law KB164; 340.6031

legal profession + reform KL84; 345.1704
UF: reform of the legal profession

legal profession + remuneration KL89; 345.1714

legal profession + structure KL84; 345.1704
UF: divided profession
UF: fused profession
UF: structure of the legal profession

legal professional conduct
USE: conduct + legal profession KL81; 345.17011

legal psychology
USE: social psychology KA63; 340.153

legal publishing
USE: law publishing K105; 340.065

legal quotations
USE: quotations K125; 340.085

legal reasoning
USE: legal logic KA55; 340.148

legal research KL155; 345.19; [Table IIA: 66]
UF: research + law

legal rights + jurisprudence KA25; 340.125

legal services + directories K168; 340.097

Legal Services Ombudsman
USE: Legal Ombudsman KL95; 345.1741

legal societies
USE: associations KN169.4; 347.41894; [Table VII: 9.4]; [Table VIII: .003]
USE: associations + legal profession KL100; 345.177; [Table IIA: 64.8]

legal statistics
USE: statistics KL300; 345.7; [Table IIA: 72]; [Table VIII: .0024]

legal style
USE: legal language K100; 340.06

legal system KL1; 345.01; [Table IIA: 61]

legal tender KN302.1; 347.711
RT: coinage KN302.2; 347.712
RT: money KN302; 347.71

legal terms KL230.18; 345.318
SN: divisions of the legal year
UF: terms + courts
RT: vacations KL230.18; 345.318

legal theory
USE: jurisprudence KA; 340.1

legal thesauri
USE: thesauri K123; 340.083

legal training
USE: legal education KL130; 345.178; [Table IIA: 65]

legal vocabulary
USE: legal dictionaries K120; 340.08; [Table IIA: 63]

legal writing K100; 340.06
RT: drama KB32; 340.372
RT: fiction (novels) KB33; 340.373

legality + war KC1353; 341.81
UF: force + war
UF: use of force + war

legations + buildings KC322.1; 341.5421
RT: diplomatic quarters KC322.2; 341.5422

legionnaire's disease KN185.69.L4; 347.44869.L4

legislation (texts) [Table IA: 15]
UF: Acts of Congress
UF: Acts of Parliament
UF: primary sources
RT: statutes + texts [Table IA: 15]; [Table VI: .Z14]

legislation (texts) + Australia KH14

legislation (texts) + Canada KG14

legislation (texts) + EU KW5

legislation (texts) + Roman law KE110; 343.419

legislation (texts) + UK KF20
UF: Public General Acts

legislation (texts) + US KG320

legislation (theory) KL36; 345.16
UF: statutes (theory)

legislation + interpretation KL35.1; 345.151

legislative bills [Table IA: 6; 12]; [Table VI: .Z11]
UF: bills + legislation

legislative bills (theory) KL36.2; 345.162

legislative bills + House of Commons (texts) KF12
UF: House of Commons (UK) + bills

legislative bills + House of Lords (texts) KF6
UF: House of Lords (UK) + bills

legislative committees [Table IA: 7; 13]
UF: select committees

legislative councils
USE: legislatures KM82; 346.21; [Table IIA: 79]

legislative definitions KL35.8; 345.158

legislative disqualification
USE: disqualification + legislators KM83.1; 346.221

legislative districts
USE: constituencies KM83.2; 346.222

legislative drafting
USE: drafting + legislation KL34.1; 345.141

legislative investigations KM86.2; 346.242
UF: Congressional investigations

legislative pensions
USE: pensions + legislators KM83.9; 346.229

legislative power KM82; 346.21

legislative procedure
USE: parliamentary procedure KM84; 346.23

legislative procedures + EU KW97.5

legislative proceedings [Table VI: .Z12]

legislators KM83; 346.22
UF: backbenchers
UF: Congressmen
UF: Members of Congress
UF: Members of Parliament
UF: representatives + parliament
UF: Senators

legislators + disabled persons KM87.5; 346.3485

legislators + pensions
USE: pensions + legislators KM83.9; 346.229

legislators + remuneration KM83.9; 346.229

legislatures KM82; 346.21; [Table IIA: 79]
UF: assemblies (legislative)
UF: legislative councils
RT: Congress (US) KM82; 346.21
RT: Parliament + UK KM82; 346.21; [Table IIA: 79]

legislatures + accommodation
USE: accommodation + Parliament KM87.1; 346.2481

legislatures + social and welfare services KM87.6; 346.2486

legitimacy + governments
USE: recognition + international law KC164; 341.274

legitimation KN176.3; 347.4263

LEIs
USE: local employment initiatives + EU KW130.6

leisure
USE: recreation KN186.6; 347.456

lending
USE: loans KN305.2; 347.752

lesbians
USE: homosexuals [Table VII: 2.3]

letters (biography) KB15; 340.33

letters of administration KN133; 347.388

letters of credit KN306.44; 347.7744

letters patent KF37.3

letting
USE: leases KN87; 347.329

Lex Aebutia KE128; 343.435

liability [Table VI: .Z45]
UF: accountability
UF: legal liability
UF: responsibility

liability + company directors KN264.7; 347.6267

liability + judiciary KL240.3; 345.43

liability + jurisprudence KA25; 340.125

liability + taxation KM336.1; 346.5211
UF: tax liability

liability + tort KN33; 347.21
UF: tortious liability

liability + trusts KN216.2; 347.562

liability for crime
USE: criminal liability KM505; 346.82; [Table IIA: 90.3]

liability insurance
USE: risks insurance KN294; 347.694

liability without fault
USE: strict liability + criminal law KM505.9; 346.828

libel KN38.21; 347.2481
RT: libel + criminal law KM541.4; 346.8612

libel + criminal law KM541.4; 346.8612
UF: criminal libel
UF: offences against reputation
UF: reputation + offences
RT: libel KN38.21; 347.2481

liberties
USE: civil rights KM201; 346.35; [Table IIA: 81]

librarianship K80; 340.05
RT: law libraries K80; 340.05

libraries KN184.4; 347.445; [Table IIA: 122.5]
UF: academic libraries
UF: college libraries
UF: public libraries
UF: university libraries
RT: law libraries K80; 340.05

libraries + accommodation K84.5; 340.0545
UF: buildings + libraries

libraries + administration K84; 340.054

libraries + automation
USE: computers in libraries K86; 340.056

libraries + directories K82; 340.054

libraries + finance K84.2; 340.0542

libraries + furniture
USE: furniture + law libraries K84.6; 340.0546

libraries + legal profession
USE: law libraries K80; 340.05

libraries + prisons
USE: prison libraries KM681.6; 346.98766; [App: 93.6]

licence fees + broadcasting
USE: broadcasting + licences + fees KN344.2; 347.8713

licences + drivers
USE: driving licences KN323.5; 347.8135

licences + equitable remedies KN221.2; 347.582

licences + intellectual property KN115.4; 347.3784

licences + marriage
USE: marriage + licences KN172.32; 347.4214

licences + motor vehicles
USE: motor vehicles + licences KN323.12; 347.8233

licensed conveyancers KN74.9; 347.3228
RT: conveyancing agents KN74.9; 347.3228

licensing + alcohol
USE: alcohol KN186.4; 347.454

licensing + competition + EU KW110.7

licensing + lawyers KL83; 345.1703
UF: disbarment
RT: admission to the Bar KL83; 345.1703
RT: practice certificates KL83; 345.1703

licensing bodies + intellectual property KN115.41; 347.3785

lie detectors KM605.2; 346.972

liens + carriage of goods by sea KN337.6; 347.8376

liens + equitable interests KN221.2; 347.582

liens + personal property KN106.3; 347.3663

liens + security + finance KN306.93; 347.7793

Lieutenant-Governors KM368.5; 346.675

life + artificial prolongation KN185.14; 347.44614
UF: artificial prolongation of life
RT: life support KN185.14; 347.44614

life insurance KN292.1; 347.683

life interests + real property KN63.13; 347.3133

life support KN185.14; 347.44614
RT: life + artificial prolongation KN185.14; 347.44614

light and air + easements KN65.11; 347.3172
UF: air + easements

lighthouses KN333.3; 347.8333

lighthouses + international maritime law KC274.5; 341.4785

lighting + roads KN322.7; 347.8127
UF: street lighting

lightships + international maritime law KC274.5; 341.4785

limitation of actions KN355; 347.915
UF: statute of limitations
UF: time limits

limitations + property KN56.1; 347.3031

limitations + real property KN79.2; 347.32312

limited liability partnerships KN267.3; 347.6363

limited partnerships KN267.4; 347.6364

Lincoln's Inn KL101.4; 345.177424

liner conferences
USE: cartels + shipping KN332.9; 347.8329

linguistic groups KM208.44; 346.3644; [Table VII: 4.4]
UF: language groups

linguistics + jurisprudence KA70.L5; 340.16.L5

linguistics : law K100.5; 340.0605

liquidated damages KN37.1; 347.231

liquidators KN312.1; 347.7921

liquor
USE: alcohol KN186.4; 347.454

Lisbon Treaty
USE: Treaty of Lisbon (2007) KW1.G07

listed buildings KN95.12; 347.34212
UF: buildings + heritage sites

Listing Officers + courts KL230.47; 345.347

literacy + EU KW143.7

literary works + intellectual property KN112.1; 347.372

literary works + Roman law KE111; 343.4191

literature : law KA70.A7; 340.16.A7

litigants + status
USE: locus standi KN370.3; 347.9303

litigants in person KN370.1; 347.9301

litigation [Table VI: .Z71]
UF: law suits

litter KN97.85; 347.3485
UF: dropping litter
UF: rubbish

livestock KN99.3; 347.3563
RT: animals + control KN186.8; 347.458

living wills KN185.157; 347.446157
UF: voluntary wills
RT: wills KN125; 347.382

loading + maritime law KN337.7; 347.8377

loan associations KN305.6; 347.766

Loan Market Association (LMA) KN304.96.L6; 347.7396.L6

loans KN305.2; 347.752
UF: borrowing
UF: lending

loans + international law
USE: investment + international law KC227; 341.415

loans + personal property KN106.1; 347.3661

loans to students
USE: student loans KN184.35; 347.4445

lobbying KM232.8; 346.3728

local acts KF24

local authorities + landlord and tenant KN86.5; 347.3285
RT: local services KM361.1; 346.611

local civil servants KM370; 346.68
UF: civil service + local government

local councillors KM367; 346.667
UF: councillors + local government
RT: elected representatives + local government KM367; 346.667

local elections
USE: elections + local government KM369; 346.679

local employment initiatives + EU KW130.6
UF: LEIs

local executive KM368; 346.67

local government KM361; 346.6; [Table IIA: 86]
RT: by-laws KF41; [Table IA: 34]

local government + finance KM361.2; 346.612
RT: local taxation KM337.8; 346.589

local government : national government KM362; 346.62
UF: national government : local government

local government districts
USE: districts + local government KM365.5; 346.655

local government officers
USE: officers + local government KM370; 346.68
USE: officials + local government KM370; 346.68

local government services
USE: local services KM361.1; 346.611

local legislation (texts) KF41; [Table IA: 34]
RT: by-laws KF41; [Table IA: 34]
RT: counties KM365.1; 346.651

local officials
USE: officers + local government KM370; 346.68
USE: officials + local government KM370; 346.68

local ombudsmen KM307.2; 346.472
UF: ombudsman + local government
RT: ombudsman KM307; 346.47

local police KM615.1; 346.9851
RT: police KM615; 346.985; [Table IIA: 92.2]

local services KM361.1; 346.611
UF: local government services
UF: services + local government
RT: local authorities + landlord and tenant KN86.5; 347.3285

local taxation KM337.8; 346.589
RT: community charge (UK) KM337.14; 346.534
RT: council tax KM337.65; 346.575
RT: local government + finance KM361.2; 346.612

lockouts KN196.4; 347.4864
RT: strikes KN196.4; 347.4864

locus standi KN370.3; 347.9303
UF: litigants + status
UF: status + litigants

logic
USE: legal logic KA55; 340.148

Lombard law KE320.5; 343.625

Lomé Conventions KW77.3

Lomé Conventions + texts KW2.5
RT: ACP-EU + publications KW35

London + local government KM391.L6; 346.69.L6
UF: Greater London Council

London Stock Exchange KN304.86.L6; 347.7386.L6

Lord Chief Justice KL241.1; 345.461

Lord Justices of Appeal KL241.1; 345.461

Lord Lieutenants KM368.5; 346.675

lorries
USE: heavy goods vehicles KN323.13; 347.81331

loss adjusters KN291.5; 347.6815

loss assessors KN291.4; 347.6814

loss of citizenship
USE: denaturalisation + international law KC192; 341.312

loss of remission KM670.4; 346.98744; [App: 92.44]

loss of rights + prisons KM670.3; 346.98743; [App: 92.43]

loss relief + taxation KM336.66; 346.5266

lotteries KN186.5; 347.455
RT: national lotteries KN186.51; 347.4551

lower chambers + legislatures KM82.4; 346.214
RT: upper chambers + legislatures KM82.3; 346.213

lower civil courts [Table V: 5.2]

lower criminal courts [Table V: 4.2]

loyalty
USE: allegiance KM172.3; 346.313

lump sum payments
USE: compensation [Table VI: .Z9]
USE: pensions KN193.4; 347.474

Lutheran churches KD410; 342.51

luxury taxes KM337.42; 346.562

lynching KM542.8; 346.8628

M'Naghten rules KM506.1; 346.8291

Maastricht Treaty
USE: Treaty on European Union (1992) KW1.F92

machinery + agriculture KN98.6; 347.3556
UF: agricultural machinery

magazines
USE: journals K1; 340.01; [Table VIII: 001]

magistrates KL243; 345.48
UF: Justices of the Peace
UF: lay magistrates
UF: police magistrates
UF: stipendiary magistrates

magistrates + criminal procedure KM574; 346.902

magistrates + training KL243.15; 345.4815

magistrates' clerks KL243.2; 345.482

Magistrates' Courts [Table V: 4.3; 5.3]
UF: petty sessions
RT: summary jurisdiction [Table V: 4.3]

Magna Carta KL401.4; 345.9424

mail KN341; 347.85
UF: postal services

mail + censorship KN349.91; 347.8991

mail + international law KC256.1; 341.461

mail + theft KM546.4; 346.8714

mail order KN285.3; 347.673

main roads KN322.15; 347.81215

maintenance + children KN176.62; 347.42662

maintenance + divorce KN173.2; 347.4245

maintenance + marriage KN172.6; 347.4216
UF: support + marriage

maintenance + tort KN38.31; 347.251

majority + children
USE: age of majority KN151.3; 347.4113; [Table VII: 1.3]

majority shareholders KN263.72; 347.62572

majority verdicts KN389.65; 347.96065

majority verdicts + criminal procedure KM583.5; 346.9335

Malabar Church KD210.M3; 342.43.M3

males [Table VII: 2.1]

malice + criminal law
USE: mens rea KM505.1; 346.821

malice + tort KN33.2; 347.212

malicious damage
USE: criminal damage KM549; 346.874

malicious prosecution KN38.32; 347.252

malpractice
USE: professional negligence KN33.33; 347.2133

malpractice + medicine
USE: medical negligence KN33.33.M4; 347.2135.M4

malpractice + personal injuries KN38.14; 347.244

management + civil service KM237.3; 346.3823

management + clients' affairs KL99; 345.1769

management + clients' money KL99; 345.1769
UF: clients + money

management + courts
USE: court management KL230; 345.3; [Table IIA: 69.2]

management + EU KW131.5

management + law offices KL96.1; 345.1761

management + legal aid KN399.6; 347.996

management + prisons KM658; 346.98718; [App: 88]

management + property KN54.6; 347.3026

management buyouts KN262.3; 347.6243
UF: buyouts
UF: MBOs

mandamus KN395.82; 347.9742

mandates + international law
USE: trusteeships + international law KC154.3; 341.2643

manslaughter KM542.2; 346.8622
UF: killing

manuals
SN: use as subdivision only

manufacturing industries + EU KW119.8
RT: industries KN270; 347.64; [Table IIA: 131]

manuscripts + intellectual property KN112.15; 347.3725; [Table VIII: 0091]

manuscripts + legal writing K102; 340.062

maps K200; 340.099
UF: plans

maps + intellectual property KN112.2; 347.373
RT: topography right KN114.7; 347.3777

Mareva injunctions
USE: freezing injunctions KN232.2; 347.5922

marine accidents
USE: collisions + international law KC274.1; 341.4781
USE: wrecks KN334.1; 347.8341

marine insurance KN335; 347.835; [Table IIA: 139]
UF: average
UF: general average
UF: insurance + maritime law

marine oil operations
USE: oil and gas + marine operations KC277.1; 341.4821

maritime law KN330; 347.83; [Table IIA: 138]
UF: admiralty law
UF: commerce + maritime law
UF: merchant marine
UF: sea law
UF: sea transport
RT: international maritime law KC260; 341.47

maritime law + international law
USE: international maritime law KC260; 341.47

maritime warfare KC1380; 341.854
UF: war at sea
RT: blockade KC1385; 341.8545

market abuse KN304.92; 347.7392

market gardens KN98.26; 347.3526
RT: horticulture + EU KW117.3.H6

market makers KN304.81; 347.7381

market manipulation **KN304.92;** **347.7392**

market rigging **KN308.7;** **347.7867**

marketing + agriculture + EU **KW115**

marketing + legal profession **KL98;** **345.1768**
RT: advertising + legal profession KL98; 345.1768

markets **KN285.2;** **347.672**

marriage **KN172;** **347.421;** **[Table IIA: 117]**
UF: husband and wife
UF: matrimony
UF: wife and husband

marriage + ceremony **KN172.5;** **347.4215**
UF: ceremony of marriage
UF: performance of marriage
UF: solemnisation of marriage

marriage + common law
USE: common law marriage KN172.9.C6; 347.422.C6

marriage + contracts **KN172.1;** **347.4211**
UF: contracts of marriage

marriage + impediments **KN172.3;** **347.4213**
UF: banns
UF: dispensations + marriage
UF: impediments to marriage
UF: prohibited degrees + marriage
RT: affinity KN172.32; 347.42132

marriage + licences **KN172.4;** **347.4214**
UF: licences + marriage

marriage + registration
USE: registration + marriages KM172.31; 346.3131

marriage + religious laws [KD Table: 8.4]

marriage breakdown KN173.11; 347.4241
UF: breakdown of marriage

marriage guidance
USE: counselling + marriage KN173.6; 347.4256

marriage settlements KN58.2; 347.3052
RT: dowry KN58.2; 347.3052
RT: matrimonial property KN58.2; 347.3052

married persons [Table VII: 3.2]

married persons + allowances + taxation KM336.61; 346.5261

married persons + taxation KM336.432; 346.52432

martial law KM416; 346.79
SN: military intervention in civil affairs
RT: military law KM400; 346.7; [Table IIA: 87]

mass media
USE: media KN343; 347.87; [Table IIA: 142]

master and servant
USE: industrial law KN190; 347.46; [Table IIA: 124]

Master of the Rolls KL241.1; 345.461

Masters + judiciary KL242; 345.47

Masters of the Supreme Court KL241.21; 345.4621

matched bargains KN304.83; 347.7383

material facts KN383.2; 347.9432
UF: certainty
UF: facts
UF: notice to admit
UF: res gestae

material facts + contracts KN15.3; 347.133

material facts + criminal procedure KM601; 346.961

maternity rights KN193.25; 347.4721

matrimonial causes
USE: matrimonial proceedings KN173; 347.423

matrimonial conveyancing KN75.M3; 347.3229.M3

matrimonial offences KN173.12; 347.4242
UF: cruelty + marriage
UF: desertion + marriage
RT: domestic violence KN175; 347.42597; [Table IIA: 117.7]

matrimonial orders KN395.21.M3; 347.9721.M3

matrimonial proceedings KN173; 347.423
UF: matrimonial causes

matrimonial property KN58.2; 347.3052
RT: marriage settlements KN58.2; 347.3052

matrimony
USE: marriage KN172; 347.421; [Table IIA: 117]

maxims + dictionaries K124; 340.084

maxims + equity KN204; 347.52

mayors KM368.1; 346.671

MBOs
USE: management buyouts KN262.3; 347.6243

meals on wheels
USE: home-based services KN182.3; 347.4423

means tests + legal aid
USE: legal aid + eligibility KN399.3; 347.933

means tests + public assistance KN181.83; 347.44183

measures and weights
USE: weights and measures KN282.5; 347.655

mechanics' liens KN306.93; 347.7793

medals
USE: honours KM114.5; 346.275

Medean law KE25.2; 343.252

media KN343; 347.87; [Table IIA: 142]
UF: mass media

media + EU KW144.5

media + international law KC258; 341.464

mediation + arbitration KN398.4; 347.984

mediation + divorce KN173.29.M4; 347.42459.M4

mediation + international disputes
USE: conciliation + international disputes KC1290.3; 341.763

medical centres + employment KN193.54; 347.4754

medical ethics
USE: ethics + medical profession KN185.18; 347.44618

medical insurance (private)
USE: health insurance (private) KN292.3; 347.685

medical law KN185; 347.446; [Table IIA: 123]

medical negligence KN33.33.M4; 347.2135.M4

medical organisations KN185.19; 347.44619

medical profession KN185.18; 347.44618

medical records KN185.112; 347.446112

medical witnesses
USE: expert evidence KN391.5; 347.9625

medical witnesses + criminal procedure
USE: expert evidence + criminal procedure KM604.9; 346.967

Medicare
USE: sickness + social security KN181.2; 347.4412

medicines
USE: drugs + medicine KN185.8; 347.4488

medieval law + England and Wales KL401.6; 345.9426
RT: feudal law + England and Wales KL401.6; 345.9426

medieval law + Europe KE355; 343.72
UF: middle ages

meetings KN164; 347.4184
UF: conventions (meetings)
UF: quorum

Members of Congress
USE: legislators KM83; 346.22

Members of Parliament
USE: legislators KM83; 346.22

membership + international organisations KC343; 341.611

membership + legislatures KM83; 346.22

membership + trade unions KN195.2; 347.482

memoirs KB15; 340.33

memorandum of association KN262.7; 347.6247
RT: company law KN261; 347.624; [Table IIA: 128]

mens rea KM505.1; 346.821
UF: criminal intent
UF: intention + criminal law
UF: malice + criminal law

mental health KN185; 347.446

mental health + EU KW149.3

mental hospitals KN185.17.M4; 347.44617.M4

mental patients KN155.2; 347.4152; [Table VII: 5.2]
RT: insane persons KN155.3; 347.4153; [Table VII: 5.3]

mercenaries
USE: foreign enlistment KM561.5; 346.8815

merchant banks KN303.63; 347.7263

merchant marine
USE: maritime law KN330; 347.83; [Table IIA: 138]

merchant seamen
USE: seamen KN332.1; 347.8321

mercy
USE: clemency KM587.3; 346.9373

mercy killing
USE: euthanasia KM542.6; 346.8626

mergers + competition KN266.12; 347.6312
UF: amalgamations
RT: transfer of undertakings + employment protection KN192.28; 347.4638

mergers + competition + EU KW110.2

mergers + incorporation KN262.1; 347.62421

mergers + states KC156; 341.266
RT: state succession KC160; 341.27

mergers + taxation KM336.493; 346.52493
UF: demergers + taxation

Methodist Church KD520; 342.6912

metro (railway)
USE: underground railways KN325.6; 347.8156

metropolitan areas
USE: conurbations KM365.2; 346.652

micro-states KC153.4; 341.2634

microforms [Table VIII: 0095]

Middle Ages
USE: medieval law + Europe KE355; 343.72

Middle East + international relations KC304; 341.514

Middle East : EU KW81.5

Middle Temple KL101.5; 345.177425

Midrash KD66.3; 342.223

midwives KN185.18.M5; 347.44618.M5

migrants + EU KW129.5

migration KM176; 346.33
UF: emigration
UF: immigration
RT: free movement KC199; 341.319
RT: quotas + immigration KM176.1; 346.331
RT: refugees [Table VII: 4.2]

migration + EU KW83.1

migration + international law KC199; 341.319
UF: emigration + international law
UF: immigration + international law
UF: international migration
RT: free movement KC199; 341.319
RT: refugees + international law KC205; 341.335

military courts
USE: courts-martial KM405; 346.74

military crimes KM409; 346.749
UF: desertion + armed forces

military government
USE: government + military occupation KC1401; 341.871

military governors KM112.7; 346.257

military law KM400; 346.7; [Table IIA: 87]
UF: armed forces
UF: articles of war
RT: air force law KM412; 346.77
RT: army law KM411; 346.76
RT: martial law KM416; 346.79
RT: naval law KM410; 346.75

military legal officers
USE: Judge-Advocates KM406; 346.745

military occupation KC1400; 341.87
UF: belligerent occupation
UF: occupied territories
RT: conquest KC142.7; 341.2527
RT: occupation + national territory KC142.3; 341.2523

military occupation + damage
USE: damage + military occupation KC1404; 341.874

military pensions KN181.7; 347.4417
UF: war pensions

military prisoners KM657; 346.98717; [App: 87]

military service (compulsory)
USE: conscription KM402; 346.715

militia KM404; 346.73

millennium bug
USE: bugs + computers KN348.5; 347.8975

mineral resources + submerged lands
USE: seabed + resources KC277; 341.482

mineral rights + taxation KM336.36; 346.5236

minerals + international maritime law
USE: seabed + resources KC277; 341.482

minerals + natural resources KN91; 347.334

mines + industrial law KN193.62; 347.4762

minicabs KN324.5; 347.8145
RT: motor vehicles + rental KN324.6; 347.8146
RT: taxis KN324.5; 347.8145

mining + natural resources KN91; 347.334

mining + taxation KM337.28.M5; 346.548.M5

ministerial responsibility KM42.2; 346.1262

ministers + diplomats KC325; 341.552

ministers + government KM113.6; 346.266

Ministers of State + UK
USE: Secretaries of State + UK KM113.5; 346.265

ministries
USE: government departments KM235; 346.38; [Table IIA: 83.2]; [Table VII: 8.3]

minitrials KN398.6; 347.986

minorities KM208; 346.36; [Table VII: 4]
RT: discrimination + industrial law KN191.2; 347.4612
RT: equal opportunities KM208; 346.36; [Table IIA: 81.5]
RT: racial discrimination KM208.43; 346.3643; [Table IIA: 81.5]
RT: religious minorities KM208.45; 346.3645

minorities + international law KC204; 341.334
RT: human rights + international law KC200; 341.33

minority problems + causes of crime [App: 15]

minority shareholders KN263.73; 347.62573

minors
USE: children KN176; 347.426; [Table IIA: 118]; [Table VII: 1.1]

mint KN302.2; 347.712

miscarriage of justice KM597; 346.957
UF: errors + criminal justice
UF: judicial error

UF: misconduct at trial
UF: trials + misconduct

mischief rule KL35.1; 345.151

misconduct at trial
USE: miscarriage of justice KM597; 346.957

misdemeanours KM503.3; 346.8153

misdirection + juries
USE: jury instructions KN389.7; 347.9607

Mishnah KD68.1; 342.231

Mishneh Torah KD70.2; 342.242

misrepresentation + contracts KN15.4; 347.134

misrepresentation + criminal law
USE: fraud + criminal law KM547; 346.872

missions + religious laws [KD Table: 3]

mistake + contract KN15.4; 347.134

mistake + criminal liability KM505.6; 346.826

mistake + equity KN222; 347.585

mistake + tort KN33.2; 347.212

Mitakshara KD714; 342.814

mitigation KM587.3; 346.9373

mixed arbitral tribunals KC1275; 341.745
UF: tribunals + conflict of laws

mixed arbitral tribunals + cases KC48; 341.143

mixed legal systems
USE: legal pluralism KB140; 340.59

mobile homes KN96.5; 347.3436

mobile phones KN342.35; 347.8635
UF: cellular phones
RT: telephone KN342.3; 347.863

mobility allowances KN181.2; 347.4412
RT: disabled persons + pensions KN181.2; 347.4412

modern law : ancient law
USE: ancient law : modern law KB125; 340.57

monarchs KM112.1; 346.252
UF: kings
UF: queens
UF: sovereigns
RT: heads of state KC189.H4; 341.299.H4
RT: monarchy KM41; 346.125

monarchy KM41; 346.125
UF: constitutional monarchy
UF: Crown
RT: monarchs KM112.1; 346.252

monetary control
USE: economic policy KM331.2; 346.502

monetary integration + EU
USE: single currency + EU KW106

monetary policy
USE: economic policy KM331.2; 346.502

monetary system KN300; 347.7

monetary system + EU KW106

money KN302; 347.71
RT: legal tender KN302.1; 347.711

money laundering KM540.6; 346.856
UF: laundering money

money laundering + international law KC226.3; 341.4143

moneylending KN305.2; 347.752

monks KD30.2; 342.182

monopolies KN266.1; 347.631; [Table IIA: 130]
RT: cartels KN266.5; 347.6345

monopolies + EU KW110.6

monorails KN325.7; 347.8157

Monroe Doctrine KC306.1; 341.5161

moonlighting
USE: multiple employment KN192.7; 347.467

moonshine
USE: alcohol KN186.4; 347.454

moorings KN336.4; 347.8364

moots KL131–149 [Table: .35]; 345.18 [Table: .35]

moral rights + intellectual property KN113; 347.3763

morality : criminal law
USE: criminal law : morality KM504; 346.818

morality : justice
USE: justice : morality KA38; 340.134

Mormon Church KD590.M6; 342.6919.M6

mortgage debentures **KN106.6;** **347.3666**

mortgage-backed securities **KN304.11;** **347.7311**

mortgages **KN56.5;** **347.3035**

mortgages + allowances + taxation **KM336.63;** **346.5263**

mortgages + real property **KN66;** **347.319**

mortmain **KN215.1;** **347.5561**

mortuary law
USE: burial KN97.3; 347.346

Mosaic law
USE: Pentateuch KD66.1; 342.221

most favoured nation clauses
USE: favoured nation clauses KC231.2; 341.4212

motability
USE: disabled persons + transport KN181.2; 347.4412

motels
USE: hotels KN186.3; 347.453

mothers
USE: parents KN176.6; 347.4266; [Table VII: 3.6]

motions **KN381.3;** **347.9413**

motor traffic
USE: road traffic KN323; 347.813

motor vehicles **KN323.1;** **347.8131**
UF: vans
UF: vehicles
RT: heavy goods vehicles KN323.13; 347.81331

motor vehicles + hijacking KM546.3; 346.8713
UF: hijacking + motor vehicles

motor vehicles + international law KC252.1; 341.4521

motor vehicles + licences KN323.12; 347.8233
UF: licences + motor vehicles

motor vehicles + manufacturing KN275.M6; 347.645.M6

motor vehicles + manufacturing + EU KW119.7

motor vehicles + rental KN324.6; 347.8146
UF: car hire
UF: hired cars
UF: rental of vehicles
RT: minicabs KN324.5; 347.8145

motor vehicles + taxation KM337.9.M6; 346.59.M6
UF: car taxes
UF: goods vehicles + taxation
RT: petroleum + taxation KM337.764; 346.5864

motor vehicles + theft KM546.3; 346.8713

motorcycles KN323.15; 347.81335

motorists + law
USE: law for motorists KL30.M6; 345.1.M6

motorways KN322.1; 347.8121
UF: freeways
UF: turnpikes
RT: trunk roads KN322.15; 347.81215

moveable property
USE: personal property KN100; 347.36; [Table IIA: 108]

mugging KM543.2; 346.8632

Muhammadan law
USE: Islamic law KD600; 342.7

multi-disciplinary partnerships + legal profession KL97; 345.1767

multiculturalism KA67; 340.157
UF: ethnic groups

multilateral agreements + EU KW85.6

multilateral peace treaties KC14; 341.124

multimedia + copyright KN112.6; 347.3756

multinational companies KN265.2; 347.6272

multinational companies + EU KW118.3

multinational companies + international law KC234; 341.424

multinational forces
USE: peace-keeping forces KC1280; 341.75

multinational forces + international law
USE: international forces KC1280; 341.75

multinational practices + legal profession KL97.2; 345.17672

multiple employment KN192.7; 347.467
UF: moonlighting

multiple occupation KN87.5; 347.3295

municipal corporations
USE: towns + local government KM365.2; 346.653

municipal law + treaties
USE: treaties : municipal law KM54.2; 346.1342

municipal law + treaties + international law KC334.2; 341.572

municipal law : international law
USE: international law : municipal law KC86; 341.196

municipal securities KN304.21; 347.7325

munitions + trade KN253.8.M8; 347.616.M8
RT: firearms KN186.1; 347.451

murder KM542.1; 346.8621
UF: assassination
UF: killing

museums KN184.4; 347.445

music + subsidies
USE: arts + subsidies KN184.8; 347.4458

musical works + intellectual property KN112.5; 347.3755

Muslim law
USE: Islamic law KD600; 342.7

mustard gas
USE: poison gas KC1395; 341.8652

mutiny KM409.9.M8; 346.7495.M8

mutual funds KN304.54; 347.7354

NAFTA
USE: North American Free Trade Association KC761; 341.6586

named reporters
USE: individual reporters

names + commercial law KN260.1; 347.621; [Table IIA: 114]
UF: business names

names + persons KN150.5; 347.405; [Table IIA: 113]
UF: aliases

nannies KN176.26; 347.42626

Nansen passports
USE: refugee passports + international law KC195.5; 341.3155

narcotics
USE: drugs + offences KM565.D7; 346.89.D7

National Assembly for Wales KM82.A15; 346.21.A15
SN: Welsh name is Cynulliad Cenedlaethol Cymru

National Assembly for Wales + publications KF162

national assistance
USE: public assistance KN181.8; 347.4418

national banks
USE: central banks KN303.5; 347.725

National Curriculum KN184.15; 347.44315

national debt
USE: public debt KM333; 346.514

national elections
USE: elections + legislatures KM83.4; 346.224

national government : local government
USE: local government : national government KM362; 346.62

National Guard (US) KM404; 346.73

National Health Service (UK) KN185.16; 347.44616

national insurance
USE: social insurance KN181; 347.44

national legal bibliography + Commonwealth K61; 340.044-9 [DDC Table 2]

national legal bibliography + England and Wales K62; 340.044–9 [DDC Table 2]

national legal bibliography + Ireland K64; 340.044–9 [DDC Table 2]

national legal bibliography + Scotland K63; 340.044–9 [DDC Table 2]

national legal bibliography + United States K71; 340.044–9 [DDC Table 2]

national lotteries KN186.51; 347.4551
RT: lotteries KN186.5; 347.455

national monuments
USE: ancient monuments KN95.11; 347.34211

national parks KN95.13; 347.34213
RT: access + countryside KN95.13; 347.34213

national police
USE: police KM615; 346.985; [Table IIA: 92.2]

National Reporter System (US) KG352

national savings KN304.2; 347.732

national security KM233; 346.373

national socialism
USE: fascist jurisprudence KA47; 340.145

national territory KC142; 341.252
UF: acquisition + territory
RT: territory + international law KC142; 341.252

national waters KC144; 341.254
UF: waters + international law

nationality KM172; 346.31; [Table IIA: 80]
UF: citizenship

nationality + aircraft
USE: aircraft + international law KC253.5; 341.4535

nationality + international law KC190; 341.31
UF: acquisition + nationality

nationality + ships
USE: ships + nationality KC272.1; 341.4751

nationality by birth
USE: birth + nationality KM172.4; 346.314

nationalisation KN56.6; 347.3036
RT: expropriation KN56.6; 347.3036

nationalisation + alien property
USE: expropriation + international law KC238; 341.438

nationalised industries + company law KN265.6; 347.6276

nations + international law
USE: states + international law KC140; 341.24

native law
USE: customary law KL8; 345.08; [Table IIA: 62]

native title KN72.4; 347.32175

NATO
USE: North Atlantic Treaty Organisation KC901; 341.671

natural disasters
USE: disaster relief KN181.6; 347.4416

natural gas
USE: gas + natural resources KN89.42; 347.33142

natural justice + administrative law KM304; 346.44

natural justice + jurisprudence K35; 340.13

natural law KA41; 340.141

natural resources KN89; 347.33; [Table IIA: 107]

natural resources of the sea
USE: sea + natural resources KC276; 341.48

naturalisation KM174; 346.32
RT: denaturalisation + international law KC192; 341.312

naturalisation + international law KC191; 341.311

nature of law
USE: legal concepts KA21; 340.121

nature reserves KN95.14; 347.34214
RT: wildlife + conservation KN95.3; 347.3423

naval courts
USE: courts-martial KM405; 346.74

naval law KM410; 346.75
RT: military law KM400; 346.7; [Table IIA: 87]

navigation + air law KC253.4; 341.4534

navigation + international maritime law KC274; 341.478
UF: rule of the road at sea

navigation + maritime law KN333; 347.833
UF: rule of the road at sea

Nazi jurisprudence
USE: fascist jurisprudence KA47; 340.145

Nazis + international law KC121; 341.221

necessity + criminal law KM505.5; 346.825
UF: superior orders

negative gearing + Australia KM336.69.N4; 346.5269.N4

negligence KN33.3; 347.213; [Table IIA: 100.5]
RT: professional negligence KN33.33; 347.2133

negligence + claimant
USE: contributory negligence KN33.32; 347.2132

negligence + criminal law KM505.6; 346.826
UF: criminal negligence

negligence + legal profession KL95.5; 345.1745
RT: professional negligence + legal profession KL95.5; 345.1745

negotiable instruments KN306; 347.77

negotiation + arbitration KN398.4; 347.984

negotiation + industrial law KN196; 347.486

negotiation + international disputes KC1290.1; 341.761
UF: diplomatic negotiations
RT: diplomacy KC320; 341.54

neighbours' rights KN72.15; 347.32155
RT: access + neighbouring land KN65.125; 347.31735

nerve gas
USE: poison gas KC1395; 341.8652

networks + computers KN347.3; 347.893

networks + international law KC257.7; 341.4627

networks + libraries K86.6; 340.0566

neutral trade KC1386; 341.8546
RT: neutrality KC1360; 341.83

neutrality KC1360; 341.83
UF: non-intervention
RT: neutral trade KC1386; 341.8546

neutralised zones KC174; 341.284

new states KC163; 341.273

new towns KN96.1; 347.3431

new trial
USE: retrial KM597.5; 346.9575

New Zealand + international relations KC307; 341.517

newspapers KN345.2; 347.882
RT: press KN345.2; 347.882

newspapers + law reporting KL33.4; 345.134

NGOs
USE: non-governmental organisations [Table VII: 9]

no cure no pay
USE: salvage KN334; 347.834; [Table IIA: 139]
USE: towage KN334.2; 347.8342

no fault liability KN33.4; 347.214

nobility
USE: peerage KN157.P4; 347.417.P4

noise KN38.81; 347.281

noise + health and safety + employment KN198.5.N6; 347.495.N6

noise + pollution KN97.72; 347.3472

noise + pollution + EU KW125.6

nolle prosequi KM582.5; 346.9325
UF: discontinuance + criminal procedure
UF: termination by prosecution
UF: withdrawal of prosecution

nolo contendere
USE: pleas + criminal procedure KM582.3; 346.9315

nominee shareholders KN263.74; 347.62574

non-aggression treaties KC336.2; 341.582

non-alignment KC317; 341.537

non-contentious cases + costs KN397.3; 347.9773

non-custodial sentences [App: 69]

non-departmental public bodies KM236.3; 346.3813
RT: quangos KM236.3; 346.3813

non-disclosure + contract KN15.4; 347.134

non-elected legislators KM83.7; 346.227
UF: appointed legislators
UF: hereditary legislators
RT: House of Lords (UK) KM82.3; 346.213

non-executive directors KN264.5; 347.6265

non-ferrous metals KN91.6; 347.3346

non-governmental organisations [Table VII: 9]
UF: NGOs

non-intervention
USE: neutrality KC1360; 341.83

non-jury list KN389.3; 347.9603

non-legal representatives + civil procedure KN370.15; 347.93015
UF: friends + civil procedure

non-legal representatives + criminal procedure KM579.3; 346.908
UF: friends + criminal procedure

non-proliferation + treaties KC336.1; 341.581
RT: arms limitation + treaties KC336.1; 341.581

non-scheduled flights + international law KC254.1; 341.4541

non-strike action KN196.5; 347.4866
RT: strikes KN196.4; 347.4864

non-voting shares KN263.59.N6; 347.62559.N6

non-wage payments
USE: benefits in kind + taxation KM336.31; 346.5231

Nordic Council KC941; 341.675

Norman law (pre-1066) KE320.6; 343.626

North American Free Trade Association KC761; 341.6586
UF: NAFTA

North American Indians
USE: aboriginals + America KE530; 343.94

North Atlantic Treaty Organisation KC901; 341.671
UF: NATO

not guilty pleas
USE: pleas + criminal procedure KM582.3; 346.9315

not proven KM586.2; 346.9362

notaries KL88; 345.171343

notaries + remuneration KL89.4; 345.17144

notice + industrial law KN192.22; 347.4632

notice to admit
USE: disclosure KN386; 347.946
USE: material facts KN383.2; 347.9432

notice to produce
USE: disclosure KN386; 347.946

notifiable diseases KN185.6; 347.4486
UF: disease + reporting
UF: reporting diseases

novation KN14.2; 347.122

Novellae (Corpus Juris Civilis) KE154; 343.475

novels
USE: fiction (novels) KB33; 340.373

nuclear disarmament
USE: arms limitation + international law KC313.5; 341.5335

nuclear energy KN89.45; 347.33145
UF: atomic energy

nuclear energy + international law KC245; 341.448

nuclear power + EU KW122.2

nuclear reprocessing KN97.822; 347.34822
RT: radioactive substances KN97.82; 347.3482

nuclear waste
USE: radioactive substances KN97.82; 347.3482

nuclear weapons + international law KC1392; 341.862
UF: atomic weapons
RT: disarmament + international law KC313; 341.533

nuisance KN38.8; 347.28
UF: public nuisance

nullity KN173.4; 347.4254
UF: annulment

nuns KD30. 2; 342.182

Nuremberg Tribunal
USE: International Military Tribunal + law reports KC35.N8; 341.136.N8

nurseries + agriculture KN98.27; 347.3527

nurseries + children KN182.45; 347.44245
UF: play groups

nurses KN185.18.N8; 347.44618.N8; [Table VII: 6.N8]

nursing homes KN185.17.N8; 347.44617.N8

OAS
USE: Organisation of American States KC751; 341.658

oaths KN391.2; 347.9622
RT: affirmations KN391.2; 347.9622

oaths + criminal procedure KM605.12; 346.9712

OAU
USE: Organisation of African Unity KC711; 341.651

obiter dicta KL32.9; 345.129

objects + evidence
USE: exhibits + evidence KN392.7; 347.9637

objects clause KN262.75; 347.62475

obligations KN5; 347.08; [Table IIA: 96]
UF: legal obligations

obscenity KM565.02; 346.89.02
UF: depravity
UF: immoral art, literature, etc.
RT: pornography KM565.P6; 346.89.P6

obstruction KM562.6; 346.8836

occupation + national territory KC142.3; 341.2523
RT: military occupation KC1400; 341.87

occupation + property KN54.3; 347.3023

occupational health
USE: health and safety KN198; 347.49

occupational pensions
USE: pensions KN193.4; 347.474

occupations KN156; 347.416; [Table VII: 6]
UF: jobs

occupied territories
USE: military occupation KC1400; 341.87

occupiers + liability KN39.03; 347.29.03

odontology + forensic science KM608.3.03; 346.9793.03

OECD
USE: Organisation for Economic Co-operation and Development KC911; 341.672

OEICs
USE: open-ended investment companies KN304.53; 347.7353

off-day working
USE: employment + onerous terms KN193.8; 347.4778

offences + prisons KM671; 346.987499; [App: 92.5]

offences against animals KM565.A5; 346.89.A5
UF: animals + cruelty
UF: cruelty + animals

offences against jurors KM563.4; 346.8854
UF: jurors + victims

offences against justice KM563; 346.885

offences against property
USE: property + offences KM545; 346.87

offences against public finance
USE: public finance + offences KM564; 346.886

offences against public order
USE: public order + offences KM562; 346.883

offences against reputation
USE: libel + criminal law KM541.5; 346.8612

offences against the person KM41; 346.86

offences against the state KM561; 346.881
UF: political offences

offences against witnesses KM563.7; 346.8857
UF: witnesses + victims

offences by jurors
USE: jurors + crimes KM563.4; 346.8854

offender management KM690; 346.9885

offenders KM587.1; 346.9371
UF: convicted persons
RT: defendants KM579; 346.905; [Table VI: .Z62]
RT: first offenders [App: 07]
RT: fugitive offenders + international law KC214; 341.354
RT: potential offenders [App: 21]

RT: prisoners KM660; 346.98715
RT: single offenders [App: 07.5]

offensive weapons
USE: weapons + criminal law KM562.2; 346.8832

offer KN13.2; 347.112

Office of Fair Trading KN266.17; 347.6317

officers + companies
USE: company officers KN264.3; 347.6263

officers + local government KM370; 346.68
UF: bureaucracy + local officials
UF: local government officers
UF: local officials

officers + trade unions KN195.6; 347.4846
UF: trade union officials

offices + automation KN347.5; 347.894

offices + buildings KN83.2; 347.3252

offices + industrial law KN193.52; 347.4752

official bodies + taxation KM336.48; 346.5248
UF: taxation + official bodies

official gazettes [Table 1A: 1]

official languages KM208.44; 346.3644
RT: language + civil rights KM208.44; 346.3644

Official Receiver (UK) KN312.4; 347.7924

Official Referees
USE: Technology and Construction Court [Table V: 8]

official secrets KM233.7; 346.3737
UF: classified information
UF: defence + information
UF: defence information
UF: defence secrets
UF: information + secrecy
RT: intelligence services KM233.8; 346.3738

official secrets + crimes KM561.3; 346.8813

Official Solicitor (UK) KL259.03; 345.59.03

officials + international organisations KC346; 341.614

officials + local government KM370; 346.68
UF: local government officers
UF: local officials

officials + public service
USE: civil service KM237; 346.382; [Table IIA: 83.3]

offshore funds + taxation KM336.76; 346.5276

offshore oil
USE: oil and gas + marine operations KC277.1; 341.4821

oil + energy policy + EU KW122.6

oil + mining KN91.3; 347.3343

oil + natural resources KN89.43; 347.33143

oil and gas + excise duties KM337.764; 346.5864
RT: petroleum + taxation KM337.764; 346.5864

oil and gas + marine operations KC277.1; 341.4821
UF: marine oil operations
UF: offshore oil
UF: petroleum + submerged lands
UF: submarine oil wells

oil and gas + mining KN91.3; 347.3343

oil and gas + seabed resources KC277.1; 341.4821

oil and gas + taxation KM337.28.04; 346.548.04

oil and gas + taxation + allowances KM336.68.04; 346.5268.04

oil industry KN91.33; 347.33433

oil refineries KN91.333; 347.334333

oil rigs KN91.336; 347.334336
RT: oil platforms KN91.336; 347.334336

oils and fats + agriculture + EU KW117.3.05

old age
USE: older people KN181.1; 347.4411; [Table VII: 1.6]

old age pensions
USE: pensions KN193.4; 347.474

Old Bailey KL230.721.05; 345.3721.05
UF: Central Criminal Court

older people KN181.1; 347.4411; [Table VII: 1.6]
UF: elderly
UF: old age
UF: old people
RT: age discrimination KM208.1; 346.361

older people + EU KW129.3

ombudsman KM307; 346.47
UF: Parliamentary Commissioner for Administration
RT: local ombudsmen KM307.2; 346.472

ombudsman + banking
USE: financial ombudsman KN304.95.F5; 347.7395.F5

ombudsman + local government
USE: local ombudsmen KM307.2; 346.472

omissions + criminal liability KM505.6; 346.826

omnibuses
USE: buses KN324.1; 347.8141

one-parent families
USE: families + single parent KN174.5; 347.42595

onerous monitoring + employment
USE: employment + onerous terms KN193.8; 347.4778

online services + libraries K86.4; 340.0564

onus of proof
USE: burden of proof KN390.1; 347.9611

OPEC
USE: Organisation of Petroleum Exporting Countries KC650; 341.6459

open-ended investment companies KN304.53; 347.7353
UF: OEICs

open prisons KM653.2; 346.987132; [App: 83.2]

opening remarks KN389.83; 347.96083

operation of law KN16.5; 347.145

operations + surgery
USE: surgery KN185.5; 347.448

opinions + evidence KN391.6; 347.9626

opinions + evidence + criminal procedure KM604.95; 346.9675

opposition to immoral laws
USE: civil disobedience KA65; 340.155

opt-outs + EU **KW97.52**

opticians **KN185.18.06;** **347.44618.06**

options **KN304.67;** **347.7367**

oral contracts **KN13.5;** **347.115**

oral evidence
USE: evidence KN390; 347.961; [Table IIA: 147]

oral pleadings
USE: statements of case KN383; 347.943; [Table IIA: 146]

oratory **KB31;** **340.371**
UF: speeches

orders + judgments **KN395.21;** **347.9721**

Orders-in-Council
USE: prerogative instruments + England and Wales KF37

Ordinances
USE: subordinate legislation KM302; 346.42; [Table IA: 20]

organ donation **KN185.51;** **347.4481**

organ transplants
USE: transplant surgery KN185.5; 347.448

Organisation Africaine et Malgache de Co-opération Economique **KC721;** **341.652**

Organisation for Economic Co-operation and Development **KC911;** **341.672**
UF: OECD

Organisation of African Unity **KC711;** **341.651**
UF: OAU

Organisation of American States KC751; 341.658
UF: OAS
UF: Pan American Union

Organisation of Eastern Caribbean States KC771; 341.6591

Organisation of Petroleum Exporting Countries KC650; 341.6459
UF: OPEC

organised crime KM540.5; 346.855
UF: gangs

oriental laws (ancient) KE500; 343.91

origin + domicile KC2066; 341.951

origin of law
USE: sources of law KA23; 340.123; [Table VI: .Z1]

orphans KN176.8; 347.4268

orthodox churches KD300; 342.45

ouster clauses KL36.6; 345.166

outer space KC280; 341.49
UF: astronautics
UF: space law

outsourcing
USE: contracting out + commercial law KN257; 347.6195
USE: contracting out + government KN236.4; 346.3814
USE: contracting out + local services KM361.15; 346.6115
USE: contracting out + office services (legal) KL96.15; 345.17615

over-the-counter market KN304.83; 347.7383

overcrowding + prisons KM658.2; 346.987182; [App: 88.2]

overdrafts KN303.3; 347.723

overdue tax + interest KM336.914; 346.52914
UF: interest + overdue tax

overflights + international law KC253.2; 341.4532

overflights + outer space KC282; 341.492

overpaid tax + refunds KM336.98; 346.5298
UF: refunds + overpaid tax

overseas earnings
USE: foreign earnings + taxation KM336.33; 346.5233

overtime KN193.1; 347.471

overtime + bans KN196.6; 347.4866

ownership KN54; 347.302
RT: possession KN54; 347.302

ozone levels
USE: air pollution KN97.71; 347.3471

pacific blockade KC1313; 341.793
RT: blockade KC1385; 341.8545

packaging + food
USE: food + packaging KN185.23; 347.44723

pacta sunt servanda KC338.2; 341.592

pacts
USE: treaties KC330; 341.56

paintings + intellectual property
USE: illustrations + intellectual property KN112.2; 347.373

palaeography K102; 340.062
UF: court hand
RT: handwriting + criminal evidence KM604.41; 346.9651

pamphlets
SN: use as subdivision only

Pan American Union
USE: Organisation of American States KC751; 341.658

papacy + international law KC153.3; 341.2633

papal bulls KD162; 342.372

papal constitutions KD163; 342.373

papal courts KD171; 342.381

papyrology KE33; 343.33

paralegals KL87.2; 345.171342
RT: legal executives KL87.2; 345.171342

pardon
USE: free pardon KM597.8; 346.9578; [App: 77]

parent and child
USE: children KN176; 347.426; [Table IIA: 118]; [Table VII: 1.1]

parental access
USE: access + children KN173.8; 347.4258

parental rights KN176.6; 347.4266

parents KN176.6; 347.4266; [Table VII: 3.6]
UF: fathers
UF: mothers

parishes + local government KM365.7; 346.657

parking + offences KM565.T7; 346.89.T7

parking + regulations KN323.75; 347.81375
UF: car parking

parks KN186.7; 347.457
UF: recreation grounds

Parliament + facilities KM87; 346.248

Parliament + UK KM82; 346.21; [Table IIA: 79]
RT: legislatures KM82; 346.21; [Table IIA: 79]

parliamentary accommodation
USE: accommodation + Parliament KM87.1; 346.2481

Parliamentary Commissioner for Administration
USE: ombudsman KM307; 346.47

parliamentary discipline
USE: discipline + legislators KM84.7; 346.2347

parliamentary dissolution
USE: dissolution + legislatures KM84.4; 346.234

parliamentary elections
USE: elections + legislatures KM83.4; 346.224

parliamentary government KM42; 346.126

parliamentary groups KM83.8; 346.228
UF: all party groups

parliamentary privileges KM85; 346.235
UF: privilege + Parliament

parliamentary procedure KM84; 346.23
UF: legislative procedure
UF: procedure + Parliament

parliamentary procedure + broadcasting KM84.8; 346.23485

parliamentary publications [Table IA: 2]

parliamentary publications + England and Wales KF2

parliamentary publishing
USE: publishing + Parliament KM84.8; 346.2348

parliamentary questions
USE: questions + Parliament KM86.1; 346.241

parliamentary sovereignty KM42.1; 346.1261

parole KM687; 346.9882; [App: 78.5]

Parsi law KD860; 342.94
UF: Zoroastrism

part 36 offer KN387.5; 347.9475
UF: Calderbank offer
UF: payment into court
UF: security for costs

part performance KN231.1; 347.5911

part-time employment KN192.6; 347.466

part-time employment + EU KW131.1

partial detention [App: 68]
UF: weekend detention

partial intestacy KN132; 347.387

particulars KN383.1; 347.9431
UF: bill of particulars
UF: statements of claim

parties KN370; 347.93; [Table VI: .Z6]

parties + contract KN14; 347.12

parties + politics
USE: political parties KM232; 346.372

parties + tort KN34; 347.22

parties + treaties KC333.1; 341.5611

partisans + war
USE: guerrilla warfare KC1368; 341.845

partition + international law KC155; 341.265

partition + states KC155; 341.265
RT: state succession KC160; 341.27

partners KN267.2; 347.6362

partnership KN267; 347.636; [Table IIA: 129]

partnerships + dissolution
USE: dissolution + partnerships KN267.7; 347.6367

partnerships + legal profession KL97; 345.1767
RT: business organisation + legal profession KL97; 345.1767; [Table IIA: 64.5]
RT: law firms KL97; 345.1767

partnerships + taxation KM336.491; 346.52491

party walls KN65.13; 347.3174

passenger traffic
USE: traffic + passengers

passing off KN116.2; 347.3792

passive smoking
USE: tobacco + public health KN186.9.T6; 347.459.T6

passports KM175; 346.328
UF: safe-conducts

passports + animals KN186.82; 347.4582
UF: animal passports
UF: cattle passports

passports + international law KC195; 341.315
UF: international travel regulation
RT: refugee passports + international law KC195.5; 341.3155

passports + withholding + punishment [App: 69.8]
UF: withholding passports

patent agents KN114.12; 347.37715

patented genes
USE: genetic modification + patents KN114.1; 347.3771

patents KN114.1; 347.3771
UF: plant variety rights

patents + EU KW142

patents + international law KC236.2; 341.432

patents + taxation KM336.37; 346.5237

Patents County Court [Table V: 9.P2]

paternity KN176.3; 347.4263
UF: affiliation

paternity rights KN193.25; 347.4721

paternity tests KN176.35; 347.42635
UF: DNA profiling + paternity
RT: blood tests KN185.52.B5; 347.4482.B5

pathological samples + identification KM604.33; 346.9646
UF: blood + samples
UF: saliva + samples
UF: semen + samples

patients KN185.11; 347.44611
UF: rights + patients

patria potestas KE216; 343.49076

patriality KM172.5; 346.315

paupers
USE: poverty KN181.82; 347.44182

pawnbroking KN305.5; 347.765
RT: second hand dealing KN285.S4; 347.679.S4

pay and file
USE: self-assessment + taxation KM336.84; 346.5284

pay as you earn KM336.93; 346.5293
UF: PAYE

payment + taxes
USE: taxes + collection KM336.9; 346.529

payment + witnesses
USE: witnesses + payment KN391.15; 347.96215

payment into court
USE: part 36 offer KN387.5; 347.9475

payroll + taxes KM337.25; 346.545

peace movements KC312; 341.53

peace treaties KC1425; 341.895
RT: termination + war KC1420; 341.89
RT: treaties + war KC338.6; 341.596
RT: truce KC1422; 341.892

peace treaties (texts) KC14; 341.124

peace-keeping forces KC1280; 341.75
UF: multinational forces
UF: police + international law
RT: international police KC1280; 341.75
RT: United Nations forces KC1281; 341.751

peaceful coexistence
USE: international relations KC300; 341.5

peaceful espionage
USE: espionage + international law KC1306; 341.7845

peaceful settlement of international disputes
USE: international disputes KC1200; 341.7

peculiar courts KD489; 342.689

pederasty KM544.7; 346.8647
UF: sexual offences against minors
RT: child abuse KN176.41; 347.42641

pedestrianisation KN322.4; 347.8124

pedestrians KN322.4; 347.8124

peerage KN157.P4; 347.417.P4
UF: nobility

peers [Table VII: 7.P4]

penal institutions [App: 80]

penal law
USE: criminal law KM500; 346.8; [Table IIA: 90]

penalties + overdue tax KM336.914; 346.52914

pensions KN193.4; 347.474
UF: lump sum payments
UF: occupational pensions

UF: old age pensions
UF: retirement pensions
UF: superannuation

pensions + civil service KM237.5; 346.3825

pensions + judiciary KL240.4; 345.44
UF: judicial pensions

pensions + legislators KM83.9; 346.229
UF: legislative pensions
UF: legislators + pensions

pensions + taxation KM336.34; 346.5234

Pensions Ombudsman KN304.95.P4; 347.7395.P4

Pentateuch KD66.1; 342.221
UF: Mosaic law

people smuggling KC199.5; 341.3195

performance + contract KN16.1; 347.141

performance + impossibility
USE: impossibility of performance KN16.4; 347.144

performance + standards + judiciary KL240.3; 345.43

performance of marriage
USE: marriage + ceremony KN172.5; 347.4215

performing arts KN112.4; 347.375

performing rights KN115.5; 347.3788

periodicals
USE: journals K1; 340.01; [Table VIII: 001]

perjury KM563.1; 346.8851

Permanent Court of Arbitration KC1261; 341.741

Permanent Court of International Justice KC1220; 341.721

Permanent Mandates Commission KC371; 341.6214

permitted acts + intellectual property KN118; 347.3794

perpetuities KN64.241; 347.31641
UF: accumulations

perquisites
USE: benefits in kind + taxation KM336.31; 346.5231

Persian law (ancient) KE25; 343.25

Personal Acts KF24

personal allowances + taxation
USE: allowances + taxation KM336.6; 346.526

personal injuries KN38.1; 347.24
UF: brain damage
UF: injuries

personal insurance KN292; 347.682

personal law
USE: persons KN150; 347.4; [Table IIA: 113]; [Table VII]

personal property KN100; 347.36; [Table IIA: 108]
UF: moveable property

personal property + remedies KN108; 347.368

personal representatives KN143; 347.39; [Table VI: .Z63]
RT: administrators + probate KN143; 347.393
RT: executors KN143; 347.39

personal taxes KM337.1; 346.531
RT: persons + taxes KM336.4; 346.524

personality
USE: legal personality KN160; 347.418

personnel management + courts KL230.17; 345.317
RT: staff + courts KL230.17; 345.317

personnel management + law offices KL96.6; 345.1766

persons KN150; 347.4; [Table IIA: 113]; [Table VII]
UF: personal law
UF: status

persons + Hindu law KD749; 342.8290751

persons + Islamic law KD649; 342.7290751

persons + taxes KM336.4; 346.524
RT: personal taxes KM337.1; 346.531

persuasive authority KL32.2; 345.122

perverting the course of justice KM563.2; 346.8852

pesticides + agricultural law KN98.53; 347.3553

pesticides + agricultural law + EU KW114.6

pesticides + environmental health KN97.81; 347.3481

Petition of Right
USE: civil rights KM201; 346.35; [Table IIA: 81]

petitions + pre-trial procedure
USE: pre-trial petitions KN381.4; 347.9414

petroleum + submerged lands
USE: oil and gas + marine operations KC277.1; 341.4821

petroleum + taxation KM337.764; 346.5864
RT: motor vehicles + taxation KM337.9.M6; 346.59.M6
RT: oil and gas + excise duties KM337.764; 346.5864

pets + passports KN186.82; 347.4582

petty jury
USE: juries KN389.6; 347.9606; [Table IIA: 70]

petty sessions
USE: Magistrates' Courts [Table V: 4.3; 5.3]

PFI
USE: private finance initiative KM333.5; 346.515

pharmaceutical drugs
USE: drugs + medicine KN185.8; 347.4488

pharmacists KN185.18.P5; 347.44618.P5

philosophy : law KA70.P5; 340.16.P5
RT: jurisprudence KA; 340.1

philosophy of law
USE: jurisprudence KA; 340.1

photographs KB35; 340.375
RT: pictures KB35; 340.375

photographs + identification KM604.31; 346.9644

photographs + intellectual property KN112.2; 347.373
RT: illustrations + intellectual property KN112.2; 347.373

photography + law reporting KL33.3; 345.133

phrases and terms
USE: legal dictionaries K120; 340.08; [Table IIA: 63]

physically disabled witnesses
USE: witnesses + disabled persons KN391.4.Q51; 347.9624.Q51

physicians
USE: doctors KN185.18.D6; 347.44618.D6

physiology + causes of crime [App: 11]

picketing KN196.5; 347.4865

pickpocketing KM546.6.P5; 346.8716.P5

pictures KB35; 340.375
UF: portraits
RT: cartoons KB35; 340.375
RT: photographs KB35; 340.375

pigs + EU KW117.3.P5

pillory [App: 62.7]

pilotage KN333.2; 347.8332
RT: collisions + maritime law KN333.1; 347.8331

pilots (air)
USE: flight crews KN327.2; 347.822

pilots (maritime) KN333.2; 347.8332

pimps
USE: prostitution KM544.1; 346.8641

Pipe rolls KF51.P4

pipelines KN96.4; 347.3435

pipes KN65.4; 347.3184

piracy + broadcasting KN344.15; 347.8712

piracy + intellectual property KN116.1; 347.3791

piracy + international law KC213.2; 341.3532
RT: crime + high seas KC213.2; 341.3532

pitch invasions
USE: crowd control + sports grounds KM562.13; 346.88313
USE: sports grounds + offences KM562.13; 346.88313

place of safety + orders KN176.42; 347.42642

plain language K100; 340.06

plaintiffs
USE: claimants [Table VI: .Z61]

planning KN96; 347.343; [Table IIA: 107.25]
UF: city planning
UF: town and country planning

planning + appeals KN96.92; 347.34492
UF: appeals + planning

planning + applications KN96.91; 347.34491

planning + control KN96.8; 347.3448

planning + enforcement KN96.96; 347.34496

planning + procedure KN96.9; 347.3449

planning + public finance KM331.8; 346.508

planning enquiries KN96.93; 347.34493

planning permission KN96.81; 347.34481

plans
USE: maps K200; 340.099

plant conservation
USE: conservation + plants KN95.6; 347.3426

plant quarantine
USE: quarantine + plants KN98.9; 347.3559

plant variety rights
USE: genetic engineering KN185.54; 347.4484
USE: patents KN114.1; 347.3771

play groups
USE: nurseries + children KN182.45; 347.44245

plays + intellectual property KN112.4; 347.375

plea bargaining KM582.3; 346.9315

pleadings
USE: statements of case KN383; 347.943; [Table IIA: 146]

pleas + criminal procedure KM582.3; 346.9315
UF: autrefois acquit
UF: autrefois convict
UF: guilty pleas
UF: nolo contendere
UF: not guilty pleas

plebiscites
USE: referendums KM56; 346.136

pledges KN106.5; 347.3665

plural nationality
USE: dual nationality KM178; 346.338

plural systems
USE: legal pluralism KB140; 340.59

poaching KM546.6.P6; 346.8716.P6

poetry KB32; 340.372
RT: drama KB32; 340.372
RT: fiction (novels) KB33; 340.373

poison gas KC1395; 341.8652
UF: asphyxiating gas
UF: mustard gas
UF: nerve gas
RT: prohibited weapons + international law KC1395; 341.865

poisoning + crimes KM543.8; 346.8638

poisons KN186.9.P6; 347.459.P6
RT: agricultural chemicals KN98.5; 347.355
RT: dangerous things KN186.9.D3; 347.459.D3
RT: toxic waste KN97.83; 347.3483

polar regions + international relations KC308; 341.518
UF: Antarctic
UF: Arctic

polders
USE: accretion + real property KN76.A3; 347.323.A3

police KM615; 346.985; [Table IIA: 92.2]
UF: constables
UF: national police
UF: policewomen
UF: sheriffs (police)
RT: emergency services KM234; 346.3739
RT: local police KM615.1; 346.9851
RT: traffic police KN323.79; 347.81379

police + complaints KM615.7; 346.9857
UF: allegations against police
UF: complaints against police
RT: Police Complaints Authority KM615.7; 346.9857

police + equipment KM615.4; 346.9854
UF: cars + police
UF: police cars

police + international law
USE: international police KC1280; 341.75
USE: peace-keeping forces KC1280; 341.75

police + powers KM615.2; 346.9852

police + questioning
USE: interrogation + criminal investigation KM580.12; 346.9112

police + remuneration KM615.9; 346.9859

police cars
USE: police + equipment KM615.4; 346.9854
USE: police vehicles KM615.42; 346.98542

police charges
USE: charges + criminal procedure KM580.4; 346.914

Police Complaints Authority KM615.7; 346.9857
RT: police + complaints KM615.7; 346.9857

police custody
USE: custody + police KM580.35; 346.9135

police discipline
USE: discipline + police KM615.8; 346.9858

police ethics KM615.25; 346.98525

police magistrates
USE: magistrates KL243; 345.48

police vehicles KM615.42; 346.98542
UF: police cars
UF: vehicles + police

policewomen
USE: police KM615; 346.985; [Table IIA: 92.2]

policies + insurance
USE: insurance policies KN290.3; 347.6803

political funds + trade unions KN195.4; 347.4835
RT: funds + trade unions

political offences
USE: offences against the state KM561; 346.881

political parties KM232; 346.372
UF: parties + politics

political parties + European Parliament KW97

political prisoners KM656; 346.98716; [App: 86]

political rights
USE: civil rights KM201; 346.35; [Table IIA: 81]

political systems KM39; 346.1235

political systems + comparative law KB177; 340.604

political uniforms
USE: uniforms + offences KM561.9.U5; 346.882.U5

politics : law KA70.P6; 340.16.P6

poll taxes KM337.14; 346.5314
UF: flat-rate taxes

polls
USE: voting + elections + legislatures KM83.45; 346.2245

pollution KN97.7; 347.347; [Table IIA: 107.4]
UF: anti-pollution laws
RT: contaminated land KN97.75; 347.3475
RT: environmental health KN97; 347.345

pollution + agriculture
USE: agricultural pollution KN97.81; 347.3481

pollution + international law KC243.1; 341.4441

pollution of the sea
USE: sea + pollution KN97.74; 347.3474

polygamy KN172.9.P6; 347.422.P6
RT: bigamy KM544.3; 346.8643

polyglot dictionaries
USE: dictionaries + polyglot K121; 340.081

polytechnics
USE: higher education KN184.3; 347.444

pools betting levy
USE: gambling + taxation KM337.9.G3; 346.59.G3

Ponzi schemes KN285.8; 347.6778
RT: pyramid selling KN285.7; 347.677

poor law KN181.82; 347.44182

popes KD181; 342.391

popular accounts KB40; 340.4

population KM172.32; 346.3132
RT: census KM172.32; 346.3132

population + EU KW126

pornography KM565.P6; 346.89.P6
RT: obscenity KM565.O2; 346.89.O2

pornography + causes of crime [App: 17.5]

portraits
USE: pictures KB35; 340.375

ports
USE: harbours KN336; 347.836

positive covenants KN65.7; 347.3187

positivism KA44; 340.144
UF: legal positivism

posses KM614.3; 346.9843

possession KN54; 347.302
RT: ownership KN54; 347.302

post feudal law KL401.7; 345.9427

post modernism KA49.P6; 340.147.P6

post mortems KM608.4; 346.9794
UF: autopsies

post-qualification training + legal education KL131–149 [Table: .9]; 345.1794–9 [Table: 9]

post-traumatic stress KN38.15; 347.245

postal services
USE: mail KN341; 347.85

potential offenders [App: 21]
RT: offenders KM587.1; 346.9371

poultry + EU KW117.3.P6

poverty KN181.82; 347.44182
UF: paupers

poverty + EU KW127.4

power of attorney KN25.2; 347.182
RT: enduring power of attorney KN25.2; 347.182

power politics
USE: international relations KC300; 341.5

power stations
USE: electricity KN89.44; 347.33144

powers
SN: use as subdivision only

practice and procedure
USE: procedure KN350; 347.9; [Table IIA: 144]; [Table VI: .Z71]
USE: trial practice KN389; 347.96

practice break-ups KL97.3; 345.17673

practice certificates KL83; 345.1703
RT: licensing + lawyers KL83; 345.1703

practice management KL96.1; 345.1761

practice mergers KL97.1; 345.17671

practice of law
USE: legal profession KL50; 345.17; [Table IIA: 64]
USE: procedure KN350; 347.9; [Table IIA: 144]; [Table VI: .Z71]

practice strategy KL97.6; 345.17676

pre-Hellenistic Egyptian law
USE: Egyptian law (pre-Hellenistic) KE27; 343.27

pre-Hellenistic Greek law
USE: Greek law (pre-Hellenistic) KE26; 343.26

pre-independence laws KM57; 346.137

pre-trial petitions KN381.4; 347.9414
UF: petitions + pre-trial procedure

pre-trial practice
USE: preliminary proceedings KN380; 347.94

pre-trial release KM580.92; 346.9192

pre-trial reviews KM580.9; 346.919

precatory trusts KN213.3; 347.544

precedent KL32; 345.12
UF: judicial precedent
UF: stare decisis

precedents
USE: forms KN360; 347.92; [Table VI: .Z3]

precious minerals KN91.5; 347.3345

preference shares KN263.59.P7; 347.62559.P7

preferred shares KN304.3; 347.733

preliminary hearings KM581; 346.92

preliminary proceedings KN380; 347.94
UF: pre-trial practice
UF: proceedings in chambers

preliminary proceedings + criminal procedure KM580; 346.91

premises
USE: buildings KN83; 347.325

premiums + insurance KN290.3; 347.681

pre-charge detention KM580.13; 346.9113

pre-pack administrations KN312.25; 347.79225

prepaid legal services KN399.2; 347.992

prerogative instruments + England and Wales KF37
UF: Orders-in-Council

prerogative of mercy KM596; 346.956

prerogative orders KN395.8; 347.974
UF: prerogative writs

Presbyterian Church KD550; 342.6915

prescription + land tenure KN76.P7; 347.323.P7

prescription + personal property KN104.6; 347.3646

prescriptions (medical) KN185.83; 347.44883

preservatives in food
USE: food + preservatives KN185.24; 347.44724

President of the Family Division KL241.1; 345.461

presidents KM112.2; 346.253

press KN345.2; 347.882
RT: newspapers KN345.2; 347.882

press freedom
USE: freedom of the press KM207; 346.357

pressure groups KM232.8; 346.3728

presumption of death KN127.1; 347.3841
RT: death KN185.15; 347.44615

presumption of innocence KM579.1; 346.906
UF: innocence + presumption

presumptions + evidence KN390.2; 347.9612

prevention of crime
USE: crime prevention KM612; 346.982; [App: 20]

preventive detention [App: 65]

preventive medicine KN185.7; 347.4487
UF: inoculations
UF: vaccination
RT: fluoridation KN185.7; 347.4487

preventive policing [App: 24]

previous convictions + evidence KM603.5; 346.9635

price fixing KN266.3; 347.633
RT: resale price maintenance KN266.3; 347.633

price fixing + EU KW110.5

price maintenance
USE: resale price maintenance KN266.3; 347.633

prices KN283; 347.658
UF: fixing prices
RT: resale price maintenance KN266.3; 347.633

prices + agriculture + EU KW114
UF: agricultural prices + EU

prices + control KN283.1; 347.6581

prices + control + EU KW109.3

prices + reductions KN283.2; 347.6582
UF: reductions of prices
RT: sales + reductions

priests [KD Table: 2]

primary sources
USE: legislation (texts) [Table IA: 15]

prime ministers KM112.3; 346.254

primitive law KE8; 343.18

principal and accessory
USE: accessories KM508; 346.84

principal and agent
USE: agency KN25; 347.18; [Table IIA: 99]

principal and surety
USE: suretyship KN18.7; 347.157

print media + censorship KN349.98; 347.8998

prison discharges
USE: discharge + prisons KM685; 346.988; [App: 76]

prison discipline
USE: discipline + prisons KM670; 346.9873

prison law KM650; 346.987; [App: 93.9]

prison libraries KM681.6; 346.98766; [App: 93.6]
UF: libraries + prisons

prison life KM683; 346.987695; [App: 94]

prison officers KM658.6; 346.987186; [App: 88.6]
UF: warders

prison punishments
USE: punishment + prisons KM670; 346.9874; [App: 92.4]

prison riots
USE: riots + prisons KM671.3; 346.9874993; [App: 92.53]

prison rules
USE: rules + prisons KM661.2; 346.98722; [App: 92.22]

prisoners KM660; 346.98715
RT: offenders KM587.1; 346.9371

prisoners + discharge
USE: discharged prisoners KM690; 346.9885; [App: 79]

prisoners + families [App: 94.8]

prisoners + human rights + international law KC209; 341.339

prisoners + privileges KM680; 346.9875; [App: 93]

prisoners + relationships KM683.3; 346.9876953; [App: 94.3]

prisoners + relationships + prisoners KM683.33; 346.98769533; [App: 94.33]

prisoners + relationships + staff KM683.32; 346.98769532; [App: 94.32]

prisoners + rights KM680; 346.9875; [App: 93]

prisoners of war KC1415; 341.885

prisons KM652; 346.98712; [App: 82]

prisons + architecture KM659; 346.98719; [App: 89]

prisons + conditions KM681; 346.9876; [App: 93.3]

prisons + inspection KM658.8; 346.987188; [App: 88.8]

prisons + population KM658.2; 346.987182; [App: 88.2]

prisons + reform [App: 99]

prisons + visits KM681.5; 346.98765; [App: 93.5]
UF: visits to prisons

prisons + work KM684; 346.987697; [App: 92.7]

privacy KM209.P7; 346.368.P7
UF: confidentiality
UF: privity

privacy + employment KN193.8; 347.4778

privacy + infringements KN38.9; 347.289

privacy + international law KC201.P7; 341.331.P7

Private Acts KF24

private armies KM614.4; 346.9844

private banks KN303.61; 347.7261

private claims + international law
USE: claims + international arbitration KC1254; 341.734

private companies KN265.1; 347.6271

private detectives KM614.2; 346.9842
UF: house detectives
UF: store detectives

private finance initiative KM333.5; 346.515
UF: PFI
RT: public projects + funding KM333.5; 346.515
RT: public-private partnerships KM333.5; 346.515

private flights + international law KC254.5; 341.4544

private international law
USE: conflict of laws KC2000; 341.9

private landlords KN86.1; 347.3281
RT: landlord and tenant KN85; 347.327; [Table IIA: 106]

private law + religious laws [KD Table: 7]

private law + unification
USE: unification of private law KB115; 340.53

private law : public law
USE: public law : private law KM5; 346.02

private postal services KN341.6; 347.855

private prisons [App: 98]

private prosecutions KM580.5; 346.915

private roads KN322.3; 347.8123

private sector tenancies KN87.7; 347.3297

private security services KM614; 346.984

privatisation + industry KN265.65; 347.62765

privatisation + property KN56.7; 347.3037

privilege + evidence KN394.8; 347.9658
UF: evidence + privilege

privilege + Parliament
USE: parliamentary privileges KM85; 346.235

privileged documents
USE: documents + privilege KN386.5; 347.9465

privileges + diplomacy
USE: diplomatic privileges KC322; 341.542

privileges + international organisations
USE: international organisations + privileges KC344; 341.612

privity
USE: privacy KM209.P7; 346.368.P7

privity of contract KN14; 347.12

Privy Council KM113; 346.26

Privy Council Judicial Committee
USE: Judicial Committee of the Privy Council [Table V: 1]

prize + international law KC1388; 341.8548

prize courts [Table V: 8.1]

pro bono work KL82.7; 345.17027

probate KN127; 347.384
RT: decedents' estates KN140; 347.39

probate courts [Table V: 7.6]

probation + employment KN192.11; 347.4622

probation + sentence [App: 70]

procedural defences + administration of justice KM584.9.P7; 346.9349.P7

procedure KN350; 347.9; [Table IIA: 144]; [Table VI: .Z71]
UF: actions and defences
UF: adjective law
UF: civil procedure
UF: practice and procedure
UF: practice of law

RT: administrative law + procedure KM304; 346.44
RT: criminal procedure KM570; 346.9; [Table IIA: 93]

procedure + assessment + taxation
USE: assessment + taxation KM336.8; 346.528

procedure + international courts KC1214; 341.714
UF: international courts + procedure

procedure + Parliament
USE: parliamentary procedure KM84; 346.23

proceedings in chambers
USE: preliminary proceedings KN380; 347.94

proceeds of crime KM594.6; 346.9486

proclamations
USE: royal proclamations KF37.1

procuration of women
USE: prostitution KM544.1; 346.8641

procurators-fiscal + Scotland KL253; 345.53

producers + co-operatives KN268.1; 347.6381

productivity + payments KN194.4; 347.4784

products + liability KN39.P7; 347.29.P7

products + liability + EU KW112.1

products + safety + EU KW112.1

profession of law
USE: legal profession KL50; 345.17; [Table IIA: 64]

professional associations [Table VII: 9.8]
RT: associations KN169.4; 347.41894; [Table VII: 9.4]; [Table VIII: .003]

professional associations + industrial law KN195.19; 347.4819

professional associations + taxation KM336.498; 346.52498

professional conduct KL81; 345.1701

professional development KN192.33; 347.4643

professional negligence KN33.33; 347.2133
UF: malpractice
RT: negligence KN33.3; 347.213; [Table IIA: 100.5]

professional negligence + legal profession KL95.5; 345.1745
RT: negligence + legal profession KL95.5; 345.1745

professional partnerships KN267.1; 347.6361

professional responsibility + legal profession KL82; 345.1702

professional training + legal education KL131–149 [Table: .8]; 345.1794–9 [Table: 8]

professions KN156; 347.416; [Table VII: 6]
RT: legal profession KL50; 345.17; [Table IIA: 64]

profit-related pay + taxation KM336.31; 346.5231

profit-sharing KN194.3; 347.4783

profits KN263.4; 347.6254

profits + taxation KM336.32; 346.5232

profits + taxes KM337.22; 346.542

profits à prendre KN65.3; 347.3183

prohibited degrees + marriage
USE: marriage + impediments KN172.3; 347.4213

prohibited drugs
USE: drugs + offences KM565.D7; 346.89.D7

prohibited names + companies KN262.85; 347.62485

prohibited weapons + international law KC1395; 341.865
UF: biological warfare
UF: warfare + prohibited methods
RT: poison gas KC1395; 341.8652

prohibition (writ) KN395.83; 347.9743

prohibition + US
USE: alcohol KN186.4; 347.454

project finance KN305.24; 347.7524

promise KN13.1; 347.111

promissory notes KN306.3; 347.773

proof
USE: burden of proof KN390.1; 347.9611

proof + criminal procedure
USE: burden of proof + criminal procedure KM 602; 346.962

proof of foreign law
USE: foreign law + proof KC2071; 341.961

proof-reading K105.5; 340.0655

propaganda KM561.2; 346.8812

property KN50; 347.3; [Table IIA: 103]

property + military occupation KC1404; 341.874

property + offences KM545; 346.87
UF: offences against property

property + taxation KM336.36; 346.5236

property + war KC1357; 341.828

property development
USE: investment + real property KN81; 347.3241

property investment
USE: investment + real property KN81; 347.3241

prophets + Jewish law KD66.2; 342.222

proportional representation KM83.41; 346.2241

proprietary medicines KN185.82; 347.44882

prosecution + alternatives KM580.8; 346.918

prosecution + trial on indictment KM582.4; 346.932

prosecutors [Table VI: .Z61]

prospectuses
SN: use as subdivision only

prostitution KM544.1; 346.8641
UF: immoral earnings
UF: pimps
UF: procuration of women
UF: soliciting

protection + civilians
USE: civilians + military occupation KC1403; 341.873

protection of citizens abroad
USE: diplomatic protection KC196; 341.316

protectorates KC154.2; 341.2642

protestant churches KD400; 342.5

protocols
USE: treaties KC330; 341.56

proverbs K124; 340.084

provinces + local government KM366.2; 346.662

provisional tax + Australia KM337.9.P7; 346.59.P7

provocation KM584.2; 346.9342

proxies
USE: voting + shareholders KN263.81; 347.62581

proximate cause KN33.1; 347.211

psychiatric injury KN38.15; 347.245

psychiatric treatment + crime prevention [App: 22]

psychiatrists KN185.18.P7; 347.44618.P7

psychology + causes of crime [App: 12]

psychology + prisoners KM683.2; 346.9876952; [App: 94.2]

psychology + sociology
USE: social psychology KA63; 340.153

psychology : law KA70.P7; 340.16.P7

public administration KM236; 346.381; [Table IIA: 83.2]

public appointments KM236.6; 346.3816

public assistance KN181.8; 347.4418

UF: national assistance

public companies KN265.4; 347.6274

public contracts KN18.4; 347.154

public debt KM333; 346.514
UF: national debt

public defenders KM599.1; 346.9591

public disclosure + employment
USE: disclosure of information + employment KN192.29; 347.4639

public display + punishment [App: 62.7]

public enquiries KM303.5; 346.435

public expenditure KM331; 346.5; [Table IIA: 84]
RT: public finance KM331; 346.5; [Table IIA: 84]

public expenditure + control KM331.3; 346.503
UF: control of public expenditure

public finance KM331; 346.5; [Table IIA: 84]
RT: public expenditure KM331; 346.5 [Table IIA: 84]

public finance + offences KM564; 346.886
UF: offences against public finance

public finance + reporting KM331.4; 346.504

public funds KM333; 346.514

Public General Acts
USE: legislation (texts) + UK KF20

public health KN185; 347.446; [Table IIA: 123]
UF: health care

public health + international law KC241; 341.441
UF: international sanitary regulations
UF: sanitation + international law

public health policy + EU KW149

public holidays KN186.2; 347.452
UF: bank holidays
RT: holidays KN193.2; 347.472

public hygiene KN97; 347.345
RT: sanitation KN97.5; 347.3463

public international law
USE: international law KC; 341

public land KN82; 347.3242

public law KM1; 346.01

public law : private law KM5; 346.02
UF: private law : public law

public lending right KN115.1; 347.3781

public liability + tort KN33.5; 347.215

public libraries
USE: libraries KN184.4; 347.445; [Table IIA: 122.5]

public nuisance
USE: nuisance KN38.8; 347.28

public officials
USE: civil service KM237; 346.382; [Table IIA: 83.3]

public opinion + EU KW74

public opinion : law KA61; 340.151

public order + offences KM562; 346.883
UF: offences against public order

public peace KM611; 346.981
UF: Queen's peace

public policy + contract KN15.1; 347.131

public policy + evidence KN394.9; 347.9659

public policy + property KN56.8; 347.304

public policy + trusts KN214.5; 347.555

public policy : law KA62; 340.152

public procurement + EU KW109.6

public projects + funding KM333.5; 346.515
RT: private finance initiative KM333.5; 346.515
RT: public-private partnerships KM333.5; 346.515

public property KN58.4; 347.3054

public prosecutors KL253; 345.53
RT: District Attorneys + US KL253; 345.53

public records KN184.5; 347.4455; [Table IIA: 122.5]
UF: archives + courts
UF: court archives
UF: court records
UF: records + courts

public relations + police KM615.6; 346.9856

public transport KN324; 347.814
UF: transit systems
RT: railways KN325; 347.815; [Table IIA: 136]
RT: trains KN325; 347.815

public trustees KN216.4; 347.564

public utilities KN275.P8; 347.645.P8
RT: electricity KN89.44; 347.33144
RT: gas + energy KN89.42; 347.33142
RT: telecommunications KN342; 347.86
RT: water KN90; 347.333

public water supply
USE: water + supply KN90.5; 347.3335

public welfare KN181; 347.44
UF: distress + social services
UF: welfare state

public-private partnerships KM333.5; 346.515
RT: private finance initiative KM333.5; 346.515
RT: public projects + funding KM333.5; 346.515

publications + supply + courts KL230.8.P8; 345.38.P8
UF: supply of publications + courts

publishers + directories K107; 340.067

publishing KN345; 347.88
RT: law publishing K105; 340.065

publishing + EU KW146

publishing + Parliament KM84.8; 346.2348
UF: parliamentary publishing

puisne judges
USE: High Court judges KL241.2; 345.462

punctuation guides K105.2; 340.0652

punishment + children + by parents KN176.45; 347.42645
RT: punishment + schools KN184.25; 347.44325

punishment + offenders
USE: sentences KM587; 346.937; [Table IIA: 93.2]; [Table VI: .Z9]

punishment + prisons KM670; 346.9874; [App: 92.4]
UF: prison punishments

punishment + schools KN184.25; 347.44325
RT: punishment + children + by parents KN176.45; 347.42645

pupillage + barristers KL86.8; 345.1713
UF: barristers + pupillage

purchase of own shares KN263.54; 347.62554
UF: companies + purchase of own shares

purchaser and vendor
USE: transfer + real property KN70; 347.32

purchasing + local government KM361.3; 346.613

purpose of criminal law
USE: criminal law : morality KM504; 346.818

purpose of punishment [App: 50.2]
UF: aims of punishment

pyramid selling KN285.7; 347.677
RT: Ponzi schemes KN285.8; 347.6778

Qiyas KD264; 342.724

Quakers
USE: Society of Friends KD570; 342.6917

qualifications KN192.12; 347.4623

qualifications + EU KW109.8

qualified majority voting + EU KW97.52

quality control KN284.3; 347.663

quangos KM236.3; 346.3813
UF: quasi-autonomous non-governmental organisations
RT: non-departmental public bodies KM236.3; 346.3813

quantum meruit KN20.1; 347.161

quantum of damages
USE: assessment + damages KN37.1; 347.331

quarantine KN185.6; 347.4486
RT: animals + quarantine KN186.82; 347.4582

quarantine + plants KN98.9; 347.3559
UF: plant quarantine

quarries + industrial law KN193.62; 347.4762

quarries + planning KN96.99.Q3; 347.34499.Q3

quashing convictions
USE: convictions + quashing KM597.3; 346.9573

quasi-autonomous non-governmental organisations
USE: quangos KM236.3; 346.3813

quasi-contract KN20; 347.16

Queen's Bench Division [Table V: 3; 5.1]
UF: King's Bench Division

Queen's Counsel KL86.5; 345.1712

Queen's peace
USE: public peace KM611; 346.981

queens
USE: monarchs KM112.1; 346.252

questioning
USE: interrogation + criminal investigation KM580.12; 346.9112

questions + Parliament KM86.1; 346.241
UF: parliamentary questions

quo warranto KN395.84; 347.9744

quorum
USE: meetings KN164; 347.4184

quotas + immigration KM176.1; 346.331
RT: migration KM176; 346.33

quotas + single market + EU KW109.4

quotations K125; 340.085
UF: legal quotations

rabies
USE: animals + quarantine KN186.82; 347.4582

race relations
USE: racial discrimination KM208.43; 346.3643; [Table IIA: 81.5]

racial conflict + causes of crime [App: 15]

racial discrimination KM208.43; 346.3643; [Table IIA: 81.5]
UF: apartheid
UF: community relations
UF: race relations
UF: segregation + race
RT: minorities KM208; 346.36; [Table VII: 4]

racial discrimination + international law KC204; 341.334

racing KN186.64; 347.4564
UF: dog racing
UF: greyhound racing
UF: horse racing

radiation KN97.82; 347.3482

radio KN344.4; 347.872
UF: wireless
RT: broadcasting KN344; 347.871
RT: wavelengths + broadcasting KN344.1; 347.8711

radio + censorship KN349.94; 347.8994

radio + international law KC258.5; 341.465
UF: wavelengths + international law
RT: television + international law KC259; 341.466

radio receivers
USE: receivers + broadcasting KN344.1; 347.8711

radioactive minerals + mining KN91.4; 347.3344

radioactive substances KN97.82; 347.3482
UF: nuclear waste
RT: nuclear reprocessing KN97.822; 347.34822

rail freight
USE: freight + railways KN328.6; 347.8286

rail routes
USE: routes + railways KN325.4; 347.8154

railroads
USE: railways KN325; 347.815; [Table IIA: 136]

railwaymen KN325.5; 347.8155
RT: train drivers KN325.5; 347.8155

railways KN325; 347.815; [Table IIA: 136]
UF: railroads
RT: public transport KN324; 347.814

railways + EU KW135.1

railways + international law KC251; 341.451

railways + safety
USE: safety + railways KN325.25; 347.81525

ransom
USE: hostage-taking KM543.5; 346.8635
USE: kidnapping KM543.4; 346.8634

rape KM544.4; 346.8644

rates + businesses
USE: business rating (taxation) KM337.65; 346.575

rates + postage KN341.1; 347.851

rates of allowances + taxation
USE: allowances + taxation KM336.6; 346.526

rates of interest
USE: interest rates KN305.3; 347.753

rates of tax
USE: tax rates KM336.89; 346.5289

ratification + treaties
USE: treaties + ratification KC333.2; 341.5612

rating + property
USE: council tax KM337.65; 346.575

ratio decidendi KL32.1; 345.121

raw materials KC232; 341.422

re-examination + witnesses KN391.3; 347.9623
RT: examination + witnesses KN391.3; 347.9623

real covenants
USE: covenants + leases KN87.4; 347.3294

real estate agents
USE: estate agents KN74.8; 347.32275

real estate finance KN305.28; 347.7528

real property KN60; 347.31; [Table IIA: 104]
UF: immoveable property
UF: land law

real property + Islamic law KD643; 342.729071

real property + taxes KM337.6; 346.57
UF: land taxes
UF: taxation + real property

reasoning + law
USE: legal logic KA55; 340.148

rebellion KM561.1; 346.8811
UF: insurrection
UF: revolution

rebellion + causes of crime [App:14]

rebellion + international law KC1365; 341.84

receivers + broadcasting KN344.1; 347.8711
UF: radio receivers
UF: television sets

receivers + insolvency KN312.4; 347.7924
RT: insolvency practitioners KN312.3; 347.7923

receiving stolen goods
USE: stolen goods KM546.9; 346.8719

reception of Roman law KE359; 343.76
RT: Roman law + Europe + medieval KE350; 343.7

recidivism [App: 09]

reciprocity + financial services KN308.8; 347.7868

reciprocity + trade KC231.1; 341.4211
UF: commercial agreements + reciprocity

reciprocity + treaties KC338.1; 341.591
UF: treaties + reciprocity

reckless driving KM565.D7; 346.89.D7
RT: careless driving KM565.D7; 346.89.D7
RT: dangerous driving KM565.D7; 346.89.D7

recklessness + criminal liability KM505.7; 346.827

recognition + international law KC164; 341.274
UF: de facto recognition
UF: de jure recognition
UF: diplomatic recognition
UF: legitimacy + governments

recognition + judgments KN395.3; 347.9729

recognition + trade unions KN195.7; 347.4847

recognisances
USE: bail KM580.6; 346.916

reconciliation + marriage KN173.6; 347.4256

Recorders KL241.32; 345.4632; [Table IIA: 69.5]

recordings + criminal evidence KM604.5; 346.966

recordings + intellectual property KN112.5; 347.3755

records + courts
USE: public records KN184.5; 347.4455; [Table IIA: 122.5]

records + law offices KL96.4; 345.1764

recreation KN186.6; 347.456
UF: amusements
UF: leisure

recreation + EU KW144.7

recreation + prisons KM681.4; 346.98764; [App: 93.4]

recreation grounds
USE: parks KN186.7; 347.457

recruitment + armed forces KM401; 346.71
UF: enlistment
UF: volunteers + armed forces

recruitment + employment KN192; 347.462

rectification KN234; 347.594

recycling KN97.87; 347.3487

recycling + EU KW125.7

Red Cross KC1412; 341.882

Red Indians
USE: American aboriginals KE530; 343.94

reductions + sentences + good behaviour KM686; 346.9881; [App: 78]
UF: good behaviour + prisoners

reductions of prices
USE: prices + reductions KN283.2; 347.6582

redundancy KN192.26; 347.4636
UF: retrenchment

reference books [Table VIII: .002]

reference books + international law KC70; 341.17

references + employment KN192.15; 347.4626

referendums KM56; 346.136
UF: direct legislation
UF: plebiscites

referendums + international law KC162; 341.272

reflexology KN185.13.R4; 347.44613.R4

reform of law
USE: law reform KL160; 345.197; [Table IIA: 66]; [Table VI: .Z53]

reform of the legal profession
USE: legal profession + reform KL84; 345.1704

reformation + punishment [App: 50.23]

reformatories KM654.2; 346.987142; [App: 84.2]

refreshment facilities + legislatures KM87.6; 346.2486

refugee governments
USE: governments in exile KC189.G6; 341.299.G6

refugee passports + international law KC195.5; 341.3155
UF: Nansen passports
RT: passports + international law KC195; 341.315

refugees [Table VII: 4.2]
RT: migration KM176; 346.33

refugees + immigration KM177.7; 346.3375

refugees + international law KC205; 341.335
UF: exiles
UF: stateless persons
RT: migration + international law KC199; 341.319
RT: statelessness KC194; 341.314

refuges + domestic violence KN175.2; 347.425972
RT: domestic violence KN175; 347.42597; [Table IIA: 117.7]

refunds + overpaid tax
USE: overpaid tax + refunds KM336.98; 346.5298

regency KM112.1; 346.252

regional aid + EU KW123

regional authorities KM366; 346.66

regional employment premiums
USE: development grants KM334; 346.518

regional policy + EU KW123

registered designs KN114.5; 347.3775

registered office + company KN262.92; 347.62492

Registrars KL241.32; 345.4632

registration + births KM172.31; 346.3131
UF: births + registration

registration + deaths KM172.31; 346.3131
UF: death + registration
RT: death KN185.15; 347.44615

registration + marriages KM172.31; 346.3131
UF: marriage + registration

registration + motor vehicles KN323.12; 347.8133

registration + shares KN263.63; 347.62563

registration + trade unions KN195.1; 347.481

regnal years KL401.1; 345.9421

regulated activities + financial services KN308.2; 347.7862

regulated tenancies KN87.73; 347.32973

regulation + financial services KN309; 347.7869

regulation + solicitors KL97.4; 345.17674

Regulations
USE: subordinate legislation KM302; 346.42; [Table IA: 20]

regulatory bodies KM302.5; 346.425

regulatory bodies + competition law KN266.17; 347.6317

regulatory bodies + insurance KN297; 347.697

regulatory bodies + investment KN304.95; 347.7395

regulatory offences KM503.6; 346.8156

rehabilitation + drugs KN185.81; 347.44881
RT: drugs + dependency KN185.81; 347.44881

rehabilitation + offenders KM690; 346.9885; [App: 79]

reinstatement + employment KN192.27; 347.4637

reinsurance KN295; 347.695

rejoinder KN385.5; 347.9455

release + prisoners KM685; 346.988; [App: 76]

relevance + criminal evidence KM602.4; 346.9624

relevance + evidence KN393.1; 347.9641
UF: irrelevant evidence

Relief and Works Agency KC458; 341.6293

reliefs + taxation KM336.6; 346.526
UF: tax reliefs

religious courts [KD Table: 9]
UF: ecclesiastical courts

religious days KN186.2; 347.452

religious groups [Table VII: 4.5]

religious laws KD; 342

religious minorities KM208.45; 346.3645
RT: minorities KM208; 346.36; [Table VII: 4]

religious personnel
USE: clergy KD30.2; 342.182

remainders KN64.22; 347.3162

remand prisons KM654.5; 346.987145; [App: 84.5]

remands KM580.7; 346.917

remarriage KN172.9.R4; 347.422.R4

remarried persons [Table VII: 3.5]

remedies KN395.1; 347.971; [Table IIA: 149]; [Table VI: .Z8]
UF: ancillary relief
RT: equitable remedies KN230; 347.59

remedies + contracts KN17; 347.148

remedies + international law KC1205; 341.705

remission + prisoners KM686.5; 346.98815; [App: 78.2]

remoteness + real property KN64.24; 347.3164

remuneration KN194; 347.478
SN: system of payments for work
UF: rewards + employment
UF: wages
RT: earnings KN194.1; 347.4781
RT: income KN194; 347.478

renewable energy KN89.3; 347.3313

renewable energy + EU KW122.9

rent KN88.1; 347.32991
RT: distress + landlord and tenant KN88.13; 347.329913

rent + taxation KM336.36; 346.5236

rent charges KN65.2; 347.3182

rent control KN88.12; 347.329912

rent review KN88.16; 347.329916

rental of vehicles
USE: motor vehicles + rental KN324.6; 347.8146

rental rights + intellectual property KN115.2; 347.3782

renunciation + contract KN16.2; 347.142

renvoi KC2060; 341.94

repairs + landlord and tenant KN88.4; 347.32994

reparation + criminal law KM594.5; 346.9485
UF: restitution orders

reparation + war KC1427; 341.897

repatriation
USE: deportation KM177.5; 346.337

repetitive strain injury
USE: industrial injuries KN198.3; 347.493

replevin KN37.2; 347.232

reply KN385; 347.945

reporting diseases
USE: notifiable diseases KN185.6; 347.4486

reporting to police [App: 69.5]

reports [Table VIII: 0052]
SN: use as subdivision only

representative actions
USE: group actions KN370.2; 347.9302

representatives + parliament
USE: legislators KM83; 346.22

reprieve KM596; 346.956

reproduction + family law KN172.7; 347.4217; [Table IIA: 117.2]

reproduction + family law + artificial techniques KN172.8; 347.4218

republics KM43; 346.127

reputation + offences
USE: libel + criminal law KM541.5; 346.8612

requests + prisoners KM680.2; 346.98752; [App: 93.2]

res gestae
USE: material facts KN383.2; 347.9432

res judicata KN384.5; 347.9445

resale price maintenance KN266.3; 347.633
UF: price maintenance
RT: price fixing KN266.3; 347.633
RT: prices KN283; 347.658

rescission + contracts KN16.2; 347.142

rescue services KM234; 346.3739
RT: emergency services KM234; 346.3739

research (academic) KN184.7; 347.4457; [Table VIII: .005]
UF: development

research + bibliography K32; 340.023
UF: bibliographical research

research + law
USE: legal research KL155; 345.19; [Table IIA: 66]

research + science KN184.7; 347.4457; [Table VIII: .005]
UF: scientific research

research and development KN273; 347.643
UF: technological change

research and development + EU KW140

reserve forces KM404; 346.73

reserves for aboriginals
USE: aboriginal reserves KN72.4; 347.32175

reservoirs KN90.5; 347.3335

residence + conflict of laws
USE: domicile + conflict of laws KC2065; 341.95

residence + taxation KM336.12; 346.5212
RT: domicile + taxation KM336.12; 346.5212

residential homes KN182.1; 347.4421
UF: almshouses

resignation + executive
USE: abdication KM112.9; 346.259

resignation + industrial law KN192.21; 347.4631

resources + conservation + international law KC243.4; 341.4444
UF: conservation of resources

responsa KD75; 342.25

responsibility
USE: liability [Table VI: .Z45]

responsibility of states
USE: states + responsibility KC180; 341.29

rest periods KN193.1; 347.471

Restatement of the law KL22.A1; 345.0973.A1

restaurants KN186.3; 347.453
UF: cafes
RT: food KN185.2; 347.447; [Table IIA: 123.3]

restitution + quasi-contract KN20.2; 347.162

restitution orders
USE: reparation + criminal law KM594.5; 346.9485

restorative justice KM594.9; 346.9489

restraint of trade KN266.2; 347.632

restraint of trade + EU KW110.3

restraint of trade + industrial law KN192.16; 347.4627

restraints on alienation KN71.2; 347.3212
UF: alienation + real property
UF: right to alienate

restrictive covenants KN65.6; 347.3186

restrictive practices + legal profession KL94; 345.173

restrictive trade practices
USE: abuse of dominant position KN266.5; 347.6345
USE: anti-competitive agreements KN266.2; 347.632

restructuring + companies KN312.7; 347.7927
UF: business restructuring

resulting trusts KN214.2; 347.552

retail + co-operatives KN268.3; 347.6383
RT: trade + retail KN286; 347.679

retail trade
USE: trade + retail KN286; 347.679

retaliation + international disputes KC1303; 341.783

retirement + employment KN192.18; 347.4629

retirement + judiciary KL240.4; 345.44
UF: judiciary + retirement

retirement + savings plans + taxation KM336.65; 346.5265

retirement age [Table VII: 1.6]
UF: age of retirement

retirement pensions
USE: pensions KN193.4; 347.474

retirement villages KN63.9.R4; 347.3149.R4

retraining KN192.35; 347.465
RT: technical education KN184.3; 347.444

retrenchment
USE: redundancy KN192.26; 347.4636

retrial KM597.5; 346.9575
UF: new trial

retribution + purpose of punishment [App: 50.25]

retroactive legislation KL36.4; 345.164
UF: ex post facto laws

revenue
USE: taxation KM335; 346.52; [Table IIA: 84.5]

Revenue and Customs (UK) KM235.R4; 346.38.R4
UF: Inland Revenue
UF: Customs and Excise

reverse mortgages KN67; 347.3191

reversions KN64.21; 347.3161

review of convictions
USE: convictions + review KM596; 346.956

Revised Reports KF53.R2

revision of law
USE: law reform KL160; 345.197; [Table IIA: 66]; [Table VI: .Z53]

revision of statute law
USE: statute law reform KL36; 345.16

revision of treaties
USE: amendments + treaties KC333.5; 341.5615

revisions
USE: amendments [Table VI: .Z53]

revocation + probate KN127.2; 347.3842

revocation + wills KN125.4; 347.3824

revolution
USE: rebellion KM561.1; 346.8811

rewards + employment
USE: remuneration KN194; 347.478

Rhodian law KE95; 343.39

rifles
USE: firearms KN186.1; 347.451

right of asylum
USE: asylum + international law KC206; 341.336

right to alienate KN71; 347.321

right to counsel KM209.C6; 346.368.C6

right to die
USE: euthanasia + medical law KN185.158; 347.3334

right to own property KM209.P8; 346.368.P8
UF: freedom of property

right to silence KM603.3; 346.9633
UF: self-incrimination
UF: silence + defendant

right to work KN191; 347.461

rights + individuals + trade unions
USE: individuals + trade unions KN195.55; 347.4845

rights + patients
USE: patients KN185.11; 347.44611

rights issues
USE: shares + issuing KN263.62; 347.62562

rights of audience KL94; 345.173

rights of way KN65.12; 347.3173
RT: bridle paths KN95.13; 347.34213
RT: footpaths KN95.13; 347.34213

riots KM562.1; 346.8831

riots + prisons KM671.3; 346.9874993; [App: 92.53]
UF: prison riots

risk management + employment KN198; 347.49

risk management + law firms KL97.5; 345.17675

risks insurance KN294; 347.694
UF: liability insurance

rivers KN90.1; 347.3331
RT: drainage basins KC144.5; 341.2545

rivers + international law KC267; 341.473

rivers + pollution KN97.73; 347.3473
RT: water + pollution KN97.73; 347.3473

rivers + transport KN326.1; 347.8161

road accidents
USE: accidents + roads KN323.9; 347.8139

road freight
USE: freight + roads KN328.5; 347.8285

road fuel duty KM337.764; 346.5864

road signs KN322.6; 347.8126
UF: signs + roads

road traffic KN323; 347.813
UF: motor traffic
UF: traffic + roads

road transport + EU KW135.2

road works KN322.55; 347.81255

roads KN322; 347.812; [Table IIA: 136]
UF: highways

roads + international law KC252; 341.452

roads + landscaping KN322.5; 347.8125
UF: landscaping + roads

roads + verges KN322.5; 347.8125
UF: verges

robbery KM546.2; 346.8712
UF: armed robbery

robes + lawyers
USE: legal dress KL81; 345.17011

rolling stock
USE: carriages + railways KN325.3; 347.8153
USE: wagons + railways KN325.3; 347.8153

Roman Catholic Church KD110; 342.31
UF: Catholic Church

Roman law KE100; 343.4
UF: Western Empire (753 BC to 600 AD)

Roman law + Europe + medieval KE357; 343.75
RT: reception of Roman law KE359; 343.76

Roman law : equity
USE: equity : Roman law KN203; 347.51

Roman-Dutch law KE400; 343.8
SN: mainly period 1473–1809

Rome Treaty
USE: Treaty of Rome (1971) KW1.F71

Rotterdam Rules + international law KC272.8; 341.4758

Rotterdam Rules + maritime law KN337; 347.837

routes + air transport KN327.3; 347.823
UF: air routes
UF: aviation routes

routes + international air law KC255.1; 341.4546
UF: international air routes

routes + railways KN325.4; 347.8154
UF: rail routes

routes + road transport KN324.4; 347.8144
UF: bus routes
UF: tramway routes

Royal Commissions KM238; 346.383

Royal Commissions + publications KF47

Royal Courts of Justice KL230.721.R6; 345.3721.R6
SN: situated in the Strand, London

royal prerogatives
USE: executive prerogatives KM114; 346.27

royal proclamations KF37.1
UF: proclamations

royal succession KM112.1; 346.252
UF: Crown + succession
UF: succession to the Crown

royalties KN115.43; 347.3787

royalties + taxation KM336.37; 346.5237

rubbish
USE: litter KN97.85; 347.3485

rubbish tips
USE: waste disposal KN97.85; 347.3485

rule of law KM34; 346.121
UF: due process of law
UF: equal protection of the law

rule of law + human rights KC202; 341.332

rule of law + jurisprudence KA34; 340.1298

rule of the road
USE: traffic regulations KN323.7; 347.8137

rule of the road at sea
USE: navigation + international maritime law KC274; 341.478
USE: navigation + maritime law KN333; 347.833

rules + employment
USE: discipline + industrial law KN192.5; 347.4655

rules + prisons KM661.2; 346.98722; [App: 92.22]
UF: prison rules

rules + trade unions KN195.5; 347.484

rules of court
USE: court rules KN360; 347.92; [Table VI: .Z72]

rural districts
USE: districts + local government KM365.5; 346.655

Russian Orthodox Church KD308.R8; 342.458.R8

sacraments [KD Table: 5]

sacrilege KM550; 346.875
UF: church desecration
UF: desecration
UF: graves + desecration

SADCC
USE: Southern African Development and Co-operation Conference
KC736; 341.656

sadism KM544.9.S2; 346.8649.S2

safe-conducts
USE: passports KM175; 346.328

safe deposits KN303.8; 347.728

safety + railways KN325.25; 347.81525
UF: railways + safety

safety + road traffic
USE: traffic regulations KN323.7; 347.8137

safety + ships + international law KC272.6; 341.4756

safety and health
USE: health and safety KN198; 347.49

sailors
USE: seamen KN332.1; 347.8321

salaries
USE: earnings KN194.1; 347.4781

salaries + civil service KM237.5; 346.3826

sale + contract
USE: contract + sale KN282.1; 347.651

sale of businesses
USE: businesses + sale KN279; 347.649

sale of goods KN280; 347.65; [Table IIA: 132]
UF: cooling off period
RT: trade + retail KN286; 347.679

sales + reductions
RT: prices + reductions KN283.2; 347.6582

sales taxes KM337.41; 346.561

Salic law
USE: Frankish law KE320.2; 343.622

saliva + samples
USE: pathological samples + identification KM604.33; 346.9646

salvage KN334; 347.834; [Table IIA: 139]
UF: civil salvage
UF: no cure no pay
RT: wrecks KN334.1; 347.8341

salvage + international law KC275; 341.479
RT: wrecks + international law KC275; 341.479

sanatoria
USE: convalescent homes KN185.17.C6; 347.44176.C6

sanctions + international disputes KC1312; 341.792
RT: embargoes + international disputes KC1311; 341.791

sanctity of life
USE: justice : morality KA38; 340.134

sanctuary + international law
USE: asylum + international law KC206; 341.336

sanctuary + medieval law KE192; 343.49055

sanitation KN97.5; 347.3463
UF: sewers + public health
RT: public hygiene KN97; 347.345

sanitation + international law
USE: public health + international law KC241; 341.441

satellite television KN344.52; 347.8732

satellite television + international law KC259.2; 341.4662

satellites + communications KN342.6; 347.866
UF: communications satellites

satellites + communications + space law KC284.2; 341.4942

satellites + international law KC257.8; 341.4628
RT: spy satellites KC1306; 341.7845

satellites + space law KC284; 341.494
UF: space satellites

satisfaction
USE: accord and satisfaction KN384.1; 347.9441

savings + taxation + reliefs KM336.65; 346.5265

savings banks KN303.7; 347.727

Saxon law (ancient) KE320.8; 343.628

Scandinavian law (ancient) KE321; 343.63

scheduled flights + international law KC255; 341.4545

schemes of arrangement KN312.71; 347.79271

Schengen agreement KW83.1

school buses KN324.2; 347.8142

school discipline
USE: discipline + schools KN184.25; 347.44325

school governors KN184.28; 347.44328
UF: governors + schools

school textbooks [Table VIII: 0085]

schools KN184.2; 347.4432
UF: comprehensive education

science + EU KW140

science : law KA70.S3; 340.16.S3

science of law
USE: jurisprudence KA; 340.1

scientific research
USE: research + science KN184.7; 347.4457; [Table VIII: .005]

Scotland + Court of Session
USE: Court of Session [Table V: 1]

Scottish Executive KM113.B2; 346.26.B2

Scottish Executive + publications KF136

Scottish legal system KL12; 345.09411

Scottish Parliament KM82.B2; 346.21.B2

Scottish Parliament + publications KF102

sea + natural resources KC276; 341.48
UF: natural resources of the sea

sea + pollution KN97.73; 347.3474
UF: pollution of the sea
RT: water + pollution KN97.72; 347.3472

sea + pollution + international law KC269; 341.474

sea law
USE: maritime law KN330; 347.83; [Table IIA: 138]

sea transport
USE: maritime law KN330; 347.83; [Table IIA: 138]

seabed + resources KC277; 341.482
UF: mineral resources + submerged lands
UF: minerals + international maritime law
RT: continental shelf KC144.2; 341.2542

sealing + contracts KN13.9; 347.119

sealing + documents KL34.22; 345.1422

sealing + international law KC276.3; 341.4813

seamen KN332.1; 347.8321
UF: merchant seamen
UF: sailors

seamen + international law KC273; 341.476

search orders KN392.7; 347.9637
UF: Anton Piller orders

search warrants
USE: searches + criminal investigation KM580.2; 346.912

searches + conveyancing KN74.2; 347.32232

searches + criminal investigation KM580.2; 346.912
UF: search warrants
UF: warrants + searches
RT: illegally obtained evidence KN394.4; 347.9654

searches + ships + international law KC272.4; 341.4754
UF: ship searches

SEATO
USE: South East Asia Treaty Organisation KC851; 341.664

SEC documents + EU KW 17

second hand dealing KN285.S4; 347.679.S4
UF: antique dealers
RT: auctions KN285.1; 347.671
RT: pawnbroking KN305.5; 347.765

secret ballot
USE: voting + elections + legislatures KM83.45; 346.2245

secret killing + international law
USE: disappearances + crimes + international law KC218.D5; 341.369.D5

secret trusts KN214.4; 347.554

secretaries + diplomacy KC325; 341.552

Secretaries of State + UK KM113.5; 346.265
UF: Ministers of State + UK

sects [KD Table: 1]

securities + finance KN304.1; 347.731
UF: blue sky law
UF: stocks + investment
RT: shares KN263.5; 347.6255

securitisation + credit KN305.23; 347.7523

security + data KN348.8; 347.8978

security + EU KW79

security + investment KN306.9; 347.779

security + networks KN347.56; 347.8946
UF: firewalls + networks

security + personal property KN106.4; 347.3664

security + prisons KM661; 346.9872; [App: 92.2]

Security Council KC416; 341.624

security for costs
USE: payment into court KN387.5; 347.9475

security of aircraft
USE: aircraft + security + international law KC255.5; 341.4549

security of employment
USE: employment protection KN192.2; 347.463

security of tenure + employment KN192.2; 347.463
UF: tenure + employment

security of tenure + judiciary KL240.1; 345.41

security of tenure + tenancies KN88.2; 347.32992

sedition
USE: subversion KM561.2; 346.8812

segregation + race
USE: racial discrimination KM208.43; 346.3643; [Table IIA: 81.5]

seizure KM580.2; 346.912
RT: illegally obtained evidence KN394.4; 347.9654

select committees
USE: legislative committees [Table IA: 7; 13]

selection + employment KN192.112; 347.46222

selection + juries KN389.61; 347.96061

selection + juries + criminal procedure KM583.1; 346.9331

selective service
USE: conscription KM402; 346.715

self-assessment + taxation KM336.84; 346.5284
UF: pay and file

self-censorship KN349.2; 347.8982

self-defence + criminal law KM584.1; 346.9341

self-defence + war KC1355.3; 341.823

self-determination + international law KC162; 341.272
RT: sovereignty KC151; 341.261

self-employment KN260.2; 347.622
RT: small businesses KN260.2; 347.622

self-government KM208.434; 346.36434

self-incrimination
USE: right to silence KM603.3; 346.9633

self-injury + prisoners KM681.31; 346.987631; [App: 93.31]

semen + samples
USE: pathological samples + identification KM604.33; 346.9646

semiotics K100.5; 340.0605

semiotics + jurisprudence KA70.L5; 340.16.L5

Senate + US KM82.3; 346.213

senators
USE: legislators KM83; 346.22

sentences KM587; 346.937; [Table IIA: 93.2]; [Table VI: .Z9]
UF: punishment + offenders

sentences + international criminal courts KC219.5; 341.395

sentences + policy [App: 40]
UF: sentencing

sentencing
USE: sentences + policy [App: 40]

separated persons [Table VII: 3.3]

separation + marriage KN173.3; 347.425
UF: judicial separation

separation of powers KM35; 346.122

sequestration KN395.25; 347.9725

serial publications
USE: journals K1; 340.01; [Table VIII: 001]

service agreements + employment KN192.11; 347.4622

service charges + landlord and tenant KN88.11; 347.329911

service defects + tort KN39.S4; 347.29.S4

service industries KN286; 347.679

service industries + EU KW119.1

service taxes KM337.44; 346.564

services + local government
USE: local services KM361.1; 346.611

servitude + religious laws [KD Table: 8.9]

servitudes + international law KC170; 341.28

servitudes + real property KN65; 347.317

set-off + defences KN384.9; 347.9449

set-off + negotiable instruments KN306.94; 347.7794

setting down
USE: cause lists KN389.1; 347.9601

settled land KN64.14; 347.3156

settlement + actions KN388; 347.95

settlement + national territory KC142.4; 341.2524

settlement systems KN304.88; 347.7388

settlements KN210; 347.54
RT: trusts KN210; 347.54; [Table IIA: 126]

settlements + taxation KM336.447; 346.52447

severance
USE: joinder and severance KM582.6; 346.9326

sewers + public health
USE: sanitation KN97.5; 347.3463

sewers + real property KN65.4; 347.3184

sex discrimination KM208.2; 346.362

sexual capacity
USE: capacity + sexual activity KM544.01; 346.86401

sexual harassment + criminal law KM544.9.H3; 346.8649.H3
UF: stalking

sexual harassment + employment KN192.57; 347.46557

sexual offences KM544; 346.864
UF: vice

sexual offences against minors
USE: pederasty KM544.7; 346.8646

sexuality + jurisprudence KA70.S4; 340.16.S4

shadow directors KN264.4; 347.6264

share-cropping KN98.14; 347.3514

shareholders KN263.7; 347.6257; [Table IIA: 129.5]

shareholders + disclosure of interests
USE: disclosure of interests + shareholders KN263.71; 347.62571

shareholders + meetings KN263.8; 347.6258

shares KN263.5; 347.6255; [Table IIA: 129.5]
RT: securities + finance KN304.1; 347.731

shares + issuing KN263.62; 347.62562
UF: rights issues

shares + options KN263.6; 347.6256

shares + sales KN263.61; 347.62561

shares + transfers KN263.61; 347.62561

shareware
USE: software KN348.4; 347.8974

sheep + EU KW117.3.S5

Sheriff Court [Table V: 3]

sheriffs (police)
USE: police KM615; 346.985; [Table IIA: 92.2]

sheriffs + England and Wales KL252; 345.52

shifts KN193.1; 347.471

Shiite law KD616; 342.716

Shinto law KD960; 342.98

ship chartering
USE: charterparties KN337.4; 347.8374

ship searches
USE: searches + ships + international law KC272.4; 341.4754

shipbuilders KN332.5; 347.8325

shipbuilding KN332.5; 347.8325

shipbuilding + EU KW119.3

shipmasters KN332.1; 347.8321

shipowners KN332.2; 347.8322

shipping KN332; 347.832

shipping lanes KN333.4; 347.8334

ships KN332.3; 347.8323
UF: boats
UF: shipping
UF: vessels

ships + EU KW135.4

ships + international law KC272; 341.475

ships + nationality KC272.1; 341.4751
UF: nationality + ships

ships + safety KC272.6; 341.4756

shipwrecks
USE: wrecks KN334.1; 347.8341

shipyards KN332.6; 347.8326

shock treatment KN185.52.S4; 347.4482.S4

shooting rights
USE: sporting rights KN65.9.S6; 347.3189.S6

shop stewards KN195.6; 347.4846

shoplifting KM546.6.S5; 346.8716.S5

shops + industrial law KN193.51; 347.4751

shops + real property KN83.2; 347.3252

short stories
USE: fiction (novels) KB33; 340.373

shorthold tenancies KN87.72; 347.32972

Shulhan Aruk KD70.6; 342.246

siblings **[Table VII: 3.8]**
UF: brothers
UF: sisters

sick leave **KN193.2;** **347.472**

sickness + social security **KN181.2;** **347.4412**
UF: Medicare
RT: health insurance (private) KN292.3; 347.685

sickness insurance (private)
USE: health insurance (private) KN292.3; 347.685

signalling + railways **KN325.2;** **347.8152**

signs + roads
USE: road signs KN322.6; 347.8126

Sikh law **KD840;** **342.93**

silence + defendant
USE: right to silence KM603.3; 346.9633

single chambers
USE: unicameral legislatures KM82.1; 346.211

single currency + EU **KW106**
UF: currency + integration + EU
UF: integration + currency + EU
UF: monetary integration + EU

Single Euro Payments Area **KW106.4**

single market + EU **KW108**
RT: harmonisation + qualifications + EU KW109.8
RT: interstate commerce + federations KN252; 347.605

single offenders **[App: 07.5]**
RT: offenders KM587.1; 346.9371

single parent families
USE: families + single parent KN174.5; 347.42595

single persons [Table VII: 3.1]
UF: unmarried persons

single transferrable vote
USE: proportional representation KM83.41; 346.2241

sisters
USE: siblings [Table VII: 3.8]

sites of historic interest
USE: historic buildings KN95.12; 347.34212
USE: historic sites + conservation KN95.11; 347.34211

sketches KB35; 340.375

skills training + legal education KL131–149 [Table: .35]; 345.1794–9 [Table: 35]

slander KN38.22; 347.2482

slaughterhouses KN185.29; 347.44729
UF: abattoirs
UF: animals + slaughter

slave labour
USE: slavery KM208.58; 346.3658

slave trade
USE: slavery KM208.58; 346.3658

slavery KM208.58; 346.3658
UF: abolition of slavery
UF: anti-slavery laws
UF: slave labour
UF: slave trade

slavery + international law KC207; 341.337

slavery + religious laws [KD Table: 8.9]

slaves [Table VII: 5.8]

Slavic law (ancient) KE340; 343.68

slum clearance KN96.25; 347.34325
RT: housing KN96.2; 347.3432

small and medium-sized enterprises KN265.15; 347.62715
UF: SMEs

small and medium-sized enterprises + EU KW118.2

small businesses KN260.2; 347.622
RT: self-employment KN260.2; 347.622

small claims court [Table V: 9.S5]

small companies KN265.16; 347.62716

small companies + taxation KM336.491; 346.52491

small holdings KN98.25; 347.3525

smart cards KN303.14; 347.7214

smartphones KN342.356; 347.86356

SMEs
USE: small and medium-sized enterprises KN265.15; 347.62715

smoking
USE: tobacco + offences KM565.T6; 346.89.T6
USE: tobacco + public health KN186.9.T6; 347.459.T6

Smriti KD722; 342.822

smuggling KM564.3; 346.8863
RT: contraband KC1385; 341.8545
RT: customs duties KM337.71; 346.581

social conditions + causes of crime [App: 13]

social conditions + EU + journals KW66.3

social contract KA41; 340.141

social impact of technology
USE: technology + social impact + EU KW131.3

social insurance KN181; 347.44
UF: national insurance
RT: insurance KN290; 347.68; [Table IIA: 133]

social law KN180; 347.43; [Table IIA: 120]

social law + international law KC240; 341.44

social media KN347.46; 347.89356
UF: social networking

social policy + EU KW127

social protection + EU + journals KW66.35

social psychology KA63; 340.153
UF: legal psychology
UF: psychology + sociology

social security KN181; 347.44; [Table IIA: 121]

social security + EU KW128

social security + offences KM564.5; 346.8865

social security + taxes KM337.9.S6; 346.59.S6

social services KN180; 347.43; [Table IIA: 121]

social services + EU KW128

social work KN180.5; 347.435

social workers + law
USE: law for social workers KL30.S6; 345.1.S6

socialism + international law KC122; 341.222

socialist jurisprudence KA48; 340.146

societies
USE: associations KN169.4; 347.41894; [Table VII: 9.4]; [Table VIII: .003]

Society of Friends KD570; 342.6917
UF: Quakers

socio-economic rights KM201.3; 346.3503

sociology : law KA70.S6; 340.16.S6

sociology of law KA60; 340.15

sodomy KM544.2; 346.8642
UF: buggery

software KN348.4; 347.8974
UF: computer programs

soil + conservation KN98.4; 347.354

soil + pollution
USE: contaminated land

solar power KN89.51; 347.3321

solatium + Scotland KN37.1; 347.231

soldiers
USE: army law KM411; 346.76

solemnisation of marriage
USE: marriage + ceremony KN172.5; 347.4215

soliciting
USE: prostitution KM544.1; 346.8641

Solicitor-General KL251; 345.51

solicitors KL87; 345.17134
RT: lawyers KL85; 345.171

solicitors + complaints
USE: complaints + legal profession KL95; 345.174

solicitors + remuneration KL89.3; 345.17143

Solicitors Regulation Authority KL97.4; 345.17674

solitary confinement KM670.5; 346.98745; [App: 92.45]

sonic booms KN38.81; 347.281

sound recordings + evidence KN392.5; 347.9635

sound recordings + evidence + criminal procedure KM604.54; 346.9664

sound recordings + intellectual property KN112.5; 347.3755

sound recordings + law reporting KL33.2; 345.132
RT: law reporting KL33; 345.13

sources of law KA23; 340.123; [Table VI: .Z1]
UF: law and custom
UF: origin of law

sources of law + conflict of laws KC2066; 341.951

sources of law + international law KC82; 341.192

sources of law + religious laws KD15; 342.15

South America + international relations KC306.3; 341.5163

South America + organisations KC780; 341.6595

South East Asia + international relations KC303.2; 341.5132

South East Asia Treaty Organisation KC851; 341.664
UF: SEATO

South Pacific Commission KC886.S6; 341.6695.S6

Southern African Development and Co-operation Conference KC736; 341.656
UF: SADCC

sovereign debt KN305.15; 347.7515

sovereigns
USE: monarchs KM112.1; 346.252

sovereignty KC151; 341.261
RT: self-determination + international law KC162; 341.272

sovereignty + airspace
USE: airspace + international law KC253.2; 341.4532

sovereignty + transfers KC161; 341.271

space + research KC284.1; 341.4941

space law
USE: outer space KC280; 341.49

space satellites
USE: satellites + space law KC284; 341.494

space stations KC284; 341.494

spam KN342.45; 347.8645

Spartan law KE94; 343.38

speakers + parliamentary procedure KM84.3; 346.233

special educational needs KN184.29; 347.44329

special representative (diplomats) KC327; 341.554

special security units KM653.3; 346.987133; [App: 83.3]

specific performance KN231; 347.591

specific restitution KN231.2; 347.5912

spectator violence
USE: sports grounds + offences KM562.13; 346.88313

speculation KN304.9; 347.739

speeches
USE: oratory KB31; 340.371

speed + traffic KN323.73; 347.81373

speed + traffic + offences KM565.T7; 346.89.T7

speed cameras KN323.73; 347.81373

spent convictions KM603.55; 346.96355

spies
USE: espionage + war + international law KC1355.5; 341.825

spirits
USE: alcohol KN186.4; 347.454

spiritualism KD590.S6; 342.6919.S6

sponsorship + legal education KL131–149 [Table: .7]; 345.1794–9 [Table: 7]

sport KN186.6; 347.456
UF: athletics

sport + EU KW144.7

sport + facilities + employment KN193.3; 347.473

sporting rights KN65.9.S6; 347.3189.S6
UF: fishing rights
UF: hunting rights
UF: shooting rights
RT: hunting KN186.63; 347.4563

sporting rights + taxation KM336.36; 346.5236

sports grounds KN186.7; 347.457
UF: football grounds
UF: stadia

sports grounds + offences KM562.13; 346.88313
UF: chanting abuse + sports grounds
UF: pitch invasions
UF: spectator violence
UF: throwing missiles + sports grounds
RT: crowd control + sports grounds KM562.13; 346.88313
RT: ticket touting KM565.T5; 346.89.T5

spy satellites KC1306; 341.7845
RT: espionage + international law KC1306; 341.7845
RT: satellites + international law KC257.8; 341.4628

spying
USE: espionage + war + international law KC1355.5; 341.825

squatting KN182.22; 347.44222

stadia
USE: sports grounds KN186.7; 347.457

staff + courts KL230.17; 345.317
RT: personnel management + courts KL230.17; 345.317

staff + legal education KL131–149 [Table: .6]; 345.1794–9 [Table: 6]

staff + libraries K84.4; 340.0544

stake holding + commercial law KN251; 347.601
SN: interests of a party in an organisation which are not fully recognised under commercial law

stalking
USE: sexual harassment + criminal law KM544.9.H3; 346.8649.H3

stamp duties KM337.5; 346.569

stamp duty reserve tax KM337.51; 346.5691

stamp duty land tax KM337.52; 346.5692

standard conditions + sale of land KN74.7; 347.3227

standard of proof
USE: burden of proof KN390.1; 347.9611

standards + courts + buildings KL230.73; 345.373

standards + industry + EU KW120

standing orders + parliamentary procedure KM84.2; 346.231

stare decisis
USE: precedent KL32; 345.12

state KM31; 346.1
UF: Crown

state : law KA27; 340.127

state aids + competition KN266.6; 347.6349
RT: subsidies + competition KN266.6; 347.6349

state aids + competition + EU KW110.1

state aircraft
USE: aircraft + international law KC253.5; 341.4535

state and church
USE: church and state KM58; 346.138

state and law
USE: law : state KA27; 340127

state compensation KM594.8; 346.9488

state constitutions + US KG391

state governors + US
USE: governors KM112.4; 346.255

state ships
USE: government ships KC272.3; 341.4753

state succession KC160; 341.27
RT: mergers + states KC156; 341.266
RT: partition + states KC155; 341.265

state succession + treaties KC338.5; 341.595

state trials + England and Wales KF70

stateless persons
USE: refugees + international law KC205; 341.335

statelessness KC194; 341.314
UF: expatriation
RT: refugees + international law KC205; 341.335

statements of case KN383; 347.943
UF: pleadings
UF: claims + statements
UF: entries + pleadings
UF: oral pleadings
UF: written pleadings

statements of claim
USE: particulars KN383.1; 347.9431

states + division KC163; 341.273

states + international law KC140; 341.24
UF: nations + international law

states + primary sources + United States KG391

states + responsibility + international law KC180; 341.29
UF: government liability + international law
UF: responsibility of states

states' rights
USE: federations + constitutional law KM44; 346.128

statistics KL300; 345.7; [Table IIA: 72]; [Table VIII: .0024]
UF: civil judicial statistics
UF: judicial statistics
UF: legal statistics
RT: criminal statistics KM620; 346.99

statistics + EU + journals KW66

statistics of crime
USE: criminal statistics KM620; 346.99

status
USE: persons KN150; 347.4; [Table IIA: 113]; [Table VII]

status + litigants
USE: locus standi KN370.3; 347.9303

statute law reform KL36; 345.16
UF: revision of statute law
RT: law reform KL160; 345.197; [Table IIA: 66]; [Table VI: .Z53]

statute of frauds
USE: fraud + criminal law KM547; 346.872

statute of limitations
USE: limitation of actions KN355; 347.915

statutes (theory)
USE: legislation (theory) KL36; 345.16

statutes + indexes + England and Wales KF26

statutes + texts [Table IA: 15]; [Table VI: .Z14]
UF: acts
RT: legislation (texts) [Table IA: 15]

statutes + texts + Australia (Commonwealth) KH15

statutes + texts + Canada (federal) KG15

statutes + texts + England and Wales KF20

statutes + texts + United States (federal) KG320

statutory companies KN265.8; 347.6278

statutory construction
USE: construction + statutes KL35; 345.15

statutory declarations KN391.2; 347.9622

statutory instruments + England and Wales
USE: subordinate legislation + texts + England and Wales KF30

statutory trusts KN214.3; 347.553

stealing
USE: theft KM546; 346.871

steel + EU KW119.2

step-children KN176.7; 347.4267; [Table VII: 3.9.S8]

step-parents KN176.7; 347.4267; [Table VII: 3.9.S8]

sterilisation + family law KN172.74; 347.42174

sterilisation + punishment [App: 75.S8]

stills + alcohol
USE: excise offences KM564.4; 346.8864

stipendiary magistrates
USE: magistrates KL243; 345.48

stock exchanges KN304.8; 347.738

stockbrokers KN304.81; 347.7381

stocks + investment
USE: securities + finance KN304.1; 347.731

stocks + punishment [App: 62.7]

stolen goods KM546.9; 346.8719
UF: receiving stolen goods

storage of food
USE: food + storage KN97.4; 347.3462

store detectives
USE: private detectives KM614.2; 346.9842

stowage KN337.7; 347.8377

stowaways KN332.7; 347.8327

straits KC265; 341.472

strata titles KN72.6; 347.32185

street cars
USE: tramways KN324.3; 347.8143

street lighting
USE: lighting + roads KN322.7; 347.8127

street plans K200; 340.099

street trading KN285.9.S8; 347.678.S8
UF: busking

stress + employment KN198.5; 347.495

strict liability + criminal law KM505.9; 346.828
UF: absolute liability
UF: liability without fault
RT: employers' liability KN198.1; 347.491
RT: vicarious liability KN33.6; 347.216

strict liability + tort KN33.4; 347.214
UF: absolute liability

strikes KN196.4; 347.4864
RT: lockouts KN196.4; 347.4864
RT: non-strike action KN196.5; 347.4866

structural funds + EU KW123.1

structural policy + EU KW123

structure of the legal profession
USE: legal profession + structure KL84; 345.1704

student grants KN184.35; 347.4445

student loans KN184.35; 347.4445
UF: loans to students

style + legal language
USE: legal language K100; 340.06

sub judice + criminal procedure KM563.33; 346.88533

sub-contractors + taxation KM336.499; 346.52499

sub-letting KN87.3; 347.3293

subjects (citizens)
USE: citizens KM171; 346.3

submarine cables KC257.5; 341.4625

submarine oil wells
USE: oil and gas + marine operations KC277.1; 341.4821

submarine warfare KC1381; 341.8541

submarines + commercial law KN332.4; 347.8324

submerged lands
USE: continental shelf KC144.2; 341.2542

subordinate legislation KM302; 346.42; [Table IA: 20]
UF: administrative legislation
UF: delegated legislation
UF: Ordinances
UF: Regulations
UF: subsidiary legislation

subordinate legislation + indexes + England and Wales KF34

subordinate legislation + texts [Table VI: .Z18]

subordinate legislation + texts + England and Wales KF30
UF: statutory instruments + England and Wales
UF: subsidiary legislation + England and Wales

subpoena
USE: witness summons KN391.1; 347.9621

subpoena + criminal procedure
USE: witness summons + criminal procedure KM605.8; 346.9778

subsidence KN92.S9; 347.335.S9

subsidiaries KN265.7; 347.6277
RT: companies KN261; 347.624; [Table IIA: 128]

subsidiaries + taxation KM336.493; 346.52493
RT: foreign subsidiary companies + taxation KM336.494; 346.52494

subsidiarity + EU KW72

subsidiary legislation
USE: subordinate legislation KM302; 346.42; [Table IA: 20]

subsidiary legislation + England and Wales
USE: subordinate legislation + texts + England and Wales KF30

subsidies + agriculture KN98.3; 347.353

subsidies + competition KN266.6; 347.6349
RT: state aids + competition KN266.6; 347.6349

subsidies + regional aid + EU KW123

subsidies to the arts
USE: arts + subsidies KN184.8; 347.4458

subversion KM561.2; 346.8812
UF: sedition

succession KN120; 347.38; [Table IIA: 110]
RT: inheritance KN120; 347.38; [Table IIA: 110]

succession to the Crown
USE: royal succession KM112.1; 346.252

suffrage KM83.3; 346.223
UF: electorate
UF: franchise (elections)

sugar + EU KW117.3.S9

suicide KM542.3; 346.8623

suicide + prisoners KM681.31; 346.987631; [App: 93.31]

suicide pacts KM542.3; 346.8623

Sumerian law KE24; 343.24

summary judgments KN395.6; 347.9736

summary jurisdiction [Table V: 4.3]
RT: Magistrates' Courts [Table V: 4.3; 5.3]

summary offences KM503.5; 346.8155

summary trial KM588; 346.94
RT: trial practice + criminal procedure KM582; 346.93

summer time
USE: time KN186.9.T5; 347.459.T5

summing up KN389.7; 347.9607

summing up + criminal procedure KM585; 346.935

summonses + criminal procedure KM580.3; 346.913

summonses + juries + civil procedure KN389.61; 347.96061

summonses + juries + criminal procedure KM583.1; 346.9331

summonses + witnesses KN391.1; 347.9621

Sundays KN186.2; 347.452
UF: blue laws

Sunnite law KD611; 342.711

superannuation
USE: pensions KN193.4; 347.474

supergrasses
USE: informers + evidence KM603.8; 346.9638

superior courts [Table V: 1]

superior judges KL241.1; 345.461

superior orders
USE: necessity + criminal law KM505.5; 346.825

supersonic flight + international law KC253.3; 341.4533

supervision of treaties
USE: treaties + supervision KC338.4; 341.594

supplementary benefits KN181.8; 347.4418

supply of publications + courts
USE: publications + supply + courts KL230.8.P8; 345.38.P8

supply procedure + public expenditure KM331.5; 346.505

support + marriage
USE: maintenance + marriage KN172.6; 347.4216

suppression + evidence KN390.4; 347.9614

supranationality KC136; 341.236

supreme courts [Table V: 1]

suretyship KN18.7; 347.157
UF: principal and surety

surgeons
USE: doctors KN185.18.D6; 347.44618.D6

surgery KN185.5; 347.448
UF: operations + surgery

surrender + war KC1421; 341.891
UF: capitulation

surrogacy KN172.85; 347.42185

surveillance + criminal investigation KM580.14; 346.9114

surveying KN72.1; 347.3215

survivors + benefits KN198.9; 347.499

suspended sentences [App: 67]

suspension + diplomatic relations KC1304; 341.784
UF: diplomatic relations + suspension

suspension + employment law KN192.23; 347.4633

suspicious persons KM562.5; 346.8835

sustainable development KN95.8; 347.3428

sustainable development + EU KW125.15

sustainable development + international law KC243.4; 341.4444

Swabian law KE320.9; 343.629

swap agreements KN306.8; 347.778

swindling
USE: fraud + criminal law KM547; 346.872

symposia
USE: collections [Table VIII: 004]

syndicated loans KN305.21; 347.7521

synonyms
USE: thesauri K123; 340.083

systems management + computers + libraries K86.2; 340.0562

table talk
USE: conversations KB15; 340.33

tabling K105.7; 340.0657

takeovers + competition KN266.12; 347.6312
UF: amalgamations
RT: transfer of undertakings + employment protection KN192.28; 347.4638

takeovers + incorporation KN262.1; 347.62421
UF: amalgamations

Talmud KD68; 342.23

tangible objects + evidence
USE: exhibits + evidence KN392.7; 347.9637

Tao law KD920; 342.96

tape-recording + criminal investigation KM580.12; 346.9112
RT: interrogation + criminal investigation KM580.12; 346.9112

tare + freight
USE: charges + freight KN328.2; 347.8282

tariffs (charges)
USE: charges + freight KN328.2; 347.8282

tariffs (customs duties)
USE: customs duties KM337.71; 346.581

tax allowances
USE: allowances + taxation KM336.6; 346.526

tax audits KM336.95; 346.5295

tax avoidance
USE: tax planning KM336.7; 346.527

tax collection
USE: taxes + collection KM336.9; 346.529

tax credits KM336.96; 346.5296

tax deducted at source KM336.92; 346.5292

tax deductions
USE: deductions + taxation KM336.6; 346.526

tax dodging
USE: tax evasion KM564.2; 346.8862

tax evasion KM564.2; 346.8862
UF: fiscal evasion
UF: tax dodging

tax exemptions
USE: exemption + taxation KM336.6; 346.526

tax havens KM336.75; 346.5275
UF: tax shelters

tax liability
USE: liability + taxation KM336.1; 346.5211

tax planning KM336.7; 346.527
UF: tax avoidance
UF: tax saving

tax planning + inheritance taxes KM337.35; 346.555

tax rates KM336.89; 346.5289
UF: rates of tax

tax reliefs
USE: reliefs + taxation KM336.6; 346.526

tax returns KM336.81; 346.5281
UF: information + taxation

tax saving
USE: tax planning KM336.7; 346.527

tax shelters
USE: tax havens KM336.75; 346.5275

tax years
USE: years + tax + assessment KM336.82; 346.5282

taxation KM335; 346.52; [Table IIA: 84.5]
UF: revenue

taxation + appeals KM336.87; 346.5287
UF: appeals + taxation

taxation + bibliography K52.2; 340.03472

taxation + comparative law KB184; 340.6047

taxation + EU KW103
RT: value added tax KM337.45; 346.565

taxation + international law KC224; 341.412

taxation + official bodies
USE: official bodies + taxation KM336.48; 346.5248

taxation + procedure
USE: assessment + taxation KM336.8; 346.528

taxation + real property
USE: real property + taxes KM337.6; 346.57

taxation + self-assessment KM336.84; 346.5284

taxation of costs
USE: assessment of costs KN397.7; 347.9777
RT: costs KN397; 347.977; [Table IIA: 150]

taxes + collection KM336.9; 346.529
UF: payment + taxes
UF: tax collection

taxis KN324.5; 347.8145
UF: cabs
RT: minicabs KN324.5; 347.8145

teachers KN184.23; 347.44323; [Table VII: 6.T4]

teachers + EU KW143.6

teachers of law
USE: law teachers KL131.6; 345.186

technical education KN184.3; 347.444
UF: day release
UF: vocational education
RT: further education KN184.3; 347.444
RT: retraining KN192.35; 347.465
RT: trainee solicitors KL87.1; 345.171341

techniques + legal profession KL90; 345.172

techniques + legal writing
USE: legal composition K101; 340.061

technological change
USE: research and development KN273; 347.643

technology + courts KL230.6; 345.36

technology + EU KW140

technology + industry + EU KW121

technology + social impact + EU KW131.3
UF: social impact of technology

Technology and Construction Court [Table V: 8]
UF: Official Referees

telecommunications KN342; 347.86; [Table IIA: 141.5]
RT: public utilities KN275.P8; 347.645.P8

telecommunications + censorship KN349.92; 347.8992

telecommunications + international law KC257; 341.462

teleconferencing + courts KL230.63; 345.363
UF: videoconferencing + courts

telegraph KN342.1; 347.861

telegraph + international law KC257.2; 341.4622

telephone KN342.3; 347.863
RT: mobile phones KN342.35; 347.8635

telephone + international law KC257.2; 341.4622

telephone sales KN285.9.T4; 347.678.T4
UF: cold calling

telephone tapping
USE: wire tapping KM604.52; 346.9662

telephones + legislatures KM87.2; 346.2482

teletext KN344.53; 347.8733

television KN344.5; 347.873
RT: broadcasting KN344; 347.871
RT: wavelengths + broadcasting KN344.1; 347.8711

television + causes of crime [App: 17]

television + censorship KN349.95; 347.8995

television + international law KC259; 341.466
UF: wavelengths + international law
RT: radio + international law KC258.5; 341.465

television + law reporting KL33.2; 345.132

television sets
USE: receivers + broadcasting KN344.1; 347.8711

telex KN342.2; 347.862

telex + international law KC257.2; 341.4622

temperance
USE: alcohol KN186.4; 347.454

temporary employment KN192.13; 347.4624

tenant and landlord
USE: landlord and tenant KN85; 347.327; [Table IIA: 106]

tenders
SN: use as subdivision only

tenure + employment
USE: security of tenure + employment KN192.2; 347.463

tenure + land
USE: land tenure KN62; 347.311; [Table IIA: 105]

termination [Table VI: .Z55]

termination + leases KN87.8; 347.3298

termination + marriage KN173; 347.423
SN: termination by all means other than death

termination + pregnancy
USE: abortion + family law KN172.73; 347.42173

termination + treaties KC338.3; 341.593

termination + war KC1420; 341.89
RT: peace treaties KC1425; 341.895

termination by prosecution
USE: nolle prosequi KM582.5; 346.9325

terminology + EU law KW7

terms + contracts KN13.4; 347.114

terms + courts
USE: legal terms KL230.18; 345.318

terms and phrases
USE: legal dictionaries K120; 340.08; [Table IIA: 63]

Territorial Army KM404; 346.73

territorial sea KC144.1; 341.2541
UF: tidelands
RT: continental shelf KC144.2; 341.2542

territories + local government KM366.2; 346.662

territory + international law KC142; 341.252
RT: national territory KC142; 341.252

terrorism KM562.22; 346.88322

terrorism + international law KC218.T4; 341.369.T4

test tube babies
USE: in vitro fertilisation KN172.82; 347.42182

testamentary freedom KN125.8; 347.3828
RT: wills KN125; 347.382

testators + capacity KN125.1; 347.3821
RT: wills KN125; 347.382

testimony
USE: evidence KN390; 347.961; [Table IIA: 147]

textbooks [Table VIII: .0085]
SN: use as subdivision only

textile industry + EU KW119.4

texts
SN: use as subdivision only

theatre KN344.7; 347.874

theatre + censorship KN349.96; 347.8996

theatre + subsidies
USE: arts + subsidies KN184.8; 347.4458

theft KM546; 346.871
UF: larceny
UF: stealing

theft by finding KM546.5; 346.8715

theory of law
USE: jurisprudence KA; 340.1

theory of punishment [App: 50]

thesauri K123; 340.083
UF: legal thesauri
UF: synonyms

thesauri + EU law KW7

thesauri + methodology K123.0099; 340.0830099

theses [Table VIII: 0055]

third market + investment KN304.84; 347.7384

third parties [Table VI: .Z65]

third parties + contract KN14.3; 347.123

third parties + partnership KN267.6; 347.6366

third parties + treaties KC334.3; 341.573

third world
USE: developing countries + international relations KC309.5; 341.5195

thirty-nine articles + Church of England KD485; 342.685

threats
USE: duress + criminal liability KM505.3; 346.823

throwing missiles + sports grounds
USE: sports grounds + offences KM562.13; 346.88313

ticket touting KM565.T5; 346.89.T5
RT: sports grounds + offences KM562.13; 346.88313

tidal power KN89.52; 347.3322

tidelands
USE: territorial sea KC144.1; 341.2541

tied accommodation KN88.25; 347.329925
UF: employees + tied accommodation

timber KN99.1; 347.3561

time KN186.9.T5; 347.459.T5
UF: British Standard Time
UF: British Summer Time
UF: daylight saving
UF: double summer time
UF: Greenwich Mean Time
UF: summer time

time charters KN337.4; 347.8374

time immemorial
USE: customary law KL8; 345.08; [Table IIA: 62]

time limits
USE: limitation of actions KN355; 347.915

timeshares KN54.55; 347.30255

tin KN91.6.T5; 347.3346.T5

tips + advice
USE: advice services KN400; 347.9991

tips + employment KN194.5; 347.4785
UF: gratuities

tithes
USE: church property [KD Table: 4]

title + personal property KN104.1; 347.3641

title + property KN54.1; 347.3021

title + real property
USE: land titles KN72; 347.3214

tobacco + excise duties KM337.761; 346.5861

tobacco + offences KM565.T6; 346.89.T6
UF: smoking

tobacco + public health KN186.9.T6; 347.459.T6
UF: passive smoking
UF: smoking

tolls + roads KN322.9; 347.8129

topography right KN114.7; 347.3777
RT: maps + intellectual property KN112.2; 347.373

Torah KD66; 342.22

Torrens system KN72.3; 347.3217
RT: land + registration KN72.2; 347.3216

tort KN30; 347.2; [Table IIA: 100]
UF: civil wrongs
UF: wrongs
RT: obligations KN5; 347.08; [Table IIA: 96]

tort + remedies KN37; 347.23

tort : criminal law
USE: criminal law : tort KM502; 346.81

tortious liability
USE: liability + tort KN33; 347.21

torture [App: 62.2]

torture + international law KC218.T6; 341.369.T6

tourism KN286.T6; 347.679.T6

tourism + EU KW136

towage KN334.2; 347.8342
UF: no cure no pay
UF: tugs

town and country planning
USE: planning KN96; 347.343; [Table IIA: 107.25]

towns + local government KM365.3; 346.653
UF: boroughs
UF: municipal corporations

toxic materials + international law KC241.3; 341.4413

toxic waste KN97.83; 347.3483
UF: dangerous waste
UF: hazardous waste
RT: dangerous things KN186.9.D3; 347.459.D3
RT: poisons KN186.9.P6; 347.459.P6

toxicology KM608.3.T6; 346.9793.T6

tracks + railways KN325.1; 347.8151

trade KN253; 347.61

trade + EU KW108
UF: trade between member states
RT: external trade + EU KW78

trade + EU + competition KW110.3

trade + international law
USE: international trade KC230; 341.42

trade + retail KN286; 347.679
UF: retail trade
RT: retail + co-operatives KN268.3; 347.6383
RT: sale of goods KN280; 347.65; [Table IIA: 132]

trade + war KC1356; 341.827

trade agreements
USE: commercial agreements + international law KC231; 341.421

trade associations [Table VII: 9.7]

trade associations + taxation KM336.497; 346.52497

trade barriers + EU KW109

trade between member states
USE: trade + EU KW108

trade descriptions KN284.1; 347.661

trade marks KN114.2; 347.3772

trade marks + EU KW142

trade marks + international law KC236.3; 341.433

trade names KN114.2; 347.3772
UF: brand names
UF: business names

trade practices + competition + Australia KN266; 347.63

Trade Related Aspects of Intellectual Property Rights Agreement KC641; 341.645
UF: TRIPS Agreement

trade secrets KN114.3; 347.3773

trade union elections
USE: elections + trade unions KN195.53; 347.4843

trade union officials
USE: officers + trade unions KN195.6; 347.4846

trade unions KN195; 347.48; [Table IIA: 124]; [Table VII: 9.7]
RT: associations KN169.4; 347.41894; [Table VII: 9.4]; [Table VIII: .003]

trade unions + accounts
USE: accounts + trade unions KN195.3; 347.483

trade unions + criminal liability KM507.Q97; 346.83.Q97

trade unions + EU KW131.6

trade unions + finance KN195.3; 347.486

trade unions + taxation KM336.497; 346.52497

trading standards KN284.6; 347.666
UF: fitness for purpose + sale of goods
RT: weights and measures KN282.5; 347.655

trading with the enemy KM561.4; 346.8814

traffic + passengers
UF: passenger traffic

traffic + roads
USE: road traffic KN323; 347.813

traffic accidents
USE: accidents + roads KN323.9; 347.8139

traffic courts [Table V: 4.4]

traffic offences KM565.T7; 346.89.T7
RT: driving offences KM565.D7; 346.89.D7

traffic police KN323.79; 347.81379
RT: police KM615; 346.985; [Table IIA: 92.2]

traffic regulations KN323.7; 347.8137
UF: highway code
UF: rule of the road
UF: safety + road traffic

traffic wardens KN323.79; 347.81379

train crews KN325.5; 347.8155

train drivers KN325.5; 347.8155
UF: drivers + railways
RT: guards + trains KN325.5; 347.8155
RT: railwaymen KN325.5; 347.8155

trainee solicitors KL87.1; 345.171341
RT: articled clerks KL87.1; 345.171341
RT: technical education KN184.3; 347.444

training KN184; 347.443
RT: education KN184; 347.443; [Table IIA: 122]

training + employment KN192.3; 347.464

training + EU KW143

training + judiciary KL240.5; 345.45
UF: judiciary + training
RT: education + judiciary KL240.5; 345.45

training and enterprise councils + taxation KM336.65; 346.5265

training centres + punishments [App: 69.6]

training directors + law firms KL131–149 [Table: .95]; 345.1794–9 [Table: 95]

trains KN325; 347.815
RT: public transport KN324; 347.814

tramps
USE: vagrancy KM562.5; 346.8835

tramway routes
USE: routes + road transport KN324.4; 347.8144

tramways KN324.3; 347.8143
UF: street cars

transcription methods + law reporting KL33.1; 345.131

transsexuals [Table VII: 2.4]

transfer + personal property KN104; 347.364

transfer + property KN56.2; 347.3032

transfer + real property KN70; 347.32
UF: purchaser and vendor
UF: vendor and purchaser

transfer of sovereignty KC161; 341.271
UF: dismantling of nations

transfer of undertakings + employment protection KN192.28; 347.4638
RT: mergers + competition KN266.12; 347.6312
RT: takeovers + competition KN266.12; 347.6312

transfer taxes KM337.3; 346.55

transit systems
USE: public transport KN324; 347.814

translation K104; 340.064
SN: the action/procedure of translating texts

translations
SN: use as subdivision only

translators + courts
USE: interpreters + courts KL230.5; 345.35

transmitters + broadcasting KN344.1; 347.8711

transnational law
USE: conflict of laws KC2000; 341.9

transplant surgery KN185.5; 347.448
UF: organ transplants
RT: human tissues KN185.5; 347.448

transport KN320; 347.8
UF: inland transport

transport + international law KC250; 341.45

transport industries + EU KW119.7

transport policy + EU KW135

transport services + legislatures KM87.9.T7; 346.2489.T7

transportation (punishment) [App: 63]

travellers' cheques KN302.4; 347.714

trawlers
USE: fishing boats KN338.3; 347.8383

treason KM561.1; 346.8811
UF: collaboration with the enemy
UF: high treason

treasure trove KN92.T7; 347.335

treaties KC330; 341.56
UF: concordats
UF: conventions (treaties)
UF: executive agreements + international law

UF: international agreements
UF: pacts
UF: protocols

treaties + breaches
USE: breach of treaty KC338.4; 341.594

treaties + commerce
USE: commercial agreements + international law KC231; 341.421

treaties + effects KC334; 341.57

treaties + EU KW85

treaties + EU + texts KW1

treaties + formation
USE: formation + treaties KC333; 341.561

treaties + history KC339; 341.599

treaties + indexes KC19; 341.129

treaties + interpretation KC334.4; 341.574

treaties + ratification KC333.2; 341.5612
UF: ratification + treaties

treaties + reciprocity
USE: reciprocity + treaties KC338.1; 341.591

treaties + supervision KC338.4; 341.594
UF: supervision of treaties
RT: breach of treaty KC338.4; 341.594

treaties + texts KC10; 341.121

treaties + trade
USE: commercial agreements + international law KC231; 341.421

treaties + war KC338.6; 341.596
RT: peace treaties KC1425; 341.895

treaties : municipal law KM54.2; 346.1342
UF: municipal law + treaties

treaties of accession + EU + texts KW2

treatment of offenders [App: 40]

Treaty of Amsterdam (1997) KW1.F97
UF: Amsterdam Treaty

Treaty of Paris (1951) KW1.F51
UF: European Coal and Steel Community Treaty

Treaty of Rome (1971) KW1.F71
UF: EU Treaty
UF: European Communities Treaty
UF: Rome Treaty

Treaty of Lisbon (2007) KW1.G07
UF: Lisbon Treaty

Treaty on European Union (1992) KW1.F92
UF: Maastricht Treaty

treaty-making power KM54; 346.134

trees + conservation KN95.6; 347.3426

trespass to goods KN38.7; 347.275

trespass to land KN38.6; 347.27

trial by impeachment
USE: impeachment KM112.9; 346.259

trial by jury
USE: juries KN389.6; 347.9606; [Table IIA: 70]

trial on indictment
USE: trial practice + criminal procedure KM582; 346.93

trial practice KN389; 347.96; [Table VI: .Z71]
UF: court practice
UF: practice and procedure

trial practice + criminal procedure KM582; 346.93
UF: trial on indictment
RT: summary trial KM588; 346.94

trial tactics KL93; 345.1723

trial within a trial KM582.1; 346.9305
UF: voire dire

trials + misconduct
USE: miscarriage of justice KM597; 346.957

trials + popular accounts KB60; 340.42

tribal law
USE: customary law KL8; 345.08; [Table IIA: 62]

tribunals
USE: administrative tribunals KM303; 346.43
USE: Copyright Tribunal KN115.42; 347.3786
USE: industrial tribunals KN196.9; 347.4869

tribunals + conflict of laws
USE: mixed arbitral tribunals KC1275; 341.745

trickery
USE: deception + criminal law KM547.2; 346.8722

TRIPS Agreement
USE: Trade Related Aspects of Intellectual Property Rights Agreement
KC641; 341.645

trojans
USE: viruses + computers KN348.5; 347.8975

trolley-buses
USE: buses KN324.1; 347.8141

trover KN38.73; 347.278

truce KC1422; 341.892
UF: flag of truce
RT: peace treaties KC1425; 341.895

trucks + road transport
USE: heavy goods vehicles KN323.13; 347.81331

trunk roads KN322.15; 347.81215
UF: turnpikes
RT: motorways KN322.1; 347.8121

trust accounts + legal profession KL99; 345.1769

trust companies + Canada + taxation KM336.4929.T7; 346.524929.T7

trust funds KN218; 347.578

trust territories KC154.4; 341.2644
UF: international trusteeships

trustees KN216; 347.56

Trusteeship Council KC441; 341.626

trusteeships + international law KC154.3; 341.2643
UF: mandates + international law

trusts KN210; 347.54; [Table IIA: 126]
RT: settlements KN210; 347.54

trusts + creation KN213; 347.541
UF: creation of trusts

trusts + taxation KM336.447; 346.52447

trusts + variation
USE: variation + trusts KN213.9; 347.549

trusts for sale KN64.13; 347.3155

tube (railway)
USE: underground railways KN325.6; 347.8156

tugs
USE: towage KN334.2; 347.8342

tunnels KN322.8; 347.8128

tunnels + railways + international law KC251.2; 341.4512

tunnels + roads + international law KC252; 341.452

Tur KD70.4; 342.244

turnpikes
USE: motorways KN322.1; 347.8121
USE: trunk roads KN322.15; 347.81215

Twelve Tables KE125; 343.43

two-counsel rule KL94; 345.173

typewriters + evidence + criminal procedure KM604.42; 346.9652

typhoid KN185.69.T9; 347.44869.T9

uberrimae fidei
USE: utmost disclosure + insurance KN290.2; 347.6802

ultimatums + international disputes KC1308; 341.785

ultra vires + companies KN262.75; 347.62475

unadopted roads KN322.2; 347.8122

unanimity + juries KN389.65; 347.96065

unanimity + juries + criminal procedure KM583.5; 346.9335

unborn children KN176.5; 347.4265
UF: foetuses

UNCITRAL
USE: United Nations Commission on International Trade Law KC465; 341.6295

UNCTAD
USE: United Nations Conference on Trade and Development KC646; 341.6456

undefended divorce KN173.17; 347.42447

underdeveloped countries
USE: developing countries + international relations KC309.5; 341.5195

underground railways KN325.6; 347.8156
UF: metro (railway)
UF: tube (railway)

underwriting
USE: insurance KN290; 347.68; [Table IIA: 133]

undue influence + contract KN15.6; 347.136

undue influence + wills KN125.1; 347.3821

unemployment KN197; 347.487

unemployment + EU KW130.5

unemployment + social security KN181.3; 347.4413
UF: dole

Unesco
USE: United Nations Educational Scientific and Cultural Organisation
KC501; 341.631

unfair competition KN266.4; 347.634

unfair contracts KN15.8; 347.138

unfair dismissal KN192.245; 347.46341
UF: wrongful dismissal

unfriendly measures + international disputes KC1300; 341.77

Uniate churches KD210; 342.43

unicameral legislatures KM82.1; 346.211
UF: single chambers

Unicef
USE: United Nations Children's Emergency Fund KC460; 341.6294

unification of private law KB115; 340.53
UF: private law + unification
RT: codification KL160; 345.197

uniform laws
USE: codification KL160; 345.197

uniforms + offences KM561.9.U5; 346.882.U5
UF: political uniforms

unincorporated associations KN169.4; 347.41894; [Table VII: 9.4]

unit trusts KN304.51; 347.7351

unit trusts + taxation KM336.4929.U5; 346.524929.U5

Unitarian churches KD560; 342.6916

United Nations KC401; 341.622

United Nations : EU KW82

United Nations Children's Emergency Fund KC460; 341.6294
UF: Unicef

United Nations Commission on International Trade Law KC465; 341.6295
UF: UNCITRAL

United Nations Conference on the Law of the Sea KC596; 341.6396

United Nations Conference on Trade and Development KC646; 341.6456
UF: UNCTAD

United Nations Educational Scientific and Cultural Organisation KC501; 341.631
UF: Unesco

United Nations Food and Agriculture Organisation
USE: Food and Agriculture Organisation KC521; 341.633

United Nations forces KC1281; 341.751
RT: peace-keeping forces KC1280; 341.75

United Nations High Commission for Refugees
USE: High Commission for Refugees KC456; 341.6292

United Nations Industrial Development Organisation KC647; 341.6457

United Nations International Law Commission
USE: International Law Commission KC450; 341.628

United States : EU KW81.3

United States legal system KL22; 345.0973

Universal Postal Union KC571; 341.638

universities KN184.3; 347.444
RT: higher education KN184.3; 347.444

university libraries
USE: libraries KN184.4; 347.445; [Table IIA: 122.5]

unjust enrichment KN20.2; 347.162

unlawful arrest
USE: wrongful arrest KM543.6; 346.8636

unlawful assembly KM562.1; 346.8831
UF: illegal assembly

unlawful killing
USE: homicide KM542; 346.862

unlawful trusts KN214.5; 347.555
UF: illegal trusts

unliquidated damages KN37.1; 347.231

unlisted securities market KN304.82; 347.7382
UF: USM

unloading + maritime law KN337.7; 347.8377

unmarried couples KN174; 347.4259
RT: cohabitation KN174; 347.4259; [Table IIA: 117.6]
RT: common law marriage KN172.9.C6; 347.422.C6
RT: de facto relationships KN174; 347.4259

unmarried couples + social security KN181.9.Q39.U5; 347.4419.Q39.U5

unmarried families KN174.1; 347.42591

unmarried persons
USE: single persons [Table VII: 3.1]

unregistered designs KN114.4; 347.3774

unsecured creditors KN305.2; 347.752

unsolicited goods KN285.9.U3; 347.678.U3

unsolicited services KN285.9.U8; 347.678.U8

unwritten constitutions KM51; 346.131

upper chambers + legislatures KM82.3; 346.213
RT: lower chambers + legislatures KM82.4; 346.214

urban districts
USE: districts + local government KM365.5; 346.655

urban renewal KN96.15; 347.34315

usage and custom
USE: customary law KL8; 345.08; [Table IIA: 62]

use of computers + law offices
USE: computers + law offices KL96.2; 345.1762

use of force + war
USE: legality + war KC1353; 341.81

use of judicial time
USE: judicial time KL230.48; 345.348

uses + real property KN64.11; 347.3153

USM
USE: unlisted securities market KN304.82; 347.7382

utmost disclosure + insurance KN290.2; 347.6802
UF: uberrimae fidei

vacant possession KN74.7; 347.3227

vacations KL230.18; 345.318
UF: courts + vacations
RT: legal terms KL230.18; 345.318

vaccination
USE: preventive medicine KN185.7; 347.4487

vagrancy KM562.5; 346.8835
UF: tramps

validity of wills
USE: wills + validity KN125.2; 347.3822

valuation + rating (taxation) KM337.65; 346.575

valuation + real property KN72.1; 347.3215

valuation + taxation KM336.8; 346.528

value added tax KM337.45; 346.565
UF: VAT
RT: goods and services tax KM337.45; 346.565
RT: taxation + EU KW103

vandalism KM549; 346.874
RT: criminal damage KM549; 346.874

vans
USE: motor vehicles KN323.1; 347.8131

variation
SN: use as subdivision only

variation + trusts KN213.9; 347.549
UF: trusts + variation

vasectomy KN172.74; 347.42174

VAT
USE: value added tax KM337.45; 346.565

Vedas KD721; 342.821

vehicles
USE: motor vehicles KN323.1; 347.8131

vehicles + police
USE: police vehicles KM615.42; 346.98542

vending machines KN285.5; 347.675

vendor and purchaser KN70.7; 347.3207

ventilation + buildings KN83.9.V4; 347.3259.V4

venture capital KN263.3; 347.6253

venture capital + credit KN305.22; 347.7522

venue
USE: jurisdiction KN353; 347.91; [Table VI: .Z4]

verdicts KN389.72; 347.96072
UF: alternative verdicts

verdicts + criminal procedure KM586; 346.936

verges
USE: roads + verges KN322.5; 347.8125

vermin + control KN97.6; 347.3464

vertical agreements + competition
USE: anti-competitive agreements KN266.2; 347.632

vessels
USE: ships KN332.3; 347.8323

veterans
USE: ex-service personnel [Table VII: 7.E9]

veterinary medicine KN186.8; 347.458
UF: animals + diseases
UF: vets
RT: animals + control KN186.8; 347.458

veto + constitutional law KM114.2; 346.272

veto + United Nations KC416; 341.624

vets
USE: veterinary medicine KN186.8; 347.458

vibration KN38.81; 347.281

vicarious liability KN33.6; 347.216
RT: strict liability + criminal law KM505.9; 346.828

vice
USE: sexual offences KM544; 346.864

victimless crime KM540.8; 346.858
UF: crimes without victims

victims of crime
USE: crime + victims KM593; 346.947

victims of war
USE: war + victims KC1410; 341.88

video games KN186.615; 347.45615

video links + witnesses KN391.37; 347.96237

video links + witnesses + criminal evidence KM605.15; 346.9715

video recordings + causes of crime [App: 17]

video recordings + criminal evidence KM604.55; 346.9665
RT: films + criminal evidence KM604.55; 346.9665

video recordings + evidence KN392.5; 347.9635

video recordings + law reporting KL33.2; 345.132

videoconferencing + courts
USE: teleconferencing + courts KL230.63; 345.363

vigilantes KM614.1; 346.9841

Viking law KE321; 343.63

village greens KN65.5; 347.3185

villages + local government KM365.7; 346.657

violent crimes KM540.1; 346.851

viruses + computers KN348.5; 347.8975
UF: trojans

visas KM175.4; 346.3284

visits to prisons
USE: prisons + visits KM681.5; 346.98765; [App: 93.5]

vivisection KN186.84; 347.4584

vocabulary of law
USE: legal dictionaries K120; 340.08; [Table IIA: 63]

vocational education
USE: technical education KN184.3; 347.444

vocational training + EU KW144

Voet KE415; 343.84

voice prints KM604.34; 346.9647

void contracts KN15.2; 347.132
UF: avoidance of contracts

voidable contracts KN15.2; 347.132

voire dire
USE: trial within a trial KM582.1; 346.9305

voluntary wills
USE: living wills KN185.157; 347.446157

volunteers + armed forces
USE: recruitment + armed forces KM401; 346.71

volunteers + trusts KN213.4; 347.545

voter registration KM83.46; 346.2246

voting + elections + legislatures KM83.45; 346.2245
UF: ballots
UF: polls
UF: secret ballot

voting + shareholders KN263.81; 347.62581
UF: proxies

voting + trade unions KN195.53; 347.4843

wagering
USE: gambling KN186.5; 347.455

wages
USE: earnings KN194.1; 347.4781
USE: remuneration KN194; 347.478

wagons + railways KN325.3; 347.8153
UF: rolling stock
RT: carriages + railways KN325.3; 347.8153

waiver
SN: use as subdivision only

Wakf KD643.1; 342.7290715

war KC1350; 341.8
UF: hostilities

war + causes of crime [App: 14]

war + contracts KN18.5; 347.155
SN: form of contracts made during wars

war + debts KC223.2; 341.4112

war + declaration
USE: declaration of war KC1355.2; 341.822

war + emergency legislation + England and Wales KF25

war + victims KC1410; 341.88
UF: victims of war
UF: war relief

war : contracts KN15.5; 347.135
SN: effect of war on contracts

war : treaties KC338.6; 341.596
SN: effect of war on treaties

war at sea
USE: maritime warfare KC1380; 341.854

war crimes KC217; 341.362
RT: International Military Tribunal + law reports KC35.N8; 341.136.N8

war in the air
USE: aerial warfare KC1375; 341.852

war on land
USE: land warfare KC1370; 341.85

war pensions
USE: military pensions KN181.7; 347.4417

war relief
USE: war + victims KC1410; 341.88

warders
USE: prison officers KM658.6; 346.987186; [App: 88.6]

wards [Table VII: 3.9.W3]
RT: guardians [Table VII: 3.9.G8]

wards of court KN176.23; 347.42623

warehouses KN83.3; 347.3253
RT: bond stores KM337.763; 346.5863

warfare + prohibited methods
USE: prohibited weapons + international law KC1395; 341.865

warranties
USE: guarantees + sale of goods KN282.4; 347.654

warrants + arrest
USE: arrest KM580.3; 346.913

warrants + searches
USE: searches + criminal investigation KM580.2; 346.912

Warsaw Pact KC1111; 341.6891

waste disposal KN97.85; 347.3485
UF: garbage disposal
UF: rubbish tips

waste disposal + EU KW125.7

water KN90; 347.333
RT: public utilities KN275.P8; 347.645.P8

water + conservation KN90.6; 347.3336

water + pollution KN97.73; 347.3473
RT: rivers + pollution KN97.73; 347.3473
RT: sea + pollution KN97.74; 347.3474

water + pollution + EU KW125.5

water + supply KN90.5; 347.3335
UF: public water supply

watercourses KN90.1; 347.3331

waters + international law
USE: national waters KC144; 341.254

wavelengths + broadcasting KN344.1; 347.8711
RT: radio KN344.4; 347.872
RT: television KN344.5; 347.873

wavelengths + international law
USE: radio + international law KC258.5; 341.465
USE: television + international law KC259; 341.466

wealth + taxation KM336.38; 346.5238
SN: type of taxable property

wealth + taxes KM337.159; 346.5359

weapons + criminal law KM562.2; 346.8832
UF: offensive weapons

weapons + international law KC1390; 341.86

weapons + police
USE: arms + police KM615.3; 346.9853

web sites
USE: internet KN347.4; 347.8935

weekend detention
USE: partial detention [App: 68]

Weekly Law Reports KF55.W2; KF60.W3

weights and measures KN282.5; 347.655
UF: measures and weights
RT: trading standards KN284.6; 347.666

weirs
USE: flood control KN90.3; 347.3333

welfare + employment KN193.3; 347.473

welfare + prisoners KM681; 346.9876; [App: 93.3]

welfare funds + trade unions KN195.3; 347.483

welfare services + crime prevention [App: 23]

welfare state
USE: public welfare KN181; 347.44

Western Empire (753 BC to 600 AD)
USE: Roman law KE100; 343.4

Western European Union KC951; 341.676
SN: terminated 31 March 2010

western law : eastern law
USE: eastern law : western law KB122; 340.56

whaling + international law KC276.2; 341.4812

whistleblowing
USE: disclosure of information + employment KN192.29; 347.4639

white-collar crime KM540.3; 346.853

white-slave traffic
USE: human trafficking KC208; 341.338

WHO
USE: World Health Organisation KC531; 341.634

wholesale co-operatives KN268.2; 347.6382

wholesaling KN287; 347.6799

widowers [Table VII: 3.4]

widows KN181.5; 347.4415; [Table VII: 3.4]

wife and husband
USE: marriage KN172; 347.421; [Table IIA: 117]

wigs + judges KL81; 345.17011

wikis KN347.49; 347.89359

wild animals
USE: animals + control KN186.8; 347.458

wildlife + conservation KN95.3; 347.3423
RT: nature reserves KN95.14; 347.34214

wildlife + conservation + EU KW125.3

wildlife + conservation + international law KC243.2; 341.4442

wills KN125; 347.382
RT: living wills KN185.157; 347.446157
RT: testamentary freedom KN125.8; 347.3828
RT: testators + capacity KN125.1; 347.3821

wills + interpretation KN125.5; 347.3825

wills + validity KN125.2; 347.3822
UF: validity of wills

wind power KN89.53; 347.3323

winding up KN312.5; 347.7925

wine
USE: alcohol KN186.4; 347.454

WIPO
USE: World Intellectual Property Organisation KC648; 341.6458

wire tapping KM604.52; 346.9662
UF: bugging
UF: telephone tapping

wireless
USE: radio KN344.4; 347.872

wit and humour
USE: humorous writings KB34; 340.374

withdrawal of actions
USE: discontinuance KN388.1; 347.951

withdrawal of prosecution
USE: nolle prosequi KM582.5; 346.9325

withdrawals + banking KN303.12; 347.7212

withholding passports
USE: passports + withholding + punishment [App: 69.8]

withholding tax KM337.9.W5; 346.59.W5

witness summons KN391.1; 347.9621
UF: subpoena

witness summons + criminal procedure KM605.8; 346.9778
UF: subpoena + criminal procedure

witnesses KN391; 347.962; [Table IIA: 147.3]

witnesses + criminal procedure KM605; 346.97; [Table IIA: 93.5]
UF: physically handicapped witnesses

witnesses + payment KN391.15; 347.96215
UF: payment + witnesses

witnesses + victims
USE: offences against witnesses KM563.7; 346.8857

women KN152.2; 347.4122; [Table VII: 2.2]
RT: equal opportunities KM208; 346.36; [Table IIA: 81.5]

women + EU KW129.1

women + prisons KM655.Q22; 346.98715.Q22; [App: 85.Q22]

women + religious laws [KD Table: 8.2]

words and phrases
USE: legal dictionaries K120; 340.08; [Table IIA: 63]

words and phrases judicially defined
USE: judicial definitions KL41; 345.1691

work life balance KN193.255; 347.47215

work-to-rule KN196.6; 347.4866

workers + company directors KN264.6; 347.6266

workers + compensation KN198.8; 347.498

workers + participation
USE: industrial democracy KN192.8; 347.468

working conditions
USE: conditions + employment KN193; 347.47

working on days off
USE: employment + onerous terms KN193.8; 347.4775

working time regulations KN193.1; 347.471

workplaces + hygiene
USE: hygiene + industrial law KN193.7; 347.477

works councils
USE: industrial democracy KN192.8; 347.468

workshops + industrial law KN193.61; 347.4761

workshops + prisons KM684.2; 346.9876972; [App: 92.72]

world + federation KC314; 341.534

World Bank
USE: International Bank for Reconstruction and Development KC601; 341.64

World Council of Churches KC1191; 341.697

World Federation of Labour KC1171; 341.695

World Federation of Trade Unions KC1161; 341.693

World Health Organisation KC531; 341.634
UF: WHO

World Intellectual Property Organisation KC648; 341.6458
UF: Bureaux Internationaux Réunis pour la Protection de la Propriété Intellectuelle
UF: WIPO

World Meteorological Organisation KC541; 341.635

World Trade Organisation KC641; 341.645
UF: WTO

world wide web
USE: internet KN347.4; 347.8935
USE: internet + international law KC257.7; 341.4627

worship [KD Table: 5]

wounding KM543.1; 346.8631

wrecks KN334.1; 347.8341
UF: marine accidents
UF: shipwrecks
RT: salvage KN334; 347.834; [Table IIA: 139]

wrecks + international law KC275; 341.479
RT: collisions + international law KC274.1; 341.4781
RT: salvage + international law KC275; 341.479

writing + law
USE: legal composition K101; 340.061

writs + judgments KN395.22; 347.9722

writs + preliminary proceedings
USE: claim forms KN381.1; 347.9411

written constitutions
USE: constitutions (theory) KM32; 346.11

written contracts KN13.5; 347.115

written pleadings
USE: statements of case KN383; 347.943; [Table IIA: 146]

wrongful arrest KM543.6; 346.8636
UF: false arrest
UF: unlawful arrest

wrongful dismissal
USE: unfair dismissal KN192.245; 347.46341

wrongs
USE: crimes KM540; 346.85; [Table IIA: 91]
USE: tort KN30; 347.2; [Table IIA: 100]

WTO
USE: World Trade Organisation KC641; 341.645

WWW
USE: internet KN347.4; 347.8935

yearbooks + texts KF50
SN: medieval reports of English cases

years + tax + assessment KM336.82; 346.5282
UF: tax years

YK2 bug
USE: bugs + computers KN348.5; 347.8975

York-Antwerp Rules KN335.3; 347.8353

young persons KN176; 347.426; [Table IIA: 118]; [Table VII: 1.2]
UF: adolescents

young persons + EU KW129.2

youth courts KL227.1; 345.3071; [Table V: 7.1]
UF: juvenile courts

zoning KN96.1; 347.3431

Zoroastrism
USE: Parsi law KD860; 342.94